Global Data Protection in the Field of Law Enforcement

W0230249

This book examines a key aspect of regulatory policy in the field of data protection, namely the frameworks governing the sharing of data for law enforcement purposes, both within the EU and between the EU and the US and other third party countries. The book features a thorough analysis of the main data-sharing instruments that have been used by law enforcement agencies and the intelligence services in the EU and in the US between 2001 and 2015. The book also explores the challenges to data protection which the current frameworks create, and explores the possible responses to those challenges at both EU and global levels.

In offering a full overview of the current EU data-sharing instruments and their data protection rules, this book will be of significant benefit to scholars and policy-makers working in areas related to privacy, data protection, national security and EU external relations.

Cristina Blasi Casagran is a Postdoctoral Researcher of EU Law at the Autonomous University of Barcelona, Spain.

Routledge Research in EU Law

Available titles in this series include:

Global Data Protection in the Field of Law Enforcement

An EU Perspective

Cristina Blasi Casagran

Routledge
Taylor & Francis Group

LONDON AND NEW YORK

First published 2017 by Routledge

2 Park Square, Milton Park, Abingdon, Oxfordshire OX14 4RN

711 Third Avenue, New York, NY 10017

Routledge is an imprint of the Taylor & Francis Group, an informa business

First issued in paperback 2018

Copyright © 2017 Cristina Blasi Casagran

British Library Cataloguing in Publication Data
A catalogue record for this book is available from the British Library

Library of Congress Cataloging-in-Publication Data
Names: Blasi Casagran, Cristina, author.
Title: Global data protection in the field of law enforcement : an EU perspective / Cristina Blasi Casagran.
Description: Abingdon, Oxon ; N.Y., NY : Routledge, 2016. | Based on author's thesis (doctoral – European University Institute, Department of Law, 2015) issued under title: Towards a global data protection framework in the field of law enforcement : an EU perspective. | Includes bibliographical references and index.
Identifiers: LCCN 2015047381| ISBN 9781138655386 (hbk) |
ISBN 9781315622521 (ebk)
Subjects: LCSH: Law enforcement—European Union countries. |
Data protection—Law and legislation—European Union countries. |
Law enforcement—International cooperation.
Classification: LCC KJE5977. B57 2016 | DDC 344.2405/2—dc23
LC record available at http://lccn.loc.gov/2015047381

ISBN: 978-1-138-65538-6 (hbk)
ISBN: 978-1-138-61417-8 (pbk)

Typeset in Baskerville by
Keystroke, Station Road, Codsall, Wolverhampton

Contents

Abbreviations

AFIS	Automated Fingerprint Identification System
AFSJ	Area of Freedom, Security and Justice
APEC	Asia-Pacific Economic Cooperation
API	Advance Passenger Information
APIS	Advance Passenger Information System
Art. 29 WP	Article 29 Data Protection Working Party
ATF	US Bureau of Alcohol, Tobacco, Firearms and Explosives
ATS	Automated Targeting System
ATS-P	Automated Targeting System-Passenger
AWF	Analysis work files
BCR	Binding Corporate Rule
BfV	Bundesamt für Verfassungsschutz
BND	Bundesnachrichtendienst
BNDD	Bureau of Narcotics and Dangerous Drugs
CAHDATA	Ad-Hoc Committee on Data Protection
CATS	Article 36 Committee
CBP	Bureau of Customs and Border Protection
CBPR	Cross-Border Privacy Rules
CBSA	Canada Border Services Agency
CEPOL	European Police College
CFSP	Common Foreign and Security Policy
CIA	US Central Intelligence Agency
CICA	Canadian Generally Accepted Privacy Principles
CIS	Customs Information System
CJEU	Court of Justice of the European Union
CNI	Centro Nacional de Inteligencia
CoE	Council of Europe
CODIS	Combined DNA Index System
COMINT	Communications Intelligence
COREPER	Permanent Representatives Committee
COSI	Standing Committee on Internal Security
COTER	Counter-terrorism Working Group
CPEA	Cross-border Privacy Enforcement Arrangement

CSDP	Common Security and Defence Policy
CSE	Canadian Communications Security Establishment
CSI	Container Security Initiative
CT	Counter-terrorism
CTG	Counter-terrorism Group
CTTF	Counter-terrorism Task Force
DEA	US Drug Enforcement Administration
DE-CIX	Deutscher Commercial Internet Exchange
DG	Directorate General
DGSE	Direction générale de la sécurité extérieure
DHS	US Department of Homeland Security
DNA	Deoxyribonucleic acid
DoJ	US Department of Justice
DoS	US Department of State
DPA	Data Protection Authority
DPO	Data Protection Office
DPPA	EU-US Data Privacy and Protection Agreement
DPR	Délégation parlementaire au renseignement
DSD	Australian Defence Signals Directorate
DST	Direction de la Surveillance du Territoire
EAS	Europol Analysis System
EC	European Communities
EC3	European Cybercrime Centre
ECB	European Central Bank
ECD	Europol Council Decision
ECDC	European Centre for Disease Prevention and Control
ECHR	European Convention for the Protection of Human Rights and Fundamental Freedoms
ECRIS	European Criminal Records Information System
ECtHR	European Court of Human Rights
EDPS	European Data Protection Supervisor
EDU	Europol Drugs Unit
EEA	European Economic Area
EEAS	European External Action Service
EES	Entry and Exit System
EEW	European Evidence Warrant
EFTA	European Free Trade Association
EIO	European Investigation Order
EIS	Europol Information System
ELINT	Electronic intelligence
EMPACT	European Multidisciplinary Platform Against Criminal Threats
ENISA	European Network and Information Security Agency
ENU	Europol National Unit
EP	European Parliament
ETA	Euskadi Ta Askatasuna

EU	European Union
EUCARIS	European Car and Driving License Information System
eu-LISA	EU Agency for large-scale IT systems
Eurojust	EU Judicial Cooperation Unit
Europol	EU law enforcement agency
EUMS	European Union Military Staff
FBI	US Federal Bureau of Investigation
FD	Framework decision
FFI	Norwegian Defence Research Establishment
FIDH	International Federation for Human Rights
FIPPs	Fair Information Practice Principles
FISA	US Foreign Intelligence Surveillance Act
FISAA	US Foreign Intelligence Surveillance Act Amendment
FISC	FISA Intelligence Surveillance Court
FISCR	FISA Intelligence Surveillance Court of Review
FIU	Financial Intelligence Unit
FOIA	Freedom of Information Act
FP	Fingerprint
FRONTEX	European Agency for the Management of Operational Cooperation at the External Borders of the Member States of the European Union
GAPP	Generally Accepted Privacy Principles
GCHQ	UK Government Communications Headquarters
GCSB	New Zealand Government Communications Security Bureau
GG	German Constitution
GPEN	Global Privacy Enforcement Network
HF	High Frequency
HLCG	High Level Contact Group
HUMINT	Human intelligence
ICC	Interception of Communications Commissioner
ICCPR	International Covenant on Civil and Political Rights
ICE	US Immigration and Customs Enforcement
IMINT	Imagery intelligence
InfoEx	Information Exchange System
INS	Immigration and Naturalisation Service
IntCen	EU Intelligence Analysis Centre
IPAHRCS	International Principles on the Application of Human Rights to Communications Surveillance
IRS	US Internal Revenue Service
ISA	UK Intelligence Services Act
ISC	Intelligence Services Commissioner
ISCP	UK Security Committee of Parliament
ISS	Internal Security Strategy
IT	Information technology
JHA	Justice and Home Affairs

JITs	Joint Investigation Teams
JSB	Joint Supervisory Body
LDH	French Human Rights League
LIBE	European Parliament Civil Liberties Committee
LPM	Loi de Programmation Militaire
MAD	Militärischer Abschirmdienst
MB	Europol Management Board
MCT	Mobile Competence Team
MEP	Member of the European Parliament
MI5	Security Service
MI6	Secret Intelligence Service
MLA	Mutual Legal Assistance
MLAT	Mutual Legal Assistance Treaty
MoU	Memorandum of Understanding
NATO	North Atlantic Treaty Organisation
NCB	National Central Bureau
NCIS	National Criminal Intelligence Service
NGO	Non-governmental organisation
NPs	National Parliaments
NSA	US National Security Agency
NSS	National Security Strategy
NTA	New Transatlantic Agenda
OAS	Organization of American States
OECD	Organisation for Economic Co-operation and Development
OIA	Office of International Affairs
OLAF	European Anti Fraud Office
OPT	Occupied Palestinian Territory
OSINT	Open Sources Intelligence
PEA	Privacy Enforcement Authority
PIU	Passenger Information Unit
PKG	Parlamentarisches Kontrollgremium
PKGrG	German Law on the Parliamentarian Control of Intelligence Services of 2009
PNR	Passenger Name Records
PPPs	Public-private partnerships
PWGT	Police Working Group on Terrorism
QMV	Qualified-majority voting
RELEX	External relations
RIPA	UK Regulation of Investigatory Powers Act
RTP	Registered Traveller Programme
SAAC	Schengen Agreement Application Convention
SIENA	Secure Information Exchange Network
SIGINT	Signals intelligence
SIRENE	Supplementary Information Request at the National Entry Bureaux

SIS	Schengen Information System
SIS II	Second Generation Schengen Information System
SitCen	Joint Situation Centre
SOC	Serious and organised crime
SPOC	Single Point of Contact
s-TESTA	Secured Trans European Services for Telematics between Administrations
SWIFT	Society for the Worldwide Interbank Financial Telecommunication
TEK	Hungarian Anti-Terrorist Centre
TEU	Treaty of the European Union
TFEU	Treaty on the Functioning of the European Union
TFTP	Terrorist Finance Tracking Program
TFTS	European Terrorist Finance Tracking System
TIDE	Terrorist Identities Datamart Environment
TLD	Transatlantic Legislators' Dialogue
TOC	Transnational Organized Crime
TREVI	Terrorism, Radicalism, Extremism and Political Violence
TSP	Telecommunication Service Provider
TWG	Terrorism Working Group
UDHR	Universal Declaration of Human Rights
UK	United Kingdom
UKIPT	UK Investigatory Powers Tribunal
UMF	Universal Message Format
UN	United Nations
UNODC	United Nations Office on Drugs and Crime
US	United States
Patriot Act	Uniting and Strengthening America by Providing Appropriate Tools Required to Intercept and Obstruct Terrorism Act
USPIS	US Postal Inspection Service
USSS	US Secret Service
VIS	Visa Information System
VoIP	Voice over IP
VRD	Vehicle Registration Data
VwGO	Code of Administrative Court Proceedings
VWP	US Visa Waiver Program
WPISP	Working Party on Information Security and Privacy

Acknowledgements

Many people have contributed in different ways to this book over the last four years. Therefore, I would like to say a word of thanks to each of them.

First, I would like to thank my PhD supervisor at the EUI, Marise Cremona, for believing in me and my project from the very beginning. She has given me unwavering support throughout all these years but, above all, she taught me all that I needed to write a PhD. Thanks to her I learned how to structure my ideas, and to develop my own arguments and reasoning. She always gave me valuable comments to improve my work, and I received her complete support in all the internships, workshops and conferences I decided to participate in. In sum, she has been my main source of inspiration during the four years of my PhD.

I would also like to thank Martin Scheinin, Steven Peers and Maria O'Neill for their helpful suggestions about parts of this book. They have all helped shaped the final version of this book. Likewise, I am very grateful to Montserrat Pi, Claudia Jiménez, Esther Zapater and Susana Beltran for facilitating my teaching experience at the UAB.

This book would never have been conceivable without the constant encouragement and advice of Dr Gregorio Garzón Clariana. Dr Garzón has been my mentor since 2007, when I decided to initiate my academic career. His valuable advice to conclude an LLM in Saarbrücken and to apply for a traineeship in the European Commission were essential in order to be awarded a PhD scholarship at the EUI.

During the years of my PhD, I had the opportunity to work as an intern at the European Data Protection Supervisor (EDPS) and at Europol. I am very grateful to Hielke Hijmans, Alba Bosch Moliné, Daniel Drewer, Jan Ellermann, Nayra Pérez Gutiérrez and Pelopidas Donos for their continual help and kindness throughout my internships. Some of the conversations I had with them have certainly influenced the argument and content of this book.

My greatest thanks go to my mother, Loles, and to my brother, Eduard, for their loving encouragement and for being a great pillar of support throughout my life. In 2008 I made the decision to continue my studies abroad. Despite the distance, I have always felt them by my side, every single day, ready to hear my problems, but also to make me laugh. I have never thanked them enough for all they have done for me. Without them my dream could have never become a reality. Therefore, I would like to dedicate this book to them, as the smallest sign of my gratitude.

Introduction

1 Subject matter and aims

We are in the midst of a war against terrorism. This is the message that governments around the world repeat to society every time they launch a new security measure. Travellers' details, financial information, facial recognition programmes and users' activity on the internet are just some of the data that are being increasingly accessed and processed by law enforcement authorities for security purposes. The main objective of such governmental surveillance is to prevent, detect, investigate and prosecute terrorism and other serious criminal offences.

Although the world has recently been subjected to several acts of terrorism, the wave of terror in which we are currently immersed has its origin in the attacks of 9/11, carried out by the terrorist group Al-Qaeda. One week after the attack, the United Nations (UN) Security Council issued a Resolution calling for global co-operation between the UN contracting parties to criminalise all forms of terrorism (United Nations Security Council 2001). Governments, therefore, deemed it necessary to establish a co-ordinated worldwide security system. After that event, they intensified their mutual co-operation to prevent and combat terrorism. Unfortunately, new attacks occurred, and this time they took place within the European borders. On the morning of 11 March 2004, co-ordinated bombings of a commuter train in Madrid (Spain) killed 191 people and wounded 1,800. Similarly, on 7 July 2005 a series of co-ordinated suicide-bomb attacks took place on London's public transport system, killing 56 people and injuring over 700. Both attacks were led by Al-Qaeda. At the time of writing, the most recent attack was on 7 January 2015, when two French nationals linked to Al-Qaeda killed 12 people in the offices of the satirical newspaper Charlie Hebdo in Paris.

All of these events have triggered the European Union (EU) to enhance its counter-terrorism policy, increasing police co-operation within and beyond the European territory. In 2009, the Treaty of Lisbon brought significant developments with regard to the Area of Freedom, Security and Justice (AFSJ). The new treaty also permitted the adoption of the Stockholm Programme (European Council 2010), as well as the EU Internal Security Strategy (COM(2010) 673 final). Both documents emphasised the importance of achieving greater coherence between external and internal elements of the work in the AFSJ.

Many of the measures the EU has adopted consist of the processing and sharing of data among law enforcement authorities. The main bone of contention for each of these instruments is their potential clash with the EU fundamental right to data protection. Data protection is a rather new issue due to the astounding advances in computer science and technology of the latter half of the twentieth century. It primarily prevents data from being misused or lost by private and public entities.

The Universal Declaration of Human Rights (UDHR) foresees in Article 12 that 'no one shall be subjected to arbitrary interference with his privacy, family, home or correspondence'. The rights to privacy and data protection are thus universal rights and, accordingly, the principles and scope of that right should be understood in the same way around the world. However, in practice, this is not the case. For instance, many security agreements regarding the collection, processing, storage and transfer of personal data for law enforcement purposes have been concluded between the United States (US) and the EU. One of the key tensions during the negotiations of each of these agreements has been related to data protection. This is because the EU and the US have numerous legal differences they had to face with respect to data protection and privacy matters, and these differences have not always been easy to reconcile in the Agreements.

However, this divergence is not only found between the EU and the US systems. The EU itself has fragmented laws regarding the processing and protection of personal data for law enforcement purposes. This internal fragmentation within the EU causes legal insecurity for the EU citizens who seek to protect their personal data. Although Article 8 of the EU Charter of Fundamental Rights enshrines the right to data protection, this has been further developed by specific EU and national laws. Yet, such sectoral laws are not consistent with each other, which ultimately causes a lack of legal protection for the individual.

The purpose of this research lies in examining the challenges and feasibility for a global data protection framework in the field of law enforcement, through looking at the EU and its network of external relations as regards data sharing for law enforcement purposes and data protection. Global standards for privacy and data protection are crucial because the sharing of data no longer has any physical borders. In the age of the internet anyone can learn about and search for just about anything, by using computers that can save, store and transmit data, as well as by using smart phones, which can do all of the above. These inventions have changed the way we live exponentially. Since any piece of information can be communicated and shared rapidly from almost anywhere in the world, global standards that pose limits to the processing of personal data are more necessary now than ever before.

Many studies have focused on the right to data protection in the area of security. For instance, De Busser (2009), Boehm (2012), Hillebrand (2012), O'Neill (2012) and Tzanou (2012) have recently published studies on data protection in the area of EU counter-terrorism and criminal law. All of these studies analyse the internal/external dichotomy of the AFSJ, as well as some data-sharing agreements between the EU and the US. Yet, the existing literature is fragmented and does not offer a full overview of the current EU data-sharing instruments and their data protection rules.

This book aims to achieve a fully-fledged analysis of the existing EU frameworks for data-sharing for law enforcement purposes within the EU and between the EU and third countries, the data protection challenges to which these give rise, and possible responses to those challenges at both the EU and global levels. In order to do so, I first analyse and expand the current literature and laws on data-sharing activities among law enforcement authorities within and beyond the EU. After that, I suggest mechanisms at the EU and international levels that could offer adequate data protection standards for the prevention and combat of terrorism and other serious crimes when the information is processed.

The ultimate goal of this book is to offer a comprehensive background on the interplay between security concerns and data protection issues within and beyond the EU. Rather than a theoretical analysis, it focuses on the examination of all EU security laws and proposals that may have an impact on the right to data protection. This study will surely help establish the right balance between security and data protection within the EU and, possibly, also in third countries.

2 Limitations of the research

The scope of this research has certain limitations. First, it is important to highlight that it is conducted solely from an EU perspective. The US legal framework is only scrutinized to the extent that it is relevant for an EU-US comparison. An analysis of the US security measures based on the processing of data is beyond the scope of the present study.

Second, this research focuses on EU law but there are some matters that are not looked at. For example, it does not include a full analysis of the existing EU legislation and Court of Justice of the European Union (CJEU) case law on data protection, but only specific data-sharing rules and cases that fall within the area of law enforcement. Moreover, it contains no details about the history of EU data protection law. The study is contemporary and the instruments under consideration have been mostly adopted in the last decade.

In addition, it does not examine data processing activities of all EU agencies within the AFSJ. Particularly, the study of Frontex and Eurojust is omitted because, even if they may process information for law enforcement purposes, they are fundamentally composed of custom and judicial authorities respectively. Therefore, the only EU agency that is an object of study is Europol.

Common Foreign and Security Policy (CFSP) measures are only considered to the extent that they are adjacent to law enforcement. Furthermore, the 'smart borders package' consisting of the Entry and Exit System (EES) and the Registered Traveller Programme (RTP) is excluded from this book since the Commission proposals note that data is not going to be used for law enforcement initially. Only after two years from the entry into force of the regulations, will the necessity for data access by law enforcement authorities be assessed.

Lastly, it must be mentioned that this study is fundamentally legal and political. Unlike other academic studies on this field (Bures 2011: 10–27), the historical and social issues related to the causes of terrorism, criminal activities, ideologies, etc are not tackled.

3 Methodology and source materials

My methodological approach combines both descriptive and normative perspectives. Regarding the descriptive approach, it explains in detail the main EU instruments for sharing information for law enforcement purposes, the EU-US international agreements for the exchange of data, the functioning of Europol and the EU data protection rules. To do so, it conducts an exhaustive study of the legal documents of the EU (treaties, regulations, Council decisions, directives, etc) as well as secondary sources such as academic articles, reports and books in the area of data protection and the AFSJ. In addition, the present work takes into consideration personal interviews that I conducted during internships at the EDPS, from July to October 2012, and at the Europol HQ, from May to July 2013. While working for these EU bodies I had the opportunity to talk to experts and officials who provided me with relevant information on data protection matters. Understanding the current EU laws on data protection for law enforcement is critical before venturing into the normative component of this book.

The normative approach focuses on the issues to be considered for the establishment of global data protection standards in the field of security. I am seeking to examine the current conflict between different regimes to look at what legal rules are available to resolve them. I also identify the appropriate level at which the rules should be adopted, and I discuss those parties that manage to strike a balance between data protection and security.

4 Terminology

This book uses a number of concepts that need further clarification. First of all, the terms 'data protection' and 'privacy' are utilised throughout the chapters according to an accepted legal meaning of each. While data protection and privacy are closely linked, they are not identical. Privacy is the individual right of control over one's body, home, property, thoughts, feelings, secrets and identity. In contrast, data protection relates to all information on identified or identifiable persons, but it does not protect legal persons. It relates to the most essential data that can identify a person – for instance, name, fingerprints, ID number or photographs (Kokott and Sobotta 2013). Despite the differences, privacy and data protection complement each other as rights. They both encompass the obligation for public and private entities to respect the most intimate information that belongs to an individual. Numerous jurisprudence of the CJEU has shown that these two rights are closely linked, although they are not identical. This is seen, for instance, in Case C-131/12 *Google v Costeja* and Cases C-293/12 and C-594/12 *Digital Rights Ireland Ltd v Minister for Communications et al.*

For the purpose of this analysis, the concept of 'law enforcement purposes' and 'counter-terrorism purposes' are not synonyms, since the former is broader than the latter. However, on some occasions, I treat counter-terrorism as an example of law enforcement, although it may also be other things.

Regarding the concepts of 'data' and 'information', these do not differentiate in meaning. Nevertheless, in strict terms, data is the unstructured, raw collected facts and figures. When such data is structured and placed within a context, it transforms into information.

The concepts of 'field of security' or 'security actors' encompass police, intelligence and military agents. Concepts of 'terrorism', 'law enforcement', 'organised crime' and 'serious crimes' do not differentiate among them for the purpose of this book. Lastly, the term 'processing of personal data' is interpreted in the sense of Article of 2(b) of the Framework Decision 2008/977/JHA. According to this provision, it includes the 'collection, recording, organisation, storage, adaptation or alteration, retrieval, consultation, use, disclosure by transmission, dissemination or otherwise making available, alignment or combination, blocking, erasure or destruction'.

5 Structure of study

This book is divided into five chapters, an introduction and a conclusion. It follows a bottom-up approach. From an EU perspective, the establishment of global data protection standards can only be conceived consistently if common laws on data protection already exist among Member States of the EU (hereinafter, Member States). Therefore, the first chapter of this book begins by studying the EU information systems and databases that fall under the 'internal' dimension of the AFSJ. It assesses both the lack of implementation and use of these EU legal instruments. It also highlights the expansion of data-sharing instruments in the EU. In the last ten years, data-sharing laws that were originally created for ensuring the border management and the internal market in the EU have been applied in the field of law enforcement. Chapter 1 critically analyses the different data protection provisions in each of these EU instruments and explains how they bring fragmentation of the data protection rules in the AFSJ.

Furthermore, in order to set a standard for global data protection laws, the EU and the US would need to agree on the right balance between security and privacy. Chapter 2 examines how, after 9/11, external pressures (especially from the US) have influenced the EU political and legal environment. In particular, a number of international agreements have been concluded between the EU and the US for the exchange of crime-related information. The chapter offers a substantive assessment of the EU-US data-sharing agreements and related issues of concern. It discusses, particularly, the divergent data protection clauses in each of the Agreements. In order to achieve global data protection standards, the EU and US laws on privacy in the field of law enforcement first need to be aligned.

Chapter 3 deals with Europol. It discusses the possibility that Europol data protection rules may become a model to follow for law enforcement authorities' data exchanges within and beyond the EU borders. It sets out the agency's procedures for the exchange of data with Member States and third countries, by focusing in particular on the use of the Secure Information Exchange Network (SIENA). It also discusses the main features of the proposed Europol regulation, and it compares the data protection standards of the agency with those applied by law enforcement authorities in the Member States. It then examines Europol's data exchanges beyond the EU, paying special attention to the relationship between the agency and the US.

There is a close co-operation between law enforcement authorities and intelligence services. In the prevention and investigation of crime, these bodies often exchange intelligence with each other. But what are the safeguards applicable for data collected or accessed by intelligence services? Chapter 4 provides an analysis of the National Security Agency (NSA) programmes and its secret collaboration with the Member States. It assesses whether the EU could set up data protection rules for the exchange of intelligence, despite the Treaty of Lisbon's exclusion of 'national security' matters. It also examines the scope and relevance of Article 39 of the Treaty of the European Union (TEU), and the feasibility of using this clause as a way to clarify the EU Intelligence Analysis Centre's (IntCen's) data transfers.

After analysing the challenges and issues of concern for the setting up of global data protection standards in the field of security, Chapter 5 presents initiatives for establishing international data protection principles. Particularly, it specifically looks at the Organisation for Economic Co-operation and Development (OECD) Privacy Guidelines, the Asia-Pacific Economic Cooperation (APEC) Privacy Framework, the UN Guidelines for the Regulation of Computerized Personal Data Files, the Council of Europe 1981 Convention and the Cybercrime Council of Europe (CoE) Convention. These are all proposals from international forums or organisations on the establishment of global data protection rules. After a careful examination, the chapter suggests a combination of the two CoE Conventions as the most adequate regulatory system to create a global data protection framework. It also explains how the EU has acquired an important role in influencing the CoE in the field of data protection.

In summary, this book identifies specific challenges that the EU needs to overcome in the field of law enforcement in order to achieve global rules on data protection and privacy. It concludes that the establishment of an international data protection framework for data processed for security purposes requires the EU first to promote consistency among its own Member States.

Bibliography

Boehm, F, 2012, *Information Sharing and Data Protection in the Area of Freedom, Security and Justice Towards Harmonised Data Protection Principles for Information Exchange at EU-level*, Springer, Berlin.

Bures, O, 2011, *EU Counterterrorism Policy. A Paper Tiger?*, Ashgate, Surrey.

Case C-131/12 *Google Spain SL, Google Inc. v Agencia Española de Protección de Datos (AEPD), Mario Costeja González* (CJEU, 13 May 2014).

Cases C-293/12 and C-594/12 *Digital Rights Ireland Ltd v Minister for Communications, Marine and Natural Resources and Others and Kärntner Landesregierung and Others* (CJEU, 8 April 2014).

Communication from the Commission to the European Parliament and the Council of 22 November 2010 – The EU Internal Security Strategy in Action: Five steps towards a more secure Europe, COM(2010)673 final.

De Busser, E, 2009, *Data Protection in EU and US Criminal Cooperation: A Substantive Law Approach to the EU Internal and Transatlantic Cooperation in Criminal Matters between Judicial and Law Enforcement Authorities*, Maklu Publishers, Antwerpen.

European Council, 2010, *European Council 2010/C 115/01 of 2 December 2009 on The Stockholm Programme – An open and secure Europe serving and protecting citizens.*

Hillebrand, C, 2012, *Networks in the European Union. Maintaining Democratic Legitimacy after 9/11*, Oxford University Press, Oxford.

Kokott, J and Sobotta, C, 2013, 'The distinction between privacy and data protection in the jurisprudence of the CJEU and the ECtHR', *International Data Privacy Law*, vol. 3, no. 4, pp. 222–228.

O'Neill, M, 2012, *The Evolving Counter-Terrorism Legal Framework*, Routledge Research in EU Law, New York.

Tzanou, M, 2012, *The added value of data protection as a fundamental right in the EU legal order in the context of law enforcement*, PhD thesis, European University Institute.

United Nations Security Council, 2001, *Threats to international peace and security caused by terrorist acts*, Resolution 1373(2001), 4385th meeting, 28 September 2001, United Nations, New York.

1 Data exchanges for law enforcement purposes within the EU

This analysis of the feasibility for the establishment of global data protection standards in the area of law enforcement begins by examining the existing European Union (EU) legislation on these matters. The first observation to be made is that Member States were originally the only competent to legislate in the field of criminal law. National governments enjoyed a wide discretion in the adoption of security measures, creating significant differences between Member States' criminal systems (Luchtman 2011). The same diversity existed for the particular rules on the collection and processing of data in the prevention, detection, investigation and prosecution of crimes. The main problem resulting from this disparity was the lack of police cross-border police co-operation in the exchange of relevant information during a criminal investigation.

Since the terrorist attacks of 9/11 (11 September 2001), and especially after the Madrid and London attacks in 2004 and 2005 respectively, the EU has significantly expanded its role within the Area of Freedom, Security and Justice (AFSJ) in the area of data exchange by adopting a number of legal instruments and systems that would add value to the traditional bilateral criminal-related data exchanges between Member States.

In the first chapter of this book, I attempt to concisely review the tools available within the EU for exchanging information between law enforcement authorities. The chapter demonstrates the growth in the creation of data-sharing tools used for security purposes at the EU level. This expansion includes systems that initially fell under the scope of border management and commercial policies. This study seeks to find out whether these multiple systems and actors are consistent with each other or not. It also examines whether these measures are actually effective in preventing and detecting crimes, or whether they are rather weak in practice (Bures and Ahern 2007: 187 and 223; Bures 2011: 245–254). After that, the EU data protection legislation covering the use of these systems and databases is studied. The chapter specifically examines whether all these instruments operating within the EU offer the same data protection standards for the individuals whose data are processed.

For the last 20 years the EU has been adopting measures in order to approximate national data protection legislations. Yet, the field of law enforcement has always been subject to special rules and conditions due to the intergovernmental nature of criminal laws. Therefore, this chapter explores the successes and shortcomings that the EU is encountering in the establishment of harmonised data protection rules in the field of law enforcement.

1 Origin, evolution and scope of the EC/EU legislation on the processing of personal data for criminal matters

In the current distribution of competences between the EU and its Member States, criminal law is, to a large extent, subject to the jurisdiction of each Member State. Consequently, 28 criminal codes coexist in the EU.[1] Some countries, due to their own national background, are characterised as having strong provisions on terrorism and other crimes (particularly, Spain, the United Kingdom (UK), France, Greece, Italy and Portugal), while others do not include many criminal offences in their national laws. In the same way, some legal jurisdictions of the Member States allow for certain elements of extraterritoriality when it comes to prosecuting for crimes, while others do not foresee it at all.[2]

Today, there is neither an EU institution with operational police powers, nor a unified EU criminal jurisdiction (Lööf 2008: 131). Yet, current crimes and offences are often difficult to locate in a well-defined country or territory. Often, these might be committed in more than one country, or even on different continents. The cross-border dimension of crime has prompted the establishment of a system of 'multilevel governance' on security matters (Lavenex and Wichmann 2009: 89), in which the EU has progressively adopted measures that co-ordinate Member States' security actions.

The first instruments enabling a cross-border co-operation among Member States date back to before the Treaty of Lisbon. Before Lisbon, there was no legal basis in the Treaties stating that the EU was competent to set up minimum rules on criminal matters. Therefore, the existing secondary legislation on that area was quite dispersed. The EU nonetheless found a way to legislate on criminal matters by enacting either intergovernmental measures within the scope of the former third pillar or directives as part of the former first pillar (the European Communities' pillar). With respect to the first-pillar legal instruments, a few instruments such as the Passenger Name Records (PNR) Agreements, the Advance Passenger Information (API) Directive and the now void Data Retention Directive were adopted. Also, regarding the former third pillar on Justice and Home Affairs (JHA), numerous intergovernmental measures for co-operation in law enforcement have come into force since the seventies.

1 Yet, it is worth noting that there is no 'criminal code' in either the United Kingdom (UK) or Ireland. In those countries, criminal law operates on the basis of a mixture of common law and statutes.
2 For instance, legal jurisdictions of England and Wales allow extraterritoriality for the prosecution of crimes, independent of the provisions in the limited number of EU framework decisions, and more recently directives, about the establishment of jurisdiction.

The Terrorism, Radicalism, Extremism and Political Violence (TREVI) Group was established by the European Council in 1976. Its function was to co-ordinate effective counter-terrorism responses among European governments by organising regular meetings at the ministerial level (Bunyan 1993). The TREVI Group worked on the development of Europol (initially called Europol Drugs Unit (EDU)) and on the definition of 'terrorism' (O'Neill 2012: 18). In 1979, two new EU initiatives were launched in the field of terrorism: an agreement on the application of the European Convention of Terrorism between the Member States, and the Police Working Group on Terrorism (PWGT). The PWGT was later absorbed by the TREVI Group (Kurth Cronin and Ludes 2004: 154), and integrated in the JHA since 1992 with the Maastricht Treaty.

In 1992, the Treaty of Maastricht introduced provisions that gave new competences to the EU in the field of criminal law. On the one hand, according to the principle of subsidiarity, the EU had competence to regulate on criminal matters as long as Member States were unable to do so (Baumeister 2008). On the other hand, Article 31(e) of the Treaty of the European Union (TEU) called for the establishment of minimum rules relating to the constituent elements of terrorist acts and penalties. The treaty set rules for the first time on JHA, and TREVI was officially dissolved (O'Neill 2012: 18). Two other working groups on criminal matters were established that year: the Terrorism Working Group (TWG) and the Working Party on Co-operation in Criminal Matters. While the first was composed of Member States' interior ministers and focused on law enforcement co-operation against internal security threats, the latter promoted mutual recognition of criminal acts and judgments within the EU. In essence, the idea of co-operating against terrorism and cross-border crimes became an EU priority with the Treaty of Maastricht.

Particularly relevant for this study is the role of Europol. Europol started functioning as the EDU within the framework of TREVI III, dealing mainly with drug-trafficking and money-laundering cases. In 1995, it extended its competences and covered also counter-terrorism investigations (O'Neill 2012: 71–72). Rules governing this body were first enclosed in the Europol Convention, which was ratified by all Member States in 1999. From that moment, Europol became the European law enforcement organisation responsible for assisting Member States 24/7 in the prevention and combat of serious forms of crime. Today, Europol is the largest AFSJ agency (Boehm 2012: 177), covering any crime that affects the common interest of the EU, as well as those serious crimes affecting two or more Member States.[3]

In 1997, three other initiatives were incorporated as part of the JHA. First, the Counter-terrorism Working Group (COTER) was established. It deals with current issues in the area of international co-operation against terrorism. Second, the Multidisciplinary Group on Organised Crime was created.[4] It draws up

---

3 Europol is thoroughly examined in Chapter 3 of this book.
4 Now replaced by the Working Party on General Matters.

guidelines for the co-ordinated fight against organised crime. Lastly, the Council established the Article 36 Committee (CATS). This committee co-ordinates the competent Council working groups in the field of police and judicial co-operation and prepares relevant work of the Permanent Representatives Committee (COREPER).[5]

The AFSJ has its origins in the Treaty of Amsterdam of 1999. Although the policy has no recognised definition to date, numerous scholars have tried to make sense of this new concept in their studies. In that sense, Wolf, Wichmann and Mounier define it as:

> An attempt to provide an overall strategic orientation to punctual measures adopted in the policy area of JHA, such as border management, the fight against terrorism and the fight against organized crime
>
> (Wolff, Wichmann and Mounier 2009: 10)

The Treaty of Amsterdam established in Article 61(e) TEU that the Council needed to adopt measures in the area of police and judicial co-operation that would enshrine a high level of security and would conform to the TEU. The Treaty amended some provisions of the JHA policy area. For instance, policies on border checks, asylum and immigration were moved from the former third pillar to the first, enhancing the Community's jurisdiction to adopt measures on criminal matters. Likewise, the Court of Justice of the European Union (CJEU) became competent to decide on the AFSJ legislation that fell under the scope of the first pillar. However, provisions on police and judicial co-operation in criminal matters remained as former third-pillar policies. Consequently, the only way for the European Communities (EC) to legislate on such areas was by widely interpreting criminal measures as part of the scope of either customs union or internal market policies.[6]

Thus, by the end of the nineties the EU had launched some initiatives to approximate national measures in the field of criminal matters. Among them, the Tampere Conclusions of 1999 are to be highlighted. They set up the European Police Chiefs Task Force as a forum where high-ranking national policemen could discuss cross-border security matters. Also, in the Tampere Conclusions the European Council pinpointed the need for a 'common effort [. . .] to prevent and fight crime and criminal organisations throughout the Union' (European Council 1999). However, the ratification of some of these measures was slow, and they were only accelerated after the 9/11 terrorist attacks.

The 9/11 attacks had a significant impact on the EU legislation, particularly on the adoption of new laws within the scope of the AFSJ (Hayes and Jones 2013). The first EU action plan on terrorism was adopted on 16 October 2001 and it

---

5 CATS has now turned into the Standing Committee on Internal Security (COSI Committee), regulated in Article 71 of the Treaty on the Functioning of the European Union (TFEU).

6 This is examined in section 3.2.3 of this chapter with respect to the void Directive 2006/24/EC.

enabled intelligence services of the Member States to exchange information and to increase their co-operation (Council of the European Union 2001). Likewise, the creation of the Counter-terrorism Group (CTG) and the CP 931 Working Party (Council Common Position 2001/931/CFSP) took place right after the attacks. The EU also adopted the European Security Strategy, in which it announced its aim of contributing to the global security through external actions (Council of the European Union 2003).

The EU security measures for the exchange of information increased dramatically after 9/11. Data exchanges between Member States and EU bodies became a crucial tool for the prevention of future similar attacks. Nevertheless, more terrorist attacks occurred: on 11 March 2004 when bombs were simultaneously detonated on the commuter train system in Madrid and, one year later, on 7 July 2005, similar bombings took place on three underground trains and a bus in central London.

The EU institutions launched several initiatives after the attacks in Madrid and London. The European Council (2004 and 2005) issued declarations, which highlighted the need to adopt common measures on the retention of telecommunications data as soon as possible. In response to both declarations, the Commission launched a series of communications suggesting ways how to improve the co-ordination of counter-terrorism activities inside the EU institutions and how to enhance the Member States' access to information (COM(2004) 376 final, COM(2004) 429 final, COM(2004) 698 final, COM(2004) 702 final, COM(2004) 701 final and COM(2004) 700 final). These communications also proposed the establishment of an integrated approach in the fight against terrorism. In 2005, two other EU instruments came into force: Council Decision on the exchange of information and co-operation concerning terrorist offences (Council Decision 2005/671/JHA), and the Hague Programme (COM(2005) 184 final). Even though this programme has been described as relatively timid by some scholars (Bures 2011: 70), it contained several recommendations for the intensification of police co-operation within the EU, and the establishment of systems for the cross-border exchange of information.

One day before the Treaty of Lisbon entered into force, several EU measures related to the exchange of information in the field of law enforcement were adopted (Council Decision 2009/917/JHA, Council Decision 2009/934/JHA, Council Decision 2009/936/JHA, Council Decision 2009/968/JHA and Council Decision 2009/902/JHA). The main reason for this was to avoid the new EU policy-making procedure, in which the European Parliament (EP) would vote for those security measures within the scope of the AFSJ in co-decision with the Council.

When the Treaty of Lisbon came into force in December 2009, the legal paradigm changed. One of the main amendments was the removal of the pillars and the shared competence between the EU and its Member States on the AFSJ,[7]

---

7 Articles 3(2) and 4(2)(j) TFEU.

including data-sharing security measures.[8] The Treaty of Lisbon also incorporates an explicit legal basis for the approximation of national criminal laws in Article 83 TFEU. According to this clause, the EU can establish:

> Minimum rules concerning the definition of criminal offences and sanctions in the areas of particularly serious crime with a cross-border dimension resulting from the nature or impact of such offences or from a special need to combat them on a common basis.

Thanks to this provision, the EU has expanded the definition of terrorism and it has also established a common list of terrorist groups. These EU common rules seek to complement national criminal laws, without replacing them. This is explicitly underlined in Article 276 TFEU, which states that:

> The Court of Justice of the European Union shall have no jurisdiction to review the validity or proportionality of operations carried out by the police or other law-enforcement services of a Member State or the exercise of the responsibilities incumbent upon member states with regard to the maintenance of law and order and the safeguarding of internal security.

The EU can also create rules on how to ensure the implementation of EU measures at the national level (Directive 2013/40/EU). According to Protocol 36, attached to the Treaty of Lisbon, Member States had to implement those EU instruments consisting of the exchange of data among law enforcement (formerly adopted under the third pillar) by 1 December 2014 (Council of the European Union 2014a). Article 10(4) of the Protocol foresaw the possibility that the UK would not implement such instruments as long as the notification was made at least six months before the expiry of the transitional period. The UK notified its intention to opt-out in 2013 (COM(2014) 596 final) and later opted back in again to 35 measures (Miller 2014). Today, the UK is bound by some of the current EU data-sharing systems – but not all of them. For instance, the UK has decided to rejoin Second Generation Schengen Information System (SIS II), Schengen Information System (SIS), European Criminal Records Information System (ECRIS), Eurojust, Europol and the Swedish initiative, to name but a few (European Parliament 2014a).

The Treaty of Lisbon also includes the participation of the EP and the CJEU in the decision and review of EU measures for the fight against terrorism and organised crime. Lastly, the solidarity clause of Article 222 TFEU binds Member States to provide assistance and to mobilise all instruments and resources at their disposal in case of a terrorist attack.

After the Treaty of Lisbon entered into force, the fear of a new terrorist attack within the EU reappeared, and France and Germany were the main targets

---

8 Articles 82(1) and 87(2)(a) TFEU.

(Kaunert 2012: 578). In consequence, new EU measures in the field of criminal law were enacted. The Commission released communications announcing its intentions to strengthen the EU counter-terrorism and criminal policies (COM (2010)386 final and COM(2011) 573 final), and the Ad Hoc Working Group on Information Exchange for an Information Management Strategy was subsequently established (Council of the European Union 2009).

Particularly relevant is the adoption of the Stockholm Programme in December 2009 (European Council 2009), in an attempt to assess the evolution and achievement of policies that were part of the AFSJ. In it, the Commission highlighted the primary concerns, and it introduced broad recommendations within the AFSJ. Likewise, the programme identified the increasing amount of data exchanged among Member States during criminal proceedings, and it referred to the current data-processing instruments.

Regarding the data-sharing measures for law enforcement purposes, the Commission released communications in 2010 and 2012 (COM(2010)385 final and COM(2012)735 final). In them, it underlined that 'no new EU-level law enforcement databases or information exchange instruments are [. . .] needed at this stage' (COM(2012)735 final, p. 2). However, the paradigm changed after the terrorist attacks occurred in Paris on 7 January 2015 and 13 November 2015. After these tragedies, Ministers of Home Affairs of the Member States have discussed the adoption of new counter-terrorism measures within the EU. These will reinforce the police and intelligence co-operation in the exchange of crime-related information. However, at the time of writing this book, there is no certainty as to the exact measures that will be adopted. Therefore, this book analyses only the data-sharing instruments and databases that are functioning today within the field of security.

2 EU data-sharing instruments for law enforcement purposes

Two methods for the exchange of crime-related information within the EU can be distinguished. The first one refers to the traditional Mutual Legal Assistance (MLA) procedure between Member States. It is a pure bilateral contract that allows Member State 'A' to request specific information from Member State 'B', and the latter has the obligation to transfer it. This system has been commonly used within the EU to gather evidence, information about previous convictions, fingerprints and many other relevant data during a criminal investigation.

However, after 9/11 and especially after the Madrid and London terrorist attacks, the EU has been seeking a stronger integration of its Member States within the AFSJ. Therefore, a number of EU instruments have been adopted to centralise and co-ordinate the exchange of information. These serve as an alternative to the traditional MLA procedures and deepen the EU integration in the field of criminal matters. The sections below analyse whether these systems work in a consistent manner, and whether they offer sufficient data protection safeguards.

2.1 The use of traditional MLA procedures within the EU

In order to understand the *raison d'être* of the European information systems, a few words about the functioning of the traditional MLA procedures are needed. The MLA procedures could be defined as the first step to reach a full mutual recognition among Member States. Mutual recognition is regulated in Article 82(2)(a) TFEU and it was first created as part of the EU economic policy. Resulting from the establishment of the single market, Member States had to find the way to recognise goods and products from other EU countries as equivalent in quality as their own domestic products. Today mutual recognition applies to other legal areas that are not harmonised at the EU level, such as criminal law. The new European Investigation Order (EIO), examined below, is one example of a measure applying mutual recognition in criminal matters.

As noted above, Member States differ in their criminal procedural systems. Thus, when a criminal investigation is carried out in one Member State by a particular national judicial authority, the procedures and laws enforced do not coincide in other EU countries (Jones 2011: 5; Sayers 2011: 3; Vernimmen-Van Tiggelen and Surano 2008: 23). This hinders the efficient co-operation between Member States in the exchange of criminal information. Therefore, both the Tampere and Hague Programmes defined mutual recognition as the cornerstone of the EU judicial co-operation (European Council 1999; Council of the European Union 2013a: 3).

In cases where mutual recognition is not possible, the traditional MLA procedures can still apply. The Commission defines the MLA procedure as:

> The cooperation between different countries for the purpose of gathering and exchanging information, and requesting and providing assistance in obtaining evidence located in one country to assist in criminal investigations or proceedings in another
>
> (European Commission 2015)

The main distinction between the mutual recognition and the MLA regimes is the power of the executing authority: under the mutual recognition system, the national judicial authority directly orders the foreign authority to recognise and execute a decision. The grounds for refusal by the foreign authorities are very limited here. In contrast, the MLA regime gives the foreign Member State the discretion to refuse the execution of the order (Mangiaracina 2014: 115–116). This section focuses exclusively on the analysis of the MLA procedure, since it predominates in the exchange of information among law enforcement forces.

MLA was originally only regulated by the Council of Europe (CoE). In particular, the Convention on mutual assistance in criminal matters (hereinafter, MLA Convention) dates back to 1959 and has been ratified by all Member States (Council of Europe 1959). It is accompanied by two protocols, signed in 1978 and 2001. Although EU Member States adopted rules on MLA since 1959, the establishment of an MLA procedure within the EU to assist cross-border exchanges of information for law enforcement purposes became a major necessity back in the mid-1990s. During those years the Treaty of Amsterdam and Tampere European Council called for an enhancement of MLA in criminal matters as part of the programme for developing an AFSJ (Jones 2011: 9).

MLA procedures were reinforced in 2000. That year, the Council adopted an act supplementing the MLA Convention between the Member States – hereinafter, EU MLA Convention – (Council Act 2000/C 197/01). It was accompanied by a protocol (Council Act of 16 October 2001), which came into force in 2005. Article 13 of the EU MLA Convention includes new mechanisms for the exchange of information within the EU such as the creation of Joint Investigation Teams (JITs). JITs were first defined in 2002 (Council Framework Decision 2002/465/JHA) as agreements signed by two or more Member States to conduct a criminal investigation together for a limited period.

Although MLA procedures have been designed to enable a fluent communication among EU police and judicial authorities, their use has been subject to several problems in practice. First, MLA procedures consist of a flexible and discretionary system that requires a case-by-case consideration by the requested Member State. This procedure creates uncertainty because it is the requested country that decides whether it wants to provide the information or not. Second, the procedure does not always involve a court authorisation over the particular information collected (European Digital Rights 2013: 18). Lastly, the MLA Convention does not include rules on automated processes and response times for requests. Although Article 5(4) of the EU MLA Convention obliges the requested authority to inform without delay, there is no mandatory rule on the length of the procedure, so it tends to be slow. All of these issues cause uncertainty for the actors participating in the MLA procedures, since the system varies from one country to the other, and from case to case.

Trying to overcome the flaws of the MLA procedures, the EU decided to adopt complementary legal instruments, which facilitated the co-operation of law enforcement authorities in the exchange of data. These are the Swedish initiative, the Prüm Decisions, the ECRIS Decisions, and the EIO initiative.

2.2 Post-9/11 data-sharing instruments

The Madrid terrorist attacks of 2004 highlighted the necessity to create a better system for accessing and exchanging crime-related information between Member States. In that sense, the Hague Programme noted that 'full use [had to] be made of new technology and that there [had to] be reciprocal access to national databases' (Council Decision 2008/615/JHA, recital 7). At that time, the EU had only a few instruments regulating cross-border law enforcement data exchanges, such as the Europol and Eurojust Conventions, the EU Convention on Mutual Assistance in Criminal Matters 2000, and the Council Framework Decision on Joint Investigation Teams.

In particular, MLA procedures had too many limitations, since they were only designed to share information bilaterally and, as described above, it can take months from the moment a Member State receives the information requested from another Member State. For those reasons, the EU established other legal instruments to be implemented by Member States in order to accelerate, simplify and intensify the co-operation between them in the exchange of information.

The first instrument adopted by the EU for improving the co-operation among EU Member States in the exchange of criminal information was the Swedish initiative (Council Framework Decision 2006/960/JHA) in 2006. According to Article 1 of the the Swedish initiative, it has the following purpose:

> To establish the rules under which Member States' law enforcement authorities may exchange existing information and intelligence effectively and expeditiously for the purpose of conducting criminal investigations or criminal intelligence operations.

Article 3 of the Swedish initiative requires complying with the 'principle of availability' (Council of the European Union 2011: 2), which guarantees the requesting Member State 'equivalent access' (COM(2012)735 final, p. 2) to that offered to the internal authorities. This principle, which was first introduced in the Hague Programme (COM(2005) 184 final, point 2.1), means that a Member State cannot request conditions stricter than those required for its national law enforcement authorities for a purely internal case. Regarding the time limits, Article 4 establishes that transfers for urgent cases should not exceed eight hours from the moment the request is sent. In contrast, non-urgent requests may take up to 14 days until the requesting Member State receives the information.

The Swedish initiative was later complemented by the Prüm procedures. Prüm is a decentralised system of national databases that dates back to 2005. That year, seven Member States – Belgium, Germany, Spain, France, Luxembourg, the Netherlands and Austria – signed the Prüm Convention (Council of the European Union 2005), which aimed at achieving a closer co-operation between Member States in the investigation of crimes with a potential cross-border dimension. As in the Swedish initiative, it sought 'to overcome lengthy mutual legal assistance bureaucratic procedures by establishing a single national contact point' (Töpfer 2011). Through these contact units, Member State 'A' could send a request to Member State 'B' to check whether the latter had DNA, fingerprint, or vehicle data for a specific target. If so, a 'hit' would be sent to the requesting Member State and, only then, would that country be able to send a second request for accessing such data (Soleto Muñoz and Fiodorova 2014: 152).

Originally, the Prüm Convention was a purely intergovernmental agreement and, therefore, it fell outside the scope of the EU treaties. Criticism about the lack of transparency (European Parliament 2007) led to a change in the Prüm Convention's nature in 2008. A proposal to integrate Prüm into the EU laws was presented in January 2007 by the German Presidency of the Council (Hernanz 2011: 8) and, one year later, the provisions of the treaty were transposed into EU instruments: the Prüm Decisions (Council Decisions 2008/615/JHA and 2008/616/JHA).

The Prüm Decisions are based on the main provisions of the former Prüm Convention, but they improve and speed up the exchange of information. Exchange mechanisms for DNA, fingerprint (FP) and vehicle registration data (VRD) of the Prüm Convention have also been transposed into the legal framework of the EU (COM(2012) 735 final, p. 4). In the new instrument, a distinction is made between DNA and exchange on the one hand, and VRD on the other. For the first two categories of data, which are biometric, the mechanism operates on a 'hit/no-hit' basis,[9] and the related personal data is only provided in response to a separate follow-up request. In other words, in the case of a hit, the national contact point conducting the search receives only a confirmation, but never the information on the DNA or samples (Hernanz 2011: 8). After a hit, the requesting authorities are required to use pre-existing bilateral or multilateral agreements (e.g. MLA procedures, the Swedish initiative, etc) for obtaining the necessary biometric data.

Along with the Swedish initiative and the Prüm Decisions, a further instrument was launched in 2004: ECRIS. Designed for the exchange of information on convictions among Member States, ECRIS was the successor of the Network of Judicial Registers, a tool set up by Germany, France, Spain and Belgium in 2003. In 2005, the Commission released a white paper shaping the initiative (COM(2005) 10 final) and, a few months later, the Council adopted on the exchange of information extracted from the criminal record (Council Decision 2005/876/JHA), which was amended in 2008 (Council Framework Decision 2008/675/JHA).

In the course of any national criminal proceeding, ECRIS allows police and judicial authorities to obtain information about all previous convictions registered in other Member States. With the same purpose, the Commission adopted two other legal instruments in 2009: a Council framework decision on the exchange of information extracted from criminal records (Council Framework Decision 2009/315/JHA), and the Council decision establishing the European Criminal Records Information System (Council Decision 2009/316/JHA) – hereinafter, the ECRIS Decisions. The ECRIS Decisions established rules among Member States for the exchange of information on convictions and data extracted from criminal records. Through this system, any EU country could access comprehensive information on the offending history of any EU citizen, irrespective of the country in which the person was convicted. As a result, the possibility for offenders to escape their criminal past simply by moving from one Member State to another was extinguished. The system allows the sending of fingerprint imagery and alphanumerical data, which are transmitted by the ECRIS software installed in every Member State. This software is programmed to notify the end of the data retention after 30 days.

---

9 The hit/no hit system means that DNA profiles or fingerprints found at a crime scene in one Member State can be compared with profiles held in databases of other Member States.

The last of the EU data-sharing instruments to be studied in this chapter is the EIO. The EIO is a judicial decision issued by a Member State in order to have one or several specific investigative measure(s) carried out in another Member State with the purpose of gathering evidence (Council of the European Union 2010). The EU decided to establish a comprehensive system for obtaining evidence in cross-border dimension cases (COM(2010) 171, para. 3.1.1) after some Member States complained that existing instruments for sharing evidence constituted a fragmentary regime.[10] These countries submitted an initiative to the EP and the Council on which they proposed a Directive for the EIO. The proposal was officially launched in April 2010, but this was not adopted until April 2014 (Directive 2014/41/EU). It is based on Article 76(2) TFEU and binds all Member States except for Denmark and Ireland.

The current ways of obtaining evidence from abroad are either by *commission rogatoires* or letters of request (Sayers 2011: 1). As seen above, MLA procedures have often been criticised for being slow and inefficient. In this sense, the EIO has partially replaced those systems of criminal evidence-exchange by integrating them into a single, efficient and flexible instrument for obtaining evidence. Based on the mutual recognition principle, it facilitates judicial co-operation, simplifying the procedure through a single instrument, and helping national law enforcement agencies become more effective in the combat of cross-border crime (Whitehead and Porter 2010).

As regards the types of data processed, the EIO applies to almost all investigative measures,[11] regardless of the type of evidence.[12] According to Articles 24–27 of the EIO Directive, it includes bank data, phone records, DNA, statements from suspects or witnesses, the interception of communications, analyses of documents, and fingerprints, to name but a few. Moreover, the EIO Directive is not only used to exchange existing evidence, but it also shares information that does not yet exist but might be necessary for an investigation. For example, France requests that Spain monitors certain suspects in real time, or asks it to obtain DNA samples and fingerprints (Mangiaracina 2014: 120). The evidence does not exist yet, but this activity can still be requested through an EIO.

In conclusion, the growth of global terrorism in the last 15 years has entailed the creation of several data-sharing instruments within the EU borders. These multilateral instruments coexist with the MLA procedures and they have the purpose of establishing better co-operation in the exchange of criminal information among Member States. Leaving aside the debated added value of these instruments in practice (Bossong 2008; Coolsaet 2010; Bures 2011), the next section identifies their shortcomings in the terms of their implementation and use.

---

10 Belgium, Bulgaria, Estonia, Spain, Austria, Slovenia and Sweden.
11 Except for two types of interceptions of telecommunications for which complex rules are provided in Articles 18–22 of the 2000 EU MLA Convention.
12 This differs from the European Evidence Warrant (EEW), whose scope is limited to specific types of 'object[s], documents and data'.

2.3 Shortcomings in the implementation and use of EU legal instruments for exchanging criminal information

The Swedish initiative, the Prüm Decisions, the ECRIS Decisions and the EIO initiative aim at facilitating the exchange of criminal information among police and judicial agents. However, these instruments have presented two main problems in practice: an enormous delay in their implementation, and confusion regarding how and when these systems should be used.

2.3.1 Delay in the implementation

There is a general transposition failure among Member States associated with the EU counter-terrorism measures (Argomaniz 2010). This problem has been apparent in all aforementioned EU data-sharing instruments except for the EIO Directive, which Member States have time to transpose until 22 May 2017.

Several Member States have not yet implemented the Swedish initiative.[13] In September 2014 the Council released new guidelines for accelerating the implementation process and use of this system. Member states were requested to fill out a factsheet with the list of information that is directly accessible to their national law enforcement authorities, other authorities, and private entities. Information that requires a prior court order to be accessed, the languages used, Single Point of Contact (SPOC) and their contact details were also requested. That information was communicated by 1 October 2014 (Council of the European Union 2014b), but the implementation process in these countries is not yet finalised.

In the case of the Prüm Decisions, although all Member States have now legally transposed them, the system is not yet fully operational. Although almost all Member States have installed the Combined DNA Index System (CODIS) 7.0 as a DNA data searches system, only a few of them have it up and running. The same occurs with the Automated Fingerprint Identification System (AFIS) for fingerprints, which is only partially operational in all Member States. The European Car and Driving License Information System (EUCARIS) for VRD searches is more successful than the previous two programmes, but it is fully active in only 19 countries. Lastly, Member States had to send a data protection questionnaire to the Council before the implementation of Prüm, but only 21 of the 28 Member States have submitted them to date (Council of the European Union 2015).

With regard to ECRIS, all Member States implemented the system by April 2012, but many of them still lack the technical infrastructure to connect their criminal records systems. In order to fix this, in October 2014 the Council released guidelines describing ECRIS technical specifications to be followed by Member

---

13 Austria, Belgium, Greece, Ireland, Italy, Luxembourg, Malta and the UK have not yet implemented the system.

States (Council of the European Union 2014c, 2014d, 2014e). Moreover, the system might change in the near future, since the Commission has considered adding a supplementary index in the programme that stores criminal records from non-EU nationals who have committed crimes in a Member State (European e-Justice Portal 2015).

There are many factors that explain the lack of implementation and usage of the EU information systems. Some of the reasons given include: the absence of political will, the existence of institutional weaknesses in some countries, and the fact that before Lisbon the Commission had no control over these measures because they were part of the third pillar (COM(2012) 735 final, p. 8; Jones 2012: 3; Argomaniz 2010: 306).

Particularly, the lack of political will is the main cause of the slow transposition of a counter-terrorism measure. Not all Member States see the establishment of law enforcement measures as a priority at national level. In fact, even the Member States that feel most threatened by terrorism do not always implement those measures on time (Argomaniz 2010: 308). Another additional problem is the lack of institutional resources. Some Member States do not have the adequate structures to make the systems fully operational. Lastly, other Member States lack the personnel training necessary to use these instruments (Politsei-ja Piirivalveamet 2013). All of these problems can be seen as part of domestic structural deficiencies.

2.3.2 Complexities in the usage

Many scholars have identified a lack of coherence in many aspects relating to the current EU counter-terrorism policy (Eckes 2011; Argomaniz 2012), which includes inconsistencies among instruments such as the Swedish initiative, the Prüm Decisions, the ECRIS Decisions and the EIO initiative. It is probable that after they are fully implemented, their use by law enforcement authorities might still be confusing. The reason is that these legal tools have been designed to complement each other but sometimes their functionalities may overlap. This will cause uncertainty for the national authorities about when to use the particular instrument. The risk is that national police forces decide to use informal mechanisms of communication instead, in a way to circumvent the complexities of the existing EU instruments.

A first difficulty detected in these legal systems refers to the channels used for exchanging the information. Some of the systems incorporate new channels, but not all. For instance, the Swedish initiative takes place via the existing channels for international law enforcement co-operation, and the choice of channel is left to the Member States. Annex B of the decision mentions Europol National Unit (ENU)/Europol Liaison Officers, Interpol National Central Bureau (Interpol NCB), Supplementary Information Request at the National Entry Bureaux (SIRENE) and Liaison Officers, but other options such as mutual assistance channels can be used. Similar channels are offered in the Prüm Decisions: Europol Liaison Officer, Interpol NCB, SIRENE and bilateral Liaison Officers (COM(2012)

732 final, p. 7). In contrast, in ECRIS the interconnection among national law enforcement authorities is carried out via the Commission's Secured Trans European Services for Telematics between Administrations (s-TESTA) network – which is a common communication infrastructure providing an encrypted network (Council Decision 2009/316/JHA, p. 3). Lastly, Article 7 of the EIO Directive states that various options for channels are available for the EIO, since data can be transmitted from the issuing authority to the executing authority 'by any means capable of producing a written record'.

Therefore, too many channels are available. In this regard, the Council is currently working on setting up a SPOC in every Member State for international law enforcement information exchanges. SPOCs seek to improve the use of all these existing platforms for exchanging information, by constituting a 'one stop shop' for all of them. The SPOC will manage under the same structure the ENU, the Interpol NCB, the SIRENE, the foreign liaison officers, the Swedish Framework Decision, the Prüm Decisions, and the regional/bilateral contact points. It will also access databases of SIS, Visa Information System (VIS), Eurodac, Customs Information System (CIS), Europol (SIENA), Interpol, etc, and will be the unit in charge of replying to any international request sent to the Member State (Council of the European Union 2014f).

In conclusion, this section has detected shortcomings in the implementation and use of the EU data-sharing systems, which are negatively affecting the EU multilateral co-operation in the AFSJ. The correct use of the measures is only possible after all Member States fully implement them. Because of the challenges mentioned above, several Member States have opted for exchanging criminal records through other traditional/CoE MLA procedures discussed above. MLA procedures are particularly attractive to law enforcement authorities because they allow free-text exchange of messages subject to lower levels of scrutiny (Vermeulen and Wills 2011: 17). However, as seen above, this procedure entails many problems regarding the efficiency and duration. Law enforcement authorities have also opted for exchanging data through regular email accounts or phone calls. A clear example of this practice was the communication between France and Spain in the past during investigations into the Spanish terrorist group ETA (Euskadi Ta Askatasuna). None of the EU provisions on cross-border policing precluded bilateral arrangements.[14] Thus, these two countries did not use any EU channel for exchanging information, nor did they involve any EU agency such as Europol or Eurojust. This is even more problematic since crime-related information is not exchanged through secure channels, meaning it can also be easily intercepted and exposed.

---

14 Bilateral arrangements had their own security arrangements and mechanisms, outside the scope of the EU.

3 Expanding the information sources of member states: data collected for non-criminal reasons but ultimately used for law enforcement

As pointed out by Hijmans and Scirocco, 'information tends to be used if it exists' (Hijmans and Scirocco 2009: 1491). The EU has gradually increased the number of information systems and databases accessible to law enforcement authorities. Particularly, the EU has amended legislation regulating the collection of personal data for commercial and border management purposes to allow the law enforcement sector to process such data. When personal data collected for one specific purpose is further accessed or processed for another purpose, this might infringe the 'purpose limitation principle'. This principle is included in Article 5(b) of the Convention for the Protection of Individuals with regard to the Automatic Processing of Personal Data (1981 CoE Data Protection Convention) (Council of Europe 1981),[15] Article 6(1)(b) of Directive 95/46/EC and Article 3 of Council Framework Decision 2008/977/JHA. The following sections examine the systems and databases through which the EU has gradually widened the use of personal information for law enforcement purposes.

3.1 Shift from border management to law enforcement purposes

In November 2010 the Commission released a Communication on a comprehensive approach on personal data protection in the EU (COM(2010) 609 final). The communication discerned 20 different AFSJ actors dealing with the collecting and processing of personal data at the EU level. The list included the following European Information Systems: SIS/SIS II, VIS, CIS and Eurodac. All of these were originally created for border control purposes; yet, terrorist attacks that have occurred in the last ten years have caused a shift in the use of these systems. Thus, since 2005, they started to alter their original objectives, becoming today effective tools in the prevention, detection and investigation of crimes, in addition to their original roles. This section examines how data collected by SIS, VIS, CIS and Eurodac can also now be processed for law enforcement purposes.

SIS has its origins in the Schengen Agreement concluded in 1985. It regulated the control of Member States' external borders, and the third-country nationals entering the EU territory. At first, only five Member States signed the Agreement: Belgium, France, the Netherlands, Luxembourg and West Germany. These Member States implemented the Agreement through the 1990 Schengen Agreement Application Convention (SAAC) (Schengen Implementation Agreement 1990). From that moment, they became part of the Schengen Area. This area was established to abolish internal checks and create a common external border, reinforcing the security measures to combat illegal immigration. The SAAC included a chapter referring to SIS and SIRENE. SIS consisted of a joint

---

15 This Convention is examined in Chapter 5.

information system composed by national sections of each Member State that could rapidly and effectively transfer data relating to border checks and movement of persons to a central database. SIRENE was the channel used to exchange information.

SIS came into operation in 1995. Its purpose is to strengthen the co-operation between immigration, police and custom authorities for the maintenance of public order and State security.[16] Member states have the possibility to issue an alert on people: (a) wanted for arrest; (b) in connection with police investigations or criminal proceedings; and (c) to be refused entry to the entire Schengen Area. It also informs on lost or stolen vehicles, firearms, identity documents and bank notes. Searches through SIS produce a 'hit', which specifies the action to be taken against the person who is denied the entry to the Schengen Area (Hayes and Vermeulen 2012: 31). There are currently more than 41,000 individuals included in SIS, and the system produces more than 1,000 hits every month (Statewatch 2014).

Law enforcement's access to the SIS is not new. In 1990, the SAAC introduced in Articles 39(1) and 46 the possibility for police authorities to access data collected by the visa part of the system. Later, the EU adopted two new legislative measures that granted competence to law enforcement authorities (Council Regulation (EC) No 871/2004; Council Decision 2005/211/JHA). Europol also gained access to a limited amount of data entered into SIS.

However, SIS was a system with limited capabilities, since it could only technically serve a maximum of 18 countries. Because of the number of entries in the system was increasing every year, the EU expressed the need to develop a second generation SIS (SIS II), which would incorporate the latest developments in the field of information technology (Hayes 2004: 17).

SIS II became operational in April 2013. It has a capacity of 100 million alerts and it introduces the possibility to gather biometric data, such as fingerprints and photographs, from persons wanted for arrest, missing persons, persons sought to assist with judicial procedures (e.g. witnesses) and persons subject to discreet checks.

With respect to the VIS, 2004 VIS Decision (Council Decision 2004/512/EC) aimed at supporting the EU common visa policy by establishing a common identification system for data on short-stay visas among Member States. In order to implement the 2004 VIS Decision a regulation was adopted in 2008 (Council Decision 2008/633/JHA). The 2008 Council Decision enhances Article 3 of the previous VIS Regulation by allowing law enforcement authorities to access VIS data. Besides immigration and asylum authorities, and authorities responsible for carrying out checks at external border crossing points, 2008 Council Decision granted access to national law enforcement authorities, Europol, as well as third countries or international organisations.

VIS did not become operative until 2011. It processed one million visa applications during the first year, and more than four million during 2012–2013

---

16 The concept and scope of 'State security' or 'national security' is discussed in Chapter 4.

(Council of the European Union 2014g: 3). The system is rapidly expanding year by year. In 2012 and 2013 it enhanced its competence to cover the entire African continent, the Near East, the Gulf Region; and it currently covers the entire world.

CIS has its origin in the Convention on the use of information technology for customs purposes (Council Act 95/C316/02), and the convention on mutual assistance and co-operation between customs administrations (Council Act 98/C 24/01). These were created to combat smuggling. CIS was signed in 1995 but it did not come into force until 2005, after being ratified by all Member States. The convention was replaced by a regulation adopted under the scope of the first pillar (Regulation (EC) No 766/2008). It regulated the collection of information on persons for the specific purposes of sighting and reporting, discreet surveillance and specific checks. CIS was thus used if there was enough evidence suggesting that the target has committed, is committing or will commit actions in breach of customs or agricultural legislation.[17]

CIS data is also used for law enforcement purposes today. Besides the 'traditional' CIS, the CIS Decision was adopted in 2008 within the scope of the third pillar (Council Decision 2009/917/JHA). According to Article 1(2) of the CIS Decision, its main purpose is 'to assist in preventing, investigating and prosecuting serious contraventions of national laws by making information available more rapidly'. Moreover, Article 5 of the CIS Decision states that data entering into CIS is to be used by law enforcement authorities for the purposes of sighting and reporting, discreet surveillance, specific checks and strategic or operational analysis.

Regarding the asylum seekers' data, in 1990 the Dublin Convention determining the state responsible for examining applications for asylum in one of the Member States of the former European Communities was signed (Convention 97/C 254/01). The examination was conducted through a centralised system that compared the asylum applicants' fingerprints. It was called Eurodac and its main purpose was to assist in determining which Member State was responsible for examining an application for asylum. At the same time, it also prevented cases of asylum shopping[18] and refugees in orbit.[19] Eurodac was first regulated in 2000 by a council regulation (Council Regulation (EC) No 2725/2000) binding those countries that had implemented the Dublin *acquis* – namely, all Member States plus the European Free Trade Association (EFTA) states.[20] Eurodac started its operations in 2003 and it established a centralised system that connected all 28 national access points.

An amendment of the Eurodac Regulation was adopted in June 2013 (Regulation (EU) No 604/2013). Similar to the aforementioned SIS II and VIS

---

17 Data in the field of agriculture refer to imported goods; businesses; goods detained, seized or confiscated; etc.
18 *Asylum shopping* is when multiple asylums applications are submitted simultaneously or successively by the same person in several Member States.
19 *Refugees in orbit* refers to a situation in which all Member States claim not to be responsible for examining an asylum application.
20 Iceland, Norway, Switzerland and Liechtenstein.

databases, introduced the possibility for Member States' law enforcement authorities and Europol to access Eurodac's central database for the purposes of the prevention, detection and investigation of serious criminal offences.

Therefore, the EU has been modifying some of the instruments originally designed to control illegal immigration within the European borders, sharing the information obtained with law enforcement authorities for the prevention and investigation of crimes.

3.2 EU data-sharing instruments created under the basis of the EU internal market clause

EU measures originally created to control external borders are not the only ones experiencing an expansion of the purposes for which they are used. As the European Data Protection Supervisor (EDPS) pointed out '[t]here is now a tendency to require that private actors co-operate with law enforcement authorities on a systematic basis' (EDPS 2013: 5). This section looks at some of the current private entities' databases that were originally established within the scope of the internal market provision (Article 114 TFEU). The data they collect was primarily used for commercial reasons, but now it is also used for purposes related to the prevention, detection, investigation and prosecution of a crime. This analysis focuses on three particular cases: (a) passenger data collected by EU airline companies; (b) financial data collected by the Belgian company SWIFT; and (c) data collected by European telecommunication service providers (TSPs) and information society services.

3.2.1 Exchange of passenger data within the EU

More than 1.7 billion passengers pass through EU airports every year (Airport Council International 2015). Aviation security has been one of the priorities within the EU internal security policy, seeking to 'keep up with the continuous innovation demonstrated by terrorist groups' (COM(2013) 179 final, p. 8). In that sense, the Commission proposed the EU Passenger Name Record Directive (EU PNR Directive) in 2011. In order to understand this instrument, it is necessary first to briefly introduce their international counterpart: the EU-US PNR Agreement.[21]

In response to the 9/11 attacks, the US authorities adopted measures that obliged airlines taking off, landing or flying through the US territory to turn over all their flight booking and departure data to the US government. This information is referred to as Passenger Name Records or PNR data. PNR data is defined as a record of the itinerary of a travelling person saved in the database of an airline, usually during the booking process (Hernanz 2011: 4).

---

21 A careful assessment of existing PNR agreements, and especially the EU-US PNR Agreement, is carried out in Chapter 2.

The EU-US PNR Agreement was signed in 2004 (Commission Decision 2004/535/EC; Council Decision 2004/496/EC). The conclusion of the Agreement was based on ex Article 95 TEC (the internal market clause)[22] in combination with the implied powers doctrine (de Busser 2009: 366). The choice of this legal basis was made upon the consideration that the collection of PNR data by private companies was a purely economic activity, necessary for the sale of an airplane ticket. In fact, for decades, airline companies had customarily stored their passengers' personal data in private databases for commercial purposes. It was only after 9/11 that the US authorities began to seize and transfer such data to public databases for the fight against terrorism.

The EP, supported by the EDPS, challenged the decisions before the CJEU. The EP argued that the EU-US PNR Agreement had been adopted under the wrong legal basis since the main objective did not concern the internal market, but a matter of public security and criminal law (third pillar). The CJEU agreed with the EP and in May 2006 it annulled the decisions that enabled the PNR Agreement (Cases C-317 and 318/04, *Parliament v Council* (2006)). The Court observed that even if it were true that data was originally collected for commercial purposes, the use of such data had later changed from private to public hands. The Court found that the main purpose of the Agreement was the prevention and combating of terrorism and, therefore, it considered that the measure should fall under the scope of the former third pillar and not as part of the Community law.

The Court's choice to annul the 2004 EU-US PNR Agreement entailed negative consequences for the enforcement of the EU data protection legislation. Subsequent EU-US PNRs adopted in 2006, 2007 and 2012 moved the matter from the first pillar (ex Article 95 TEC) to the third pillar (ex Article 24(1) TEU) and, therefore, Directive 95/46/EC was no longer applicable.[23]

During the negotiations of the PNR agreements, the EP voiced its concerns about the lack of reciprocity on PNR matters. With the adoption of these international agreements, passenger data was transferred from the EU to the US, but not vice versa. The trigger for the initial discussions on the possibility to create an EU PNR scheme was the failed car bomb attacks in London and at Glasgow Airport in June 2007 (Argomaniz 2009: 130). In November that year, the Commission launched a proposal for a Council framework decision with the aim to:

> [H]armonise Member State's provisions on obligations for air carriers operating flights to or from the territory of at least one Member State regarding the transmission of PNR data to the competent authorities for the purpose of preventing and fighting terrorist offences and organised crime.
>
> (COM(2007) 654 final, p. 6)

22　This is not expressly stated in the Agreement, which only refers to Directive 95/46/EC as the legal basis.

23　This issue is better assessed in Chapter 2.

However, in November 2008 the EP refused to issue a formal opinion on the proposal for not granting enough protection for the individual rights (European Parliament 2008). Therefore, in February 2011, the Commission presented a new proposal for an EU PNR Directive, this time with an impact assessment attached (SEC(2011) 132 and SEC(2011) 133 final). As in the current EU-US PNR Agreement, the main purpose is the prevention, detection, investigation and prosecution of terrorist offences, serious crimes, and serious transnational crimes. Unlike the 2004 EU-US PNR Agreement, the EU PNR Directive is based on Articles 82(1)(d) and 87(2)(a) TFEU and its main purpose is the prevention, combat and investigation of crimes (COM(2011) 32 final). Thus, we can observe a change in the purpose for collecting passenger data in the 2004 EU-US PNR Agreement and this EU PNR Directive.

The EU PNR Proposal allows the collection of up to 19 categories of data from both EU and non-EU citizens by airline companies at the moment of the ticket purchase. These will be sent to specific Passenger Information Units (PIUs) in the Member State prior the flight departure (Bellanova and Duez 2012: 115). The PIUs will be in charge of cross-checking the data for predetermined criteria. In the case of a positive match, the specific data will be evaluated. Data will be encrypted from the moment it is collected by airline companies. It will then be stored in the specific PIU for five years. The goal is that, during that period of time, such data will produce information linked to subsequent passengers (Bellanova and Duez 2012: 120).

The EP was doubtful about the necessity of collecting data from all types of passengers – suspects and non-suspects. Therefore, in April 2013 the proposal was rejected by the European Parliament Civil Liberties Committee (LIBE) and, consequently, the EP suspended its voting in 2014. However, the terrorist attacks that occurred in Paris on 7 January 2015 revived the debate as to the necessity for an EU PNR system to combat terrorism. In order to prevent Member States from installing national PNR regimes or the Commission from launching a new proposal, the LIBE Committee finally suggested amendments on the 2011 proposal (European Parliament 2015). Among them, it suggests replacing the broad concept of 'serious crimes' for 'serious transnational crimes', retaining data for only four years in cases of serious transnational crimes, collect data for intra-EU flights, and enhancing the conditions for transferring PNR data to third countries (Blasi Casagran 2015). The new text is now being discussed by the Council, the Commission and the EP through trilogues.

3.2.2 Exchange of financial data within the EU

Law enforcement authorities of the Member States also expressed interest in accessing EU citizens' financial data. In 2000, a Council decision on the cooperation between financial intelligence units of the Member States for exchanging information was adopted.[24] Yet, the creation of an EU system for the exchange

---

24 OJ L 271, 24 October 2000, pp. 4–6.

of financial data was postponed in 2001 due to the 9/11 attacks: at the time the exchange of financial data between the US and the EU was the priority.

In December 2001, two Europol-US agreements were concluded for the exchange of information related to global financial movements (Agreement 2001 and Supplemental Agreement 2002). They were part of the so-called Terrorist Finance Tracking Program (TFTP), established in secret by the Bush Administration to pull EU citizens' data from a private company, the Society for the Worldwide Interbank Financial Telecommunication (SWIFT). SWIFT was based in Belgium, but the US authorities were able to access the data because it also had servers located in the US. Thus, depending on where the EU citizens' data was being processed, the company had to comply with either Belgian national laws implementing Directive 95/46/EC (first pillar)[25] or US laws. In this sense, the company always processed EU citizens' data through its servers located in the US in order to avoid potential clashes with European laws.

The TFTP was uncovered in 2006 by the *New York Times* (Lichtblau and Risen 2006). It created a big debate within the EU and as a result SWIFT decided to move all of its servers completely to the territory of the EU Member States (Cremona 2011: 13; Curtin 2011: 6). Since financial data from EU citizens was now processed on EU soil, the company had to comply with EU data protection laws. Consequently, the Commission urged the drafting of an agreement enabling data transfers from the EU to the US.

In 2005, the EU had only one instrument for the prevention and combat of terrorist financing (Directive 2005/60/EC). This was introduced as a consequence of the Madrid attacks and it obliged financial institutions within the EU to control and store their clients' data. If any suspicious transaction was noticed, it was to be communicated to the designated authorities. Nevertheless, that directive raised concerns about data protection, transparency and accountability rights (Wesseling 2014: 21). Also, the fact that the banks were responsible for detecting terrorist transactions made the system quite ineffective since, clearly, the banks' primary mission is not related to national security (Wesseling 2014: 24).

On 30 November 2009, the SWIFT Agreement came into force. The Agreement was adopted under the scope of the ex-third pillar, with a combined legal basis of former Articles 24 and 38 TEU. The SWIFT Agreement was provisionally applied after signature, but this was then abrogated after the negative EP vote in February 2010.[26]

In the summer of 2010, a second SWIFT Agreement (SWIFT II) was adopted. One of the changes it included was the future creation of an EU programme equivalent to the US TFTP, called the European Terrorist Finance Tracking System (TFTS). In 2015, the scope and features of this system are still unclear. The only thing that is known is that the main goal of the TFTS will be to restrict

---

25 Transfers originally responded to 'commercial purposes' and therefore they fell under the scope of the internal market clause.
26 SWIFT and SWIFT II Agreements are thoroughly examined in Chapter 2.

the amount of bulk information that the US selects, processes and decrypts, by setting a control on EU soil. Likewise, the system seeks to increase the EU contribution to the detection of terrorist financing (Archick 2013: 11), gaining autonomy from the US leads.

In July 2011, the Commission launched a communication called *A European terrorist finance tracking system: available options* (COM(2011) 429 final), which was amended in November 2013 (COM(2013) 842 final). The Commission proposed three different available options for the TFTS.[27] All of them conform to Article 72 TFEU about the EU legal limitations in the field of internal security: (a) the EU TFTS Coordination and Analytical Service; (b) the EU TFTS Extraction Service; and (c) the Financial Intelligence Unit (FIU) Coordination Service. They are hybrids between a full EU-centralised database and a decentralised national system. However, their feasibility in practice is still doubtful. The EU has not yet reached full co-operation among its Member States in the field of security, and the EP argues that the necessity for such a system has not been sufficiently justified (Porter and Bendiek 2012: 503).

In contrast, the Council has always supported the initiative, stating that it will ensure grater efficiency in the processing of information by police and intelligence agencies (Council of the European Union 2008: 39). Indeed, the system might be advantageous in the sense that it will increase the exchange of intelligence within the EU, which many national intelligence services have long resisted.

The Commission has not launched any formal proposal for a TFTS yet, but other new initiatives seem to be accommodating the creation of this future system: on the one hand, the Commission has adopted a regulation on information accompanying transfers of funds (Regulation (EU) 2015/847). It is based on Article 114 TFEU (the internal market provision) so the data collected, processed and stored by FIUs will have to comply with Directive 95/46/EC. On the other hand, the Council has included a provision on the co-operation between Europol and national FIUs in the proposed Europol Regulation. Although some Member States have expressed their reservation on that issue, the provision as suggested by the Council allows the FIUs to collaborate with the EU agency through ENUs. It makes the aforementioned option for establishing a FIU Coordination System very probable, considering that the mirroring TFTP Agreement also involves Europol in the supervision of data requests.

The establishment of the TFTS would require the adjustment of the existing EU-US TFTP Agreement. In this sense, the EDPS has argued that a better analysis should be conducted on the impact that a future EU TFTS will have on the SWIFT Agreement (EDPS 2014). This issue might be one of the reasons why the Commission has delayed the proposal. In any event, if a proposal is finally released, the TFTS will be another example of how police authorities in EU Member States are progressively expanding the EU security measures.

---

27 The first option would be the creation of an EU TFTS co-ordination and analytical service, the second an EU TFTS extradition service and the third would be an FIU co-ordination.

3.2.3 Exchange of telecommunication data within the EU.
The annulled Data Retention Directive

Information collected and stored by TSPs and information society services has also been increasingly accessed by law enforcement authorities in the last 15 years. The reason is the emerging use of broadband, internet and mobile devices by organised criminal bands and terrorists. One example is found in the Madrid bombings of 2004, where terrorists used pre-paid SIM cards to detonate the bombs. Consequently, the EU adopted the Data Retention Directive, which gave police authorities access to telecommunication data for the prevention, detection, investigation and prosecution of crimes. This directive has been highly controversial, as shown in the following paragraphs.

Before 2006, the only mechanism to request telecommunication data was through the MLA procedures. As seen above, MLA requests can often be a very lengthy and inefficient process. Therefore, the Commission decided to adopt an instrument that would facilitate the retention, access and use of telecommunication data for law enforcement purposes: the Data Retention Directive (Directive 2006/24/EC). It was adopted in 2006 with the purpose of harmonising domestic rules on the retention of traffic data stored by TSP for 'the investigation, detection and prosecution of serious crimes' (Article 1.1).

The Data Retention Directive was annulled by the CJEU in April 2014. The annulment did not come as a surprise, since the directive was controversial from the outset. The proposal was launched by the Council in order to establish in the EU a similar tool to the Uniting and Strengthening America by Providing Appropriate Tools Required to Intercept and Obstruct Terrorism Act (USA Patriot Act 2001). The Patriot Act was enacted in October 2001 following the 9/11 attacks as a measure to combat terrorism and money laundering activities. Section 215 of the Patriot Act allows US law enforcement officials to collect metadata from TSPs located within the US territory during a criminal investigation. Yet, it is not only data from US citizens and residents that is processed through the Patriot Act. Third countries' data (including EU citizens' data) can also be accessed by the US authorities if they have been collected by a TSP located in the US, according to Section 702 of the Patriot Act.[28]

In order to prevent alleged clashes between the Patriot Act and the EU laws, the adoption of a similar piece of law in the EU became a necessity. Originally, the Council proposed that a retention provision was included in Directive 95/46/EC, but the EP rejected that proposal. Finally, the provision was included in the Directive on privacy and electronic communications (Directive 2002/58/EC). According to Article 15, 'Member States may, *inter alia*, adopt legislative measures providing for the retention of data for a limited period justified on the grounds laid down in this paragraph'.

The nature of the instrument was also an issue of debate. The Council proposed to draft a framework decision on data retention – a third-pillar instrument) – whereas

28 This is examined further in Chapter 4.

the EP suggested adopting it in the form of a directive – a first-pillar instrument – (Ni Loideain 2011: 258–259). In the end, the Commission followed the EP's suggestions and it launched a first-pillar proposal for a directive on data retention based on ex Article 95 TEC. The directive came into force in March 2006.

Four months later, Ireland, supported by Slovakia, challenged the directive before the CJEU. Ireland argued that the legislation should be adopted as a third-pillar measure because its purpose was clearly to combat serious crimes. That was the argument that the Court itself had followed in the previous PNR case, in which the Court concluded that when private companies collected personal data, even if the original purpose was purely economic, the measure could not fall under the scope of the internal market provision if data was later used for law enforcement. On the contrary, the Commission justified the legal basis for the Data Retention Directive by stating that it imposed direct obligations on TSP, rather than on governments.

Although it was expected that the Court would follow the precedent established in the PNR decision, this was not the case. In Case C-301/06 *Ireland v European Parliament* (2009), the Court contradicted its own jurisprudence by creating an artificial distinction between the reason for storing data and the purpose for processing such data (Boehm 2011: 193). Under that new test, the Court held that as long as the data was initially stored by a TSP to cover commercial activities, the directive was correctly adopted under the basis of ex Article 95 TEC. The Court added that 'the obligations relating to data retention have significant economic implications for service providers in so far as they may involve substantial investment and operating costs' (para. 68).

The argument used by the Court for PNR data transfers was then no longer valid.[29] Many scholars have speculated about the reasons why the Court changed its own argument (Hijmans and Scirocco 2009: 1506; Pateraki 2011: 318; Ni Loideain 2011: 260). A possible justification could be related to the different nature of the two instruments. The EU internal market clause was easier to justify in a directive than in an international agreement, whose scope exceeds the territory of the 'EU internal market'. Another justification could be found in the categories of the data collected. In the PNR case, airlines were required to collect specific data that, before the Agreement, was not collected at all. In contrast, the Data Retention Directive required operators to retain data that was already collected for commercial purposes (Hijmans and Scirocco 2009: 1506). Lastly, another explanation could be that the Court sought to harmonise data retention rules within the EU with its new decision. Such harmonisation would have been difficult to achieve in the PNR agreements because third countries were involved (Docksey 2014).

The Directive established that Member States could adopt domestic laws that obliged TSPs to retain data for a period of no less than six months and no more

29 The argument in the PNR decision was that the internal market provision does not apply when personal data is originally collected for commercial purposes by private companies and later transferred to government authorities for the purposes of national security and law enforcement.

than two years. Article 5 stated the categories of data retained in a communication were: (a) the source; (b) the destination; (c) the time, date and duration; (d) the type; (e) the equipment; and (f) the location. However, in 2011 the Commission released an evaluation report that found that many provisions of the directive were too broad. For example, the main purpose was the prevention, combat and investigation of 'serious crimes', but the scope of that term was interpreted differently depending on the Member State. Some countries decided that a serious crime would be any offence with a minimum of one-year of prison; whereas others decided to retain data related to all kinds of criminal offences. Another controversial issue concerned the public actors that were able to access the data. These were not the same in all Member States, and nor was the type of authorisation required for that access (COM(2011) 225 final, pp. 6 and 9).

In 2012, two new preliminary rulings on the validity of the Data Retention Directive were issued before the CJEU (Cases C-293/12 and C-594/12, *Digital Rights Ireland Ltd v Minister for Communications et al* (2014)). This time, the challenges did not concern the adequacy of its legal basis, but they questioned the substance of the instrument. The preliminary rulings claimed a potential clash between the directive and the rights enclosed in Directive 95/46/EC, the Charter of Fundamental Rights (the Charter) and the European Convention for the Protection of Human Rights and Fundamental Freedoms (ECHR) (especially, the right to privacy and data protection). In that sense, between 2008 and 2012, several constitutional courts of the Member States had found that national laws implementing the directive were contrary to their constitutional rights[30] The two preliminary rulings were supported by the EDPS, who argued that the Directive did not comply with the necessity principle, its purpose was not sufficiently precise and it had not considered less-intrusive data retention mechanisms (EDPS 2011).

In its defence, the Commission released a report with numerous cases in which the Data Retention Directive had helped in preventing and investigating crimes (European Commission 2013).[31] However, the report did not convince the CJEU, and in April 2014 the Court followed the Opinion of AG Cruz Villalón and ruled that the Directive was invalid for violating Directive 95/46/EC, as well as Articles 7, 8 and 52(1) of the Charter:

> [T]he obligation to retain for a certain period, data relating to a person's private life and to his communications, constitutes in itself an interference with the right guaranteed by Article 7 of the Charter. Furthermore, the access of the competent national authorities to the data constitutes a further interference with that fundamental right. [. . .] The fact that data are retained and subsequently used without the subscriber or registered user being

30 Particularly, Bulgaria, Hungary, Germany, Romania, Czech Republic, Slovakia and Cyprus.
31 For instance, it helped German police to identify individuals supporting the Al-Qaeda and the Uzbekistan Islamic Movement by distributing propaganda over the internet, and it allowed the identification of the person who uploaded a video on a terrorirst organisation in an internet forum in 2010.

informed is likely to generate in the minds of the persons concerned the feeling that their private lives are the subject of constant surveillance.

(Cases C-293/12 and C-594/12, *Digital Rights Ireland Ltd v Minister for Communications et al* (2014), paras 34, 35 and 37)

The case is especially relevant since it is the first time that the CJEU has annulled an entire directive because of its incompatibility with the provisions of the Charter. Specifically, the main reason for the annulment was that the data retained failed to comply with the necessity and proportionality tests. Law enforcement authorities were able to access all EU citizens' communications even if there was no link to or evidence of any threat. No exceptions and distinctions depending on the categories of data were provided, either. Therefore, the Court considered that the nature of that measure was abusive.

After the ruling, the Article 29 Data Protection Working Party (hereinafter, Art. 29 WP) urged Member States and the Commission to evaluate the consequences at the domestic and the EU level (Article 29 Data Protection Working Party 2014). Moreover, as Peers explains, national laws have to comply with the provisions of the Charter (and the general principles of law) when implementing EU law (Peers 2014). In that sense, several Member States have started to invalidate or amend their implementation laws after the judgment, in conformity with the provisions of the Charter.[32] As for a future data retention directive, the Commission has not yet started any preparations, and no replacement is expected in the near future. It could be that the EU will not adopt a new data retention instrument at all in the future, considering that the court has been very clear in highlighting the intrusion it causes to the EU fundamental rights to data protection and privacy.

The potential implications of this decision for other data retention measures in the EU are unclear. Many questions still need to find an answer, one of these issues being the future of other large-scale data retention systems after this judgment. Likewise, it is unclear to what extent the EU legislation/agreement needs to specify how Charter rights will be complied with. In this regard, a study concluded that the EU-US PNR Agreement, the EU PNR proposal, the EU-US TFTP agreement and the future EU TFTS could all be affected by this decision (Boehm and Cole 2014). Any of these measures could be now challenged before the CJEU using the same arguments as in the Data Retention decision.

In contrast, the Legal Service of the EP has noted that the Data Retention judgment 'does not [. . .] have any direct consequences for the validity of any other EU act' (European Parliament 2014b: para. 52). The Legal Service has thus underlined that each EU act benefits from a 'presumption of legality', so formally they remain valid. It has also noted that existing international agreements like PNR and SWIFT will not be reviewed by the CJEU in the sense of Article 218(11)

---

32 Particularly, Austria, Romania, Slovenia, the UK, Poland, Belgium and Slovakia. However, the Dutch government decided to maintain its data retention laws.

TFEU, since this procedure can only be conducted before the international agreement is adopted.[33]

Lastly, another important issue emerging from the CJEU decision is the link the court poses between Articles 7 and 8 of the Charter and Article 8 ECHR. This close connection shows the important role of the EU in referencing other international organisations in the field of data protection. There is no doubt that the decision will be taken into consideration in the event of the establishment of global principles for data protection.

Since there is no Data Retention Directive, police and judicial authorities have, in principle, returned to the traditional mechanism to access telecommunication data from a TSP located in another Member State: The MLA procedure.

This procedure is established in Articles 17 to 22 of the EU MLA Convention. It can also apply when law enforcement authorities need data collected and stored beyond the EU territory (e.g. in the US), but only if the two countries have previously signed a MLAT. For instance, the US has Mutual Legal Assistance Treaties (MLATs) with the majority of Member States, and even with the EU as a whole.[34] They co-operate with each other, sharing electronic information between their law enforcement authorities.

If police officers need to request specific information from a TSP, the first thing they need to know is where the headquarters of that particular private company is located as this will indicate the jurisdiction that the company is bound to. There are two ways to send a request to a TSP located in another Member State or a third country: (a) the informal process, developing a direct relationship with the private entity or making the request through the police authorities of the requested country; and (b) the formal process, sending the MLA request to the department of justice of the requested country, which will submit it to the competent court for the necessary warrant (United Nations Office on Drugs and Crime 2012: 90–91).

Each private company decides in which circumstances it will accept an informal request. For instance, the popular social network Twitter, which has its main headquarters in the US, answers requests made by governmental authorities of EU Member States by distinguishing between: (a) emergency requests, where there is a risk of death or serious injury to a person; and (b) non-emergency requests. Regarding the emergency requests, Twitter is available 24/7 and in such cases it responds without delay. In the non-emergency cases, requests need to be issued formally via the US courts through MLA (Blasi Casagran 2013: 423).

Within the EU, one of the main problems with the use of MLA procedures is that each Member State has its own criminal legal system, which contains specific requirements and conditions for accessing TSPs' data. For instance, some Member States require a prior court order, whereas others permit the authorisation by the Secretary of State or a senior official.

---

33 This is actually the case of the proposed EU-Canada PNR Agreement, which has been reviewed by the CJEU since November 2014.

34 MLATs with third countries and especially with the US are thoroughly analysed in Chapter 2.

In sum, as demonstrated by this study, the EU has adopted many instruments for the purpose of facilitating the exchange of information among law enforcement authorities. However, all of them reveal shortcomings with regard to their use and implementation. The next section examines an additional problem: all these data-sharing instruments contain different data protection rules, which leads to a fragmented EU data protection framework in the field of law enforcement.

3.2.4 The EU data protection legislation under the scope of the AFSJ

This study has identified and analysed the main EU instruments for processing information for law enforcement purposes. Any data processing requires compliance with data protection rules. In this sense, the Council of the European Union has emphasised that:

> Information exchange in the context of EU law enforcement cooperation will at all times respect the fundamental rights of citizens, in particular where it concerns the protection of personal data.
>
> (Council of the European Union 2013b: 3)

The main object of this section is to analyse the current and future laws regulating the protection of personal data collected, processed, stored and transferred within the EU for law enforcement purposes. It attempts to discern whether the EU has an effective data protection framework in the field of law enforcement, since this is the first step forward for achieving the establishment of global data protection principles in the area of security.

The analysis starts with an examination of the origins and evolution of the general data protection legislation before and after the Treaty of Lisbon. The specific data protection laws within the AFSJ are detailed next. The premise is that, although data protection legislation is harmonised at the EU level when it is encompassed within the internal market clause, the scope and limits of the EU protection of personal data are still very unclear when the processing is carried out for law enforcement purposes. This is added to the fact that general EU data protection laws might overlap with those data protection provisions included in each of the existing data-sharing instruments and systems in the field of criminal matters. The overall goal of this last analysis is to identify the flaws, if any, of the EU data protection rules applicable for data processing in the field of law enforcement.

4. The EU data protection legislation under the scope of the AFSJ

4.1. General data protection rules in connection with the AFSJ

4.1.1 Origins of the EU data protection legislation

The CoE and the Organisation for Economic Co-operation and Development (OECD) play an important role as the main influences of the EU data protection framework. On the one hand, the OECD released a *Recommendation of the Council concerning Guidelines governing the Protection of Privacy and Transborder Flows of Personal Data in September 1980* (OECD Privacy Guidelines) (Organisation for Economic Co-operation and Development 1980). On the other hand, in 1981 the CoE adopted the 1981 CoE Data Protection Convention (Council of Europe 1981). Unlike the OECD Privacy Guidelines, the standards and values of the 1981 CoE Data Protection Convention are binding for all CoE Contracting Parties.[35]

Both frameworks served as the source of inspiration for the later EU data protection legislation. At first, the EU based data protection laws on its internal market clauses: Article 100a TEC (later amended as Article 95 TEC) and Article 286 TEC. Therefore, the Community had full competence to legislate on data protection matters. The reason behind the choice of the legal basis was simple. The creation of a common market had brought the free movement of goods, persons, services and capital, and with it a free flow of personal data from one Member State to another. The objective was to systematise the substantial increase in the cross-border movement of personal data because of the intensification of social and economic activities within the EU. That came along with the technological progress for processing and exchanging data that emerged during the early nineties. Directive 95/46/EC was thus crucial to avoid a situation where Member States adopted different national laws on data protection.

4.1.2 Impact and scope of Directive 95/46/EC

Directive 95/46/EC is the first and main EU legislative act that regulates the protection of personal data within the EU. As explained above, the establishment of the EU internal market by the Maastricht Treaty increased significantly the quantity of personal data collected and stored for economic purposes. The free circulation of goods, services, persons and capital among Member States led to the proliferation of databases in private companies and industries that interacted in the European market. Under these circumstances, Directive 95/46/EC was drafted as the legislative tool that would co-ordinate the collection, processing and storage of various personal data obtained for commercial reasons.

Directive 95/46/EC was inspired by the core privacy principles established in the OECD Privacy Guidelines and the 1981 CoE Data Protection Convention. These were included in Directive 95/46/EC, and later implemented in the domestic legal frameworks of the Member States.

From the moment Directive 95/46/EC came into force, Member States started a reform of their domestic laws on data protection. However, the scope of the directive included a limitation: Article 3(2) expressly refrained from addressing those activities concerning public security, defence or state security. Hence, the Member States retained the sole competence to legislate on the data processed by the judicial and police authorities.

---

35 Chapter 5 examines in depth the nature and content of these instruments.

The scope and limits of Article 3 was not always fully clear to Member States during the implementation process. Therefore, the CJEU set jurisprudence on the interpretation of this provision. In Cases C-465/00, C-138/01 and C-139/01, *Rechnungshof v Österreichischer Rundfunk et al* (2003) and Case C-101/01, *Lindqvist* (2003), the Court showed a great flexibility in the interpretation of Article 3 regarding the connection between the internal market and the economic activity at stake (Tzanou 2011: 284–285). In the first case, the Court found that the Austrian provision requiring private entities to inform the Austrian Court of Audit about the names and salary of their employees fell under the scope of the directive. In particular, the Court ruled that:

> The applicability of Directive 95/46 to situations where there is no direct link with the exercise of the fundamental freedoms cf movement guaranteed by the Treaty is confirmed by the wording of Article 3(1) of the directive, which defines its scope in very broad terms.
>
> (Cases C-465/00, C-138/01 and C-139/01,
> *Rechnungshof v Österreichischer Rundfunk et al* (2003), para. 40)

Therefore, the directive has often applied even when the data processing activity was not directly linked to the internal market. Likewise, in *Lindqvist*, a catechist had set up a home page on the Internet containing information about herself and various members of her parish, without their consent. The Court found that the mention of an individual on an internet home page fell under the scope of Directive 95/46/EC. Even if the creation of a web page did not constitute any economic activity (it was a non-profit-making activity), it concluded that:

> Charitable or religious activities such as those carried out by Mrs. Lindqvist cannot be considered equivalent to the activities listed in [. . .] Article 3(2) of Directive 95/46 and are thus not covered by that exception.
>
> (Case C-101/01, *Lindqvist* (2003), para. 45)

In both cases the CJEU interpreted the scope of the directive broadly. The same occurred a few years later in Case C-301/06, *Ireland v European Parliament* (2009) on the Data Retention Directive, mentioned above. In that case the CJEU inferred that a measure related to criminal law fell under the former EC competence if it was necessary to achieve the effectiveness of an EU policy (Hijmans and Scirocco 2009: 1507). In conclusion, the Court has often[36] offered a wide interpretation of the scope of Directive 95/46/EC when determining whether the purpose for processing data was linked to the EU internal market policy.

---

36 However, the PNR court decision did not follow this background, as examined in Chapter 2.

4.1.3 The Treaty of Lisbon and the new data protection paradigm

Before Lisbon, Article 286 TEC was the provision regulating data protection within the first pillar. For data processing within the scope of the second and third pillars, the EU competence was limited to secondary legislation in the field. According to several CJEU decisions,[37] international law was usually ranked more highly than EU secondary law but below EU primary law (EU Treaty provisions). Consequently, international agreements confronting EU secondary legislation on data protection for law enforcement purposes would always prevail.

The Treaty of Lisbon significantly changed the European framework regarding the protection of personal data. With the abolishment of pillars, the EU and its Member States shared competences for legislation on data processed for criminal matters. Also, Articles 16 TFEU and 39 TEU were introduced as new legal bases for the right to data protection.

Article 16 TFEU replaces former Article 286 TEC. According to this new provision, the right to data protection is now applicable to all EU sectors. This right is entirely EU primary law and prevails over any international agreement confronting it. Likewise, Article 16(2) TFEU expands the scope of the provision by stating that rules on data protection are not only bound to EU institutions, bodies, agencies and offices, but also to 'Member States when carrying out activities which fall within the scope of Union law'. Hence, EU data protection legislation is today not only applicable to former first-pillar activities, but also to former second- and third-pillar matters, including data processing activities in the field of law enforcement. Some of these activities are expressly foreseen in the Treaty. This is the case for the use of biometrics (Article 77(3) TFEU), the freezing of funds (Article 75 TFEU), border management (Article 77(2)(d) TFEU) and the data processed for the prevention, detection and investigation of crimes (Article 87(2) (a) TFEU), to name a few. Moreover, Article 216 TFEU enables the EU to conclude international agreements in cases specified by the Treaty, when it is necessary for achieving an EU objective, or if is provided for a legally binding EU act. This is, for example, the legal basis of the most recent EU-US PNR Agreement, studied in Chapter 2.

Regarding the institutional amendments, before the Treaty of Lisbon the EP did not have any legislative role to play in the formulation of third-pillar laws. It was consulted but its opinion was not always taken into account in the negotiations of an international agreement. Since the Treaty of Lisbon, the EP participates in the ordinary legislative procedure and, therefore, it now has the right to veto EU international agreements. In this sense, Article 218 TFEU enshrines the so-called 'consent procedure', in which the EP needs to approve those international agreements adopted through ordinary legislative procedure. Likewise, the EDPS has enjoyed greater powers since the Treaty of Lisbon. The role of this body is no longer limited to the areas falling under the former first pillar. Now, the EDPS'

---

37 For instance, Case C-162/96 *Racke v Hauptzollamt Mainz* [1998] ECR I-3633, para. 46.

supervisory tasks cover all EU institutions and bodies, including areas outside the scope of what used to be 'Community law'.

The new EU data protection legislation increases the role of the CJEU on these issues, too. For example, before the Treaty, the Court did not address aspects relating to data protection when it clashed with individual restrictive measures in the field of security. Now, according to Article 218(11) TFEU, the Court is able to examine any EU act and international agreement based on the processing of information for law enforcement purposes and to issue an opinion on the compatibility with the provisions of the Treaty. Therefore, the fact that there is an explicit EU provision on the right to data protection, together with the new binding nature of the Charter, provides the Court with more instruments to protect that right.

The status of the Charter is also amended with the Treaty of Lisbon. Before the Treaty, the Charter was considered as part of the soft law for the courts, being a quasi-legal instrument with no legally binding force. In contrast, the provisions of the Charter are now part of the hard law. Thus, they have a binding nature and the same value as the treaties (Blasi Casagran 2012: 79–80). As seen above, the right to data protection is included as a fundamental right in Article 8 of the Charter.

It is worth mention here that the Treaty of Lisbon also includes Article 6(2) TEU on the EU accession to the ECHR. Although the accession procedure has been recently put back by the CJEU Opinion 2/13 (CJEU 2014), a future adhesion would allow the use of Article 8 ECHR on the right to respect for private and family life within the scope of the EU law.

In the view of the foregoing, Article 16 TFEU, the new nature of the Charter and the anticipated EU accession to the ECHR have caused a reinforcement of the EU right to data protection. However, in line with the exception of the 1981 CoE Data Protection Convention, Article 8(2) ECHR recognises that interferences of a public authority with a person's right to privacy may be justified as necessary in the interest of national security, public safety or the prevention of crime. This paragraph justifies that, in some circumstances, the EU and the Member States can put collective security before the right to privacy.

In the same way, the Treaty of Lisbon has foreseen specific data protection rules in the context of the Common Foreign and Security Policy (CFSP). According to Article 39 TEU, the Council can adopt a special decision laying down the rules relating to data protection. If that occurs, Article 16 TFEU would be derogated for the processing of personal data for activities under the scope of the CFSP, and new rules would apply.

The relationship between Articles 16 TFEU and 39 TEU is today still unclear, since it is unknown in which situations Article 39 TEU will be applicable. It is presumed that Article 39 TEU, together with Declarations 20 and 21,[38] was

---

38 Declaration 20 recalls that this legal framework includes specific derogations when rules on the protection of personal data have direct implications for national security; and Declaration 21 acknowledges that data protection in the fields of judicial co-operation in criminal matters and police co-operation may require provisions specific to this area.

introduced with the expectation that there will be situations in which general EU data protection laws might clash with third countries' security rules. In such situations, new standards will be adopted.

As part of the CFSP, rules adopted under Article 39 will exclude the control of the CJEU and the EP. In particular, no instrument based on this provision can be challenged before the CJEU,[39] and the decision-making process will only involve the Council, but not the EP. However, Article 39 TEU has never been used to date. Therefore, it remains to be seen what purpose lies behind this provision, and the level of data protection that it will introduce for data processing activities within the scope of external security.

The Treaty of Lisbon has also introduced two protocols that weaken Article 16 TFEU. On the one hand, Protocol 21 states that the UK and Ireland are not always bound to Article 16 TFEU in the processing of personal data within the field of police and judicial co-operation. On the other hand, Protocol 36 foresees a number of transitional provisions, by which EU acts and international agreements adopted before the treaty will be preserved. According to this protocol, the Commission has only been able to challenge an ex-third-pillar instrument under Article 258 TFEU since 1 December 2014, and this has not occurred yet. The same condition applies for the CJEU revision of third-pillar instruments adopted before the Treaty of Lisbon. Therefore, with these new powers, the CJEU could now start procedures against pre-Lisbon instruments like Council Framework Decision 2008/977/JHA or the Prüm Decisions.

4.2 Sector-specific data protection legislation within the AFSJ

Today there is no unified EU approach on data protection within the field of law enforcement. In fact, many data exchanges conducted by national law enforcement authorities are still entirely subject to national criminal laws. According to Article 3(2) of Directive 95/46/EC, EU data protection laws do not apply 'in any case to processing operations concerning public security, defence, State security [. . .] and the activities of the State in areas of criminal law'. This provision has been an obstacle every time the EC has attempted to incorporate new data-sharing instruments in the field of security. The third pillar had its own provisions, which regulated transnational law enforcement as opposed to national and state security, but no provisions were originally foreseen to protect data within the scope of that pillar. Thus, before 2008, the only solution for that was to 'mask' these laws as part of one of the EC former policies, as occurred with the 2004 EU-US PNR Agreement and the Data Retention Directive.

In 2008 that paradigm changed. The EU adopted a framework decision under the former third-pillar on data protection aspects falling within the scope of police

---

39 However, a possible way for the Court to review data processing agreements under the basis of Article 39 TEU is examined below.

and judicial matters. Although it was seen as an improvement, the instrument was criticised from the beginning for being very broad, for giving too much room for implementation to the Member States. This section analyses the scope and short-comings resulting of Council Framework Decision 2008/977/JHA. After that, a comparison is made between the framework decision and the new directive on data protection in the field of criminal matters.

4.2.1 The limited scope of Council Framework Decision 2008/977/JHA

The Council Framework Decision 2008/977/JHA on the protection of personal data processed in the framework of police and judicial co-operation in criminal matters (Council Framework Decision 2008/977/JHA) – hereinafter, FD 2008/977 – was adopted as the first EU data protection instrument in the field of the former third pillar. The necessity to have EU law that would regulate cross-border exchanges of law-enforcement information was first stressed in the Hague Programme four years earlier.

FD 2008/977 was proposed in 2005 and it included rules on data subjects' rights, supervisory authorities, data processing and data transfer similar to those established in Directive 95/46/EC. However, the first draft proposal was signifi-cantly modified because of its lack of precision in several provisions (de Hert and Papakonstantinou 2009: 407). A new proposal was not launched until 2008.

FD 2008/977 was based on former Articles 30(a) and (b) TEU – today Articles 87 to 88 TFEU. The main purpose of the act was to ensure that data made available between Member States had a high level of data protection while guaranteeing public safety. It included data protection rules such as the lawfulness and fairness of data processing; the purpose limitation principle; accuracy of the processing; the rights to erasure, blocking and deletion of data; appropriate technical meas-ures against destruction, loss, alteration or unauthorised access or disclosure; rules on confidentiality and data security; remedies, liability and sanctions; and the obligation for an independent supervision.

Law enforcement authorities would need to comply with the act every time data was transferred to another Member State for the 'prevention, investigation, detec-tion or prosecution of criminal offences or the execution of criminal penalties' (recital 6 of Council Framework Decision 2008/977/JHA). However, it would not apply to purely internal situations in which information was collected and used for one single Member State. That was a criticism that was levelled at the instru-ment after its adoption (de Hert and Bellanova 2009: 6). Other issues of complaint referred to the nature of the instrument: on the one hand, Member States' com-pliance with a framework decision cannot be enforced by the Commission and, on the other hand, the instrument was limited by the subsidiarity principle. Being the AFSJ, an area of shared competence between the EU and the Member States, national laws on data processing for security purposes might still apply if an action can be more effectively taken at national, regional or local levels.

The fact that data protection principles of FD 2008/977 were not fully equivalent to Directive 95/46/EC was also seen as controversial (de Hert and

Papakonstantinou 2009; de Hert and Bellanova 2009: 6–7; Boehm 2012: 138–144; Hijmans and Scirocco 2009: 1494; Nino 2010: 67–69). For instance, FD 2008/ 977 does not contain any provision prohibiting the processing of special categories of data. Instead, Article 6 of FD 2008/977 states that data on race, politics, religion or philosophical beliefs, trade-union membership, health or sex life are permitted if strictly necessary and under adequate safeguards.[40] Another difference is found in the requirement to notify and inform the data subject. This condition is included in recital 26 of FD 2008/977, but according to recital 27 national laws can determine exceptions to it. The individual right to access is not equivalent in the two instruments either. Recital 29 of the Framework Decision introduces that right similarly to Directive 95/46/EC. Yet, paragraph 2 of Article 17 of FD 2008/977 establishes a number of restrictions in its applicability. Also, unlike Directive 95/46/EC, the Framework Decision does not foresee the individual's right to object, and includes several vague derogations of the requirement of prior consent before transferring data to third countries or international bodies. Lastly, both the Directive and FD 2008/977 specify powers for an independent data protection authority for the oversight; but the Framework Decision does not establish any body similar to the Art. 29 WP within its scope.

The major disappointment as regards the content of FD 2008/977 was the exclusion of several sector-specific EU legislative instruments from its scope in the terms of recital 39.[41] For instance, the framework decision does not apply to data processed by Europol, Eurojust, SIS, CIS, Prüm, existing agreements with third countries (e.g. PNR agreements) and other existing EU acts on the exchange of criminal-related information. Although such instruments contain their own particular data protection rules and usually refer to the data protection principles of the CoE, a general fully-fledged regime through FD 2008/977 would have ensured a minimum data protection threshold for all EU information systems.[42]

That said, it could be concluded that, although the adoption of FD 2008/977 brought some progress with respect to the protection applicable to that data processed within the field of criminal law, the instrument has several shortcomings. One of them is the exclusion of data processed by Europol, Eurojust, SIS, CIS, Prüm, international agreements with third countries and any other existing EU act on data exchanges (e.g. the Swedish initiative). FD 2008/977 is thus only applicable to data exchanges through mutual assistance procedures (according

---

40 Interestingly, Europol (which is excluded from the scope of FD 2008/977) offers in this respect a higher level of data protection, since Article 10 Europol Council Decision (ECD) does not allow any processing of personal data revealing racial or ethnic origin, political opinions, religious or philosophical beliefs or trade-union membership and the processing of data concerning health or sex life. A complete analysis of the Europol data protection framework is examined in Chapter 3.

41 This restriction regarding the scope was not foreseen in the original proposal by the Commission in 2005, but it was added afterwards due to the political interest of some Member States.

42 As for this lack of a minimum common denominator for data processed in the field of law enforcement, Chapter 3 suggests using Europol's data protection framework as the model system for every cross-border exchange of crime-related information.

to CoE and EU MLA provisions), Visa Information System (VIS), ECRIS and Eurodac systems. The need for a new legislative act on data protection for police and judicial matters in the EU emerged because of these limitations, especially after the entry into force of the Treaty of Lisbon.

4.2.2 New directive on data protection for police and judicial co-operation in criminal matters

FD 2008/977 does not fulfil the criteria of Article 16 TFEU because it does not apply to domestic data processing activities and it excludes the participation of the EP (Hijmans and Scirocco 2009: 1519; de Hert and Bellanova 2009: 7).

On 25 January 2012 the Commission launched two proposals, which were adopted by the EP and the Council in December 2015: the General Data Protection Regulation (COM(2012) 11 final) – hereinafter, the GDPR – and the Police and Criminal Justice Data Protection Directive (COM(2012) 10 final) – hereinafter, the new Directive. This study focuses only on the latter.

According to Article 58 of the new Directive, it will repeal current FD 2008/977. If we compare the two instruments, a number of improvements can be discerned in the future act. For instance, the new Directive will confer direct effect on individuals; it will be subject to the Charter; it involves the EP in the legislative procedure and it will fall within the jurisdiction of the CJEU (Peers 2012).

As for the substance of the new Directive, it enhances the scope of application of the FD 2008/977: it will not only apply to cross-border data exchanges within the EU, but also to the processing of personal data at the purely national level. Some Member States have opposed to this new issue, arguing that if the directive regulates national data processing, it might be contrary to the EU subsidiarity principle. Other Member States have expressed doubts about the feasibility of harmonising data protection laws in the field of law enforcement (Council of the European Union 2013c: 4), or they simply find the data protection rules in the current FD 2008/977 sufficient (Council of the European Union 2013c: 2–3).

The new Directive also includes small improvements as for individual rights, like the obligation to notify data subjects about the processing of their data (Article 11). Unfortunately, rights like the duty to inform and the right of access are subject to numerous exceptions established in Articles 11 and 13. In this regard, the Art. 29 WP has argued that the possibility to exempt entire categories of personal data from these rights should be deleted from the proposal (Article 29 Data Protection Working Party 2013a, p. 3).

Particularly interesting is Article 5 on different data processing procedures depending on the category of the data subjects (suspects, convicts, victims, witnesses, contacts or associated persons and other persons). Also, Article 8(1) states that personal data classified as 'sensitive'[43] cannot in principle be processed.

43　Sensitive data are those personal data revealing race or ethnic origin, political opinions, religion or beliefs, trade-union membership, genetic data or data concerning health or sex life.

This general rule has been another issue of debate at the domestic level, since many national law enforcement authorities consider that sensitive data may be relevant for a criminal investigation and, therefore, should be processed (Council of the European Union 2013c: 23, 58–59). In fact, the majority of Member States prefer the wording in the FD 2008/977, which is not formulated as a prohibition.

Although the new Directive improves the current framework decision, numerous aspects have brought disappointment among the pro-privacy community. One of these issues was that an unofficial proposal leaked in November 2011 offered better safeguards for the individuals than the final version released in January 2012 (Bäcker and Hornung 2012: 628 and fn. 9). By way of example, the final version of the Directive does not contain any mention of data protection impact assessments, which was originally included in the leaked draft (Bäcker and Hornung 2012: 629). Another criticism refers to the removal of Article 1(5) of the FD 977/2008. This provision establishes that the framework decision cannot preclude Member States from providing higher data protection safeguards than those established in the law. A similar provision is not found in the current version of the directive, even though some Member States have already expressed the will to adopt stricter domestic rules than those in the new Directive.

Further discontent relates to the data retention rules in the new Directive. Article 24 of the new Directive states that personal identification will be allowed for the data processing 'as far as possible'. This ambiguity is reinforced in Article 4, paragraph (e) of the new Directive, which establishes that 'data will be kept in a form which permits identification of data subjects for no longer than it is necessary for the purposes for which the personal data are processed'. The risk of this wording is that the information could be used for multiple investigative purposes with no temporal limitation.

The annulment of the Data Retention Directive has also stirred up debate over the lack of precise rules on public-private co-operation, profiling measures and the need to define the term 'serious crime' in the new Directive. As Boehm and Cole noted, the new Directive should be revised to include the Court's argumentation on such aspects (Boehm and Cole 2014: 85–87).

Although the inclusion of an independent supervisory authority supposes 'a big step forward' (Article 29 Data Protection Working Party 2013a: 5), these authorities will have very limited powers. In that sense, the Art. 29 WP recommended extending Article 46 of the new Directive on supervisory authorities' powers and adding the possibility to access 'all necessary documents for the exercise of their investigative powers' (Article 29 Data Protection Working Party 2013a: 7). That change would offer a complete supervision on the processing of data within the field of police and judicial co-operation, aligning it to Directive 95/46/EC.

Furthermore, the fact that the new Directive has not been adopted in the form of a regulation has drawn criticism from various EU data protection 'watchdogs'. In particular, the EDPS (EDPS 2012a: iv), the Art. 29 WP (Article 29 Data Protection Working Party 2012: 26) and the EP (European Parliament 2012: point 26) expressed their disappointment about this issue. They highlighted the inadequate level of protection in the new Directive as being greatly inferior to the General Data Protection Regulation (Bäcker and Hornung 2012: 628–629). In contrast, some Member States have argued that the whole data protection package should have been released in the form of a directive as a way to overcome any overlap between the two instruments. In the end, the separation of instruments (a regulation and a directive) has remained. The Commission has justified the specific nature of the new Directive by referring to Declaration 21 of the Treaty of Lisbon, which acknowledges specific rules for the protection of personal data in the field of criminal matters. In addition, the majority of Member States prefer a directive to a regulation because they do not want to lose national sovereignty in the field of criminal law.

The new Directive does not specify if it will operate in cases where data is collected by private entities for internal market purposes but later processed by police authorities. In my view, it will depend on who is conducting the data processing activity. If it is carried out by a public authority then the new Directive will apply; but if a private company is the data processor instead, it will fall under the scope of the GDPR. In this regard, the Council has clarified that if a private entity collects data for commercial purposes and it has a legal obligation to share it with law enforcement bodies, the GDPR applies – for example, data stored by TSPs, airline companies and financial entities – (Council of the European Union 2014h: 5).

Article 2(3) of the new Directive explicitly excludes from the scope of application the processing of data by EU institutions, bodies and agencies. It means that, for instance, data processed by Europol will not be covered by the new Directive.[44] As a result, the divergence of data protection frameworks within the AFSJ will remain in the future. The new Directive has thus missed the opportunity to finally set up minimum EU rules for data exchanges carried out within the field of police and judicial co-operation.

In conclusion, despite the proposed Directive bringing significant progress with regard to the data protection rules in the field of law enforcement, it will not end the current fragmentation of rules. Many EU information systems will be excluded from the scope of the proposal, which means that it will not achieve full harmonisation of EU data protection rules in the field of law enforcement.

4.3 Comparative study of the specific data protection provisions in EU data-sharing instruments

As mentioned above, both the current FD 2008/977 and the new data protection directive on police and judicial matters explicitly exclude numerous EU data-sharing instruments. The reason for such limitation was mainly political, since some Member States thought that by centralising data protection rules in one single act, they would lose authority over the way they regulate security

---

44 This is addressed in Chapter 3.

measures. Both the current FD 2008/977 and the new directive include a clause stating that any prior specific rules on data protection will always take preference over the act.[45] Yet, only the framework decision foresees that if sector-specific rules on data protection are more restrictive than those in the act, the former will apply (recital 40).

The majority[46] of EU data-sharing instruments within the AFSJ include data protection provisions. Some of these instruments are preventive measures and store data from untargeted individuals, while others process data as a response to a specific criminal investigation. The main problem stemming from these instruments is that they do not have their data protection rules aligned with each other. Not even the preventive measures themselves contain similar rules.

Preventive tools are specifically the proposals for an EU PNR system and an EU TFTS, the Advance Passenger Information System (APIS), the SIS/SIS II, the VIS, the Eurodac and the CIS.[47] Table 1.2. presents a comparison of such instruments in light of four different criteria: data retention, data items collected, entities with data access and individual rights.

The first thing that is evident from Table 1.1 is that none of these measures for the prevention of crimes coincides from a data protection perspective. The retention of information goes from 30 days, in the case of EU PNR Directive, up to ten years in SIS and Eurodac systems (Kabera Karanja 2008). After the CJEU declared void the Data Retention Directive, many conclusions can be made regarding these retention rules. The first is that the majority of these retention periods are longer than that established in the annulled directive, which ranged from six months to two years. In the case of the PNR Directive, the period of 30 days does not impede PIUs from accessing unmasked data after that period, so the real retention period is five years. Therefore, in line with the aforementioned Court decision Case C-301/06 *Ireland v European Parliament* (2009) and/or Cases C-293/12 and C-594/12, *Digital Rights Ireland*, these periods of time could be contrary to the EU principles of necessity and proportionality (Boehm and Cole 2014: 67–68 and 80).

As for the number of items collected, they also vary significantly from one instrument to another. For example, CIS has 14 data categories, whereas VIS collects 34 different items. In all cases the data can easily disclose a wide range of information about individuals, such as what their dietary habits are, what type of card they are paying with, who they are travelling with, etc. All this information can easily clash with the right to private life (Boehm and Cole 2014: 69) and, similarly to the Data Retention Directive, be contrary to Articles 7 and 8 of the Charter.

---

45 Article 28 of FD 2008/977 and Article 59 of the new directive.
46 This is not the case in Council Decision 2005/671/JHA of 20 September 2005 on the exchange of information and co-operation concerning terrorist offences.
47 The Data Retention Directive was initially included in the matrix, but it was removed after it was declared void by the CJEU.

Table 1.1

	Duration of data storage	Categories of data collected	Entities with data access	Rights of data subject
EU PNR	30 days, and 5 years in a masked out state	19	PIUs	Access, deletion/correction, blockage, judicial redress, compensation
EU TFTS	*Undefined*	*Undefined*	FIUs or Europol/Eurojust	*Undefined*
SIS/SIS II	5 or 10 years max. Review after 1 or 3 years	10/15	Border authorities; police and customs authorities; judicial authorities; visa and immigration authorities; Europol and Eurojust; vehicle registration authorities; Interpol	Access, deletion/correction, judicial redress, compensation
VIS	5 years max	34	Border authorities; visa and immigration authorities; designated law enforcement authorities; Europol; third countries or international organisations	Access, deletion/correction, judicial redress
Eurodac	10 years; or 2 years	12	National asylum authorities; designed law enforcement authorities; Europol	Access, deletion/correction, judicial redress, compensation
CIS	3 years; 6 years, or 10 years max. Review after 1 year	14	Designated customs administrations; other national authorities; third countries, international/regional organisations	Access, deletion/correction, blockage

Regarding the authorities and institutions allowed to access the information, all allow access to law enforcement authorities,[48] or even Europol[49] and Eurojust.[50] The main issue of concern is that these broad categories of actors may translate into a very high number of people with access to personal data. For instance, nobody knows what the composition of the PIUs in the PNR Directive is going to be, or who the 'verifying authorities' of Eurodac are. As Boehm and Cole point out, this imprecision 'leaves room for an arbitrary expansion of the persons who may access the data sets' (Boehm and Cole 2014: 70 and 79). They also propose the appointment of an independent body among law enforcement authorities for the control of the access (Boehm and Cole 2014: 70).

Lastly, the rights guaranteed to individuals are insufficient in most of the measures. In fact, only the proposed EU PNR Directive offers all basic rights – i.e. right to access, right to delete or correct, blockage of data, judicial redress, right to compensation – aligned to Directive 95/46/EC.

Considerably different is Table 1.2 on EU instruments processing information for specific criminal investigations, rather than as a preventive tool. I refer particularly to the Prüm Decisions, the ECRIS initiative, the EIO and the Swedish Initiative.

Following the same matrix as before, Table 1.2 shows that, rather than a divergence among data protection rules, the main problem among these instruments is a lack of rules *per se*. Therefore, it is not possible to carry out an adequate comparison.

Table 1.2

	Duration of data storage	Categories of data collected	Entities with data access	Rights of data subject
Prüm Decisions	2 years max	10	Competent law enforcement authority	Right to access, right to delete or correct, judicial redress, right to compensation
Swedish Initiative	–	15	Competent law enforcement authority	–
ECRIS	Until they are deleted in the Member State	13	Competent law enforcement authority	–
EIO	–	11	Competent judicial and law enforcement authority	General mention Art.14, judicial redress

48 This is the case of SIS/SIS II, VIS, Eurodac, CIS and the Data Retention Directive. See Article 27 of the SIS II Regulation, Article 3 of theVIS Decision, Articles 5 and 6 of the 2012 Eurodac Proposal, Article 7 of the CIS Decision and Article 21 of the ECD.

49 Like in SIS/SIS II, VIS, Eurodac and perhaps the EU TFTS. See Article 7 of the VIS Decision, Article 7 of the Eurodac Regulation and section 6 of the TFTS communication.

50 Like in SIS/SIS II and perhaps the EU TFTS.

The consequence of having a data-sharing instrument with poor data protection rules is that it might lead to abuses by law enforcement authorities. For example, in ECRIS the consequence of not restricting data processing to specific purposes means that Member States can easily use the data for purposes other than criminal proceedings. Likewise, in the case of the EIO Directive, nothing is said about the possibility to make copies of the evidence – nor the retention periods for such copies (Mangiaracina 2014: 125). For all these measures, except for Prüm, the FD 2008/977 applies subsidiarily. However, as explained above, the framework decision is very broad and does not cover certain aspects of the particular data processing activity.

It is not a coincidence that the Prüm Decision is the only instrument offering a full-fledged data protection framework. A data protection regime in Prüm is particularly important due to the explicit exclusion of this measure from the FD 2008/977 and from the proposed Directive. This exclusion does not translate into a lower data protection framework, but quite the opposite: Article 25 of Council Decision 2008/615 establishes the condition that a Member State can only participate in the exchange of Prüm data if it demonstrates a compliance with all data protection requirements (Soleto Muñoz and Fiodorova 2014: 159). No similar provision is found in the FD 2008/977 and the Police and Criminal Justice Data Protection Directive.

Data security provisions included in FD 2008/977 will also apply to those systems which do not contain specific rules on classified information. For instance, the proposed EU TFTS and SIS II include data security requirements, whereas the Prüm Decisions, the Swedish initiative, the EIO and the ECRIS do not. In the cases where no reference is made on data security, the general rules established in Council Decision 2001/264/EC and its amendment in Council Decision 2011/292/EU apply by default (O'Neill 2012: 80).

When looking to understand the reason for the lack of a consistent data protection framework in almost all of the aforementioned instruments we might consider their specific *raison d'être*: all these instruments are used as a response to specific criminal investigations and data processed is already focused on a particular target. Therefore, any data protection limitation could potentially obstruct the ongoing criminal investigation. In any case, the EDPS has already called for an alignment of such instruments with the Police and Criminal Justice Data Protection Directive (EDPS 2013: 7).

4.4 The purpose limitation and the necessity principles

There are two data protection principles that have been especially controversial in all EU data-sharing systems. These are the purpose limitation principle and the necessity principle.

Looking first at the purpose limitation principle, it is established in Article 6(1)(b) of Directive 95/46/EC. According to the Art. 29 WP, it consists of collecting personal data 'for specified, explicit and legitimate purposes' that must 'not be further processed in a way incompatible with those purposes' (Article 29 Data Protection Working Party 2013b; Bygrave 2002: 337–341). This has often been challenged by the increasing 'function creep' of the existing European information systems. A function creep is the gradual expansion of the use of a system or database, beyond the purpose for which it was originally intended, which is exactly what has happened in many of the aforementioned systems. They were initially created either to develop the European borders or for commercial purposes, but they have been ultimately used – or are expected to be used – as tools for the detection and investigation of crimes.

For instance, the VIS was created to support the common visa policy, and Eurodac was established to prevent asylum seekers from filing multiple asylum applications in different Member States simultaneously. Yet, data processed through these systems are now accessed by law enforcement authorities of Member States and by Europol to fight terrorism. Therefore, once the information is collected and stored in the EU centralised systems, it can easily be used for other purposes. Likewise, before the adoption of PNR agreements, booking details (PNR data) collected by airline companies were only processed for commercial purposes. However, the initial collection of PNR data does not correspond today to the final processing based on law enforcement purposes. Another example is found in Article 5(5) of the EU PNR Proposal. It leaves the door open to add other offences to the list established in Articles 1 and 2 of the EU PNR Proposal. According to this provision, it could occur that a police agent requests PNR data invoking the exception of Article 5(5) to investigate a minor offence that is not included on the list (Boehm and Cole 2014: 66). That would weaken the original purpose for which the proposal was drafted. In this sense, the Art. 29 WP has considered that all the above-mentioned cases are incompatible with the purpose limitation principle (Article 29 Data Protection Working Party 2013b: 68–69).

At this stage, one might wonder what limits should apply in the processing of personal data. According to the Art. 29 WP, the limit should be set by the necessity principle. All instruments include a clause about their compliance with the necessity and proportionality principles. The Art. 29 WP has stressed that the purpose limitation principle should be restricted for any processing in which the data is not necessary to safeguard important interests (Article 13 of Directive 95/46/EC). However, the problem is that there are no strict parameters for assessing the necessity to access EU information systems' data by law enforcement authorities. Therefore, in order to conduct an objective examination of the necessity and proportionality, impact assessments in the use of instruments should be always conducted. Unfortunately, the Commission has not always carried out impact assessments before adopting data-sharing systems. For example, the Eurodac proposal launched by the Commission in May 2012 did not include any impact assessment. The EDPS was the first to react to this, arguing that the Commission did not demonstrate any substantive reason for which asylum seekers' data was needed. It then urged the Commission to provide solid evidence and reliable statistics for the need to access Eurodac data (EDPS 2012b). The Europol Joint Supervisory Body (JSB) also published a report in October 2012 examining that particular aspect on Eurodac access. It stated that there was a 'lack of evidence that such access is actually necessary and proportionate for countering terrorism and other serious crimes' (Joint Supervisory Body 2012). The JSB also noted that:

> Europol's mission to support the EU in preventing and combating all forms of serious international crime and terrorism cannot be seen as separate from the mission of national law enforcement authorities in these crime areas.
>
> (Joint Supervisory Body 2012: 3)

The JSB also called for a careful assessment and demonstrable evidence of the necessity for Europol's access. Consequently, the Council later issued a document with examples of real cases where the comparison of fingerprint data taken at a crime scene had contributed to a criminal investigation (Council of the European Union 2012). In fact, Member States are interested in encouraging the function creep, allowing them to expand accessible systems during the investigation of a crime.

The principles of purpose limitation and necessity were acknowledged by the CJEU in the recent ruling Case C-301/06 *Ireland v European Parliament* (2009) and C-293/12 and C-594/12 *Digital Rights Ireland* (2014). The Court annulled that directive precisely because the necessity of the retained data was not justified. The argument of the Court was that the interference applied 'even to persons for whom there is no evidence capable of suggesting that their conduct might have a link, even an indirect or remote one, with serious crime' (para. 58).

The same processing of an untargeted person's data occurs in all other instruments studied in this chapter. Therefore, it remains to be seen if the fact that since December 2014 the CJEU has had jurisdiction over former third-pillar measures results in more challenges before the court. Using the same argumentation as in the Data Retention case, other data-sharing instruments are likewise to be disputed in the future.

5 Conclusion

In the last 15 years, the EU has contributed significantly to the adoption of instruments for the prevention and combat of terrorism and other serious crimes. This first chapter has conducted a comprehensive analysis of the measures facilitating the exchange of information among Member States for law enforcement purposes. Many legal instruments (e.g. the Swedish Initiative and the Prüm Decisions) and information systems (e.g. SIS, VIS and Eurodac) have been added to the traditional MLA mechanism for exchanging crime-related data.

This chapter has identified divergent data protection rules in the existing EU data-sharing instruments, which would ultimately impede the establishment of global data protection standards for security purposes. Moreover, there is a delay in the implementation and a lack of use of these measures. As a result, law enforcement authorities often apply MLA procedures or even informal communication tools for the exchange of data with other Member States.

This chapter has also scrutinised whether it is possible to approximate these rules and achieve a common EU data protection framework for the information shared for law enforcement purposes. In order to do that, an in-depth analysis of the data protection laws within the AFSJ has been conducted. It has determined that the Treaty of Lisbon has clearly reinforced the protection of personal data. However, the Treaty establishes limitations when data is processed for law enforcement purposes. These restrictions are seen in Article 39 TEU, Declaration 21 and Protocol 36.

Moreover, FD 2008/977 and the new Directive on data protection for police and judicial co-operation in criminal matters have been minutely examined and compared. Although the new Directive introduces many new aspects (e.g. the coverage of pure domestic data transfers, a bigger role from the EP and the CJEU revision), its wording is still disappointing from a data protection perspective. The main dissatisfaction stemming from the new Directive is the restricted scope of the instrument. It excludes data processed by EU agencies such as Europol and Eurojust, Prüm transfers, data exchanged through SIS and CIS, as well as data collected by private companies and later processed by law enforcement authorities. This last limitation sets aside the processing of PNR data, SWIFT data and data collected by TSPs. Another problem is that other EU instruments might find their provisions overlapping with the new Directive, causing confusion and uncertainty: in some situations there will be two or more systems applicable; while in others there will be no applicable instrument at the EU level at all (Hijmans and Scirocco 2009: 1524).

In light of the foregoing considerations, it can be concluded that too many instruments and data protection frameworks are converging in the AFSJ. The current complexity of the security environment within the EU blocks the possibility to apply common data protection standards for the information shared among law enforcement agents. The major consequence of this issue is that, if personal data is not equally protected within the EU, the risk of disparities increases for data transfers between the EU and a third country. This is precisely the object of study in the next chapter.

Bibliography

Agreement between the United States of America and the European Police Office, 6 December 2001.

Airport Council International, 2015, *Fast Facts*, www.aci-europe.org/policy/fast-facts.html (accessed 4 November 2015).

Archick K, 2013, 'U.S.-EU Cooperation against terrorism', *Congressional Research Service*, Report RS22030, pp. 1–24.

Argomaniz, J, 2009, 'When the EU is the "norm-taker": The Passenger Name Records Agreement and the EU's internalization of US border security norms', *Journal of European Integration*, vol. 31, no. 1, pp. 119–136.

Argomaniz, J, 2010, 'Before and after Lisbon: Legal implementation as the "Achilles heel" in EU counter-terrorism?', *European Security*, vol. 19, no. 2, pp. 297–316.

Argomaniz, J, 2012, 'A coordination nightmare. Institutional coherence in European Union Counterterrorism' in C Kaunert, S Léonard and P Pawlak (eds), *European Homeland Security. A European Strategy in the Making?*, Routledge, New York, pp. 72–93.

Article 29 Data Protection Working Party, 2012, *Opinion 01/2012 on the data protection reform proposals*, WP 191, 23 March 2012.

Article 29 Data Protection Working Party, 2013a, *Opinion 01/2013 providing further input into the discussions on the draft Police and Criminal Justice Data Protection Directive*, WP 201, 26 February 2013.

Article 29 Data Protection Working Party, 2013b, *Opinion 03/2013 on purpose limitation*, WP 203, 2 April 2013;

Article 29 Data Protection Working Party, 2014, *Statement on the Ruling of the Court of Justice of the European Union (CJEU) which invalidates the Data Retention Directive*, WP 220, 1 August 2014.

Bäcker, M and Hornung, G, 2012, 'Data processing by police and criminal justice authorities in Europe – The influence of the Commission's draft on the national police laws and laws of criminal procedure', *Computer Law & Security Review*, vol. 28 no. 6, pp. 627–663.

Baumeister, P, 2008, 'Das Subsidiaritätprinzip und seine Bedeutung im Bereich der polizeilichen und justiziellen Zusammenarbeit in Strafsachen' in J Wolter, WR Schenke, H Hilger, J Ruthig and MA Zoller (eds), *Alternativenentwurf Europol und europäischer Datenschutz*, C.F.Müller Wissenschaft, Heidelberg, pp. 158–169.

Bellanova, R and Duez, D, 2012, 'A different view on the "making" of European security: The EU Passenger Name Record System as a socio-technical assemblage', *European Foreign Affairs Review*, vol. 17, no. 1/2, pp. 109–124.

Blasi Casagran, C, 2012, 'The reinforcement of fundamental rights in the Lisbon Treaty' in S Dosenrode (ed), *The European Union after Lisbon*, Ashgate Publishing Ltd, Surrey, pp. 75–94.

Blasi Casagran, C, 2013, 'People c. Harris: El lado oscuro de la libertad de expresión en las redes sociales' in L Cotino Hueso and L Corredoira Alfonso (eds), *Libertad de expresión e información en internet. Amenazas y protección de los derechos personales*, Centro Estudios Políticos y Constitucionales, Madrid, pp. 306–319.

Blasi Casagran, C, 2015, 'The future EU PNR system: Will passenger data be protected?', *European Journal of Crime, Criminal Law and Criminal Justice*, vol. 23, no. 3, pp. 241–257.

Boehm, F, 2011, 'EU PNR: European flight passengers under general suspicion. The envisaged European Model of Analyzing Flight Passenger Data' in S Gutwirth, Y Poullet, P de Hert and R Leenes (eds), *Computers, Privacy and Data Protection: An Element of Choice*, Springer, Berlin, pp. 171–199.

Boehm, F, 2012, 'Information sharing in the area of freedom, security and justice – Towards a common standard for data exchange between agencies and EU information systems' in S Gutwirth, R Leenes, P de Hert and Y Poullet (eds), *European Data Protection: In Good Health?*, Springer, Berlin, pp. 143–184.

Boehm, F and Cole, MD, 2014, 'Data retention after the Judgment of the Court of Justice of the European Union', Greens/EFA Group, European Parliament, Brussels, www.janalbrecht.eu/fileadmin/material/Dokumente/Boehm_Cole_-_Data_Retention_Study_-_June_2014.pdf (accessed 5 November 2015).

Bossong, RS, 2008, 'The Action Plan on combating terrorism – A flawed instrument of EU security governance', *Journal of Common Market Studies*, vol. 46 no. 1, pp. 27–48.

Bunyan, T, 1993, 'Trevi, Europol and the European state', *Statewatching the new Europe*, pp. 1–15, www.statewatch.org/news/handbook-trevi.pdf (accessed 3 November 2015).

Bures, O, 2011, *EU Counterterrorism Policy. A Paper Tiger?*, Ashgate, Surrey.

Bures, O and Ahern, S, 2007, 'The European Model of Building Regional Cooperation against Terrorism' in D Cortright and GA López (eds), *Uniting against Terror. Cooperative*

Nonmilitary Responses to the Global Terrorist Threat, Massachusetts Institute of Technology Press, Massachusetts, pp. 187–236.

Bygrave, LA, 2002, *Data Protection Law. Approaching Its Rationale, Logic and Limits*, Kluwer Law International, The Hague.

Cases C-465/00, C-138/01 and C-139/01, *Rechnungshof v Österreichischer Rundfunk and Others; and Christa Neukomm and Joseph Lauermann v Österreichischer Rundfunk* (CJEU, 20 May 2003).

Case C-101/01, *Lindqvist* (CJEU, 6 November 2003).

Case C-301/06, *Ireland v European Parliament and Council of the European Union* (CJEU, 10 February 2009).

Cases C-317 and 318/04, *Parliament v Council and Commission* (CJEU, 30 May 2006).

Cases C-293/12 and C-594/12, *Digital Rights Ireland Ltd v Minister for Communications, Marine and Natural Resources and Others and Kärntner Landesregierung and Others* (CJEU, 8 April 2014).

Cases C-293/12 and C-594/12, *Digital Rights Ireland Ltd v Minister for Communications, Marine and Natural Resources and Others and Kärntner Landesregierung and Others* (2014), Opinion of AG Cruz Villalón, 12 December 2013.

Commission Decision 2004/535/EC of 14 May 2004 on the adequate protection of personal data contained in the Passenger Name Record of air passengers transferred to the United States' Bureau of Customs and Border Protection (notified under document number.)

Communication from the Commission to the Council and the European Parliament of 10 May 2005 – The Hague Programme: ten priorities for the next five years. The Partnership for European renewal in the field of Freedom, Security and Justice, COM(2005) 184 final.

Communication from the Commission to the European Parliament and the Council of 18 May 2004 – Enhancing police and customs co-operation in the European Union, COM(2004) 376 final.

Communication from the Commission to the European Parliament and the Council of 16 June 2004 – Towards enhancing access to information by law enforcement agencies, COM (2004) 429 final.

Communication from the Commission to the European Parliament and the Council of 20 October 2004 – Prevention, preparedness and response to terrorist attacks, COM(2004) 698 final.

Communication from the Commission to the European Parliament and the Council of 20 October 2004 – Critical Infrastructure Protection in the fight against terrorism, COM(2004) 702 final.

Communication from the Commission to the European Parliament and the Council of 20 October 2004 – Preparedness and consequence management in the fight against terrorism, COM(2004) 701 final.

Communication from the Commission to the European Parliament, the Council, the European Economic and Social Committee and the Committee of the Regions of 4 November 2010 – A comprehensive approach on personal data protection in the European Union, COM(2010) 609 final.

Communication from the Commission to the European Parliament and the Council of 20 October 2004 – the Prevention of and the Fight against Terrorist Financing, COM(2004) 700 final.

Communication from the Commission to the European Parliament and the Council of 20 July 2010 – The EU Counter-Terrorism Policy: main achievements and future challenges, COM(2010) 386 final.

Communication from the Commission to the European Parliament and the Council of 20 July 2010 – Overview of information management in the area of freedom, security and justice, COM(2010)385 final.

Communication from the Commission to the European Parliament, the Council, the European Economic and Social Committee and the Committee of the Regions of 20 April 2010 – Delivering an area of freedom, security and justice for Europe's citizens – Action Plan Implementing the Stockholm Programme, COM(2010) 171.

Communication from the Commission to the European Parliament, the Council, the European Economic and Social Committee and the Committee of the Regions of 20 September 2011 – Towards an EU Criminal Policy: Ensuring the effective implementation of EU policies through criminal law, COM(2011) 573 final.

Communication from the Commission to the European Parliament, the Council, the European Economic and Social Committee and the Committee of the Regions of 13 July 2011 – A European terrorist finance tracking system: available options, COM(2011) 429 final.

Communication from the Commission to the European Parliament and the Council of 7 December 2012 – Strengthening law enforcement cooperation in the EU: The European Information Exchange Model (EIXM), COM(2012) 735 final.

Communication from the Commission to the European Parliament and the Council of 10 April 2013 – Second Report on the implementation of the EU Internal Security Strategy, COM(2013) 179 final.

Communication from the Commission to the European Parliament and the Council of 27 November 2013 – A European terrorist finance tracking system (EU TFTS), COM(2013) 842 final.

Convention Implementing the Schengen Agreement of 14 June 1985 between the Governments of the States of the Benelux Economic Union, the Federal Republic of Germany and the French Republic, on the Gradual Abolition of Checks at their Common Borders ('Schengen Implementation Agreement'), 19 June 1990.

Convention 97/C 254/01 determining the State responsible for examining applications for asylum lodged in one of the Member States of the European Communities, Dublin, 15 June 1990.

Coolsaet R, 2010, 'EU counterterrorism strategy: Value added or chimera?', *International Affairs,* vol. 86, no. 4, pp. 857–873.

Council Act 95/C316/02 of 26 July 1995 drawing up the Convention on the use of information technology for customs purposes.

Council Act 98/C 24/01 of 18 December 1997 drawing up, on the basis of Article K.3 of the Treaty on European Union, the Convention on mutual assistance and cooperation between customs administrations.

Council Act 2000/C 197/01 of 29 May 2000 establishing in accordance with Article 34 of the Treaty on European Union the Convention on Mutual Assistance in Criminal Matters between the Member States of the European Union.

Council Act of 16 October 2001 establishing, in accordance with Article 34 of the Treaty on European Union, the Protocol to the Convention on Mutual Assistance in Criminal Matters between the Member States of the European Union.

Council Common Position 2001/931/CFSP of 27 December 2001 on the application of specific measures to combat terrorism.

Council Decision 2001/264/EC of 19 March 2001 adopting the Council's security regulations.

Council Decision 2004/496/EC of 17 May 2004 on the conclusion of an Agreement between the European Community and the United States of America on the processing and transfer of PNR data by Air Carriers to the United States Department of Homeland Security, Bureau of Customs and Border Protection.

Council Decision 2004/512/EC of 8 June 2004 establishing the Visa Information System (VIS).

Council Decision 2005/211/JHA of 24 February 2005 concerning the introduction of some new functions for the Schengen Information System in the fight against terrorism.

Council Decision 2005/671/JHA of 20 September 2005 on the exchange of information and cooperation concerning terrorist offences.

Council Decision 2005/876/JHA of 21 November 2005 on the exchange of information extracted from the criminal record.

Council Decision 2008/615/JHA of 23 June 2008 on the stepping up of cross-border cooperation, particularly in combating terrorism and cross-border crime.

Council Decision 2008/616/JHA of 23 June 2008 on the implementation of Decision 2008/615/JHA on the stepping up of cross-border cooperation, particularly in combating terrorism and cross-border crime.

Council Decision 2008/633/JHA of 23 June 2008 concerning access for consultation of the Visa Information System (VIS) by designated authorities of Member States and by Europol for the purposes of the prevention, detection and investigation of terrorist offences and of other serious criminal offences.

Council Decision 2009/316/JHA of 6 April 2009 on the establishment of the European Criminal Records Information System (ECRIS) in application of Article 11 of Framework Decision 2009/315/JHA.

Council Decision 2009/917/JHA of 30 November 2009 on the use of information technology for customs purposes.

Council Decision 2009/934/JHA of 30 November 2009 adopting the implementing rules governing Europol's relations with partners, including the exchange of personal data and classified information.

Council Decision 2009/936/JHA of 30 November 2009 adopting the implementing rules for Europol analysis work files.

Council Decision 2009/968/JHA of 30 November 2009 adopting the rules on the confidentiality of Europol information.

Council Decision 2009/902/JHA of 30 November 2009 setting up a European Crime Prevention Network (EUCPN) and repealing Decision 2001/427.

Council Decision 2011/292/EU of 31 March 2011 on the security rules for protecting EU classified information.

Council Framework Decision 2002/465/JHA of 13 June 2002 on joint investigation teams.

Council Framework Decision 2006/960/JHA of 18 December 2006 on simplifying the exchange of information and intelligence between law enforcement authorities of the Member States of the European Union.

Council Framework Decision 2008/675/JHA of 24 July 2008 on taking account of convictions in the Member States of the European Union in the course of new criminal proceedings.

Council Framework Decision 2008/977/JHA of 27 November 2008 on the protection of personal data processed in the framework of police and judicial cooperation in criminal matters.

Council Framework Decision 2009/315/JHA of 26 February 2009 on the organisation and content of the exchange of information extracted from the criminal record between Member States.

Council of Europe, 1959, *European Convention on Mutual Assistance in Criminal Matters*, 20 April 1959.

Council of Europe, 1981, *Convention for the Protection of Individuals with regard to Automatic Processing of Personal Data*, CETS No. 108, 28 January 1981.

Council of the European Union, 2001, *'Note from the Presidency. Co-ordination of Implementation of the Plan of Action to Combat Terrorism'*, Doc. 12800/01, 16 October 2001.

Council of the European Union, 2003, *European Security Strategy. A secure Europe in a better World*, 12 December 2003.

Council of the European Union, 2005, *Prüm Convention*, Doc. 10900/05, 7 July 2005.

Council of the European Union, 2008, *Freedom, Security, Privacy – European Home Affairs in an open world – Report of the Informal High-Level Advisory Group on the Future of European*, Doc. 11657/08, 9 July 2008.

Council of the European Union, 2009, *Draft Council Conclusions on an Information Management Strategy for EU internal security*, Doc. 16637/09, 25 November 2009.

Council of the European Union, 2010, *Initiative for a Directive of the European Parliament and of the Council regarding the European Investigation Order in criminal matters*, Doc. 9145/10, 29 April 2010.

Council of the European Union, 2011, *Council Framework Decision 2006/960/JHA on simplifying the exchange of information and intelligence between law enforcement authorities of the Member States of the European Union ('Swedish Framework Decision')*, Doc. 15278/11, 14 October 2011.

Council of the European Union, 2012, *Amended proposal for a Regulation of the European Parliament and of the Council on the establishment of 'EURODAC' for the comparison of fingerprints for the effective application of Regulation (EU) No [. . ./. . .] (establishing the criteria and mechanisms for determining the Member State responsible for examining an application for international protection lodged in one of the Member States by a third-country national or a stateless person) and to request comparisons with EURODAC data by Member States' law enforcement authorities and Europol for law enforcement purposes and amending Regulation (EU) No 1077/2011 establishing a European Agency for the operational management of large-scale IT systems in the area of freedom, security and justice (Recast version)*, Doc. 16990/12, 3 December 2012.

Council of the European Union, 2013a, *Discussion Paper on the future development of the JHA area*, Doc. 14898/13, 16 October 2013.

Council of the European Union, 2013b, *Target information management architecture (IMS Action 10) – Draft vision on EU law enforcement information exchange*, Doc. 7903/13, 25 March 2013.

Council of the European Union, 2013c, *Proposal for a directive of the European Parliament and of the Council on the protection of individuals with regard to the processing of personal data by competent authorities for the purposes of prevention, investigation, detection or prosecution of criminal offences or the execution of criminal penalties, and the free movement of such data, Chapters I–IV*, Doc. 14901/2/13, 30 October 2013.

Council of the European Union, 2014a, *List of the former third pillar acquis*, Doc. 9930/14, 19 May 2014.

Council of the European Union, 2014b, *Guidelines on the implementation of Council Framework Decision 2006/960/JHA ('Swedish Framework Decision' – SFD) – Update of national fact sheets*, Doc. 13034/14, 17 September 2014.

Council of the European Union, 2014c, *ECRIS-DTS-Detailed Technical Specifications*, Doc. 14264/14, 17 October 2014.

Council of the European Union, 2014d, *ECRIS Technical Specifications – Proposal of changes for the implementation of the Directive 2011/93/EU in ECRIS*, Doc. 14266/14, 17 October 2014.

Council of the European Union, 2014e, *ECRIS-BA-Business Analysis*, Doc. 14269/14, 17 October 2014.

Council of the European Union, 2014f, *Draft Guidelines for a Single Point of Contact (SPOC) for international law enforcement information exchange – International law enforcement cooperation structures in each Member State*, Doc. 10492/14, 15 December 2014.

Council of the European Union, 2014g, *Report on the technical functioning of the Visa Information System (VIS)*, Doc. 7996/14, 21 March 2014.

Council of the European Union, 2014h, *Proposal for a Directive of the European Parliament and of the Council on the protection of individuals with regard to the processing of personal data by competent authorities for the purposes of prevention, investigation, detection or prosecution of criminal offences or the execution of criminal penalties, and the free movement of such data*, Doc. 11109/14, 30 June 2014.

Council of the European Union, 2015, *Implementation of the provisions on information exchange of the 'Prüm Decisions'. Overview of documents and procedures, overview of declarations, state of play of implementation of automated data exchange*, Doc. 5010/3/15, 23 April 2015.

Council Regulation (EC) No 2725/2000 of 11 December 2000 concerning the establishment of 'Eurodac' for the comparison of fingerprints for the effective application of the Dublin Convention.

Council Regulation (EC) No 871/2004 of 29 April 2004 concerning the introduction of some new functions for the Schengen Information System, including in the fight against terrorism.

CJEU, 2014, *Opinion 2/13 of 18 December 2014 on the accession of the European Union to the European Convention for the Protection of Human Rights and Fundamental Freedoms.*

Cremona, M, 2011, 'Justice and Home Affairs in a globalised world: Ambitions and reality in the tale of the EU-US SWIFT Agreement', *Austrian Academy of Sciences, Institute for European Integration Research*, Working Paper No. 04/2011, pp. 1–30.

Curtin, D, 2011, 'Top Secret Europe', Inaugural Lecture, *Universiteit van Amsterdam*, http://dare.uva.nl/document/2/103309 (accessed 4 November 2015).

de Busser, E, 2009, *Data Protection in EU and US Criminal Cooperation: A Substantive Law Approach to the EU Internal and Transatlantic Cooperation in Criminal Matters between Judicial and Law Enforcement Authorities*, Maklu Publishers, Antwerpen.

de Hert, P and Bellanova, R, 2009, 'Data protection in the Area of Freedom, Security and Justice. A system still to be fully developed?', *European Parliament, Directorate General Internal Policies of the Union, Policy Department C, Citizens' Rights and Constitutional Affairs*, Doc. PE 410.692, pp. 1–32.

de Hert, P and Papakonstantinou, V, 2009, 'The data protection framework decision of 27 November 2008 regarding police and judicial cooperation in criminal matters – A modest achievement however not the improvement some have hoped for', *Computer Law & Security Review*, vol. 25, pp. 403–414.

Directive 95/46/EC of the European Parliament and of the Council of 24 October 1995 on the protection of individuals with regard to the processing of personal data and on the free movement of such data.

Directive 2002/58/EC of the European Parliament and of the Council of 12 July 2002 concerning the processing of personal data and the protection of privacy in the electronic communications sector.

Directive 2005/60/EC of the European Parliament and of the Council of 26 October 2005 on the prevention of the use of the financial system for the purpose of money laundering and terrorist financing.

Directive 2006/24/EC of the European Parliament and of the Council of 15 March 2006 on the retention of data generated or processed in connection with the provision of publicly available electronic communications services or of public communications networks and amending Directive 2002/58/EC.

Directive 2013/40/EU of the European Parliament and of the Council of 12 August 2013 on attacks against information systems and replacing Council Framework Decision 2005/222/JHA.

Directive 2014/41/EU of the European Parliament and the Council of 3 April 2014 regarding the European Investigation Order in criminal matters.

Docksey, C, 2014, 'The European Court of Justice and the decade of surveillance' in H Hijmans and H Kranenborg (eds), *Data Protection Anno 2014: How to Restore Trust? Contributions in Honour of Peter Hustinx European Data Protection Supervisor 2004–2014*, Intersentia, Cambridge.

Eckes, C, 2011, 'The legal framework of the European Union's counter-terrorist policies: Full of good intentions?' in C Eckes and T Konstadinides (eds), *Crime within the Area of Freedom, Security and Justice: A European Public Order*, Cambridge University Press, Cambridge, pp. 127–158.

EDPS, 2011, *Opinion of the EDPS on the Evaluation report from the Commission to the Council and the European Parliament on the Data Retention Directive (Directive 2006/24/EC)*, 31 May 2011.

EDPS, 2012a, *Opinion on the data protection reform package*, 7 March 2012.

EDPS, 2012b, *Opinion on Eurodac*, 5 September 2012.

EDPS, 2013, *Opinion on the Communication from the Commission to the European Parliament and the Council entitled 'Strengthening law enforcement cooperation in the EU: the European Information Exchange Model (EIXM)'*, 29 April 2013.

EDPS, 2014, Comments on the Communication from the Commission to the European Parliament and the Council on a European Terrorist Finance Tracking System (TFTS) and on the Commission Staff Working Document – Impact Assessment accompanying the Communication from the Commission to the European Parliament and the Council on a European Terrorist Finance Tracking System (TFTS), 17 April 2014.

European Commission, 2013, *DG Home, Evidence for necessity of data retention in the EU, March 2013*, http://ec.europa.eu (accessed 5 November 2015).

European Commission, 2015, *Mutual Legal Assistance and Extradition*, http://ec.europa.eu/justice/criminal/judicial-cooperation/legal-assistance/index_en.htm (accessed 3 November 2015).

European Commission, Commission Staff Working Paper. Operation of the Council Framework Decision 2006/960/JHA of 18 December 2006 ('Swedish Initiative'), SEC(2011) 593, 13 May 2011.

European Commission, Commission Staff Working Paper. Impact Assessment Accompanying document to the Proposal for a European Parliament and Council Directive on the use of Passenger Name Record data for the prevention, detection, investigation and prosecution of terrorist offences and serious crime, SEC(2011) 132 and SEC(2011) 133 final, 2 February 2011.

European Commission Evaluation Report on Data Retention Directive, COM(2011) 225 final, 18 April 2011.

European Commission Proposal for a Council framework decision on the use of Passenger Name Record (PNR) for law enforcement purposes, COM(2007) 654 final, 6 November 2007.

European Commission Proposal for a European Parliament and Council Directive on the use of Passenger Name Record data for the prevention, detection, investigation and prosecution of terrorist offences and serious crime, COM(2011) 32 final, 2 February 2011.

European Commission Proposal for a Regulation of the European Parliament and of the Council on the protection of individuals with regard to the processing of personal data and on the free movement of such data (General Data Protection Regulation), COM(2012) 11 final, 25 January 2012.

European Commission Proposal for a Directive on the protection of individuals with regard to the processing of personal data by competent authorities for the purposes of prevention, investigation, detection or prosecution of criminal offences or the execution of criminal penalties, and the free movement of such data, COM(2012) 10 final, 25 January 2012.

European Commission Proposal for a Council Decision determining certain consequential and transitional arrangements concerning the cessation of participation of the United Kingdom of Great Britain and Northern Ireland in certain acts of the Union in the field of police cooperation and judicial cooperation in criminal matters adopted before the entry into force of the Treaty of Lisbon, COM(2014) 596 final, 26 September 2014.

European Commission White Paper on exchanges of information on convictions and the effect of such convictions in the European Union, COM(2005) 10 final, 25 January 2005.

European Council, 1999, *Tampere Conclusions of 15–16 October 1999*.

European Council, 2004, *Declaration on combating terrorism*, 25 March 2004.

European Council, 2005, *Declaration on condemning the terrorist attacks on London*, 13 July 2005.

European Council, 2009, *The Stockholm Programme – An open and secure Europe serving and protecting citizens*, 2 December 2009.

European Digital Rights, 2013, 'An introduction to Data Protection', *The EDRI Papers*, Issue 6, pp. 1–21, https://edri.org/files/paper06_datap.pdf (accessed 3 November 2015).

European e-Justice Portal, 2015, *Criminal Records* (online), https://e-justice.europa.eu/content_criminal_records-95-en.do (accessed 4 November 2015).

European Parliament, 2007, 'Working Document on a Council Decision on the stepping up of crossborder cooperation, particularly in combating terrorism and cross-border crime', Rapporteur: Fausto Correia, *Committee on Civil Liberties, Justice and Home Affairs*, 10 April 2007.

European Parliament, 2008, *European Parliament resolution on the proposal for a Council framework decision on the use of Passenger Name Record (PNR) for law enforcement purposes*, Doc. B6-0615/2008, 20 November 2008.

European Parliament, 2012, *Resolution of 22 May 2012 on the European Union's Internal Security Strategy* ((2010)2308 (INI)).

European Parliament, 2014a, *Protocol 36 to the Treaty of Lisbon on transitional provision: the position of the United Kingdom*, Committee on Civil Liberties, Justice and Home Affairs 2014–2019, November 2014.

European Parliament, 2014b, *LIBE-Questions relating to the judgment of the Court of Justice or 8 April 2014 in Joined Cases C-293/12 and C-594/12, Digital Rights Ireland and Seitlinger and others – Directive 2006/24/EC on data retention – Consequences of the judgement*, Legal Opinion of the EP.

European Parliament, 2015, *Second Report on the proposal for a directive of the European Parliament and of the Council on the use of Passenger Name Record data for the prevention, detection, investigation and prosecution of terrorist offences and serious crime*, Doc. PE 549.223v03-00, 7 September 2015.

Hayes, B, 2004, 'From the Schengen Information System to SIS II and the Visa Information (VIS): The proposals explained', *Statewatch Analysis*, www.statewatch.org/news/2005/may/analysis-sisII.pdf (accessed 4 November 2015).

Hayes, B and Jones, C, 2013, 'Catalogue of EU Counter-Terrorism Measures adopted since 11 September 2001', *SECILE: Securing Europe through Counter-Terrorism – Impact, Legitimacy & Effectiveness*, www.statewatch.org (accessed 3 November 2015).

Hayes, B and Vermeulen, M, 2012, *Borderline. The EU's New Border Surveillance Initiatives Assessing the Costs and Fundamental Rights Implications of EUROSUR and the 'Smart Borders' Proposals*, Heinrich Böll Foundation, Berlin.

Hernanz, N, 2011, 'More surveillance, more security? The landscape of surveillance in Europe and challenges to data protection and privacy – Policy report on the proceedings of a conference at the European Parliament', *SAPIENT Deliverable 6.4*, www.sapientproject.eu/docs/D6.4-Policy-Brief-submitted-January-2012-29.pdf (accessed 3 November 2015).

Hijmans, H and Scirocco, A, 2009, 'Shortcomings in EU data protection in the third and the second pillars. Can the Lisbon Treaty be expected to help?', *Common Market Law Review*, vol. 46, no. 5, pp. 1485–1525.

Joint Supervisory Body, 2012, *Opinion of the Joint Supervisory Body of Europol 12/52, with respect to the amended proposal for a Regulation of the European Parliament and of the Council on the establishment of EURODAC*, 10 October 2012.

Jones, C, 2011, 'Implementing the "principle of availability": The European Criminal Records Information System, The European Police Records Index System, The Information Exchange Platform for Law Enforcement Authorities', *Statewatch Analysis*, www.statewatch.com (accessed 3 November 2015).

Jones, C, 2012, 'Complex, technologically fraught and expensive – The problematic implementation of the Prüm Decision', *Statewatch Analysis*, www.statewatch.com (accessed 4 November 2015).

Kabera Karanja, S, 2008, *Transparency and Proportionality in the Schengen Information System and Border Control Cooperation*, Martinus Nijhoff Publishers, Leiden.

Kaunert, C, 2012, 'Conclusion: assessing the external dimension of EU counter-terrorism – Ten years on', *European Security*, vol. 21 no. 4, pp. 578–587.

Kurth Cronin, A and Ludes, JM, 2004, *Attacking Terrorism: Elements of a Grand Strategy*, Georgetown University Press, Washington DC.

Lavenex, S and Wichmann, N, 2009, 'The external governance of EU Internal Security', *Journal of European Integration*, vol. 31, no. 1, pp. 83–102.

Lichtblau, E and Risen, J, 2006, 'Bank data is sifted by U.S. in secret to block terror', *The New York Times*, 23 June 2006.

Lööf, R, 2008, *Defending liberty and structural integrity: A social contractual analysis of criminal justice in the EU*, PhD thesis, European University Institute.

Luchtman, M, 2011, 'Choice of forum in an area of freedom, security and justice', *Utrecht Law Review*, vol. 7, no. 1, pp. 44–101.

Mangiaracina, A, 2014, 'A new and controversial scenario in the gathering of evidence at the European level: The proposal for a Directive on the European Investigation Order', *Utrecht Law Review*, vol. 10, no. 1, pp. 113–133.

Miller, V, 2014, 'The UK block opt-out in police and judicial cooperation in criminal matters: Recent developments', *House of Commons, International Affairs and Defence Section, Standard Note: SN/IA/6930*, 10 November 2014.

Ni Loideain, N, 2011, 'The EC Data Retention Directive: Legal implications for privacy and data protection' in C Akrivopoulou and A Psygkas (eds), *Personal Data Privacy and Protection in a Surveillance Era: Technologies and Practices*, IGI Global, Hershey, pp. 256–272.

Nino, M, 2010, 'The protection of personal data in the fight against terrorism. New perspectives of PNR European Union instruments in the light of the Treaty of Lisbon', *Utrecht Law Review*, vol. 6, no. 1, pp. 62–85.

Organisation for Economic Co-operation and Development, 1980, Recommendation of the Council concerning Guidelines Governing the Protection of Privacy and Transborder Flows of Personal Data, 23 September 1980.

O'Neill, M, 2012, *The Evolving Counter-Terrorism Legal Framework*, Routledge Research in EU Law, New York.

Pateraki, A, 2011, 'The implementation of the Data Retention Directive' in C Akrivopoulou and A Psygkas (eds), *Personal Data Privacy and Protection in a Surveillance Era: Technologies and Practices*, IGI Global, Hershey, pp. 317–328.

Peers, S, 2012, 'Analysis. The Directive on data protection and law enforcement: A missed opportunity?', *Statewatch*, pp. 2–3, www.statewatch.com (accessed 4 November 2015).

Peers, S, 2014, 'Are data retention laws within the scope of the Charter?', *EU Law Analysis. Blog about developments in EU Law*, 20 April 2014, http://eulawanalysis.blogspot.com.es (accessed 5 November 2015).

Politsei- ja Piirivalveamet, 2013, *Police officers are being trained to use on of cooperation tools of the PRUM decision – Joint police operations* (online), www.politsei.ee/en/uudised/uudis.dot?id= 258362 (accessed 4 November 2015).

Porter, AL and Bendiek, A, 2012, 'Counterterrorism cooperation in the transatlantic security community', *European Security*, vol. 21, no. 4, pp. 497–517.

Regulation (EC) No 766/2008 of the European Parliament and of the Council of 9 July 2008 amending Council Regulation (EC) No 515/97 on mutual assistance between the administrative authorities of the Member States and cooperation between the latter and the Commission to ensure the correct application of the law on customs and agricultural matters.

Regulation (EU) No 604/2013 of 26 June 2013 establishing the criteria and mechanisms for determining the Member State responsible for examining an application for international protection lodged in one of the Member States by a third-country national or a stateless person.

Regulation (EU) 2015/847 of the European Parliament and of the Council of 20 May 2015 on information accompanying transfers of funds and repealing Regulation (EC) No 1781/2006.

Report from the Commission to the European Parliament and the Council on the implementation of Council Decision 2008/615/JHA of 23 June 2008 on the stepping up of cross-border cooperation, particularly in combating terrorism and cross-border crime (the 'Prüm Decision'), COM(2012) 732 final, 7 December 2012.

Sayers, D, 2011, 'The European Investigation Order Travelling without a "roadmap"', *CEPS Paper in Liberty and Security in Europe,* pp. 1–25.

Soleto Muñoz, H and Fiodorova, A, 2014, 'DNA and law enforcement in the European Union: Tools and human rights protection', *Utrecht Law Review,* vol. 10, no. 1, pp. 149–162.

Statewatch, 2014, *Schengen Information System: 41,000 people subject to 'discreet surveillance or specific checks'* (online), 9 September 2014, http://statewatch.org/news/2014/sep/sis-stats.htm (accessed 4 November 2015).

Supplemental Agreement between the Europol Police Office and the United States of America on the exchange of personal data and related information, 20 December 2002.

Töpfer, E, 2011, 'Europe's emerging web of DNA databases', *Statewatch Journal,* vol. 21, no.1, http://database.statewatch.org/article.asp?aid=30566 (accessed 3 November 2015).

Tzanou, M, 2011, 'Data protection in EU Law: An analysis of the EU legal framework and the ECJ jurisprudence' in C Akrivopoulou and A Psygkas (eds), *Personal Data Privacy and Protection in a Surveillance Era: Technologies and Practices,* IGI Global, Hershey, pp. 273–297.

United Nations Office on Drugs and Crime, 2012, 'The use of the Internet for terrorist purposes', September 2012, New York, www.unodc.org (accessed 5 November 2015).

Uniting and Strengthening America by Providing Appropriate Tools Required to Intercept and Obstruct Terrorism (USA Patriot Act) Act of 2001, H.R.3162, 107th Congress (2001–2002).

Vermeulen, M and Wills, A, 2011, 'Parliamentary oversight of security and intelligence agencies in the European Union', European Parliament, Directorate General for Internal Policies, Policy Department C, Citizens' Rights and Constitutional Affairs, Brussels.

Vernimmen-Van Tiggelen, G and Surano, L, 2008, 'Analysis of the future of mutual recognition in criminal matters in the European Union', Institute for European Studies, Université Libre de Bruxelle, ECLAN Report, http://ec.europa.eu/justice/criminal/files/mutual_recognition_en.pdf (accessed 3 November 2015).

Wesseling, M, 2014, 'Evaluation of EU measures to combat terrorist financing', European Parliament, Directorate General for Internal Policies, Policy Department C, Citizens' Rights and Constitutional Affairs, Brussels.

Whitehead, T and Porter, A, 2010, 'Britons to be spied on by foreign police', *The Telegraph,* 26 July 2010, www.telegraph.co.uk/news/uknews/law-and-order/7909314/Britons-to-be-spied-on-by-foreign-police.html (accessed 4 November 2015).

Wolff, S, Wichmann, N and Mounier, G, 2009, 'The external dimension of justice and home affairs: A different security agenda for the EU?', *European Integration,* vol. 31, no. 1, pp. 9–23.

2 Data exchanges for law enforcement purposes between the EU and a third state

Terrorism and other serious crimes are not always demarcated within a specific territory. A terrorist group might commit an attack in France today, and repeat a similar atrocity in Chicago tomorrow. Therefore, Member States and the EU itself have strengthened their co-operation with police forces in third countries. As a result, the EU is now competent to adopt international agreements with third countries in the fight against globalised terrorism and other serious crimes.

After an examination of the EU instruments that collect and exchange information among Member States for the prevention, combat, investigation and prosecution of crimes, this chapter focuses on the exchange of information beyond the European borders. The feasibility of a global data protection framework will depend to a great extent on the consistency among current agreements between the EU and third countries. If international agreements for the exchange of information among law enforcement authorities do not yet have common data protection rules, it will make the establishment of a universal catalogue of data protection principles difficult to achieve.

This chapter is divided into two parts. The first part examines the great external influences, especially from the US, on current EU counter-terrorism measures. The terrorist attacks of 9/11 (11 September 2001) caused an increase in the number of measures taken by the EU for the collection, processing and storage of personal data. These measures regulate not only the exchange of information within the EU but also with non-EU countries. Within this context, I assess the main EU external data-sharing instruments. My contention is that, although the EU has influenced certain third countries' norms, the US rules have mostly shaped the EU security norms. In other words, as the EU is widening its role in the global security environment, it also becomes a 'norm-taker' when US counter-terrorism measures based on the exchange of information are at stake. In order to prove this point I thoroughly analyse the Agreements on mutual legal assistance, PNR, financial data, as well as air and maritime security partnerships between the EU and the US.

The second part of this chapter studies the data protection safeguards for transfers carried out between the EU and a third country. In Chapter 1, I concluded that there is no consistent EU data protection framework in the field of law enforcement. Does it imply that data protection provisions of international agreements between the EU and a third country are likewise discrepant? I examine this below.

1 The external dimension of the AFSJ in the fight against terrorism

1.1 Origins and evolution

Although the original purpose of the AFSJ was to provide a framework in which the EU and its Member States could co-operate for increasing public order, internal peace and security, a parallel external mission has been developed over the last ten years. Threats to the EU internal security have often been originated outside the EU territory (Wolff, Wichmann and Mounier 2009: 11; Lavenex and Wichmann 2009: 84; Wesser, Marin and Matera 2011: 277). To respond to these threats, the EU institutions have engaged in joint actions with third countries (Pawlak 2009a: 33).

The external dimension of the AFSJ stemmed from three correlative events: (a) the initiatives in the Tampere European Council of 1999; (b) the global impact of the terrorist attacks of 9/11; and (c) the external strategy proposed in the Hague Programme since 2005 (Wesser, Marin and Matera 2011: 179–180). These three episodes acted as 'critical junctures' or key moments that led the EU to conduct institutional reforms in its external security policy. Yet, differences need to be distinguished between the Tampere European Council and the other two events.

First, the main goal of the Tampere European Council (European Council 1999) was to make better use of the EU competences in the field of external relations. In that sense, the Conclusions of the Presidency underlined the need to achieve a greater coherence between internal and external policies of the EU (point 59 of the Conclusions). A closer co-operation between the Council and the Commission was encouraged. The external dimension of the AFSJ as defined in Tampere was not supposed to be an independent policy, but rather an action complementing the internal AFSJ (Wesser, Marin and Matera 2011: 180; Cremona 2008a: 3). In this sense, the declaration stated:

> All competences and instruments at the disposal of the Union, and in particular, in external relations must be used in an integrated and consistent way to build the area of freedom, security and justice.
>
> (European Council 1999: 59)

The purpose of enhancing external relations within the AFSJ launched in Tampere was later reiterated in the Santa Maria da Feira European Council (European Council 2000), as well as in the 'Multi-Presidency Work Programme' on external relations released by the Council in July 2001 (Council of the European Union 2001a).

The 9/11 terrorist attacks had a substantial political impact on the AFSJ legislation. Only ten days after the attacks, the European Council conducted a meeting with all the heads of the Member States in order to discuss the EU co-operation with the US and how to achieve the strengthening of EU counter-terrorism measures (European Council 2001). The same discourse took place during the European Council of Seville one year later (European Council 2002: 31–34).

In 2003, the former High Representative for CFSP, Javier Solana, drafted a European Security Strategy. It stressed the new multidimensional nature of security (Longo 2013: 37) in which the EU had to contribute to global security through its external action (Council of the European Union 2003). Frequent dialogue began between the EU and US officials in order to harmonise police, judicial and border control policy matters. The counter-terrorism policy thus became a priority on both sides of the Atlantic.

Many international agreements on border security and criminal matters were signed between the EU and the US shortly after the attacks. The EU-US agreements on extradition and mutual legal assistance,[1] as well as the Agreements between Europol and the US[2] were two of these. In addition, the External Security Strategy of 2003 increased the role of the Council in the decision-making process for measures falling under the external dimension of the AFSJ.

Lastly, the Hague Programme, approved in November 2004, also had a significant impact on the expansion of the external dimension of the AFSJ. The programme was a direct consequence of the Madrid terrorist attack of 2004, in which synchronised detonations of bombs were carried out in the city's commuter train system. The Hague Programme aimed at strengthening the co-operation between law enforcement agencies of Member States, while consolidating the internal/external nexus of the AFSJ. On 7 July 2005, a similar attack occurred on three underground trains on a bus in central London. The European Council issued several declarations after these attacks (Council of the European Union 2004a, 2005a), highlighting the need to adopt common measures on the retention of telecommunications data as soon as possible.

The Commission also launched a series of communications (COM(2004) 376 final; COM (2004) 429 final; COM(2004) 698 final, COM(2004) 702 final, COM(2004) 701 final and COM(2004) 700 final) encouraging the co-ordination of counter-terrorism activities among EU institutions and Member States. These communications suggested the establishment of an integrated approach on the fight against terrorism, which would give the Commission a more direct involvement in both internal and external security policies. During that period, the COTER and the European Union Counter-Terrorism Strategy were also established. Both initiatives dealt with external aspects of terrorism.

The Hague Programme emphasised the necessity to establish coherence between the internal and the external dimensions of the AFSJ in the fight against terrorism. As in the former Tampere Declaration, the Hague Programme

---

1 These agreements are examined in section 2 of this chapter.
2 These agreements are examined in Chapter 3.

considered that external police operations had the ultimate purpose of improving the internal security of the EU (European Council 2005: point 2.4). The external dimension of the AFSJ became a priority in the EU agenda and, therefore, the European Council invited the Council and the Commission to draft strategies on that matter (European Council 2005: point 4). As a result, in 2005 the Commission released a communication for 'a strategy on the external dimension of the Area of Freedom, Security and Justice' (COM(2005) 491 final). The communication underlined that the external dimension of the AFSJ had to be conceived as a projection of the internal AFSJ. That communication served as a basis for the Council's *A Strategy for the External Dimension of JHA: Global Freedom, Security and Justice* (Council of the European Union 2005b). Together with the Council and the Commission, the EP also promoted the external dimension of the fight against international terrorism, despite its limited competences in the EU decision-making process at that time (O'Neill 2012: 166).

In order to comply with the US demands, the EU concluded many international agreements in the field of security. However, the appropriate legal basis for those agreements was not entirely clear since they had a cross-pillar nature (Wesser 2010; Cremona 2008a: 16; Wesser, Marin and Matera 2011: 291). Some of them were adopted under the internal market clause (e.g. the 2004 EU-US PNR Agreement)[3] through the Community implied powers (Cremona 2008a: 5–6; Monar 2012: 22–23); while others were adopted under the scope of the third pillar. That was the case of the 2006 and 2007 EU-US PNR Agreements.[4] The Commission used Article 24 TEU in conjunction with Article 38 TEU as the legal bases for concluding such agreements (Wesser, Marin and Matera 2011: 289–290; Cremona 2008a: 13).

New legal bases for the AFSJ were included in the Treaty of Lisbon. Particularly, the treaty includes express provisions in Articles 78(2)(g) and 79(3) TFEU for the conclusion of international agreements in two matters: immigration and asylum. However, it does not add any general legal basis for the conclusion of international agreements in the AFSJ. It is a step backwards compared to the pre-Lisbon legal framework. Before Lisbon, Article 38 TEU was the legal basis to conclude international agreements under the scope of the AFSJ, but the provision was removed with the Treaty of Lisbon, so now agreements on criminal co-operation are based on EU implied powers.

There are, however, many issues in the Treaty of Lisbon that have contributed to the strengthening of the external dimension of the AFSJ. According to Article 21(3) TEU, external objectives of the EU do not only refer to general external policy issues, but also to those 'external aspects of its other policies' like the external dimension of the AFSJ (Cremona 2008a: 5 and 8). Also, the abolishment of pillars ends with the distinction between the first- and third-pillar matters of the AFSJ. All fields are now reviewable by the CJEU. Likewise, the

3 2004 EU-US PNR Agreement is examined in section 2.2.1 of this chapter.
4 2006 and 2007 EU-US PNR Agreements are also examined in section 2.1.2 of this chapter.

Treaty of Lisbon removes the separation between the EU and EC international agreements, now gathered under one single legal basis: Article 218 TFEU. The new procedure for concluding international agreements allows both Member States and the EU to participate in the negotiations. The EP is involved in the legislative procedure too, but in a more limited way: in some cases it has to approve the Agreement (Article 218(6)(a) TFEU);[5] whereas in others it only has a consultative role (Article 218(6)(b) TFEU).[6]

Since the Treaty of Lisbon, new initiatives within the scope of the external dimension of the AFSJ have been released. The first instrument launched was the Stockholm Programme in December 2009 (European Council 2009). The programme highlighted that the external dimension was crucial to the successful implementation of the objectives of the programme. Also, it sought a 'greater coherence between external and internal elements of the work' in the AFSJ. The two main priorities of the programme in relation to the external dimension of the AFSJ were the control of migration flows on the one hand, and the improvement of security in Europe on the other. The programme also included new policies connected to external threats such as the fight against cybercrime (European Council 2009: 4–6, 22 and 34).

According to the Stockholm Programme, an Internal Security Strategy (ISS) was to be drafted by the Council and the Commission. In this regard, the Council released a 'Draft Internal Security Strategy for the European Union: Towards a European Security Model' (Council of the European Union 2010a), and the Commission issued a communication on *The EU Internal Security Strategy in Action: Five steps towards a more secure Europe* (COM(2010) 673 final). The Commission's communication established clear objectives, which included the disruption of international crime networks with the creation of an EU PNR Directive, and the prevention of terrorism by cutting off terrorists' access to funding and materials and by following their transactions. The ISS, like the Stockholm Programme, considered that the internal security was increasingly dependent on external security matters (Cremona 2011: 6).

All the EU institutions approve the existing link between the ISS and external security measures (European Parliament 2012: point 9; Council of the European Union 2012a; COM(2013) 179 final, p. 17). They acknowledge that internal and external aspects of the EU security are complementary and, therefore, stronger co-ordination between policies should be promoted. Likewise, AFSJ agencies such as Europol, Eurojust and FRONTEX have strengthened their competences in the field of external action, and they are currently able to conclude co-operation agreements with third countries and non-EU organisations.

---

5 The involvement of the EP in the adoption of the SWIFT agreement is discussed in section 3.2 of this chapter.
6 This is the case, for example, of operational co-operation in internal security matters (Article 87(3) TFEU) and family law matters with cross-border implications (Article 81(3) TFEU).

1.2 Data exchanges for security purposes. The blurry line between the AFSJ and the CFSP/CSDP

As Cremona states, there is not one single external policy within the scope of the AFSJ (Cremona 2008a: 1 and 7). Instead, this area is constituted by several integrated policies that, to some extent, are to be achieved in co-operation with third countries. These include the immigration policy, the counter-terrorism policy and the fight against organised and serious crime, among others (Trauner and Carrapiço 2012: 4). For the purpose of this study, the following paragraphs focus solely on the law enforcement area and, particularly, on measures consisting of the processing of information for security purposes.

As seen earlier, the number of counter-terrorism measures adopted by the EU institutions has dramatically increased in the last decade, leading to an expansion of the AFSJ. Yet, counter-terrorism is not an exclusive AFSJ matter. The events of 9/11 also strengthened the CFSP and the Common Security and Defence Policy (CSDP) areas through new military missions and partnership agreements with third countries (Wolf 2009: 146). Before the attacks, neither the CFSP nor the CSDP were conceptualised as tools for fighting terrorism (Ferreira-Pereira and Oliveira Martins 2012: 541) but, in the aftermath of 9/11, many EU institutional documents started to consider the CFSP/CSDP as necessary tools in this area (European Council 2001; Council of the European Union 2004a; European Council 2004). As a result, it has not always been easy to distinguish which counter-terrorism activities belong to the AFSJ and which are part of the CFSP/CSDP (Cremona 2008a: 7; Longo 2013: 29–46; Monar 2012: 46; Wesser, Marin and Matera 2011: 277; Trauner and Carrapiço 2012: 11–12; Wolff, Wichmann and Mounier 2009, Kurowska and Pawlak 2009).

The Treaty of Lisbon has sought to ensure consistency between the CFSP/ CSDP and the AFSJ by incorporating Article 21(3) TEU.[7] The Treaty has also created a new body: the European External Action Service (EEAS), which is led by the EU High Representative of the Union for Foreign Affairs and Security Policy. The fact that the High Representative is both president of the Foreign Affairs Council and Vice-President of the Commission (Article 18(4) TEU) shows the EU's aim of ensuring consistency of the Union's external action. The strategic link between the CFSP/CSDP and the AFSJ is also stressed in the Stockholm Programme. It highlights that 'CSDP missions also make an important contribution to the Union's internal security in their efforts to support the fight against serious transnational crime' (European Council 2009: point 7.1).

Determining which counter-terrorist activities are part of the CSDP and which fall under the AFSJ is not always clear-cut. That debate is found, for instance, in missions carried out by police agents beyond the EU territory. The EU

---

7 It establishes that 'the Union shall ensure consistency between the different areas of its external action and between these and its other policies. The Council and the Commission, assisted by the High Representative of the Union for Foreign Affairs and Security Policy, shall ensure that consistency and shall cooperate to that effect'.

has ten civilian CSDP operations ongoing in Ukraine, Georgia, the Palestinian Territories, Kosovo, Libya, Afghanistan, Mali, Niger, and the group of Djibouti, Somalia, Seychelles and Tanzania. Likewise, it has seven military missions in Somalia, the Democratic Republic of Congo, Mali, Central African Republic and Bosnia Herzegovinia (EEAS 2015a). In the theoretical framework, Article 43(1) TEU establishes that civilian and military operations 'may contribute to the fight against terrorism', but the added value of these civilian/military missions in the field of counter-terrorism has been often questioned (Coolsaet 2010: 871; Oliveira Martins and Ferreira-Pereira 2012; Ferreira-Pereira and Oliveira Martins 2012: 467; Argomaniz 2012: 50). In practice, military bodies are often seen on the scene after a terrorist attack. For instance, Spanish military forces were deployed at several train stations in Spain after the attacks of 11 March 2004 (Pulido Gragera 2004: 79), and France deployed more than 10,000 military troops after shootings in Paris in January 2015 (Blachier and Irish 2015).

A lot of information is processed during civilian and military missions. Police agents who are part of a CSDP mission often gather intelligence and pass it to agencies concerned with internal security (e.g. Europol, FRONTEX and the European Police College (CEPOL)) and Member States' law enforcement officers (Statewatch 2012). For instance, one of the main focuses of the civilian mission in Niger is to find 'ways for the different authorities responsible for security to collect and share information' (EEAS 2015b). Likewise, the mission strategy in Mali includes the exchange of operational information for combating the illicit trafficking of cocaine (EEAS 2015c). As for the mission taking place in Moldova and Ukraine, the mandate includes the improvement of cross-border co-operation and information exchange to prevent and detect smuggling, trafficking of goods and human beings and customs fraud (EEAS 2015d).

Another example of data processing in the area of external security is found in the different associations,[8] partnerships[9] and co-operation agreements that the EU concludes with third countries.[10] The majority of these agreements are not CFSP instruments, but mixed agreements. Yet, they tackle issues related to international security and defence diplomacy. Since 2005 they have included clauses on confidentiality of data for the fight against terrorism (EUROMED 2005). These provisions are called 'counter-terrorism clauses' and allow the EU to obtain information collected by third countries on terrorist groups and networks. They are usually elaborated on a case-by-case basis (Wolf 2009: 148), but follow similar templates.

Despite the recent EEAS efforts to clarify the way data is exchanged between CFSP bodies and AFSJ agencies (EEAS 2013), more detailed information is

---

8 For instance, Article 90 of the Euro-Mediterranean Agreement establishing an Association between the European Community and its Member States, of the one part, and the People's Democratic Republic of Algeria, of the other part.

9 The notion of 'partnership' was first introduced in the Council's JHA External Strategy of 2005.

10 For instance, Article 5 of the Framework Agreement on Comprehensive Partnership and cooperation between the European Community and its Member States, of the one part, and the Republic of Indonesia, of the other part.

needed. It is unclear, for example, how information gathered during CSDP missions is disseminated at the EU level by the EU Intelligence Analysis Centre (IntCen) and by the Intelligence Division of the European Military Staff (Statewatch 2012). IntCen belongs to the EEAS and its mandate tackles both internal and external security areas. It is composed of more than 100 staff members, 70 per cent of which are intelligence officials in the Member States (Hillebrand 2012: 30). One of IntCen's basic functions is the exchange of intelligence and the drafting of terrorism assessments as part of its counter-terrorism analytical task (Argomaniz 2012: 50). IntCen analysts often travel to crisis zones and CSDP operation locations to gain the necessary data for their counter-terrorism reports (Cross 2013: 393). Yet, it is not clear whether all IntCen data exchanges fall under the scope of the CFSP, or whether some of them belong to the AFSJ.[11]

1.3 Questioning the scope and purposes of Article 39 TEU

In light of the foregoing considerations, it is important to examine the legal consequences of considering a counter-terrorism measure as part of the external dimension of the AFSJ, or as part of the CFSP/CSDP.

In certain areas, the Treaty of Lisbon has incorporated dual legal bases, one under the scope of the CFSP and one as a non-CFSP policy. The reason for that is to offer two different decision-making processes for the same purpose: one is adopted under the ordinary legislative procedure, while the other falls under the unanimous decision of the Council. There is no prioritisation in the application of these two legal bases. According to Article 40 TEU, the CJEU has the responsibility to decide case by case the suitable legal basis.

The CJEU has issued a landmark case that will probably have an impact on the unclear dichotomy between CFSP and AFSJ. In the ruling, the CJEU decided the adequate legal basis on EU restrictive measures on the freezing of assets. Before the Treaty of Lisbon, restrictive measures against individuals within the EU were adopted under ex Articles 60 and 301 TEC. Article 301 TEC was the basis for economic sanctions against third states, and Article 60 was the legal basis for necessary urgent measures on the movement of capital on payments to the third countries concerned (e.g. freezing funds). However, it was not clear whether economic sanctions could be adopted against individuals, since they were not explicitly regulated in the treaties. In Cases C-402/05 P and C-415/05 P, *Kadi* (2008), the CJEU solved that question by applying together ex Articles 60, 301 and 308 TEC as the legal basis for economic sanctions against individuals (Cremona 2009).

The Treaty of Lisbon incorporates two different legal bases dealing with restrictive measures regarding the freezing of assets. Each of them has specific aims and functions: Article 215 TFEU (replacing Article 301 TEC) regulates the

---

11 Further analysis about IntCen is carried out in Chapter 4, section 5.1.

adoption of restrictive measures against individuals – economic and non-economic. In contrast, Article 75 TFEU establishes that the EP and the Council, through the ordinary legislative procedure, need to adopt administrative measures on capital movements and payments such as 'the freezing of funds, financial assets or economic gains belonging to, or owned or held by, natural or legal persons, groups or non-State entities'.

Thus, instruments under Article 75(1) TFEU are adopted under the ordinary legislative procedure by the EP and the Council, whereas measures authorised under Article 215 TFEU require a CFSP act approved by the Council on a joint proposal from the High Representative and the Commission. Here, the EP is only informed thereof.

The controversy arose with regard to the EU Council Regulation amending Regulation (EC) No 881/2002 (Council Regulation (EU) No 1286/2009). That Regulation implemented a UN Resolution about the freezing of funds of certain persons and entities associated with Osama bin Laden, the Al-Qaeda network and the Taliban. It was adopted on the basis of Article 215(2) TFEU and not on the basis of Article 75 TFEU. The EP argued that the contested regulation was adopted under the wrong legal basis. It maintained that Article 75 TFEU was the right basis for adopting restrictive measures aimed at combating terrorism. However, the Council took the opposite position. It claimed that the contested regulation against international terrorism pertained to the CFSP, because it fell under the scope of the EU's external action. Furthermore, the Council made a distinction between international or external terrorism, on the one hand, and internal terrorism, on the other.

This lack of clarity on the proper legal basis persisted among the EU institutions (European Parliament 2012: point 14) and legal scholars (Cremona 2008b; Hinarejos 2009) until the CJEU issued the decision in July 2012. In Case C-130/10, *European Parliament v Council of the European Union* (2012), the CJEU decided that the proper legal basis for adopting the EU Council Regulation of freezing of funds was Article 215 TFEU (Van Elsuwege 2014: 130–135). That decision supported AG Bot's reasoning (Case C-130/10, AG Bot 2012). Bot had considered that the action came from the international stage and, therefore, the objective of preserving peace and strengthening international security had to be regarded as falling within the sphere of the CFSP. To the same conclusion, the CJEU explained that ex Articles 60 and 301 TEC mirrored Article 215 TFEU and not Article 75 TFEU (C-130/10, paras 51–54). The court's arguments were based on the idea that Article 215 is appropriate where the EU is implementing an UN policy and there is a CSdecision to that effect. In contrast, Article 75 TFEU may be used for the non-UN security measures. The judgment is a clear evidence of how decisive the interpretation of the CJEU can be, even when the contested legislation falls within the scope of the CFSP.

However, the argument used by the court to justify the legal basis of restrictive measures have not fully solved the blurry delimitation of CFSP and AFSJ competences in the field of external security measures. Another CFSP/AFSJ duality of legal basis needs to be interpreted by the Court. This time the controversy arises with regard to Article 16 TFEU and Article 39 TEU concerning the right to data protection. The Treaty of Lisbon offers in Article 16 TFEU a specific provision regarding the protection of personal data within the EU territory. It establishes that 'everyone has the right to the protection of personal data concerning them'. Yet, the Treaty has also included a way of enacting specific data protection rules in the context of the CFSP. Article 39 TEU states that, in derogation of Article 16(2) TFEU, the Council can adopt a special decision laying down the rules relating to data protection and the free movement of such data when Member States are acting within the field of CFSP.

The relationship between Article 16 TFEU and Article 39 TEU is unclear. There is no document specifying in which cases Article 39 TEU should apply, derogating the EU data protection general rules. It is, however, apparent that Article 39 will limit the role of the CJEU and the EP. The CJEU will not solve any question relating to the interpretation and application of Article 39, unless it refers to the determination of the proper scope of the two articles to ensure compliance with Article 40 TEU. Regarding the EP, this institution will be excluded from the decision-making process of any instrument based on Article 39 TEU.

However, there is a positive way of interpreting the existence of Article 39 TEU. One could see the provision as a tool for ensuring that data protection also applies in the CFSP sphere, in contrast to the pre-Lisbon regime. For instance, recent PNR Agreements with the US, Canada and Australia have been based on Article 82(1)(d) TFEU and 87(2)(a) TFEU, in conjunction with Article 218(6)(a) TFEU. These international agreements fall under the scope of the AFSJ and they have been brought forward under Article 16 TFEU. Yet, it could occur that a future data-sharing agreement for security purposes is based on Article 39 TEU. This legal basis would guarantee minimum data protection safeguards, avoiding a divergent regulation among Member States.

As is examined in Chapter 4 of this book, a possible use of Article 39 could emerge from the information gathered by EU IntCen as well as police agents in CSDP missions. From the Opinion of AG Bot in Case C-658/11, *European Parliament v Council of the European Union* (AG Bot 2014) it could also be deduced that Article 39 TEU applies in the collection of records of pirates operating off Somalia, which are then made available to the Union.

Either way, the fact that Article 39 TEU has never been used today shows how far the external dimension of the AFSJ can reach. The EDPS has recommended the Commission present, as soon as possible, common rules for the CFSP based on Article 39 TEU (EDPS 2012: 6). Only with a clarification from the Commission or from the CJEU will we be able to discover what purpose this provision intends to fulfil.

2 Exchange of information between the EU and the US

The EU has developed many partnerships with strategic countries for co-operating in the exchange of crime-related information. For instance, a special link has been established between the EU and Russia for the fight against terrorism based on a

Memorandum of Understanding (MoU) (COM(2008) 740 final), a co-operation agreement with Europol[12] and a Joint Statement on counter-terrorism (EU-Russia Summit 2002). Another example is found in the Agreement on mutual legal assistance in criminal matters between the EU and Japan (Council Decision 2010/88/CFSP/JHA, p. 3). That agreement brought both parties closer in terms of the management of criminal justice. Lastly, it is no coincidence that any partnership agreement between the EU and a third country would include a 'counter-terrorism clause'.

The following analysis focuses mainly on the bilateral co-operation between the EU and the US. The reason for this delimitation is that the co-operation between these parties constitutes the most developed to date, tackling numerous (if not all) important legal issues regarding the EU external security instruments.

The EU maintains a very close relationship with the US authorities. They established diplomatic relations as early as 1953, and their co-operation was formalised for the first time in 1990 (European Communities 1990). In the last decade, numerous agreements have been adopted between the two parties. Also, foreign policy, collective security and trade issues have been discussed in regular transatlantic meetings (European Parliament 2006). In the particular field of security, the EU has always co-operated closely with the US. After the Second World War, the US became the protector of the European countries against the Soviet Union through the Marshall Plan and the establishment of the North Atlantic Treaty Organisation (NATO). In exchange, the EU supported the US interests during the American-Russian confrontation. In the post-Cold War era, the US interests in protecting Europe decreased and this brought uncertainty about what role NATO was going to play.

However, during the nineties both actors continued co-operating in diverse security issues (Rees 2011: 1–11). They set up a partnership for security areas through the following events: (a) annual EU-US Summit meetings;[13] (b) the 1995 New Transatlantic Agenda (NTA); (c) the Joint EU-US Action Plan; (d) the 1999 Transatlantic Legislators' Dialogue (TLD); and (e) the Transatlantic Group on Counter-terrorism.

The existing security co-operation between the two has expanded into the field of criminal matters since 2001, following the 9/11 terrorist attacks. The US enlarged its counter-terrorism policy on the basis of the start of a 'war on terror', and it called for the support of all countries, threatening that they were either with them or against them (Kaunert, Léonard and MacKenzie 2012: 475). Essentially, the US authorities were interested in establishing closer co-operation with the EU institutions and its Member States because there were at that time many visa-exempt Western European jihadists (Argomaniz 2009: 125) who could easily fly to the US. In fact, Al-Qaeda cells had already been detected in some Member States, and several individuals were arrested in Belgium, France, Germany, Italy, Spain

---

12 Europol agreements are examined in Chapter 4.
13 US-EU Summit in London on 18 May 1998; US-EU Summit in Bonn, Germany on 21 June 1999; US-EU Joint Statements on 17 December 1999.

and the UK as co-ordinators of the 9/11 terrorist attacks (Archick 2013: 1). NATO invoked its collective defence clause six hours after the event (Monar 2005: 411). According to Article 5 of the Washington Treaty '[t]he Parties agree that an armed attack against one or more of them in Europe or North America shall be considered an attack against them'. Moreover, on 20 September of that year, the EU Justice and Home Affairs Council adopted eight broad initiatives encouraging co-operation with the US (Council of the European Union 2001b: 10–12) and, one month later, George W Bush suggested the Commission enhance its co-operation on counter-terrorism measures (Statewatch 2001).

Collaboration with the US in the field of law enforcement became a top priority within the EU. Many US agencies included international relations departments and, simultaneously, the Directorate General (DG) JHA in the European Commission enhanced its external competences (Pawlak 2009b: 567). However, initially the EU and the US developed different counter-terrorism approaches: while the US counter-terrorism strategy focused on the increase of military measures and the use of force, the EU counter-terrorism programme tended to prioritise preventive measures through law enforcement and intelligence agencies (Porter and Bendiek 2012: 498). Therefore, the EU has usually been identified as a 'civilian' or 'soft power' because it promotes non-military and non-coercive measures; whereas the US has been defined as a 'hard power', which exports its values with the use of force if necessary (Rees 2011: 22–28).

The influence of the US security strategy within the EU is today unquestionable. Specific examples of this impact are found in the 2003 European Security Strategy, which was adopted after the US National Security Strategy in 2002 (Ferreira-Pereira and Oliveira Martins 2012: 465); the EU-US agreements on security matters, influenced by the 2004 Intelligence Reform and Terrorism Prevention Act (Pub.L. 108–458) and the 2004 EU-US Declaration on combating terrorism (Council of the European Union 2004b); or the creation of the overall EU Counter-terrorism Strategy of 2005 (Council of the European Union 2005c: 7). They all indicate the important role played by the US authorities in shaping EU interests.

Under the Treaty of Lisbon, new forms of co-operation between the EU and the US were established. The EU-US 'Declaration on Counter-terrorism' of 2010 (Council of the European Union 2010b), and President Obama's National Security Strategy (NSS) for Counter-terrorism of 2011 (White House 2011: 15) show how the EU-US partnership continues to be a priority on both sides of the Atlantic. Through these strategies, both parties have agreed to prioritise preventive measures over military intervention (Porter and Bendiek 2012: 500). As a result, they organise regular meetings between the EU institutions and the Secretary of State, the US Attorney General and the Secretary of Homeland Security to address counter-terrorism issues (Archick 2013: 4).

Many divergences remain, however, between the EU and the US in addressing security challenges. They have tried to prove their similar goals by emphasising shared transatlantic values such as democracy, rule of law, market economy and human rights (Rees 2011: 29). However, in reality, the two parties have not always shared the same objectives in addressing security challenges. This lack of an 'alliance of values' has resulted in a decrease of mutual trust between them, especially after the Snowden revelations, which is analysed in Chapter 4.

The next section analyses the current data-sharing agreements between the EU and the US based on security matters. It focuses specifically on the MLA Agreement, the PNR Agreement, the SWIFT Agreement and the EU-US Agreements on air and maritime security partnership. The analysis demonstrates that there is a clear US influence in each of these agreements. After that, returning to the already mentioned blurry line between the CFSP and the AFSJ, the implications resulting from the choice of an AFSJ legal basis for all international agreements adopted between the EU and the US are examined.

2.1 EU-US data-sharing agreements

There are different ways to exchange crime-related information between the EU and the US. De Busser distinguishes between judicial requests through rogatory letters, subpoenas issued by national courts, informal contacts between police authorities and the prior adoption of an agreement between both parties (de Busser 2009: 307–310). This section examines only the latter of these four suppositions.

As explained above, not only are Member States able to conclude data-sharing agreements in the field of law enforcement with third countries[14] but the EU itself also has the competence for that. A few agreements between the EU and the US on the collection, storage, processing, analysis and exchange of relevant information have been concluded using Articles 87(2)(a) and 218 TFEU (ex Articles 24 and 38 TEU). In fact, having the EU as a partner has been very attractive for third countries, which have often preferred to submit one single initiative to the EU as a whole, rather than to negotiate criminal issues with each Member State individually (Monar 2012: 71).

The necessity for data-sharing agreements has emerged from the increasingly transnational nature of crimes, which often affect multiple countries or even multiple continents. These agreements have expanded considerably after 9/11. They are part of the external dimension of the AFSJ, and they mainly address issues on international criminal justice (e.g. the MLA treaties) and co-operation on law enforcement (e.g. the PNR Agreements). The following sub-sections examine the main agreements concluded between the EU and the US consisting in the exchange of information for the prevention, combat, investigation and prosecution of crimes.

2.1.1 The EU-US Mutual Legal Assistance Agreement

The EU-US Mutual Legal Assistance Agreement (EU-US MLA Agreement) was concluded two years after the 9/11 terrorist attacks, because of the continuous US

---

14 For instance, the existing agreement between Germany and the US on the exchange of DNA and fingerprint data.

pressures expressing the need to access data from police authorities and TSPs located in any of the EU countries. As an example, since the EU-US MLA Agreement came into force, judiciary authorities on both sides have access to bank accounts and can get financial data for the investigation of a crime.

The EU-US MLA Agreement was not the first instrument of mutual assistance between both parties. Before the conclusion of that agreement, 16 countries in Europe had already signed bilateral MLATs with the US authorities,[15] and some existing UN Conventions also included mutual legal assistance clauses (de Busser 2009: 312–313).[16] At the EU level, the CoE has had a Convention on MLA since 1959, and the EU adopted a Convention on Mutual Assistance in Criminal Matters between the Member States and the EU a year before the 9/11 terrorist attacks (Council Act 2000/C 197/01 2000).

On 20 September 2001, the JHA Council announced the initiation of negotiations for an EU-US judicial co-operation agreement. In a letter sent by the former US President George W Bush to the Commission President Prodi on 16 October 2001, it was requested that '[w]henever possible, permit urgent MLAT requests to be made orally, with follow-up by formal written requests' (Statewatch 2001). The mandate for negotiating the Agreement was adopted on 26 April 2002, the day that the Commission negotiations with the US Department of Justice (DoJ) began. The Agreement was signed the following year on 25 July 2003. For the first time[17] the Commission used ex Articles 24 and 38 TEU as legal bases for concluding an international agreement between the EU and a third country in the field of judicial co-operation in criminal matters (Faull and Soreca 2008: 406).

When the EU-US MLA Agreement was adopted, only Bulgaria, Finland, Malta, Portugal, Slovakia and Slovenia did not already have a bilateral MLAT with the US (MacKenzie 2012: 107). According to Article 3 of the Agreement, existing bilateral treaties between Member States and the US would remain in force, so there would be no replacement with the EU-US MLA Agreement. Moreover, pursuant to Article 14 a possibility to conclude future bilateral treaties with the US remained open. As for the new provisions included in the Agreement, Article 4 restricted banking secrecy, Article 5 allowed the creation of JITs, Article 6 permitted video-conferences and Article 9 gave the possibility to share information as evidence before a court.

However, a lack of use of MLA instruments between the EU (or its Member States) and the US has been identified in recent years. Problems commenced with

---

15 These were: Austria (1995), Belgium (1988), Cyprus (1999), the Czech Republic (1998), Estonia (1998), France (1998), Greece (1999), Hungary (1994), Italy (1982), Latvia (1997), Lithuania (1998), Luxembourg (1997), Poland (1996), Romania (1999), Spain (1990), the UK (1994 and amended 2001).

16 For instance the Convention against Illicit Trafficking in Drugs, the Convention for the Suppression of the Financing of Terrorism, the Convention against Transnational Organized Crime (TOC), the Convention against Corruption.

17 Together with the EU-US Extradition Agreement, also signed on that very same day.

the ratification process of the EU-US MLA Agreement. Some of the Member States have been extremely slow in ratifying the Agreement, which only came into force on 1 February 2010 (Council of the European Union 2009). But even after the ratification, Member States have raised other issues of concern about the use of this instrument. In the last questionnaire sent by the Council, the Czech Republic, Malta, Poland, Romania and Slovakia complained about the enormous length of time that the whole procedure takes from the issuing of a request to its execution. Likewise, Spain highlighted obstacles in executing requests about email content information at an early stage of an investigation because, according to the Spanish system, information can only be provided by a Spanish judge after the pre-trial investigation. Finally, a problem regarding the lack of use of the MLA channel among Member States has been identified. Many countries often acquire data stored by companies in another country without any mutual legal assistance request. The same occurs with data stored by US authorities; Member States usually contact them informally through email (Council of the European Union 2012b: 2–4, 11 and 13–14).

From the US side, the Review Group on Intelligence and Communications Technologies also detected some current problems regarding the use of MLA procedures. First of all, the Group noted that the procedure is slow, taking on average ten months or longer. There is also no online submission form for such procedures, so many governments do not know how to send a request, or what the formal requirements are. In addition, the steps to follow are too long. When a MLA request is sent to the US, the Office of International Affairs (OIA) first examines it; then it sends it to the US Attorney of the district where data is held; and finally the DoJ also needs to explore the request (White House 2013: 226–228). It makes the procedure significantly protracted and inefficient.

2.1.2 Agreements on PNRs

Another agreement influenced by the US counter-terrorism policies is the PNR Agreement. Although the Commission confirmed that the need for an EU-US PNR Agreement derived from the general EU counter-terrorism strategy, scholars have demonstrated that it has been shaped by the US requirements (Kaunert, Léonard and MacKenzie 2012). In fact, the Agreement was a direct consequence of a US law adopted in November 2001 (Pub.L. 107–71, 115 STAT. 597), under which any EU airline company with flights taking off or landing within the US territory was obliged to provide the Bureau of Customs and Border Protection (CBP) with electronic access to PNR data (de Busser 2009: 360–362).

Airline companies have been collecting and exchanging registration data for passenger arrangement purposes for more than 60 years now. However, before 2001, US law enforcement authorities could only access the necessary data by manual means, on a case-by-case basis and with a prior court order by a European judge (Barros 2012: 7). After 9/11, new US laws obliged all airline companies to systematically transfer passenger data of flights arriving in, transiting through and exiting the country through electronic means before the flight departure.

If any airline company decided not to comply with the post-9/11 mandate, it could suffer serious consequences, such as the removal of all landing rights within the US territory, the exclusion from the American market, and fines of up to US$5,000 for each passenger whose data were not transferred. However, by complying with the US laws, EU airline companies were infringing the EU legal framework, and particularly Directive 95/46/EC on the protection of personal data. Article 25 of the Directive establishes that any third country receiving data from Member States needs a prior adequacy decision from the Commission; and the US border control authorities did not have any.

In an effort to avoid conflicts between the US law and the existing EU data protection legislation, the Commission asked the US authorities for an extension to comply with the new rules (Kaunert, Léonard and MacKenzie 2012: 484) and decided to start formal negotiations for the establishment of a PNR agreement with the US. The Agreement would solve the problem of infringing Directive 95/46/EC because it would include adequate data protection standards in the sense of Article 25 of the Directive.

The Commission, in December 2003, launched a communication on the PNR global approach (COM(2003) 826 final) and, two months later, the Council authorised the start of negotiations with the US (de Hert and de Schutter 2008: 327). The main institutions that took part in the negotiations were the Commission (DG of External Relations (RELEX)) from the side of the EU, and the Department of State (DoS) on behalf of the US (Pawlak 2009b: 563). The EP was only consulted under ex Article 300 TEC. Therefore, neither the EP resolution opposing the EU-US PNR Agreement (European Parliament 2004), nor the warning to go to the CJEU for an opinion of compatibility with the Treaties (Statewatch 2004) were taken into consideration by the Commission.

After the adoption of a Council decision (Council Decision 2004/496/EC), the (first) EU-US PNR Agreement was formally concluded in Washington DC on 28 May 2004. As seen in Chapter 1, the EU-US PNR Agreement was signed under ex Article 95 TEC. Since the main debate referred to the adequacy of the data protection in the Agreement, the US guaranteed an adequate protection of passenger data on 6 July 2004 (US Federal Register 2004). Similarly, the *Official Journal of the European Communities* published (on the same day) a Commission decision on the adequate protection of personal data contained in PNR transfers (Commission Decision 2004/535/EC).

The EP challenged Council Decision 2004/496/EC and Commission Decision 2004/535/EC before the CJEU. It argued that, on the one hand, the Agreement constituted a breach of the fundamental principles of Directive 95/46/EC and, on the other hand, it was based on the wrong legal basis.

It is explained in Chapter 1 that in May 2006 the Court based its decision exclusively on the legal basis matter, and it annulled the Commission decision and the Council decision for not being founded on the appropriate provision. The EU rushed the negotiations and the adoption of a second EU-US PNR Agreement, which was provisionally adopted in October 2006. This time the Agreement fell under the scope of the former third pillar and it was concluded between the EU (not the EC) and the US (Council Decision 2006/729/CFSP/JHA). As noted above, international agreements on data transfers signed under the basis of the first pillar had to comply with the 'adequacy principle' of Article 25 of Directive 95/46/EC. Yet, it was not the case when the Agreements fell under the third pillar, where Member States could apply their own standards. Thus, while that new agreement solved airline companies' concerns of infringing the EU data protection legislation, new concerns arose within the EU, this time because the new agreement no longer required 'adequate' data protection safeguards for international transfers.

According to ex Article 24(1) TEU, the negotiations of the second PNR Agreement were conducted by the Council, which authorised the participation of the Presidency and the Commission. As for the role of the EP, it enjoyed only an 'observer' status, despite maintaining bilateral contact with the US authorities (Pawlak 2009b: 571).

The second PNR Agreement expired on 31 July 2007 and it was immediately replaced by a third agreement. The third EU-US PNR Agreement was signed and provisionally applied through a Council decision (Council Decision 2007/551/CFSP/JHA). That agreement was considered an effective tool by the US authorities. Americans stated that, thanks to the Agreement, they identi-fied during 2008 and 2009 more than 3,000 individuals with potential ties to terrorism. For example, the Mumbai attacks' plotter David Headley, who was arrested in 2008 at a Chicago airport, was identified through his PNR data. Faisal Shahzad, the perpetrator of the failed New York Times Square bombing in May 2010, and Najibullah Zazi, who pleaded guilty to plotting to bomb New York City subways, were also arrested after the US police had access to their PNR.

However, the 2007 EU-US PNR Agreement was never formally concluded because the EP never gave consent to the proposal (European Parliament 2010a). The reason for this was mainly that many Members of the European Parliament (MEPs) were not convinced by the Agreement but they did not want to reject it because they thought it could create legal uncertainties for travellers and airline companies (Archick 2013: 12). Therefore, they decided to postpone the vote. As in the previous agreement, the role of the EP, the national Data Protection Authorities (DPAs) and the EDPS was very limited. However, the establishment of the EU-US High Level Contact Group (HLCG) on data protection offered a new oversight on data transfers.[18]

In 2009 the Treaty of Lisbon abolished the previous division of EU policies in pillars. Although the 2007 EU-US PNR Agreement was expected to remain operational until 2014, the EP's postponement of the vote, combined with the fact that not all Member States had ratified the Agreement (US Department of Homeland Security 2013), made the drafting of a new PNR agreement between the EU and the US a matter of urgency.

18 This group is examined in section 3.3.2 of this chapter.

Negotiations for the fourth PNR Agreement with the US authorities were officially launched in December 2010 (Archick 2013: 13). Despite the opposition from the US government to modify the 2007 EU-US PNR Agreement (US House Committee on Homeland Security 2011), these negotiations between the Commission and the US were successfully concluded in May 2011 (Archick 2013: 13). A new proposal for the EU-US PNR Agreement was officially released in November 2011. It was signed on 14 December 2011 under the substantive legal basis of Articles 82(1)(d) and 87(2)(a) TFEU. The procedure for the adoption of the Agreement followed the wording of Article 218 TFEU. Particularly, paragraph 6 of Article 218 TFEU gives new competences to the EP, which is now required to give its consent before concluding specific international agreements.

Compared to the previous agreement, the current EU-US PNR Agreement includes new safeguards for passengers. For instance, data is only retained for six months, before it passes to another database where it is depersonalised and 'marked'. In addition, there are more restrictions regarding the personnel authorised to access data, and there is more legal certainty regarding the judicial redress.[19] Finally, airline companies are now obliged to provide passenger details up to 96 hours before the flight departure, in comparison with the 72 hours required under the 2007 EU-US PNR Agreement (Travis 2011).

The Agreement was very well received among Member States.[20] Even the EP, which voiced initial concerns, found that having that agreement was better than having no agreement at all, thus the majority of MEPs voted in favour – 409 in favour and 226 against – (Archick 2013: 15). After being approved by the EP and the Council, the Agreement entered into force on 1 July 2012 and it will be up for automatic renewal by 2019 at the latest.

2.1.3 SWIFT agreements

Another EU-US agreement that has been largely influenced by US requirements is the SWIFT agreement. Although the EU has always tried to justify the adoption of such an agreement as beneficial for the fight against terrorism in Europe and necessary to ensure protection of EU citizens' privacy (MEMO/13/1060), the present section proves that the EU followed the US mandate as regards the content of both the first and the second SWIFT agreements.

On 11 September 2001 the US and the EU started to exchange financial data. In December 2001, two US-Europol agreements were concluded in order to facilitate the exchange of information related to global financial movements (Agreement 2001; Supplemental Agreement 2002). They were part of the TFTP, created by the Bush administration after 9/11 as one of the counter-terrorism measures resulting from Executive Order 13224 and the UN Resolution 1373 (2001) (United Nations Security Council 2001).

19 Further analysis on data protection safeguards in PNR agreements is found in section 3.2.1 of this chapter.
20 All Member States except Austria and Germany approved the Agreement in December 2011.

Under the TFTP the US authorities were able to pull EU citizens' data from the private company SWIFT. The programme was secret and it did not involve the EU at all, since the company was based in Belgium but had servers located in the US territory, particularly in Virginia. The US could only get the financial data from SWIFT in the form of standardised messages by sending administrative subpoenas to the institution. The programme was very attractive for the US law enforcement sector, since the company collects personal data from 10,000 financial institutions in more than 200 countries (MacKenzie 2012: 107). Although SWIFT executives always insisted that the transfers were not voluntary (Pell 2012: 253) SWIFT never contested the subpoenas (de Goede 2012: 221). The US gathered information from up to 12.7 million financial transactions a day (Pell 2012: 253), and once the information was pulled, messages were stored for a period of 124 days (de Hert and de Schutter 2008: 331).

The TFTP was uncovered in 2006 by the *New York Times* (Lichtblau and Risen 2006) and from that moment many concerns were raised within the EU about its potential violation of EU data protection laws. Even though the company always processed EU citizens' data through its servers located in the US, due to the fact that SWIFT headquarters were in Belgium the company had to comply with Belgian national law implementing Directive 95/46/EC.

In November 2006, the Art. 29 WP issued an opinion stating that the programme breached EU data protection laws (Article 29 Data Protection Working Party 2006). SWIFT joined the now void Safe Harbour principles in 2007 and, that same year, the company decided to move its servers completely to Europe (Cremona 2011: 13, Curtin 2011: 6), relocating its servers in Virginia (US) to Switzerland (MacKenzie 2012: 107). This made the need for an agreement enabling SWIFT transfers in compliance with EU laws particularly urgent. The EP released two resolutions in 2006 and 2007 (European Parliament 2007) calling for the adoption of an agreement, which would regulate SWIFT data transfers to the US. These claims convinced the German Presidency of the Council about the necessity for an agreement with the US Department of the Treasury that avoided potential clashes with EU data protection laws.

On 30 November 2009, under the legal basis of the former Articles 24 and 38 TEU, the EU and the US signed the first official SWIFT Agreement, exactly one day before the Treaty of Lisbon came into force. The Agreement became operational on 1 February 2010 and it was supposed to be applied temporarily until 31 December of that year. However, the legal basis to conclude international agreements changed with the Treaty of Lisbon and so did the powers of the EP: since the Treaty of Lisbon the Council can only adopt a decision authorising the conclusion of an agreement after obtaining the consent of the EP in the terms of Article 218(6) TFEU. Under these new competences, the LIBE Committee wrote a report on 5 February 2010 recommending the rejection of the interim SWIFT agreement (European Parliament 2010b).

The main concerns expressed by the EP related to privacy. In particular, it stated that: (a) there was a lack of necessity and proportionality of the Agreement; (b) it did not respect the purpose limitation principle; (c) it did not foresee any judicial remedy for EU citizens; (d) data were transferred by a pull system, causing the storage of 'bulk data'; and (e) it was necessary to establish an EU TFTP to process the data within the EU.

Despite intense lobbying from the Commission, Member States and the US authorities, on 11 February 2010 the EP rejected the adoption of the SWIFT Agreement (European Parliament 2010c). The rejection was interpreted as a protest by the EP against the Commission and the Council because it was not consulted during the negotiations (Cremona 2011: 16; Ripoll Servent and MacKenzie 2011: 400). Also, the EP rejection reflected the significant power that the institution gained with the Treaty of Lisbon. The EP now plays an important role in the negotiation of international agreements.

The adoption of a second SWIFT agreement was imperative. In the months that followed there was no agreement in place so data transfers to the US were conducted through the existing EU-US MLA Agreement, as well as through the MLATs between Member States and the US (Cremona 2011: 18). Yet, as seen earlier, this procedure is usually quite slow and inefficient.

The Council restarted negotiations with the US authorities for the new agreement during the spring of 2010. Unsurprisingly, the EP played a predominant role during the negotiations. Yet, not all the changes proposed by this institution were finally fulfilled (Ripoll Servent and MacKenzie 2011: 401). In any case, the EP voted in favour of that second agreement by 484 votes to 109 (European Parliament 2010d), and it was signed on 28 June 2010.

The second SWIFT agreement was based on Articles 87(2)(a) and 88(2) TFEU on police co-operation. It certainly introduced many of the EP suggestions such as: (a) the possibility of administrative and legal redress for EU citizens in the US (Article 18) – although it does not apply in practice (Ripoll Servent and MacKenzie 2012: 81) – (b) the competence for Europol to approve the requests sent by the US Treasury Department (Article 4); (c) the introduction of an independent observer appointed by the Commission based in Washington DC (Article 12); (d) provisions on retention and deletion of data (Article 6); and (e) plans for and equivalent TFTP in the EU (Article 11).

The EP's demands that were not included in the Agreement referred particularly to the removal of bulk data and the pull system, as well as the establishment of a judicial oversight. Since these issues are important safeguards to be considered in any adequate data protection framework, some scholars believe that this second permanent agreement is not very different from the first interim agreement (Ripoll Servent and MacKenzie 2011: 391 and 396). Other aspects subject to criticism in the new SWIFT agreement relate to the lack of necessity, the length of the retention period (five years) and the vagueness of the US requests in order to collect SWIFT data (Archick 2013: 11).

As analysed in Chapter 3, the new SWIFT agreement involves Europol in the transfer of financial data to the US. In this regard, the EP raised concerns because Europol, which is in charge of verifying the US compliance of the Agreement, did not initially provide any updated written information about the requests from the US Treasury Department and the compliance with the European data protection standards. A dispute on document secrecy between the Council and the EP ended up with a CJEU decision in favour of the EP in July 2014 (C-350/12 P). The Council argued that the disclosure of the US requests to the EP would have a '[negative] impact on the European Union's negotiating position'. However, the argument did not convince the Court because no evidence had been provided showing that the secrecy was necessary to prevent a 'risk of a threat to the public interest'. Thus, that CJEU decision reinforces EU transparency rules in the context of international agreements.

2.2 Issues of concern in the Agreements

2.2.1 Legal basis implications

Before Lisbon, the EU divided its policies in three pillars: the first on Community policies, the second on CFSP, and the third on Police and Judicial Cooperation in Criminal Matters. This structural division had significant legal implications since the role of the EU (formerly, the EC) was greater for policies under the scope of the first pillar than in the other two intergovernmental pillars. The legislative procedure under the first pillar required qualified-majority voting (QMV) in the Council and simple majority in the EP. In contrast, for second- and third-pillar decisions there was no participation of the EP and any country could block a proposal in the Council because it required unanimity of its members.

Questions about the adequacy of the legal basis were raised regarding those measures that intertwined different policy areas. The process was known as cross-pillarisation and the choice of legal basis ultimately depended on the preferences of Member States and EU actors. For example, there were cases in which Member States preferred to conclude an international agreement under the former third pillar to get more control in the decision-making and implementation process. For instance, as mentioned above, an international agreement in the third pillar was only adopted if all Member States voted in favour: once approved, the Commission lacked the competence to force any Member State to comply with it.

Thus, the choice of the legal basis of any legislative act depends on the main objective that such law seeks to achieve. It is quite common that an EU instrument pursues more than one goal. For example, a law can protect the environment and criminalise a particular behaviour at the same time. If that law establishes that the protection of the environment is the main objective, then the proper legal basis falls under the former first pillar (ex Article 174 TEC). Yet, if the law mainly focuses on sanctioning individuals and companies that conduct non-environmentally friendly activities, then a third-pillar legal basis should apply.

As regards the first/third pillar dichotomy, a debate arose because the former EC adopted several EC acts that involved internal security matters (Randazzo 2009: 507). That was the case of first EU-US PNR Agreement. Airline companies initially collected PNR data for commercial reasons, and only later law enforcement authorities started to request them for security purposes. The fact that the processing of data was based on two purposes allowed a margin of discretion as for the most 'adequate' legal basis for the measure. The first EU-US PNR Agreement in 2004 used ex Article 95 TEC as legal basis (first pillar), while subsequent EU-US PNR Agreements of 2006, 2007 and 2012 were based on third-pillar provisions.[21]

The choice of different PNR legal bases had enormous implications. The first PNR Agreement was adopted under the scope of the first pillar and, therefore, it involved both the Council and the EP in the decision-making process. According to ex Article 300(7) TEC, it also bound all Member States without any room for exceptions. One of the reasons why Member States and EU institutions decided to resort to a first-pillar instrument was because they wanted to gain more control in the way they executed sensitive security-related problems (Randazzo 2009: 509). Also, by choosing a first-pillar legal basis for the first EU-US PNR Agreement, they ensured that it would comply with Directive 95/46/EC. In contrast, the 2006 and 2007 PNR Agreements were subject to other decision-making rules. They were intergovernmental instruments so they needed unanimous consent in the Council, with no approval by the EP. As for the data protection safeguards, Directive 95/46/EC was no longer applicable. Member States (and not the EC) were the main competent authorities to control the data protection 'adequacy' of the transfers.

The Treaty of Lisbon kept the legal basis in the 'third pillar' for the 2012 EU-US PNR Agreement, but here the EP participated in the negotiations. Regarding the data protection standards, the Agreement includes provisions regulating the protection of personal information, but it falls outside the scope of the general EU data protection legal framework. These provisions are carefully examined in section 3.2.1 of this chapter.

Besides the confusing first-/third-pillar division, another recent legal debate has referred to the ambiguous separation between second- and third-pillar measures. It was not always clear when a measure fell under the scope of CFSP, and when it was an AFSJ instrument. The reason for this confusion is that there is no specific provision in the EU treaties indicating the objectives of AFSJ external actions: Article 67 TFEU enumerates the general purposes of the AFSJ, but nothing is said about its external dimension. Likewise, Article 21 TEU lists the EU overall security objectives to be fulfilled through the EU external policies but it does not concretise which policy conducts what. In that regard, the AG Bot stated in Case C-658/11, *European Parliament v Council of the European Union*:

> The distinction between these two Union policies [the CFSP and the AFSJ] is made difficult because they are both connected to the imperative of security. The objectives of safeguarding the security of the Union and strengthening international security are assigned to the Union as objectives of the Union's external action under Article 21(2)(a) and (c) TEU. At the same time, ensuring a high level of security is also an objective of the AFSJ in accordance with Article 67(3) TFEU.
>
> (Case C-658/11, AG Bot 2014, para. 107)

---

21 In particular, Articles 24 and 38 TEU before Lisbon, and Articles 81(1)(d) and 87(2)(a) TFEU.

Precisely because of this lack of specific rules, the EU has made use of its implied powers to adopt international agreements within the scope of the external dimension of the AFSJ.

The Council has had some political discretion for deciding whether a measure falls under the scope of the CFSP or under the AFSJ – former second-/third-pillar division – (Randazzo 2009: 516). This appreciation is ultimately subject to interpretation by the CJEU in the terms of Article 40 TEU. Interestingly, the Council has usually chosen to adopt data-sharing security measures under the scope of the external dimension of the AFSJ instead of using a CFSP provision. For instance, agreements on security procedures for the exchange of classified information, the 2006 and 2007 EU-US PNR Agreements and the first temporary SWIFT agreement were all adopted under the basis of ex Articles 24 and 38 TEU. However, as seen above, intelligence gathered by organisations such as the European Union Military Staff (EUMS) and IntCen would fall under the scope of the former second pillar.

My theory, after a careful examination of this CFSP/AFSJ division, is as follows. The choice of pillar on security issues depends on two factors: (a) the specific purpose of the law; and (b) the actors involved.

Following the argument of AG Bot in Case C-658/11, *European Parliament v Council of the European Union*, if the main purpose of the measure is the internal security of the EU then it should be adopted on an AFSJ legal basis; whereas if the main purpose is preserving the international security, then the CFSP should be used (e.g. Case C-658/11). However, the difficulty here is in deciding when the security objective is really internal or international.

As regards the subjects involved, two main categories of actors can process information for security purposes: law enforcement authorities and intelligence services. If data is gathered by the diplomatic or intelligence services, then the legal basis for data-sharing agreements falls under the scope of the second pillar. In contrast, agreements on data processed by law enforcement authorities fall under the third-pillar framework.

As in the first-/third-pillar discussion, the choice of legal basis under the second or the third pillars has legal implications. Agreements adopted under a third-pillar legal basis need the approval from both the EP and the Council, and they can be challenged before the CJEU. Contrary to this, second-pillar measures require unanimous consent by the Council, no participation of the EP and no control by the CJEU. Member States are here the only competent authorities to control the 'adequacy' of data processing; at least until the scope of Article 39 TEU is finally determined.

2.2.2 Public-private partnership

During the investigation of a crime, law enforcement authorities often require information that has been originally collected by private companies. The privatisation of security gained importance during the nineties (Ortiz 2013: 216), and it increased significantly after the 9/11 terrorist attacks. The public-private partnerships (PPPs) are present in all Member States and they work both ways: law enforcement agencies are able to access information collected by private parties, and these companies can also access some police databases (see, for instance, the TIDE database[22]).

This section focuses only on the access that the law enforcement sector has to data collected by private companies. The phenomenon is seen with regard to passenger data collected by airline companies through PNR systems, financial records collected by banks and other similar institutions such as SWIFT and, above all, data stored by TSPs.

A great number of TSPs are located in the US and, therefore, they are bound by US laws. This is the case of Google, Yahoo, Twitter, Facebook, LinkedIn, Dropbox Inc and Whatsapp, to name a few. Despite having their headquarters in the US, these companies process personal data from users around the world. Such valuable information has not only caught the attention of publicity and marketing companies, but also of police and judicial authorities within and beyond the US borders.

Companies such as Google, Twitter, Facebook, LinkedIn, Dropbox and Apple publish transparency reports every six months (or yearly, in the case of Dropbox) with the aim of keeping users informed about governments' requests for access or suppression of their data. The number of requests varies from country to country. In the EU, Germany, France and the UK are leading the lists of data requests, as shown in a recent comparative study conducted by the non-governmental organisation (NGO) Silk (Silk 2015).

It has been seen above that MLA procedures are normally used by law enforcement authorities in the EU to request information located in the US, and vice versa. For instance, if Spanish authorities ask Facebook to disclose an inbox message of a Spanish user, they will need to follow the procedure established in the MLA concluded between the US and Spain. The procedure consists of a request to the Office of International Affairs of the US DoJ, which will then be reviewed by the Counter-terrorism Department and, finally, submitted to a federal court, which will issue the court order that authorises the data transfer (United Nations Office on Drugs and Crime 2012: 90–91).

In principle, the provider (e.g. Facebook) will not send the records directly to the requesting country, but this is not always the case. Besides the formal MLA procedure, US companies can decide to provide law enforcement authorities with information through an alternative informal process. In fact, employees of big tech companies do not always understand the functioning of the MLA procedure when they receive a government request (Vodafone 2014: 65). Therefore, they often choose the informal approach over the formal MLA, because they simply find it is easier.

Informal contact can be established directly with the TSP or by sending an application to the Federal Bureau of Investigation (FBI). For instance, as

---

22 The Terrorist Identities Datamart Environment (TIDE) is a US classified database where names of suspects of terrorists are registered.

mentioned in Chapter 1, Twitter replies to requests made by governmental authorities of Member States only if these are emergency requests. In contrast, for the rest of cases, requests should be issued via US courts by a letter rogatory, or through MLATs (Blasi Casagran 2013: 423). Likewise, Facebook, according to its privacy policy, will informally provide information to law enforcement bodies if the company has strong reason to believe it is necessary in order to: detect, prevent and address fraud and other illegal activity; to protect ourselves, you and others, including as part of investigations; or to prevent death or imminent bodily harm.

The situation is made much more complex when law enforcement agencies requesting information are located within the US and the data is stored in servers placed within the EU borders. In theory, rules should be the same, but in practice the US police authorities barely use MLATs when data is in the EU. Even when the general rule is that US judicial authorities should send a MLA request to the EU judicial courts of the country where the information is stored, a US judgment shows that it rarely occurs. In the *Microsoft* case (Case No. 13-Mag-2814), the company was requested to hand over information stored in its Irish servers to the US authorities. The request was accompanied by a search warrant[23] but it did not use the MLA procedures. Search warrants need to prove probable cause but their effects are limited to the US territory. Even though the information was stored within the EU borders (particularly, in Ireland), on 25 April 2014, Judge James C Francis obliged Microsoft to provide the data. The US judge concluded that no extraterritoriality principles would apply to the case, since Microsoft has no verification system checking every user who registers in the system. For that reason, the judge considered that denying search warrants in the EU would be advantageous to those individuals who are aware of this flaw and use the account for criminal purposes.

From the judgment it can be deduced that US judicial and police authorities see MLA procedures as slow and laborious and, consequently, they are constantly looking for other ways to circumvent such laws. Judge Francis was concerned about a clause included in most of the MLATs which allows the requested party to deny assistance if it deems that the request would be 'contrary to important public policy' or involves 'an offense of a political character'. He also noted that any search using MLATs had to be executed in accordance with the laws of the requested party (Case No. 13-Mag-2814: 20, *Microsoft*). Since the US does not have MLATs with all countries, relying only on these procedures would, in his view, be extremely risky.

Therefore, it can be concluded that non-MLA means of obtaining information from private entities are increasingly used by law enforcement authorities on both sides of the Atlantic, but especially by the US. The main concern from the privacy perspective is that police authorities do not always have a court order for accessing

---

23 In the US, the Government has three formal ways to obtain information from a TSP: a subpoena (18 USC 2703(b)(1)(B)(i)), a court order (18 USC 2703(d)) and a warrant (18 USC 2703(a)).

content data stored in TSPs, so this practice lacks external oversight.[24] Within this context, the former Vice-president of the European Commission Viviane Reding stated that, as a general rule, data should only be exchanged via judicial authorities, and not directly through a citizen or company. She added that 'asking the companies directly should only be possible under clearly defined, exceptional and judicially reviewable situations' (Reding 2013).

3 The EU data protection legislation for international data transfers in the field of law enforcement

As seen in previous sections, EU citizens' data is not only exchanged among law enforcement authorities in the Member States, but might also be transferred beyond the EU. One of the main debates on international data transfers concerns the applicable data protection standards. The EU has often been accused of applying double standards when conducting data transfers, depending on whether these are sent to third countries or are purely intra-European data flows. This section focuses on the data protection safeguards that apply to data transfers beyond the EU. It will be crucial for determining the feasibility of global data protection rules. If the EU already has a consistent data protection framework for data transferred to third countries, EU laws could be used as a model at the international level.

This analysis is divided into three parts. First, it examines the provisions on international data transfers included in Council Framework Decision 2008/977/JHA as well as the draft Directive on Police and Criminal Justice Data Protection. The main goal of this analysis is to determine whether these provisions offer the same level of protection as the provisions applicable for internal EU data transfers. Second, it evaluates the data protection provisions included in the main international agreements between the EU and the US. Particularly, the EU-US PNR Agreement, the SWIFT agreement and the EU-US agreement on data security are examined. Lastly, the EU and the US data protection regimes are compared. This comparison starts by identifying the differences in the conception of the right to privacy, followed by an analysis of the current attempts to approximate the two legal frameworks in the field of privacy.

3.1 EU secondary law

3.1.1 International data transfers according to Council Framework Decision 2008/977/JHA

When the EU adopted the first data protection law in 1995, it included a provision for data exchanges beyond the EU borders. It specified the conditions that a third

---

24 For instance, Vodafone, which has its headquarters in the UK, admitted that it received numerous requests without warrant for accessing its users' data between 1 April 2013 and 31 March 2014.

country had to comply with for sharing personal data with an EU country. According to Article 25(1) of Directive 95/46/EC:

> The Member States shall provide that the transfer to a third country of personal data which are undergoing processing or are intended for processing after transfer may take place only if, without prejudice to compliance with the national provisions adopted pursuant to the other provisions of this Directive, the third country in question ensures *an adequate level of protection.* (emphasis added)

The Art. 29 WP later clarified that the level of protection of a third country is considered 'adequate' if it complies with the following principles: (a) purpose limitation principle; (b) data quality and proportionality; (c) transparency; (d) security principle; (e) sensitive data; (f) the right of access, rectification and opposition; and (g) restrictions on onward transfers (Art. 29 WP 1998).

However, Directive 95/46/EC does not cover data transfers to third countries for law enforcement purposes. Member States were initially the only competent authorities to adopt legislation regulating data transfers in the field of security. As a result, there were situations in which one Member State could consider data protection standards of a particular third country (e.g. Nigeria) to be adequate, whereas another Member State could prohibit any exportation of data to that same third country because its data protection standards were not deemed to be high enough (de Hert and de Schutter 2008: 337; de Hert and Papakonstantinou 2009a: 412).

In 2001 an additional protocol of the Convention for the Protection of Individuals with regard to the Automatic Processing of Personal Data (1981 CoE Data Protection Convention) (Council of Europe 1981) was adopted. This solved the problems of the disparity of rules regarding data were transferred to third countries for law enforcement purposes. According to Article 2 of the protocol, parties could send data to non-Contracting Parties *only* 'if that State or organisation ensures an adequate level of protection for the intended data transfer'. However, that article presented two main limitations. First, paragraph 2 included broad derogations of the adequacy requirement (Council of Europe 2001), and second, the adequacy requirement for transborder flows did not apply if a Contracting Party had not ratified the protocol, and not all CoE members have ratified it (de Busser 2009: 119).

Eight years later, the Commission adopted Framework Decision on the protection of personal data processed in the framework of police and judicial co-operation in criminal matters – hereinafter, FD 2008/977 – (Council Framework Decision 2008/977/JHA). According to recitals 23 and 24, and Article 13(1)(d), data transfers to third countries could only take place if 'the third state or international body concerned ensures an adequate level of protection for the intended data processing'. Also, that provision establishes an equivalent adequacy mechanism to that of Article 25 of Directive 95/46/EC for international data transfers in the field of the common market. In both cases, the criteria taken into account for any data transfer operation are:

[T]he nature of the data, the purpose and duration of the proposed processing operation or operations, the State of origin and the State or international body of final destination of the data, the rules of law, both general and sectoral, in force in the third State or international body in question and the professional rules and security measures.

(Article 13(4) of Council Framework Decision
2008/977/JHA and Article 25(2) of Directive 95/46/EC)

The main disappointment of Article 13 is that it includes the same broad and ambiguous derogations as the additional protocol of the 1981 CoE Data Protection Convention (de Busser 2009: 119). In this regard, a Member State can still send data to non-EU members without complying with the adequacy criteria if it is for a legitimate specific interest or a public interest. Moreover, in contrast to Directive 95/46/EC, FD 2008/977 gives a broad margin to Member States to decide on specific adequacy parameters. In other words, each Member State assesses the adequacy level according to its own discretion. We must not forget that it is still the competence of the Member States, and not the EU, to regulate in the field of criminal matters.

It is worth highlighting here that council framework decisions do not have direct effects for individuals. In consequence, EU citizens whose domestic legislation opposes or does not fully comply with the EU instrument cannot invoke it directly. Another debate stems from recital 38 and Article 26 of FD 2008/977. These provisions state that this framework decision is:

[W]ithout prejudice to any obligations and commitments incumbent upon Member States or upon the Union by virtue of bilateral and/or multilateral agreements with third States existing at the time of adoption of this Framework Decision.

Hence, the 2007 EU-US PNR Agreement existing at that time fell outside of the scope of this law. In fact, every international data-sharing agreement has its own data protection provisions.

Therefore, it can be concluded that there is today no common EU legal framework regulating data transfers in the field of law enforcement. This situation will probably remain the same in the coming years, considering that the EU data protection law on crime-related data transfers does not include any change on that issue.

3.1.2 International data transfers according to the new Police and Criminal Justice Data Protection Directive

On 25 January 2012, the European Commission launched two proposals dealing with data protection matters: the General Data Protection Regulation (COM(2012) 11 final) and the Police and Criminal Justice Data Protection Directive (COM(2012) 10 final). This section examines only the latter, which regulates the processing of personal data for law enforcement purposes.

The new Police and Criminal Justice Data Protection Directive (hereinafter, the new directive) will repeal the current FD 2008/977 when it enters into force. As seen in Chapter 1, the wording of the new Directive is ambiguous. Although it states that it does not apply to data processing operations falling outside the scope of EU law (COM(2012) 10 final, p. 7), Chapter V and recitals 45, 46, 48 and 49 regulate transfers of personal data to third countries and international organisations. Unfortunately, neither the current FD 2008/977 nor the new Directive includes a definition of an 'international data transfer'. A proper definition of this term would clarify, for example, whether the countries that are part of the European Economic Area (EEA) are considered third countries or not (Guasch Portas 2014).

Regarding the specific provisions dealing with international data transfers, Article 33 of the proposal establishes that transfers to third countries may only take place if they are necessary for the prevention, investigation, detection or prosecution of criminal offences or the execution of criminal penalties. Moreover, Articles 34 and 35 of the new Directive establish that the Commission will be the institution in charge of deciding whether or not an international transfer is adequate in terms of data protection. So it will no longer be the Member State deciding on the adequacy of data protection rules in the third country, but any international data transfer bill needs the consent of the Commission. Despite the criticism from some Member States, this new role of the Commission will approximate the new Directive to the current adequacy procedure of Directive 95/46/EC (Peers 2012: 4).

Lastly, Article 36 of the new Directive enables the derogation of appropriate data protection safeguards when: (a) it is necessary to protect the vital or legitimate interests of the data subject; (b) it is essential for the prevention of an immediate and serious threat to the public security; (c) for the purposes of prevention, investigation, detection or prosecution of criminal offences or the execution of criminal penalties; and (d) for the establishment, exercise or defence of legal claims. From this provision it can be deduced that future clashes between data protection safeguards and counter-terrorism measures will be solved by derogating individual rights in the best interest of collective security.

Thirteen non-EU countries have adequate data protection systems to date.[25] It means that, in the remainder of third countries, derogations of data protection standards can be accepted as long as they are proved to be 'necessary'. In Chapter 1, it is shown that the scope and limits of the necessity principle are often ambiguous, and there is the risk that it is interpreted too broadly. In this sense, the EDPS has argued that 'any derogation used to justify a transfer needs to be interpreted restrictively and should not allow the frequent, massive and structural transfer of personal data' (EDPS 2012: 65).

---

25 These are Uruguay, Switzerland, Israel, Canada, Argentina, Guernsey, Isle of Man, Andorra, Australia, Faeroe Islands, Jersey, New Zealand and the US.

Article 36 of the new Directive does not guarantee that data transferred to third countries with no adequacy decision will not be misused. Given the recent decision from the CJEU considering the Data Retention Directive as contrary to the EU laws, Article 36 should be modified. The Court highlighted the importance of an independent overseer for data transfers to third countries. Yet, neither national DPAs nor the EDPS can control the use of the data once it is transferred to a third country with no adequate legal framework (Boehm and Cole 2014: 84).

A further obstacle is detected in the data protection principles of Article 4 of the new Directive. Although this provision lists the same data protection principles as those in Article 6 of Directive 95/46/EC, the new Directive is more limited in terms of its scope. For instance, these principles will not apply for previous international agreements in the field of police and judicial co-operation. According to Article 60, previous international agreements (e.g. the EU-US MLA Agreement) will remain unamended for five years after the directive enters into force. Assuming that the proposal enters into force in 2016, they would not be amended until 2021.

Another limitation is found in those EU instruments that regulate the processing of data collected by private entities for commercial purposes and then transferred to law enforcement authorities. This is the case of PNR data. The General Data Protection Regulation will deal with cross-border data flows resulting from the functioning of the internal market. In contrast, the directive will address the processing of personal data for police and criminal matters. But what legal instrument will bind data processing operations combining both commercial and security purposes? As noted by the EDPS, that might be a controversial issue in the future, since both legislative instruments do not have the same level of data protection (EDPS 2012: 7 and 51). It might occur that, for the same operation, one country applies the regulation standards, whereas another Member State bases its laws on the new directive.

In conclusion, neither the current FD 2008/977 nor the new directive on data protection in the field of law enforcement offer a full-fledged legal framework when a Member State transfers personal data to law enforcement authorities beyond the EU. One of the obstacles mentioned in this section is that these instruments do not apply for data transfers that fall within the scope of a specific data-sharing agreement concluded between the EU and a third country. Therefore, it is now necessary to examine whether data protection provisions in the main international agreements are similar to those foreseen in the new directive.

3.2 Data protection provisions in the main international agreements between the EU and the US

Many international agreements regarding the exchange of information for law enforcement purposes have been signed between the EU and the US to date. Each of these agreements includes their own data protection provisions. This section examines the data protection provisions of the main EU-US agreements based on the exchange of information for security reasons: the PNR Agreement, the

SWIFT Agreement and the Agreement on the security of classified information. No study is carried out on the Container Security Initiative (CSI), because the maritime information that the EU transfers to the US does not contain personal data. Likewise, no analysis is conducted as regards the EU-US MLAT because the Agreement does not include provisions on data protection, except for the purpose limitation rule in Article 9. This lack of data protection clauses in the MLAT is however corrected by the fact that the Agreement is currently subject to the FD 2008/977.

This study seeks to unveil whether all these agreements have the same data protection provisions or not. If it is concluded that each agreement has it own provisions, it means that different levels of protection are applied to EU citizens' data depending on the particular instrument. It would ultimately complicate the establishment of global data protection rules in the field of security.

3.2.1 Data protection in the EU-US PNR Agreement

The current EU-US PNR Agreement was adopted in 2012. Before examining it, it is pertinent to observe what data protection provisions were included in the previous PNR agreements.

The first draft of the 2004 EU-US PNR Agreement collected 38 PNR categories of data. However, during the negotiations of the Agreement, this dropped from 38 to 34 (de Busser 2009: 373). Moreover, there was no possibility for EU citizens to access their data and to have judicial redress (Pawlak 2012: 18). Two particular aspects of that first agreement are, however, positive. The first is that data was retained for only three years and six months (de Busser 2009: 381). The other is that the CBP used a 'push-system', through which airlines retained control over their databases for the CBP requests. That system lowered the chances for abuses by law enforcement agencies (de Busser 2009: 371).

As seen above, the 2004 EU-US PNR Agreement was found to be in breach of EU laws. The ground used by the EP to challenge the Agreement was mainly an infringement of the fundamental principles of Directive 95/46/EC. Yet, that issue was never properly examined by the CJEU, which focused its decision on the examination of the applicable legal basis. The CJEU ruling gave airline companies an escape route, as before the judgment they found themselves in a Catch-22 situation because they could not comply with the conflicting US and Community obligations. As for the EU citizens, the court decision resulted in lower data protection safeguards: prior to the ruling, the Agreement fitted under the scope of the internal market provision and, consequently, European institutions had competence to enforce citizens' fundamental rights and principles. In contrast, subsequent agreements of 2006 and 2007 fell outside the scope of the first pillar and, therefore, adequacy levels required by Directive 95/46/EC were no longer applicable. The Council became the only institution entitled to decide on the mandate of the Agreement, and the EP had no formal say in the negotiations.

The 2007 EU-US PNR Agreement decreased the protection of personal data in the following issues: first, data was no longer processed through the push method, but through the pull method. This means that the subjects in charge of processing personal data changed from private actors (air carriers) to public entities (law enforcement agencies), and the US authorities were now competent to extract data from the airlines' databases. Second, data was to be kept for seven years from the moment of collection, and then moved to an inactive database for a further eight years. This meant a total retention period of 15 years, in contrast to the three and a half years of the previous agreement. Third, the US Department of Homeland Security (DHS), and not the CBP, was the competent authority for the processing of data. This change had negative implications, since it gave access to PNR data not only to that specific body, but also to all other US agencies with counter-terrorism functions. Fourth, information (including sensitive data)[26] received at the DHS could be easily transferred to foreign authorities. Lastly, PNR data was used to detect more criminal offences than the previous agreement (Archick 2013: 14).

Notwithstanding the general decrease of data protection, a few positive aspects of the 2007 EU-US PNR Agreement need to be highlighted. The main one is the fact that the number of categories of PNR data collected was reduced from 34 to 19. However, many scholars have stated that the shorter list did not necessarily mean that less data were included. De Busser used the example of the number of bags. The 2007 Agreement included a single category of 'all baggage information', whereas the 2004 Agreement added the elements 'bag tag numbers', 'number of bags' and 'general remarks' regarding a passenger's luggage (de Busser 2009: 374). Another positive feature was that the 2007 EU-US PNR Agreement foresaw the conducting of periodical reviews to check the compliance with privacy measures. That was not required in the 2004 Agreement.

The current 2012 EU-US PNR Agreement (Council Decision 2012/471/EU) includes many improvements in terms of data protection in comparison with the previous Agreements. With regard to the method used to transfer data, it prescribes the 'push method', a process by which airline companies collect PNR data in their databases and then transfer such data to the respective government authorities. The push system is a sign of progress, considering that the 2007 EU-US PNR Agreement used the 'pull method' for transferring data. Under the old pull method, the US authorities had access to all data in airline companies' databases. Consequently, data was collected and processed under US laws, preventing EU data protection laws from being enforced.

However, this 'push method' is not fully implemented in practice: in 2013 the Privacy Office found that the 68 per cent of air carriers had already transitioned to that system, but the 'pull' method was still used by 15 air carriers (US Department of Homeland Security 2013: 5 and 17). In that sense, the Commission has asked airline companies to fully move to the 'push' method, since it is required by Article 15(4) of the Agreement (COM(2013) 844 final).

---

26 Sensitive data can be defined as data revealing racial or ethnic origin, political opinions, religious or philosophical beliefs, trade union membership or concerning the health or sex life of the individual.

Data retention periods are also improved in the current agreement. In fact, the DHS had to introduce changes to the technology of the Automated Targeting System (ATS) in order to adapt to the requirements of Article 8. Authorised ATS users have access to an active database up to five years. Yet, PNR data are depersonalised after six months. That means that after that period, authorised ATS users can only see the record locator, the reservation system, the date record and the itinerary (US Department of Homeland Security 2013: 16). Thus personal data are no longer visible. A repersonalisation is still possible, but it lasts for a maximum of 24 hours. In addition, it requires prior authorisation by a supervisory agent and proof that there is a specific threat or risk. After five years, data is moved to a dormant, non-operational database. Data transferred to this dormant database will be retained for ten years in cases of transnational crime information (five years less than under the previous 2007 EU-US PNR Agreement), and for 15 years in cases of terrorism information. During that period, access will only be possible with the approval of a senior DHS official designated by the Secretary of Homeland Security. After ten or 15 years, PNR data will be automatically deleted, and no repersonalisation will be possible.

As for the categories of data collected, the Agreement keeps the same number of items as those in the 2007 Agreement: air carriers will provide a maximum of 19 data categories, which are the following:

Table 2.1

1 PNR record locator code
2 Date of reservation/issue of ticket
3 Date(s) of intended travel
4 Name(s)
5 Available frequent flier and benefit information (i.e. free tickets, upgrades, etc)
6 Other names on PNR, including number of travellers on PNR
7 All available contact information (including originator of reservation)
8 All available payment/billing information (e.g. credit card number)
9 Travel itinerary for specific PNR
10 Travel agency/travel agent
11 Code share information
12 Split/divided information (e.g. when one PNR contains a reference to another PNR)
13 Travel status of passenger (including confirmations and check-in status)
14 Ticketing information, including ticket number, one-way tickets and automated ticket fare quote
15 All baggage information
16 Seat information, including seat number
17 General remarks including Other Service Indicated (OSI), Special Service Indicated (SSI) and Supplemental Service Request (SSR) information
18 Any collected Advance Passenger Information (API)
19 All historical changes to the PNR listed under points 1 to 18

As seen in the Table 2.1, there is no information on racial or ethnic origin, political views, religion or sex life of the individual. However, if sensitive data is collected by an air carrier (e.g. concerning the health or dietary requirements of the passenger), it will be automatically masked to prevent routine viewing. As for the individual rights included in the current EU-US PNR Agreement, any passenger of any nationality has in principle the right to access, rectify and delete the information that the CBP has processed about him/her. Data can be accessed by sending a Freedom of Information Act (FOIA) request. If the disclosure is rejected, there is an appeal procedure and the individual can go to the federal court as the last instance. In 2011 there were 220,000 FOIA requests (US Homeland Security Committee 2011), and from July 2012 to March 2013, the CBP received a total of 21,606 requests, 27 of which were specifically on PNR – none of them was from EU citizens – (SEC(2013) 630 final, p. 12). The majority of requests came from immigration and custom agencies (US Homeland Security Committee 2011), and they were apparently processed within 38 days on average (SEC(2013) 630 final, p. 12).

For the purposes of this study, I followed the procedure of three data requests to the CBP from EU citizens (in particular, from France, Spain and Hungary) during the years 2013 and 2014. None of them was completed in 38 days. In fact, in 2015 none of the applicants has received the information yet. The only application to which the CBP replied was to inform the applicant that his/her request had been rejected. The other two remain unanswered by the US government. Even if the CBP eventually sends the data, this delay of over one year must be viewed with disappointment, especially considering that a similar PNR data request I sent to the Australian government was completed after only 15 days.

Provisions on onward transfers are also found in the Agreement. Data stored in ATS can be shared with non-DHS governmental agencies (within or beyond the US) after verifying that the requester has a need to know the information.

The use and disclosure of PNR data is regulated in the Customs and Border Protection Directive. According to this law, requesters need to sign specific PNR disclosure forms in which they agree to treat the information provided as confidential and not to send it on other third parties without prior DHS authorisation. The system logged 589 disclosures when the last PNR joint review took place in April 2013, and only one came from the EU (SEC(2013) 630 final, pp. 8 and 16).

Data security measures are also present in the Agreement. The DHS has noted that:

> [U]sers may only access PNR through ATS-P, which can only be accessed through a web-based user interface over the DHS infrastructure or remotely through secure-encrypted mobile devices for certain CBP officers in foreign locations and at Ports of Entry.
>
> (SEC(2013) 630 final, p. 29)

Thus, the CBP network can only be accessed by authorised users through secure encrypted devices requiring a password. Any internal sharing is logged locally on hard copy, and data requests from non-DHS agencies are also retained and audited.

Regarding the overseeing of PNR transfers, audits of the use of Automated Targeting System-Passenger (ATS-P)[27] are carried out every six months by the CBP's Office of Internal Affairs. If the audits show that a user has conducted an unauthorised access or disclosure, it may result in criminal sanctions (US Department of Homeland Security 2013: 23). Therefore, all PNR users need to undergo privacy training and pass an examination before using ATS. Lastly, independent supervision is conducted by the Chief Privacy Officer, the DHS Office of Inspector General, the US Government Accountability Office and the US Congress. Also, since February 2012, a new Privacy Oversight Team has been incorporated in the DHS Privacy Office. It deals with privacy investigations, privacy complaint handlings and redress, among other tasks (US Department of Homeland Security 2013: 6).

The Agreement explicitly states that decisions cannot be based solely on automated processed data. This provision aims to prevent illegal profiling (Archick 2013: 14). This clause is particularly important considering the numerous errors that have been committed in the past due to the lack of investigation into hits of potential suspects of terrorism. The case of Maher Arar is an example. Arar is a dual citizen of Canada and Syria who was denied entry into US territory on 26 September 2002. The decision was taken after the DoS's cross-matched passenger information from the APIS and identified Arar as a 'special interest' alien who was suspected of terrorism and described as armed and dangerous. The inspectors of the Immigration and Naturalisation Service (INS) arrested him at the US airport and returned him to Syria, where he was subjected to beatings and torture for over a year. Finally, he was found innocent and released to Canada (US Department of Homeland Security 2008).

Even though the EU-US PNR Agreement incorporates several provisions that limit the collection, use and storage of EU citizens' data by the DHS, some rules may still be contrary to EU laws. The recent CJEU decision to annul the Data Retention Directive provided valuable guidance about what practices by which law enforcement authorities violate the right to data protection of EU citizens. In a study requested by the LIBE Committee, Boehm identified many provisions of the Agreement that would contradict the CJEU judgment. Particularly, these are Article 4 on the purpose, Article 8 on the data retention, Article 14 on the oversight, Article 15(5) on the ad-hoc 'pull' method, Article 17(1) on the onward transfers and Article 21 on the rights of the data subject (Boehm and Cole 2014: 58–65). Therefore, after the judgment (Cases C-293/12 and C-594/12, *Digital Rights Ireland Ltd v Minister for Communications et al* (2014)), this Agreement would need to be revised and adapted in accordance with the parameters established by the Court.

---

27 ATS-P is a component of ATS, which collects PNR information obtained from commercial aircrafts.

3.2.2 Data protection in the SWIFT Agreement

From 2001 to 2009, the Belgian company SWIFT transferred financial data from EU citizens to the US authorities without any formal agreement. As mentioned earlier, SWIFT's headquarters were in Belgium and, consequently, Belgian Data Protection Law (which implemented Directive 95/46/EC) was applicable. On 30 November 2009 the EU and the US signed the first SWIFT Agreement, which authorised the transfer of financial data to the US Department of the Treasury for the prevention, investigation, detection or prosecution of terrorism or terrorist financing. The Agreement was vetoed by the EP in February 2010, on the basis that adequate data protection safeguards were lacking (see section 2.1.3 above). By mid-June 2010, the second and current SWIFT Agreement was adopted, this time approved by the EP.

Regarding the data protection provisions of the current SWIFT Agreement, some of them differ from those found in the EU-US PNR Agreement. For instance, according to Article 5(7) of the SWIFT Agreement, data categories in SWIFT refer to the originator and/or recipient of a transaction, including name, account number, address and national identification number. Once the data enters the database of the US Department of the Treasury, it is retained for 'no longer than necessary to combat terrorism or its financing', with five years being the maximum retention period (Article 6(4) of the SWIFT Agreement). This does not coincide with the provisions established in the EU-US PNR Agreement, which processes up to 19 categories of data and permits passenger data to be retained for up to 15 years.

Articles 12 and 13 of the SWIFT Agreement regulate the supervision of data transfers. It requires the establishment of independent overseers, one appointed by the Commission and the other by the US Department of the Treasury. They perform regular checks on the TFTP database (or 'black box') to confirm that it complies with the extraction requirements (de Busser 2009: 388). In particular, overseers control that any extraction is based on the value of data for the investigation, prevention, detection or prosecution of terrorism or its financing; the processing is necessary and proportional; and it includes adequate data security measures (Article 5 of the Agreement). If any search or extraction appears to be in breach of the data protection safeguards of Article 5, overseers will then report and block that operation.

Articles 14, 15, 16 and 18 of the Agreement refer to the individual rights, namely, the rights to data access, right to rectification, erasure and blocking of inaccurate data, and non-discriminatory administrative and judicial redress. In the particular case of data access, any individual can request data that the US Department of the Treasury has control over via the national DPA. The DPA then sends the formal request to the US authorities.

During the current study, I myself sent a request for my own SWIFT data to the Spanish DPA. I requested access to my financial data in April 2014, and the Spanish DPA sent the request to the US Department of the Treasury. One year later, I received as a response that the US Department of the Treasury was 'unable to confirm or deny the existence of any responsive records'. The letter then added that the disclosure of such information could identify subjects of ongoing counter-terrorism investigations or harm national security. From this response, there are two possible conclusions: either I have been particularly targeted as a suspect of a serious crime by the US authorities, or the letter I received is a standardised answer for any data request. Either way, it is very worrying. Therefore, in line with the recommendation made in an EP study about the TFTP, there is a real need for 'making the right to access, rectification, erasure, blocking and administrative and judicial redress a reality' (Wesseling 2014: 33).

Some data protection provisions are the same in the PNR and SWIFT agreements. For instance, data is extracted via the push method in both agreements. Article 4(6) of the SWIFT agreement establishes that it is the designated provider (i.e. SWIFT) that provides the data directly to the US Treasury Department. Moreover, SWIFT needs to keep a detailed log of all data transferred to the US.

Another similarity is found in the provision regulating onward transfers (Article 7 of the Agreement). In line with the current PNR Agreement, data can be shared with law enforcement, public security and counter-terrorism authorities in the US; with Member States; and with third countries. SWIFT also mentions Europol as a possible receptor of the data. The narrow link between the US Department of the Treasury and Europol stems from the fact that the latter verifies that each request 'is tailored as narrowly as possible to minimise the amount of data requested' (MEMO/13/1060). This practice is thoroughly examined in Chapter 3. Lastly, the Agreement also coincides with the current PNR Agreement in the obligation to obtain prior consent of the competent Member States' authorities before EU citizens' data are shared.

It can therefore be concluded that, although there are some equivalences as regards the push method and the onward transfers in both the PNR and SWIFT data exchanges, we find many differences in the data protection provisions included in SWIFT and PNR Agreements. Moreover, as with the EU-US PNR Agreement, the recent CJEU decision on the Data Retention Directive might have some implications for the SWIFT agreement. In particular, the fact that SWIFT data is transferred in bulk, the lack of an independent administrative oversight and the absence of notification to the data subjects contradict the Court's core arguments (Boehm and Cole 2014: 72–75).

3.3 EU-US data protection regimes

3.3.1 Different conceptions of privacy in the US and the EU

Although the EU and the US have made huge efforts to show to the world that they share common values, common interests and common responsibilities (US Mission to the EU 2012), in practice many important divergences as regards their privacy laws are evident. This section focuses precisely on examining the differences between the EU and the US regarding the notion of privacy.

The main difference to be highlighted is that the EU considers 'privacy' as a human right, whereas the US tends to value it as a liberty over and against the state. This distinction has a historical explanation. The sensitivity that the EU has on privacy has its origins in the horror suffered by Jews during the Holocaust. The Nazis used public and church records to identify Jewish people, so that they might be persecuted and ultimately be sent to concentration camps (Sullivan 2006). As a result of those abuses, the idea of human dignity, as well as the protection of one's identity have been significantly reinforced within the EU during the twentieth and twentieth-first centuries (Hughes 2013).

Besides the idea that every individual has the right to enjoy a private life (Article 7 of the EU Charter of Fundamental Rights), the EU has taken a step further by establishing a 'right to data protection' (Article 8 of the Charter). In general terms, the main difference between the right to privacy and the right to data protection is that the latter is linked to the idea of self-determination, by which any individual should be able to decide how their data is processed. The right to data protection is thus connected to natural persons and it safeguards the human identity. In the US, laws only refer to the right to privacy, but EU laws treat these two concepts separately (Hondius 1983; González Fuster 2014: 257–262).

The right to data protection constitutes a 'general principle of law' within the EU, and it is also regulated in Article 16 TFEU. This fundamental right has long been protected by many rulings issued by the highest European and Member State courts, including the European Court of Human Rights (ECtHR).[28] Likewise, the idea of data protection has been included in the constitutions of almost all Member States.

In the US, the Fourth Amendment of the US Constitution is the main binding provision as regards the right to privacy. Unlike the EU laws, the Fourth Amendment does not regulate the right to privacy against all circumstances, but only protects US citizens – or non-US citizens who are long-term residents in the US – against unreasonable searches and seizures conducted by the government. Yet, the Fourth Amendment does not protect individuals against violations committed by non-governmental actors. In such cases, the right to privacy can only be enforced through sectoral laws,[29] self-regulation[30] and privacy-enhancing technologies.[31]

---

28 See, for instance, the case law of the CJEU: Case C-450/00, *Commission v Luxembourg*, 4 October 2001; Cases C-465/00 and C-138/01, *Rechnungshof v Osterreichischer Rundfunk*, 20 May 2003, Case C-101/01, *Lindquist*, 6 November 2003; Case C-524/06, *Huber v Germany*, 16 December 2008; Case C-73/07, *Tietosuojavaltuutettu [Finnish data protection ombudsman] v Satakunnan Markkinaporssi Oy and Satamedia Oy*, 16 December 2008; Case C-28/08, *Commission v Bavarian Lager Co.*, 29 June 2010; Case C-92/09, *Volker und Markus Schecke GbR v Land Hessen*, 9 November 2010, and Case C-93/09, *Eifert v Land Hessen and Bundesanstalt fur Landwirtschaft und Ernahrung*, 9 November 2010, among others.

29 For instance, the 1986 Electronic Communications Privacy Act (ECPA), the 1974 Family Educational Rights and Privacy Act (FERPA), the 1994 Driver's Privacy Protection Act and the 1978 Right to Financial Privacy Act.

30 Industries are expected to take responsibility for their own data protection safeguards.

31 For instance, the use of encryption or smartcards systems to enhance the protection of personal data.

The EU-US divergence is also seen in the fact that in the US privacy is associated with a governmental obligation to refrain from taking specific actions. In other words, it is linked to a negative duty. Instead, the EU perceives the right to privacy as a positive duty: the government must not only abstain from conducting certain activities, but it has to 'affirmatively protect privacy rights' (Kuner 2013).[32] Thus, according to the EU perspective, it is not sufficient that EU governments refrain from carrying out unreasonable searches, but they have an additional positive obligation to make sure that no individual is unlawfully monitored by a third person (either governmental or non-governmental).

At this point, one might ask: Are privacy standards higher in the EU than in the US in the field of law enforcement? Although several academic studies conclude that privacy rights are similar on both sides of the Atlantic (US State Department 2012: 2; Bamberger and Mulligan 2013; Tene 2014; Bender 2014; Schwartz 2014; Rosenzweig 2014), I believe they are not.

One of the main privacy flaws in the US (not present in the EU laws) relates to the great number of exemptions to the applicability of the purpose limitation principle. This principle is one of the core requirements of adequate data protection standards in the EU. However, it is not regulated in the US legal framework at all. In fact, since the adoption of the Patriot Act in 2001, the US government has been processing data that was originally collected for other purposes (Smith 2003). Particularly, Section 215 of the Patriot Act increased the US government's control over all communications collected by TSPs. Under that provision, US law enforcement and intelligence authorities are able to collect phone metadata of any US citizen without prior warrant.[33]

Similarly, the EU adopted the Data Retention Directive. This law obliged European TSPs to store metadata for a period between six months and two years, depending on the Member State. The directive, however, was annulled by the CJEU in April 2014. As mentioned in Chapter 1, the grounds were the infringement of the purpose limitation, the proportionality and the necessity principles as stated in Directive 95/46/EC, as well as Articles 7 and 8 of the Charter.[34]

Another difference between the EU and the US concerns the retention periods. Precisely, the Data Retention Directive obliged phone companies to keep users' data for a period of between six months and two years. As mentioned above, the Directive was annulled by the CJEU for violating EU fundamental rights. If we compare this ruling with the situation in the US, we notice that there are no US laws for retention periods. Each TSP decides for how long it wants to retain its users' data. For instance, Verizon keeps subscriber information from three to five years and call records for one year; whereas Sprint preserves subscriber information for an unlimited period, and keeps call details for approximately 18 months.

---

32 This same positive obligation is seen in the case law of the ECtHR. See, for example, *Marckx v Belgium*, Judgment of 21 April 1979; *Mikuli v Croatia*, Judgment of 7 February 2002; *Cotley v Romania*, Judgment of 3 September 2003; *Von Hannover v Germany*, Judgment of 24 June 2004; among others.

33 This law is examined in Chapter 4.

34 See Chapter 1, section 3.2.3.

Another privacy weakness that we find in the US and not in the EU concerns the publication of criminal records, and the subsequent difficulties of 'being forgotten' even after having served a sentence. One example is found in several US States with regard to the so-called 'Megan's Law'. Megan was a seven-year-old girl who was tragically raped and killed in 1994 by her neighbour in New Jersey. The murderer had been found guilty of committing several sex offences on other young girls before, but people living in his neighbourhood were not aware of this. Therefore, a month after the murder, New Jersey passed the first 'Megan's Law', by which any sex offender would be registered and publically identified on the Megan's Law website of the State. The law had the purpose of informing other neighbours about the location of sex offenders, including the name, picture, address, nature of crime and the incarceration date.

Megan's Law directories show how in the US the freedom of expression, regulated in the US First Amendment, may often override the right to privacy if the purpose is justified, as in the case of sex offenders. No similar public database could ever exist in the EU. The right to freedom of speech is regulated differently in each Member State, and some give it higher importance than others. The EU courts have also been reluctant to keep criminal records indefinitely. In that sense, the ECtHR ruled in 2008 that DNA data of EU citizens arrested but never charged could not be retained permanently in police databases (*S. and Marper v the United Kingdom* [2008] ECHR 1581). As for the publication of criminal records on the internet, judgments of national courts – except for constitutional courts' rulings (Blasi Casagran and Blasi Casagran 2012) – are excluded from the indexes of search engines through robots.txt. This is a measure that avoids linking police and judicial records to the name of a person via search engines. Likewise, the CJEU has demonstrated that someone can be formally 'forgotten' from the indexes of search engines, even if their name is linked to the website of a newspaper, as long as the information is no longer accurate and relevant to society (Case C-131/12, *Google v Costeja* (2012)). In that particular case, the information to be removed revealed high social security debts that an individual had already paid off a long time ago. The CJEU argumentation for erasing information could also be used to remove criminal data once the EU citizen has already served their sentence.

3.3.2 Attempts to approximate the EU and the US privacy legislations

The EU and the US have launched many initiatives to approximate their privacy laws, basing them on global principles and conventions that they have both signed. They have also already adopted a few bilateral instruments that seek to establish common privacy rules.

As regards global principles subscribed to by the EU and the US, four main instruments can be distinguished: the OECD Privacy Guidelines, the APEC Privacy Framework, the Fair Information Practice Principles (FIPPs), and the CoE Cybercrime Convention.

The OECD released recommendations concerning Guidelines governing the Protection of Privacy and Transborder Flows of Personal Data (OECD Privacy Guidelines) in September 1980. The EU and the US are both members of the OECD. In fact, the OECD Privacy Principles are similar to those included in Directive 95/46/EC and Member States' data protection legislations. Therefore, the OECD is a key organisation for the establishment of adequate data protection safeguards for EU-US data transfers in the field of law enforcement.

The US became a formal participant of the Asia-Pacific Economic Cooperation's (APEC's) Cross-Border Privacy Rules (CBPR) framework on 25 July 2012. This framework creates privacy obligations for all APEC economies. With regard to the EU, it is not a formal member but the Art. 29 WP has produced a common referential[35] for the requirements of the CBPR system and the EU Binding Corporate Rules.[36] Therefore, this framework could also serve as the basis to get the two legal frameworks closer. However, the main problem with the APEC and the OECD privacy rules is that they constitute non-binding instruments. Consequently, the US has not always implemented the principles enshrined in the OECD Privacy Guidelines and the APEC Privacy Framework accurately. For instance, rules on data quality or purpose limitation (both well-defined by the conventions) have not been transposed in the US legislation (de Busser 2009: 305).

The US and the EU are also both subject to the FIPPs, released in 1973. These are core elements for all privacy laws around the world. In particular, they include principles such as transparency, individual participation, purpose limitation, data security, data usage, data access, auditing and accountability and redress. The FIPPs were first embedded in the US Privacy Act of 1974, and they influenced later rules such as the aforementioned 1980 OECD Privacy Guidelines and Directive 95/46/EC. The FIPPs were created with the aim of harmonising privacy legislation applicable to any international data flow. Yet, as Wolf and Maxwell have pointed out, '[h]istorically, the EU and United States have taken divergent approaches to implementing the FIPPs' (Wolf and Maxwell 2012: 8). Similarly, de Busser concluded that the FIPPs have not been sufficient to make EU and US data protection systems fully compatible (de Busser 2009: 297). For data transfers in the field of law enforcement these principles have not been very helpful in approximating EU-US rules either. The US has often stated that all EU-US data-sharing agreements have been adopted in line with the FIPPs (US Homeland Security Committee 2011), but these principles are so broad that they have not prevented different privacy provisions from existing in each of the current EU-US data-sharing agreements (see section 3.2).

The CoE Cybercrime Convention was signed by the US and all EU Member States on 23 November 2001. It sets out a legal framework for police and judicial

---

35 *Joint work between experts from the Article 29 Working Party and from APEC Economies, on a referential for requirements for Binding Corporate Rules submitted to national Data Protection Authorities in the EU and Cross Border Privacy Rules submitted to APEC CBPR Accountability Agents.*

36 It is examined in Chapter 5.

access to computer data. Among the safeguards guaranteed in the Convention, there is the need for independent supervision (Article 15), and the use of mutual assistance requests in the absence of applicable international agreements (Article 27). Therefore, to some extent, the CoE Cybercrime Convention could provide a secure and effective EU-US framework for ensuring that electronic data is available to law enforcement authorities when needed for the investigation and prosecution of crimes. However, the scope of this Convention is very specific, so it does not offer a complete data protection regime for the parties.

Besides these multilateral instruments signed by the EU and the US, there are also bilateral initiatives. Two groups have been created with the purpose of bringing the two legal frameworks closer: the HLCG and the EU-US working group of data protection and privacy. The HLCG was established in 2006. It is composed of senior officers of both the EU[37] and the US[38] sides, who are in charge of discussing the exchange of data between both parties in the field of law enforcement. In the words of the Council of the EU:

> [T]he goal of the HLCG was to explore ways that would enable the EU and the US to work more closely and efficiently together in the exchange of law enforcement information while ensuring that the protection of personal data and privacy are guaranteed.
>
> (Council of the European Union 2008)

This group identifies common principles and definitions within the field of data processing for law enforcement. In particular, these are the purpose specification/purpose limitation; integrity/data quality; relevant and necessary/proportionality; information security; special categories of personal information (sensitive data); accountability; independent and effective oversight; individual access and rectification; transparency and notice; redress; automated individual decisions; and restrictions on onward transfers to third countries (Council of the European Union 2008).

The EU-US working group on data protection and privacy was set up in July 2013 (MEMO/13/1059), after the US National Security Agency (NSA) scandal took place.[39] The goal was 'to establish the facts around U.S. surveillance programmes and their impact on personal data of EU citizens' (MEMO/13/1059, p. 8). On the one hand, it comprised members of the Commission, the Presidency of the Council of the EU, the EEAS, the EU Counter-Terrorism Co-ordinator, the Art. 29 WP and ten experts from EU Member States. On the other hand, it involved the participation of the US DoJ, the US Office of the Director of National Intelligence, the US State Department and the DHS (MEMO/13/1059, p. 9).

---

37 They come from the European Commission and the EU Presidency (supported by the Council Secretariat).
38 They come from the DOJ, DHS and DoS.
39 See Chapter 4, section 3.

The Group organised three meetings in 2013[40] and issued an exhaustive report in which it clarified all the legal issues regarding the controversial Section 215 of the Patriot Act and Section 207 of Foreign Intelligence Surveillance Act Amendment (FISAA) 8 (MEMO/13/1059, pp. 9–10).[41] Yet, no new report has been published in 2014, and it is not fully clear what the input of this group is, apart from clarifying technical questions on the transatlantic exchanges of personal data.

Taking the above into account, we can conclude that none of the instruments seems to be sufficient for establishing a common data protection framework in the EU and the US, at least for the moment. It is precisely this need for a common regulatory system that triggered the negotiations for another legal instrument: the EU-US Data Protection Agreement, which is examined below.

3.3.3 The umbrella EU-US Data Protection Agreement

Parallel to the specific agreements on data transfers concluded between the EU and the US in the last ten years, many attempts have been made in order to reach a general framework on data protection.

The EP launched the first call for this Data Privacy and Protection Agreement (DPPA) in March 2009. One year later, in May 2010, the Commission drafted a mandate on the negotiation terms, which the Council authorised on 3 December 2010. Negotiations officially commenced in March 2011. Since then, several meetings have taken place between the Commission and the US authorities. Also, the DHS Chief Privacy Officer has participated in these discussions, giving valuable input on the current US privacy laws (US Department of Homeland Security 2013: 69).

The Agreement was finalised by the Commission in September 2015, and the EU and the US have agreed on the following provisions that the Agreement will include. First of all, the Agreement will only cover data transfers between the EU and the US for the prevention, investigation, detection and prosecution of crimes. Moreover, it is now clear that the Agreement will not be used as a specific legal basis for bilateral data-sharing agreements, but rather will be a general mandate for transatlantic data exchanges. Thus, the current PNR and SWIFT agreements will fall out of the scope of the DPPA, having these agreements their own data safeguards.

Regarding the substantive provisions of the Agreement, the EU has moved forward to incorporate as many safeguards as possible. Although the US authorities were originally leading the negotiations on the content of the DPPA, the NSA revelations of 2013 brought a change of leadership. After the revelations, the US needed to rebuild trust within the EU and, therefore, it gave greater consideration to the initial recommendations made by Commission.

---

40 One in Brussels on 22–23 July, one in Washington DC on 19–20 September and another in Brussels on 6 November.
41 These provisions are examined in Chapter 4, section 2.

The EU has achieved the inclusion of a provision on the need of prior consent of the original authority for onward transfers. Also, other stronger requirements will also be required if such onward transfer involves bulk data extracted from systems such as PNR. Other EU successes are the establishment of a non-discrimination clause between national and non-national data, the prohibition of basing decisions solely on the automatic processing of personal data (e.g. profiling systems), and provisions on data quality and integrity. Likewise, general provisions on access, modification and administrative redress will be available to any individual. Unfortunately, this might not be enough to stop the enormous delays that EU citizens encounter today when they request access to their PNR or SWIFT data.[42]

The US has also committed to establish oversight mechanisms similar to those conducted by DPAs within the EU. It is not clear what US supervisory authority will be in charge of the oversight, but it will probably be a combination of Chief Privacy Officers, Inspector Generals and the Privacy and Civil Liberties Oversight Board. The fact that a number of different supervisory authorities operate in the US could pose a problem. However, the US authority will need to be independent, in line with the EU DPA's characteristics. In addition, EU and US oversight authorities will co-operate and consult each other through national contact points.

For its part, the US has imposed its preferences in some of the provisions, especially in terms of data retention and data breach notification. As for data retention, the US has always resisted setting specific data retention periods, suggesting that these should be decided in accordance to each party's domestic laws. Therefore, the DPPA will not include specific periods of retention, but it will only state that data should not be kept 'for longer than necessary and appropriate'. The DPPA will also add that any specific data-sharing agreement will have to contain precise provisions on retention periods. However, these retention periods will probably differ from one agreement to another, as is the case today with regard to the PNR and SWIFT agreements.

Three issues remain unresolved: (a) the judicial redress – particularly the possibility for EU citizens to obtain redress in the US; (b) the purpose limitation principle; and (c) the processing of sensitive data. As for the judicial redress, the Commission has been trying to enable EU citizens to obtain judicial redress in the US by establishing enforceable legal provisions in the Agreement. The Commission has even requested that the US authorities amend the US Privacy Act of 1974 in order to include judicial redress for non-US citizens. However, the US Congress has been reluctant to do so. It has long maintained that EU citizens already have the possibility to use the US FOIA to get judicial redress and, therefore, the amendment is unnecessary (Archick 2013: 16). Yet, after the Snowden revelations,[43] the Attorney General of the US, Eric Holder, finally promised to take action in order to guarantee that Europeans who do not live in

---

42 The author's own experiences in this regard are detailed in sections 3.2.1 and 3.2.2 of this chapter.
43 It is examined in Chapter 4.

the US can also have judicial redress. Thus, subject to the approval of the US Judicial Redress Bill, the DPPA will allow EU citizens to seek judicial redress before US courts under the US Privacy Act where US authorities have processed their personal data unlawfully.

Now it remains to be seen whether the EP will approve this agreement. Korff has already claimed that it is violation with the EU data protection laws since it allows the sharing of data with the US security agencies, it does not prohibit onward data transfers, it does not give adequate remedies for EU citizens and the oversight mechanisms are not sufficient (Korff 2015). What is clear is that the Agreement is not as ambitious as it was initially presented to be, and it will only partially help to establish common minimal standards on data protection between the EU and US.

3.3.4 The norm-taking role of the EU

Many studies have concluded that the US has shaped the EU's security policy (Argomaniz 2009: 119–121; de Hert and Papakonstantinou 2009b; Hillebrand 2012: 127–128; Trauner and Carrapiço 2012: 6; Quesada Gámez and Mincheva 2012: 292). This section examines whether the EU has been a pure 'norm-taker' (Argomaniz 2009: 127) of US counter-terrorism rules, or whether it has also influenced the US in the negotiations of data-sharing agreements.

There is no doubt that, after the 9/11 terrorist attacks, the US strategy triggered the adoption of all the EU-US Agreements described above. In 2001, the Bush administration called upon its allies (including the EU) to provide support and assistance to the US in order to combat terrorism. The US pushed the EU to change their national policies if necessary. The National Strategy for Combating Terrorism was clear on this point:

> When states prove reluctant or unwilling to meet their international obligations to deny support and sanctuary to terrorists, the United States, in cooperation with friends and allies, or if necessary, acting independently, will take appropriate steps to convince them to change their policies.
>
> (US Central Intelligence Agency 2003)

It has been confirmed by this study that when the EU adopted the SWIFT, PNR and CSI Agreements, the negotiations were mainly led by the US needs. As for the PNR saga, the transfer of air passenger data to the US was not on the EU agenda as a counter-terrorism measure before the adoption of the first PNR Agreement (Argomaniz 2009: 125). The US power over the EU legal framework was then seen in Cases C-317 and 318/04, *Parliament v Council* (2006). The Court's reasoning on the applicable legal basis revealed the increasing influence of US counter-terrorism measures on the EU. The US has also shaped subsequent PNR Agreements, softening their data protection provisions. In fact, the EU passed the Agreements because it was afraid that a refusal would cause the removal of some Member States from the Visa Waiver Program (VWP) (Suda 2013: 779).

With regard to the SWIFT Agreement, this is another example of the EU becoming a 'norm-taker' of US interests, especially considering that the EP could not fulfil all its expectations regarding SWIFT II, after it rejected the first agreement (Kaunert, Léonard and MacKenzie 2012: 476 and 487; Ripoll Servent and MacKenzie 2012: 73). SWIFT was due for renewal in 2015 (Archick 2013: 9). There is a possibility that the EU will propose some changes for the renewal, especially with regard to data protection, but for the moment it is mainly the US at the helm. Lastly, the CSI was also established because the US wanted to have US officers at EU ports.

All these international Agreements have brought changes to the EU's internal security policy. For instance, the future TFTS will mirror a similar US system (Bigo *et al* 2012: 5), and the EU PNR proposal resembles to a great extent the EU-US PNR Agreement. The EU-US data-sharing agreements have also influenced international Agreements between the EU and other third countries. Specially, PNR Agreements between the EU and Australia or Canada show this tendency.

I provide a brief outline of these two Agreements. About the EU-Canada PNR Agreement, the Canadian Government adopted a Customs Act requiring API and PNR data from all passengers arriving from outside the Canadian frontiers. As in the US, the Canada Border Services Agency (CBSA) threatened to fine all those airline companies that failed to comply with the mandate. However, the EU had a temporary derogation of such requirements since the EU law on data protection was seen as contrary to the Canadian measures. Hence, an EU agreement needed to be adopted. In 2005 the Commission launched a proposal for a Council decision on the conclusion of an agreement between the European Community and the Government of Canada on the processing of API and PNR data (COM(2005) 200 final). The proposed legislation had the purpose of preventing and combating terrorism and other serious crimes. As with the first EU-US PNR Agreement, it fell under the scope of the former Article 95 TEC. That international Agreement was signed in 2006, together with an adequacy decision (Commission Decision 2006/253/EC).

Nonetheless, at that time, the CJEU was reviewing the adequacy of the legal basis used for the EU-US PNR Agreement, so the EP adopted a legislative resolution rejecting the Canadian proposal (European Parliament 2005), as well as instructing the Council not to conclude the Agreement until the CJEU had delivered a verdict on the pending judgment. As seen earlier, the CJEU finally annulled Council Decision 2004/496/EC and Commission Decision 2004/535/EC so, consequently, the proposed council decision on PNR between the Community and Canada was never adopted. The adequacy decision expired in September 2009, and thus a new and permanent agreement was required by that time. In November 2010, the EP adopted a resolution encouraging the Commission to open new negotiations on behalf of the EU (European Parliament 2010e). A new EU-Canada Agreement was signed on 26 June 2014, but it is now awaiting the EP's consent.

Since the Lisbon Treaty, the EP can refer international agreements to the CJEU before voting if the institution has doubts on their legality. The EP has decided to make use of these new powers for the proposed EU-Canada PNR Agreement. Thus, using the arguments of the CJEU decision on the annulled Data Retention Directive, the EP has referred the proposal to the CJEU before it grants the approval. According to the EP:

> [T]here is legal uncertainty as to whether the draft agreement is compatible with the provisions of the Treaties (Article 16) and the Charter of Fundamental Rights of the European Union (Articles 7, 8 and 52(1)) as regards the right of individuals to protection of personal data; questions, further, the choice of legal basis, i.e. Articles 82(1)(d) and 87(2)(a) TFEU (police and judicial cooperation) rather than Article 16 TFEU (data protection).
>
> (European Parliament 2014: 4)

It remains to be seen whether the Court decides that the proposed EU-Canada PNR Agreement contradicts EU laws. If so, it could affect the validity of the current EU-US PNR Agreement as well as the EU-Australia PNR Agreement.

A few years after 9/11 the EU decided to sign a PNR agreement with Australia. It was concluded in June 2008 between the Australian Customs Service and the EU (Agreement 2008). However, with the entry into force of the Treaty of Lisbon the EU found a need to amend that Agreement. Negotiations for a new PNR agreement started on 2 December 2010 and, six months later, the Commission launched the proposal for the new EU-Australia PNR Agreement. On 22 September 2011 the Council gave the Agreement the green light and it was successfully voted on by the EP on 27 October 2011. The EU-Australia PNR Agreement was adopted under the framework of the Treaty of Lisbon and, therefore, it required the EP's approval.

The EU-Australia PNR Agreement clearly benefited from all the experience that the Commission had built up over many years during the negotiations of the EU-US PNR Agreements. At the same time, the EU-Australia PNR Agreement served as a reference for subsequent PNR agreements with the US (adopted in 2012) and Canada (still pending adoption). The three PNR Agreements that the EU has with the US, Australia and Canada have several similarities. They have the same provisions on purpose, adequacy level, processing of sensitive data, data security measures, oversight, transparency, access and correction of individual data, judicial redress, decisions based on automated processing, retention of data (five years),[44] logging and documentation of data processing, transfers through the push method[45] and the number of categories of collected data (19).

However, it would be incorrect to say that all EU agreements for the exchange of data follow the US interests. It is today beyond a doubt that, like the US, the

---

44 Surprisingly, the Australian Customs Service retains data for five and a half years, six months longer than the US and Canada.

45 Canada applied a push method from the beginning, in its first PNR Agreement in 2005; and even though Australia did not define it clearly in its first Agreement of 2008, the push method is expressly stated in its current PNR Agreement with the EU.

EU also has an enormous potential to influence third countries with respect to security policies. For example, in the SWIFT agreement, the EP promoted the elimination of bulk data transfers. Likewise, in the negotiations of the EU-US PNR Agreement, the US originally sought to retain the data for 50 years (Suda 2013: 780). Thanks to the EP this period was finally reduced to 15 years. Similarly, the EP succeeded in ensuring that the PNR transfers were carried out via the push method.

Moreover, the experience acquired by the Commission during the negotiations of the EU-US PNR Agreements was of great help for drafting other PNR agreements with third countries. The EU-Canada PNR Agreement is less intrusive than the EU-US PNR Agreement in terms of use of data (they will be used for offences punishable by at least four years in prison, versus the three years of imprisonment in the US agreement); deletion of sensitive data (in Canada data has to be deleted after 15 days, whereas in the US it is after 30 days), notification of the use of sensitive data (not existing in the US agreement), depersonalisation of data (after 30 days in Canada, and after six months in the US), disclosure of data (in Canada there is no onward transfer of data), and the frequency of transfers for a particular flight (there is no similar provision in the US agreement). Australia also applies these safeguards as for the scope of serious crime (the offences need to be of at least four years' imprisonment) and the frequency of transfers.[46]

It can be thus concluded that, when security norms arrived from the US, the EU 'did not simply subordinate to the security rules that the United States unilaterally strengthened' (Suda 2013: 783–784). The PNR schemes demonstrate that the EU has also contributed in establishing some limits to the US will. Recent improvements of data protection clauses are the result of years of negotiations and dialogue between the US authorities and the EU institutions. These same data protection provisions are also found in the Australian and Canadian PNR Agreements. Therefore, the EU also has an influence beyond the European borders on security issues, ensuring the compatibility of its international agreements with the EU data protection laws.

The number of PNR agreements concluded between the EU and third countries might increase in the coming years, including countries such as Japan, South Korea and the Kingdom of Saudi Arabia (Hernanz 2011: 6–7). As Argomaniz points out, US norms in the field of counter-terrorism could easily become universal standards (Argomaniz 2009: 132). However, there is one issue in which the EU could contribute and export its model globally: the EU data protection framework. The EU has always been characterised for having strong data protection and privacy laws, which have had an impact on many third countries, including the US.

---

46 Yet, Australia establishes stricter security measures than Canada and the US as regards the depersonalisation of PNR data, which is only conducted after three years, in contrast to the 30 days in Canada and six months in the US.

4 Concluding remarks

This analysis has demonstrated the increasing influence of the US authorities in shaping EU security measures consisting of transatlantic data exchanges. The EU emergence as an international actor goes hand in hand with the US lead in the adoption of international agreements between the two within the counter-terrorism environment. In line with the argument of many scholars (Matlary 2009; Kaunert and Zwolski 2013) the EU's role as foreign and security policy actor appears to be quite weak in practice. This study has confirmed that the EU has often adopted the US's own approach in the trade-off between security and data protection.

Each of the current EU-US data-sharing agreements has different data protection provisions. They also differ from the sections dedicated to data transfers to third countries in the current FD 2008/977 and the EU Police and Criminal Justice Data Protection Directive. The lack of harmonisation among these laws complicates the future establishment of an umbrella EU-US data protection agreement, as well as global data protection standards in the field of law enforcement.

As for the question of whether the right to data protection is equally applicable when the data is only processed within the EU territory – rather than beyond the EU borders, the answer is partially negative. Although the general EU provisions of FD 2008/977 on international data transfers are very limited in scope, specific EU-US data-sharing agreements (and mainly, the PNR Agreement) offer a complete data protection scheme for the exchange of information. The right to data protection is thus only weakened when the need for those data comes from beyond the EU territory and there is no specific international agreement in place. It has also been shown that, although the EU enjoys a specific legal basis on the right to data protection under Article 16 of the TFEU, the Treaty of Lisbon leaves the door open for the derogation of this provision if specific legislation is based on Article 39 TEU. This legal basis has never been used but it could eventually apply for CFSP measures.

Therefore, it can be concluded that external factors have played a fundamental role in the existing data protection legislation within the EU. The US, in particular, has exerted powerful external pressures in order to establish the right balance between security and data protection within the EU, even if it has entailed the weakening of the latter in certain circumstances. Following this same path, global data protection standards in the area of security might also come to be largely influenced by US needs in the future.

Bibliography

Agreement Between the United States of America and the European Police Office, 6 December 2001.

Agreement between the European Union and Australia on the processing and transfer of European Union-sourced passenger name record (PNR) data by air carriers to the Australian customs service, 8 August 2008.

Archick, K, 2013, 'U.S.-EU Cooperation against terrorism', *Congressional Research Service*, Report RS22030, pp. 1–24.

Argomaniz, J, 2009, 'When the EU is the "norm-taker": The Passenger Name Records Agreement and the EU's internalization of US border security norms', *Journal of European Integration*, vol. 31, no. 1, pp. 119–136.

Argomaniz, J, 2012, 'A rhetorical spillover? Exploring the link between the European Union Common Security and Defence Policy (CSDF) and the external dimension in the EU counterterrorism', *European Foreign Affairs Review*, vol. 17, no. 2/1, pp. 35–52.

Article 29 Data Protection Working Party, 1998, *Transfers of personal data to third countries: Applying Articles 25 and 26 of the EU data protection directive*, WP 12, 24 July 1998.

Article 29 Data Protection Working Party, 2006, *Opinion 10/2006 on the processing of personal data by the Society for Worldwide Interbank Financial Telecommunication (SWIFT)*, WP128, 22 November 2006.

Bamberger, K and Mulligan, D, 2013, 'Privacy on the ground: Governance choices and corporate practice in the U.S. and Europe', *George Washington Law Review*, vol. 81, no. 5, pp. 1529–1664.

Barros, X, 2012, 'The external dimension of EU counter-terrorism: The challenges of the European Parliament in front of the European Court of Justice', *European Security*, vol. 21, no. 4, pp. 518–536.

Bender, D, 2014, 'Why is the U.S. on the defensive?', *IAPP*, 14 March, https:// privacyassociation.org (accessed 8 November 2015).

Bigo, B, Carrera, C, Hayes, H, Hernanz, N and Jeandesboz, J, 2012, 'Justice and Home Affairs databases and a smart borders system at EU external borders. An evaluation of current and forthcoming proposals', *CEPS Paper in Liberty and Security in Europe*, no. 52, Brussels.

Blachier, G and Irish, J, 2015, 'France mobilizes 10,000 troops at home after Paris shootings', *Reuters*, 12 January, www.reuters.com (accessed 6 November 2015).

Blasi Casagran, C, 2013, 'People c. Harris: El lado oscuro de la libertad de expresión en las redes sociales' in L Cotino Hueso and L Corredoira Alfonso (eds), *Libertad de expresión e información en internet. Amenazas y protección de los derechos personales*, Centro Estudios Políticos y Constitucionales, Madrid, pp. 306–319.

Blasi Casagran, C and Blasi Casagran, E, 2012, 'Spain makes Google remove personal information from index', *Privacy, Laws & Business, International Report*, no. 120, pp. 27–30.

Boehm, F and Cole, MD, 2014, 'Data retention after the Judgement of the Court of Justice of the European Union', Greens/EFA Group, European Parliament, Brussels, www. janalbrecht.eu/fileadmin/material/Dokumente/Boehm_Cole_-_Data_Retention_ Study_-_June_2014.pdf (accessed 5 November 2015).

Cases C-317 and 318/04, *Parliament v Council and Commission* (CJEU, 30 May 2006).

Cases C-402/05 P and C-415/05 P, *Kadi and Al Barakaat International Foundation v Council and Commission* (CJEU, 3 September 2008).

Case *S. and Marper v the United Kingdom* [2008] ECHR 1581 (ECtHR, 4 December 2008).

Case C-130/10, *European Parliament v Council of the European Union* (CJEU, 19 July 2012).

Case C-130/10, *European Parliament v Council of the European Union*, Opinion of AG Bot, 31 January 2012.

Case C-658/11, *European Parliament v Council of the European Union*, Opinion of AG Bot, 30 January 2014.

Cases C-293/12 and C-594/12 *Digital Rights Ireland Ltd v Minister for Communications, Marine and Natural Resources and Others and Kärntner Landesregierung and Others* (CJEU, 8 April 2014).

Case C-131/12 *Google Spain SL, Google Inc. v Agencia Española de Protección de Datos (AEPD), Mario Costeja González* (CJEU, 13 May 2014).

Case No. 13-Mag-2814, *In the Matter of a Warrant to Search a Certain Email Account Controlled and Maintained by Microsoft Corporation* (United States District Court, Southern District of New York, 13 June 2014).

Case C-350/12 P, *Council of the European Union v Sophie in 't Veld* (CJEU, 3 July 2014).

Commission Decision 2004/535/EC of 14 May 2004 on the adequate protection of personal data contained in the Passenger Name Record of air passengers transferred to the United States' Bureau of Customs and Border Protection.

Commission Decision 2006/253/EC of 6 September 2005 on the adequate protection of personal data contained in the Passenger Name Record of air passengers transferred to the Canada Border Services Agency.

Communication from the Commission to the European Parliament and the Council – Transfer of Air Passenger Name Record (PNR) Data: A Global EU Approach, COM(2003) 826 final, 16 December 2003.

Communication from the Commission to the European Parliament and the Council enhancing police and customs co-operation in the European Union, COM(2004) 376 final, 18 May 2004.

Communication from the Commission to the European Parliament and the Council Towards enhancing access to information by law enforcement agencies, COM (2004) 429 final, 16 June 2004.

Communication from the Commission to the European Parliament and the Council on the prevention, preparedness and response to terrorist attack, COM(2004) 698 final, 20 October 2004.

Communication from the Commission to the European Parliament and the Council – Critical Infrastructure Protection in the fight against terrorism, COM(2004) 702 final, 20 October 2004.

Communication from the Commission to the European Parliament and the Council – Preparedness and consequence management in the fight against terrorism, COM(2004) 701 final, 20 October 2004.

Communication from the Commission to the European Parliament and the Council – On the Prevention of and the Fight against Terrorist Financing through measures to improve the exchange of information, to strengthen transparency and enhance the traceability of financial transactions, COM(2004) 700 final, 20 October 2004.

Communication from the Commission – A strategy on the external dimension of the area of freedom, security and justice, COM(2005) 491 final, 12 October 2005.

Communication from the Commission to the Council – Review of EU-Russia relations, COM(2008) 740 final, 5 November 2008.

Communication from the Commission to the European Parliament and the Council – The EU Internal Security Strategy in Action: Five steps towards a more secure Europe, COM(2010) 673 final, 22 November 2010.

Communication from the Commission to the European Parliament and the Council – Second Report on the implementation of the EU Internal Security Strategy, COM(2013) 179 final, 10 April 2013.

Coolsaet, R, 2010, 'EU counterterrorism strategy: Value added or chimera?', *International Affairs*, vol. 86, no. 4, pp. 857–873.

Council Act 2000/C 197/01 of 29 May 2000 establishing in accordance with Article 34 of the Treaty on European Union the Convention on Mutual Assistance in Criminal Matters between the Member States of the European Union.

Council Decision 2004/496/EC of 17 May 2004 on the conclusion of an Agreement between the European Community and the United States of America on the processing and transfer of PNR data by Air Carriers to the United States Department of Homeland Security, Bureau of Customs and Border Protection.

Council Decision 2006/729/CFSP/JHA of 16 October 2006 on the signing, on behalf of the European Union, of an Agreement between the European Union and the United States of America on the processing and transfer of passenger name record (PNR) data by air carriers to the United States Department of Homeland Security.

Council Decision 2007/551/CFSP/JHA of 23 July 2007 on the signing, on behalf of the European Union, of an Agreement between the European Union and the United States of America on the processing and transfer of Passenger Name Record (PNR) data by air carriers to the United States Department of Homeland Security (DHS) (2007 PNR Agreement).

Council Decision 2010/88/CFSP/JHA of 30 November 2009 on the signing, on behalf of the European Union, of the Agreement between the European Union and Japan on mutual legal assistance in criminal matters.

Council Decision 2012/471/EU of 13 December 2011 on the signing, on behalf of the Union, of the Agreement between the United States of America and the European Union on the use and transfer of Passenger Name Records to the United States Department of Homeland Security.

Council Framework Decision 2008/977/JHA of 27 November 2008 on the protection of personal data processed in the framework of police and judicial cooperation in criminal matters.

Council of Europe, 1981, *Convention for the Protection of Individuals with regard to Automatic Processing of Personal Data*, CETS no. 108, 28 January 1981.

Council of Europe, 2001, *Additional Protocol to the Convention for the Protection of Individuals with regard to Automatic Processing of Personal Data regarding supervisory authorities and transborder data flows*, ETS no. 181, November 2001.

Council of the European Union, 2001a, *Multi-Presidency Work Programme on external relations in the area of Justice and Home Affairs (2001–2002)*, Doc. 10741/01, 12 July 2001.

Council of the European Union, 2001b, *Conclusions adopted by the Council (Justice and Home Affairs)*, Doc. 12156/01, 25 September 2001.

Council of the European Union, 2003, *European Security Strategy A secure Europe in a better World*, 12 December 2003.

Council of the European Union 2004a, *Declaration on combating terrorism*, 25 March 2004.

Council of the European Union, 2004b, *EU-U.S. declaration on combating terrorism*, Doc. 10760/04 (Presse 205), 26 June 2004.

Council of the European Union 2005a, *Declaration on condemning the terrorist attacks on London*, 13 July 2005.

Council of the European Union, 2005b, *A Strategy for the External Dimension of JHA: Global Freedom, Security and Justice*, Doc. 14366/3/05, 30 November 2005.

Council of the European Union 2005c, *The European Union Counter-Terrorism Strategy*, Doc. 14469/05, 15 November 2005.

Council of the European Union, 2008, *Final Report by EU-US High Level Contact Group on information sharing and privacy and personal data protection*, 9831/08, 28 May 2008.

Council of the European Union, 2009, *EU/US agreements on extradition and on mutual legal assistance*, Doc. 14826/09 (Presse 303), 23 October 2009.

Council of the European Union, 2010a, *Draft Internal Security Strategy for the European Union: 'Towards a European Security Model'*, Doc. 5842/2/10, 23 February 2010.

Council of the European Union, 2010b, *EU-US and Member States 2010 Declaration on Counterterrorism*, 3 June 2010.

Council of the European Union, 2012a, *Implementation report on the Council Conclusions on enhancing the links between internal and external aspects of counter-terrorism*, Doc. 14819/1/12, 19 October 2012.

Council of the European Union, 2012b, *Questionnaire in preparation for the workshop on the application of the mutual legal assistance (MLA) and extradition agreements between the European*

Union and the United States of America (Eurojust, 25–26 October 2012), Doc. 14253/2/12, 24 October 2012.

Council Regulation (EU) No 1286/2009 of 22 December 2009 amending Regulation (EC) No 881/2002 imposing certain specific restrictive measures directed against certain persons and entities associated with Osama bin Laden, the Al-Qaeda network and the Taliban

Cremona, M, 2008a, *EU External Action in the JHA Domain: A Legal Perspective*, EUI Working Papers Law 2008/24, European University Institute, Florence, pp. 1–31.

Cremona, M, 2008b, 'Defining competence in EU external relations: Lessons from the treaty reform process' in A Dashwood and M Maresceau (eds), *Law and Practice of EU External Relations*, Cambridge University Press, Cambridge, pp. 34–69.

Cremona, M, 2009, 'EC competence, 'Smart Sanctions' and the Kadi case' in M Cremona, F Francioni and P Poli (eds), *Challenging the EU Counter-terrorism Measures through the Courts*, EUI Working Papers AEL 2009/10, Florence, pp. 71–98.

Cremona, M, 2011, *Justice and Home Affairs in a Globalised World: Ambitions and Reality in the Tale of the EU-US SWIFT Agreement*, Austrian Academy of Sciences, Institute for European Integration Research, Working Paper No. 04/2011, pp. 1–30.

Cross, MKC, 2013, 'A European transgovernmental intelligence network and the role of IntCen', *Perspectives on European Politics and Society*, vol. 14, no. 3, pp. 388–402.

Curtin, D, 2011, 'Top Secret Europe', Inaugural Lecture, *Universiteit van Amsterdam*, http:// dare.uva.nl/document/2/103309 (accessed 2 November 2015).

de Busser, E, 2009, *Data Protection in EU and US Criminal Cooperation: A Substantive Law Approach to the EU Internal and Transatlantic Cooperation in Criminal Matters between Judicial and Law Enforcement Authorities*, Maklu Publishers, Antwerpen.

de Goede, M, 2012, 'The SWIFT Affair and the global politics of European security', *Journal of Common Market Studies*, vol. 50, no. 2, pp. 214–230.

de Hert, P and Papakonstantinou, V, 2009a, 'The data protection framework decision of 27 November 2008 regarding police and judicial cooperation in criminal matters – A modest achievement however not the improvement some have hoped for', *Computer Law & Security Review*, vol. 25, pp. 403–414.

de Hert, P and Papakonstantinou, V, 2009b, 'The PNR Agreement and transatlantic anti-terrorism co-operation: No firm human rights framework on either side of the Atlantic', *Common Market Law Review*, vol. 46, pp. 885–919,

de Hert P and de Schutter, B, 2008, 'International transfers of data in the field of JHA: The lessons of Europol, PNR and Swift' in B Martenczuk and S van Thiel (eds), *Justice, Liberty, Security: New Challenges for EU External Relations, from Justice, Liberty, Security: New Challenges for EU External Relations*, VUBPress, Brussels, pp. 299–334.

Directive 95/46/EC of the European Parliament and of the Council of 24 October 1995 on the protection of individuals with regard to the processing of personal data and on the free movement of such data.

EDPS, 2012, *Opinion of the European Data Protection Supervisor on the data protection reform package*, 7 March 2012.

EEAS, 2013, *Strengthening Ties between CSDP and FSJ: Road Map implementation. Second annual progress report*, Doc. 02230/13, 14 November 2013.

EEAS, 2015a, *Ongoing Missions and Operations* (online), www.eeas.europa.eu/csdp/missions-and-operations/index_en.htm (accessed 6 November 2015).

EEAS, 2015b, *EUCAP SAHEL Niger* (online), www.eeas.europa.eu (accessed 6 November 2015).

EEAS, 2015c, *Strategy for Security and Development in the Sahel* (online), www.eeas.europa.eu (accessed 6 November 2015).

EEAS, 2015d, *European Union Border Assistance Mission to Moldova and Ukraine* (online), www.eeas.europa.eu (accessed 6 November 2015).

EUROMED, 2005, 'Code of Conduct on the Prevention of Terrorism', Barcelona, http://eeas.europa.eu/euromed/summit1105/terrorism_en.pdf (accessed 6 November 2015).

European Commission, 2013a, *The EU-US TFTP Agreement: Main elements*, MEMO/13/1060, 27 November 2013.

European Commission, 2013b, *Restoring Trust in EU-US data flows – Frequently Asked Questions*, MEMO/13/1059, 27 November 2013.

European Commission Proposal for a Regulation of the European Parliament and of the Council on the protection of individuals with regard to the processing of personal data and on the free movement of such data (General Data Protection Regulation), COM(2012) 11 final, 25 January 2012.

European Commission Proposal for a Directive on the protection of individuals with regard to the processing of personal data by competent authorities for the purposes of prevention, investigation, detection or prosecution of criminal offences or the execution of criminal penalties, and the free movement of such data, COM(2012) 10 final, 25 January 2012.

European Communities, 1990, Transatlantic Declaration on EC-US Relations, 1990, www.eeas.europa.eu/us/docs/trans_declaration_90_en.pdf (accessed 6 November 2015).

EU-Russia Summit, 2002, 'EU-Russia Joint Statement on Counter-terrorism', Brussels, 11 November 2002.

European Council, 1999, *Presidency conclusions of the Tampere European Council*, 15–16 October 1999.

European Council, 2000, *Santa Maria da Feira European Council, Conclusion of the Presidency*, 19–20 June 2000.

European Council, 2001, *Conclusions and Plan of Action of the Extraordinary European Council Meeting*, 21 September 2001.

European Council, 2002, *Seville European Council Presidency Conclusions*, 21–22 June 2002.

European Council, 2004, *Conceptual Framework on the ECDP dimension of the fight against terrorism*, 18 November 2004.

European Council, 2005, *The Hague Programme: Strengthening freedom, security and justice in the European Union*, 3 March 2005.

European Council, 2009, *The Stockholm Programme — An open and secure Europe serving and protecting citizens*, 2 December 2009.

European Parliament, 2004, *Resolution on the draft Commission decision noting the adequate level of protection provided for personal data contained in the Passenger Name Records (PNRs) transferred to the US Bureau of Customs and Border Protection (2004/2011(INI))*, 31 March 2004.

European Parliament, 2005, *Report on the proposal for a Council decision on the conclusion of an Agreement between the European Community and the Government of Canada on the processing of Advance Passenger Information (API)/Passenger Name Record (PNR) data (COM(2005)0200 – C6-0184/2005 – 2005/0095(CNS)) — Committee on Civil Liberties, Justice and Home Affairs*, 7 July 2005.

European Parliament, 2006, *EU-USA Transatlantic Partnership Agreement*, Doc. P6_TA(2006)0238, 1 June 2006.

European Parliament, 2007, *Resolution on SWIFT, the PNR agreement and the transatlantic dialogue on these issues*, Doc. P6_TA(2007)0039, 14 February 2007.

European Parliament, 2010a, *Resolution of 5 May 2010 on the launch of negotiations for Passenger Name Record (PNR) agreements with the United States, Australia and Canada*, Doc. P7_TA(2010)0144.

European Parliament, 2010b, *Recommendation on the proposal for a Council decision on the conclusion of the Agreement between the European Union and the United States of America on the processing and transfer of Financial Messaging Data from the European Union to the United States for purposes of the Terrorist Finance Tracking Program*, Doc. PE 438.440v02-00, 5 February 2010.

European Parliament, 2010c, *Legislative resolution of 11 February 2010 on the proposal for a Council decision on the conclusion of the Agreement between the European Union and the United States of America on the processing and transfer of Financial Messaging Data from the European Union to the United States for purposes of the Terrorist Finance Tracking Program (05305/1/2010 REV 1 – C7-0004/2010 – 2009/0190(NLE))*.

European Parliament, 2010d, *Recommendation on the draft Council decision on the conclusion of the Agreement between the European Union and the United States of America on the processing and transfer of Financial Messaging Data from the European Union to the United States for the purposes of the Terrorist Finance Tracking Program*, Doc. PE 445.596v02-00, 5 July 2010.

European Parliament, 2010e, *Resolution of 11 November 2010 on the global approach to transfers of passenger name record (PNR) data to third countries, and on the recommendations from the Commission to the Council to authorise the opening of negotiations between the European Union and Australia, Canada and the United States*, P7_TA-PROV(2010)0397.

European Parliament, 2012, *Resolution of 22 May 2012 on the European Union's Internal Security Strategy*, Doc. (2010)2308 (INI).

European Parliament, 2014, *Draft Motion for a Resolution pursuant to Rule 108(6) of the Rules of Procedure on seeking an opinion from the Court of Justice on the compatibility with the Treaties of the Agreement between Canada and the European Union on the transfer and processing of Passenger Name Record data (2014/2966(RSP))*, 19 November 2014.

Faull, J and Soreca, L, 2008, 'EU-US Relations in justice and Home Affairs' in B Martenczuk and S van Thiel (eds), *Justice, Liberty, Security: New Challenges for EU External Relations*, VUBPress, Brussels, pp. 393–420.

Ferreira-Pereira, LC and Oliveira Martins, B, 2012, 'The external dimension of the European Union's counter-terrorism: An introduction to empirical and theoretical developments', *European Security*, vol. 21, no. 4, pp. 459–473.

González Fuster, G, 2014, *The Emergence of Personal Data Protection as a Fundamental Right of the EU*, Springer, London.

Guasch Portas, V, 2014, *Las transferencias internacionales de datos en la normativa española y comunitaria*, Agencia Estatal Boletín Oficial del Estado, Madrid, pp. 46–55.

Hernanz, N, 2011, 'More surveillance, more security? The landscape of surveillance in Europe and challenges to data protection and privacy – Policy report on the proceedings of a conference at the European Parliament', *SAPIENT Deliverable 6.4*, www.sapient project.eu/docs/D6.4-Policy-Brief-submitted-January-2012-29.pdf (accessed 8 November 2015).

Hillebrand, C, 2012, *Networks in the European Union. Maintaining Democratic Legitimacy after 9/11*, Oxford University Press, Oxford.

Hinarejos, A, 2009, *Judicial Control in the European Union. Reforming Jurisdiction in the Intergovernmental Pillars*, Oxford Studies in European Law, Oxford University Press, Oxford, pp. 154–163.

Hondius, FW, 1983, 'A decade of international data protection', *Netherlands International Law Review*, vol. 30, no. 2, pp. 103–128.

Hughes, JT, 2013, 'Bridging the EU-US privacy gap', *IAPP*, 22 April, www.privacyassociation.org (accessed 8 November 2015).

Joint Review of the implementation of the Agreement between the European Union and the United States of America on the processing and transfer of passenger name records to the United States Department of

Homeland Security Accompanying the Report from the Commission to the European Parliament and to the Council on the joint review of the implementation of the Agreement between the European Union and the United States of America on the processing and transfer of passenger name records to the United States Department of Homeland Security, SEC(2013) 630 final, 27 Novemebr 2013.

Kaunert, C, Léonard, S and MacKenzie, A, 2012, 'The social construction of an EU interest in counter-terrorism: US influence and internal struggles in the cases of PNR and SWIFT', *European Security*, vol. 21, no. 4, pp. 474–496.

Kaunert, C and Zwolski, K, 2013, *The EU as a Global Security Actor: A Comprenhensive Analysis beyond CFSP and JHA*, Palgrave Studies in European Union Politics, Palgrave, Basingstoke.

Korff, D, 2015, 'Note on the EU-US Umbrella Data Protection Agreement', Fundamental Rights European Experts Group (FREE), DK/151014, 14 October 2015.

Kuner, C, 2013, 'The transatlantic divide over data privacy rights', *IAPP*, 20 May, www.privacyassociation.org (accessed 8 November 2015).

Kurowska, X and Pawlak, P, 2009, 'Introduction: The politics of European security policies', *Perspectives on European Politics and Society*, vol. 10 no. 4, pp. 474–485.

Lavenex, S and Wichmann N, 2009, 'The external governance of EU Internal Security', *Journal of European Integration*, vol. 31, no. 1, pp. 83–102.

Lichtblau, E and Risen, J, 2006, 'Bank data is sifted by U.S. in secret to block terror', *New York Times*, June 23, www.nytimes.com (accessed 7 November 2015).

Longo, F, 2013, 'Justice and Home Affairs as the new dimension of the European security concept', *European Foreign Affairs Review*, vol. 18, no. 1, pp. 29–46.

MacKenzie, A, 2012, 'The external dimension of European homeland security' in C Kaunert, S Léonard and P Pawlak (eds), *European Homeland Security. A European Strategy in the Making?*, Routledge, New York.

Matlary, JH, 2009, *European Union Security Dynamics. In the New National Interest*, Palgrave Macmillan, Basingstoke.

Monar, J, 2005, 'The European Union and the challenge of September 11, 2001: Potential and limits of a "new" actor in the fight against international terrorism' in P Eden and O'Donnell (eds), *September 11, 2001: A Turning Point in International and Domestic Law?*, Transnational Publishers, Inc, Ardsley, New York, pp. 387–419.

Monar, J, 2012, *The External Dimension of the EU's Area of Freedom, Security and Justice. Progress, Potential and Limitations after the Treaty of Lisbon*, Swedish Institute for European Policy Studies, report no.1, Stockholm.

Oliveira Martins, B and Ferreira-Pereira, LC, 2012, 'Stepping inside? CSDP missions and EU counter-terrorism', *European Security*, vol. 21, no. 4, pp. 537–556.

O'Neill, M, 2012, *The Evolving Counter-terrorism Legal Framework*, Routledge Research in EU Law, New York.

Ortiz, C, 2013, 'Security partnerships, intelligence and the recasting of the UK monopoly of violence in the 21st Century' in C Kaunert and S Léonard (eds), *Counter-terrorism and Intelligence in Europe*, Palgrave Macmillan, Basingstoke, pp. 215–228.

Pawlak, P, 2009a, 'The external dimension of the Area of Freedom, Security and Justice: Hijacker or hostage of cross-pillarization?', *Journal of European Integration*, vol. 31, no. 1, pp. 25–44.

Pawlak, P, 2009b, 'Network politics in transatlantic homeland security cooperation', *Perspectives on European Politics and Society*, vol. 10, no. 4, pp. 560–581.

Pawlak, P, 2012, 'Homeland security in the making American and European patterns of transformation' in C Kaunert, S Léonard and P Pawlak (eds), *European Homeland Security. A European Strategy in the Making?*, Routledge, New York, pp. 15–34.

Peers, S, 2012, 'Analysis. The Directive on data protection and law enforcement: A missed opportunity?', *Statewatch*, pp. 2–3, www.statewatch.com (accessed 4 November 2015).

Pell, SK, 2012, 'Systematic government access to private-sector data in the United States', *International Data Privacy Law*, vol. 2, no. 4, pp. 245–254.

Porter, AL and Bendiek, A, 2012, 'Counterterrorism cooperation in the transatlantic security community', *European Security*, vol. 21, no. 4, pp. 497–517.

Proposal for a Council Decision on the conclusion of an Agreement between the European Community and the Government of Canada on the processing of Advance Passenger Information (API) / Passenger Name Record (PNR) data, COM(2005) 200 final, 19 May 2005.

Pulido Gragera, J, 2004, 'El papel de la inteligencia en la PESD', *El papel de la inteligencia ante los retos de la seguridad y la defensa internacional*, Dirección General de Relaciones Institucionales de la Defensa. Instituto Español de Estudios Estratégicos, Grupo de Trabajo número 5/04, pp. 62–83.

Quesada Gámez, M and Mincheva, E, 2012, 'No data without protection? Re-thinking transatlantic information exchange for law enforcement purposes after Lisbon' in PJ Cardwell (ed), *EU external relations law and policy in the post-Lisbon era*, Springer, Berlin, pp. 287–312.

Randazzo, V, 2009, 'EU security policies and the pillar structure: A legal analysis', *Perspectives on European Politics and Society*, vol. 10, no. 4, pp. 506–522.

Reding, V, 2013, Speech on data protection at the Delegation of the European Union to the United States of America (online video), Washington, DC, 18 November 2013, www.euractiv.com/video/eu-commissioner-reding-us-meetin-531789 (accessed 7 November 2015).

Rees, W, 2011, *The US-EU Security Relationship: The Tensions between a European and a Global Agenda*, Palgrave Macmillan, Basingstoke.

Report from the Commission to the European Parliament and the Council on the joint review of the implementation of the Agreement between the European Union and the United States of America on the processing and transfer of passenger name records to the United States Department of Homeland Security, COM(2013) 844 final, 27 November 2013.

Ripoll Servent, A and MacKenzie, A, 2011, 'Is the EP still a data protection champion? The case of SWIFT', *Perspectives on European Politics and Society*, vol. 12, no. 4, pp. 390–406.

Ripoll Servent, A and MacKenzie, A, 2012, 'The European Parliament as a "norm taker"? EU-US relations after the SWIFT Agreement', *European Foreign Affairs Review*, vol. 17, Special Issue, pp. 71–86.

Rosenzweig, R, 2014, 'American privacy values vs. European perceptions', *The Business of General Technologies*, 8 August, http://fcw.com/ (accessed 8 November 2015).

Schroeder, UC, 2009, 'Strategy by stealth? The development of EU internal and external security strategies', *Perspectives on European Politics and Society*, vol. 10, no. 4, pp. 486–505.

Schwartz, PM, 2014, 'Differing privacy regimes: A mini-poll on mutual EU-US distrust', *IAPP*, 22 July, https://privacyassociation.org (accessed 8 November 2015).

Silk, 2015, *Transparency Reports Database* (online), https://transparency-reports.silk.co (accessed 7 November 2015).

Smith, JC, 2003, 'The USA Patriot Act: Violating reasonable expectations of privacy protected by the Fourth Amendment without advancing national security', *North Carolina Law Review*, vol. 82, pp. 412–455.

Statewatch, 2001, 'Text of US letter from Bush with demands for EU for cooperation', 1 November 2001, www.statewatch.org (accessed 6 November 2015).

Statewatch, 2004, 'European Parliament votes to go to court on EU-US PNR deal', 21 April 2004, www.statewatch.org (accessed 6 November 2015).

Statewatch, 2012, 'Plans emerge for the collection of personal data outside European borders to obtain comprehensive situational awareness and intelligence support', 30 October 2012, www.statewatch.org (accessed 6 November 2015).

Suda, Y, 2013, 'Transatlantic politics of data transfer: Extraterritoriality, counter-extraterritoriality and counter-terrorism', *Journal of Common Market Studies*, vol. 51, no. 4, pp. 772–788.

Sullivan, B, 2006, '"La difference" is stark in the EU, US privacy laws', *NBC News*, 1 October, www.nbcnews.com (accessed 8 November 2015).

Supplemental Agreement Between the Europol Police Office and the United States of America on the Exchange of Personal Data and Related Information, 20 December 2002.

Tene, O, 2014, 'The U.S.-EU privacy debate: Conventional wisdom is wrong', *Privacy Perspectives*, 4 March, https://privacyassociation.org (accessed 8 November 2015).

Trauner, F and Carrapiço, H, 2012, 'The external dimension of EU Justice and Home Affairs after the Lisbon Treaty: Analysing the dynamics of expansion and diversification', *European Foreign Affairs Review*, vol. 17, no. 2/1, pp. 1–18.

Travis, A, 2011, 'US to store passenger data for 15 years', *The Guardian*, 25 May, www.theguardian.com (accessed 6 November 2015).

United Nations Office on Drugs and Crime, 2012, *The Use of the Internet for Terrorist Purposes*, September 2012, New York, pp. 90–91, www.unodc.org (accessed 6 November 2015).

United Nations Security Council, 2001, *Threats to international peace and security caused by terrorist acts*, Resolution 1373(2001), 4385th meeting, 28 September 2001, United Nations, New York.

US Act to reform the intelligence community and the intelligence and intelligence-related activities of the United States Government, and for other purposes, Pub.L. 108–458, December 2004, www.gpo.gov/fdsys/pkg/PLAW-108publ458/pdf/PLAW-108publ458.pdf (accessed 6 November 2015).

US Aviation and Transportation Security Act, Pub.L. 107–71, 115 STAT. 597, 19 November 2001.

US Central Intelligence Agency, 2003, 'The national strategy for combating terrorism', 17 December 2003, www.cia.gov (accessed 8 November 2015).

US Department of Homeland Security, 2008, 'The removal of a Canadian citizen to Syria', *Office of Inspector General*, OIG-08-18, March 2008, www.oig.dhs.gov/assets/Mgmt/OIGr_08-18_Jun08.pdf (accessed 8 November 2015).

US Department of Homeland Security, 2013, 'A report on the use and transfer of Passenger Name Records between the European Union and the United States', Privacy Office, 3 July 2013.

US Federal Register, 2004, *Undertakings of the Department of Homeland Security, Customs and Border Protection*, vol. 69, no.131, 6 July 2004.

US Homeland Security Committee, 2011, Subcommittee Hearing: Intelligence Sharing and Terrorist Travel: How DHS Addresses the Mission of Providing Security, Facilitating Commerce and Protecting Privacy for Passengers Engaged in International Travel, 5 November 2011, http://homeland.house.gov (accessed 8 November 2015).

US House Committee on Homeland Security, 2011, 'How DHS Addresses the Mission of Providing Security, Facilitating Commerce and Protecting Privacy for Passengers Engaged in International Travel', Subcommittee on Counterterrorism and Intelligence, 112th Congress, 5 October 2011.

US Mission to the EU, 2012, Remarks by U.S. Ambassador to the EU, William E. Kennard, at Forum Europe's 3rd Annual European Data Protection and Privacy Conference, 4 December 2012, http://useu.usmission.gov/data_privacy.html (accessed 8 November 2015).

US State Department, 2012, 'Five Myths Regarding Privacy and Law Enforcement Access to Personal Information in the European Union and the United States', 4 December 2012.

Van Elsuwege, P, 2014, 'The interface between the Area of Freedom, Security and Justice and the Common Foreign and Security Policy in the European Union: Legal constraints to political objectives' in RL Holzhacker and P Luif (eds), *Freedom, Security and Justice in the European Union. Internal and External Dimensions of Increased Cooperation after the Lisbon Treaty*, Springer, Berlin, pp. 119–135.

Vodafone, 2014, 'Law Enforcement Disclosure Report', June 2014, www.vodafone.com (accessed 7 November 2015).

Wesseling, M, 2014, 'Evaluation of EU measures to combat terrorist financing', European Parliament, Directorate General for Internal Policies, Policy Department C, Citizens' rights and Constitutional Affairs, Brussels.

Wesser, RA, 2010, 'Cross-pillar mixity: Combining competences in the conclusion of EU international agreements' in C Hillion and P Koutrakos (eds), *Mixed Agreements Revisited. The EU and its Member States in the World*, Hart Publishing, pp. 30–55.

Wesser, RA, Marin, L and Matera, C, 2011, 'The external dimension of the EU's Area of Freedom, Security and Justice' in C Eckes and T Konstadinides (eds), *Crime within the Area of Freedom, Security and Justice. A European Public Order*, Cambridge University Press, Cambridge, pp. 272–300.

White House, 2011, National Agenda for Counterterrorism, 6 June 2011, www.whitehouse. gov/sites/default/files/counterterrorism_strategy.pdf (accessed 6 November 2015).

White House, 2013, 'Liberty and Security on a changing world. Report and Recommendations of The President's Review Group on Intelligence and Communications Technologies', 12 December 2013.

Wolf, C and Maxwell, W, 2012, 'So close, yet so far apart: The EU and U.S. visions of a new privacy framework', *Antitrust*, vol. 26, no. 3, pp. 8–13.

Wolf, S, 2009, 'The Mediterranean dimension of EU counter-terrorism', *European Integration*, vol. 31, no. 1, pp. 137–156.

Wolff, S, Wichmann, N and Mounier, G, 2009, 'The external dimension of justice and home affairs: A different security agenda for the EU?', *European Integration*, vol. 31, no. 1, pp. 9–23.

3 The role of Europol in the exchange of information within and beyond the EU

Within the EU AFSJ, Europol is the agency that stores the largest amount of information. Its scope covers any crime affecting a common interest within the EU, organised crime, terrorism and other forms of serious crimes involving two or more Member States. As noted in the Stockholm Programme, Europol is a 'hub for information exchange between the law enforcement authorities of the Member States, a service provider and a platform for law enforcement services' (European Council 2009: 20). Europol also processes information from non-EU countries, since third countries have been increasingly involving it in their criminal investigations.

The previous chapters illustrate the challenges that the EU encounters in the exchange of crime-related information within and outside the European territory. After examining the main failures in the functioning of the EU data-sharing tools, this chapter analyses whether the EU could enhance the use of Europol as a way to reduce the existing diversity of communication channels available for law enforcement authorities.

In addition, it examines whether Europol's legal framework offers strong data protection rules that could inspire the future data protection legal framework at the international level. As concluded in the previous chapters, the EU cannot become a global regulator on data protection in the field of law enforcement without first achieving a coherent framework among its own Member States. Neither Member States nor the Commission have been capable of achieving that coherence so far, and the Police and Criminal Justice Data Protection Directive does not seem to improve this situation either.

This chapter is divided into three parts. The first part is an examination of whether Europol's data protection regime could be used as a reference for Member States when processing data within the EU for law enforcement purposes. The second part looks at the international actorness of Europol in the field of security. It analyses to what extent Europol influences (and will continue to influence) third countries' data protection rules. I reserve the final section of this chapter for the analysis of the difficulties that currently exist with regard to the use of the agency's data protection and data security standards within and beyond the EU. In short, this study helps to conclude whether Europol's data protection system could be the solution for achieving an approximation of national data protection regimes for data transfers conducted within and beyond the EU borders.

1 The origins and aim of Europol

Europol was first regulated in the Treaty of Maastricht[1] as a way to contribute to a safer Europe (Council of the European Union 2012a: 13). It began functioning in 1994 as the EDU, within the framework of TREVI III, which dealt with drug-trafficking and money-laundering cases. EDU had no competence to store personal data and the information collected could not be transferred to third countries or international bodies (Hillebrand 2012: 61).

Europol extended its competences in 1995, covering for the first time counter-terrorism (CT) investigations (O'Neill 2012: 71–72). Rules governing that body were enclosed in the Europol Convention, which was ratified by all Member States in 1999. From that moment, Europol became the European law enforcement organisation in charge of assisting 24/7 the competent authorities in Member States and third countries for the prevention and combat of serious forms of crime. Yet, one of the main Europol's limitations is that its officers are not armed and they have no power to arrest. Europol is principally a hub of information, which interconnects national law enforcement activities within the EU, co-ordinates joint operations and receives and distributes information (Europol 2010).

Since 9/11, several structural changes have been implemented at Europol's headquarters. One of them was the establishment of a new unit, the so-called Counter-terrorism Task Force (CTTF), comprised of police agents and intelligence analysts from the Member States. In 2003, the mandate of this unit was amended and taken over by the Serious Crime Unit (Bures and Ahern 2007: 199). The Commission encouraged Member States to give enhanced operational competences to this unit (MEMO/04/66, p. 8). However, even today numerous Member States are reluctant to do this, so the unit maintains its original powers.

Europol's tasks have evolved since the moment the Europol Convention came into force. In fact, in Tampere (1999), Hague (2004) and Stockholm (2009) the Commission suggested enhancing the role of Europol in co-operation with the Member States and other EU bodies. The main amendment has been the replacement of the convention by a Council decision. The ECD was proposed by the Commission in late 2006 and finally adopted in April 2009 (Council Decision 2009/371/JHA). It came into force in January 2010, when Europol became a full EU agency.

Today, Europol is the largest AFSJ agency. The list of crimes in which Europol can be involved is found in the annexes of the current ECD and the proposed Europol Regulation (COM(2013) 173 final, Annex 1). The Treaty of Lisbon introduced significant changes with respect to Europol. First, the agency now has

---

1 The first legal basis for the establishment of Europol was Articles K1(9) and K3 of the Maastricht Treaty.

an explicit legal basis in Article 88 TFEU. This provision permits the amendment of Europol's laws without having to be ratified first by the 28 Member States. In fact, the existence of Article 88 has triggered a process to replace the current ECD with the above-mentioned Europol Regulation, proposed by the Commission in 2013. Another important change since the Treaty of Lisbon is that Europol's activities are scrutinised by both the EP and the national parliaments (NPs). Moreover, Europol is now financed by the EU, and the agency is composed of EU staff (Boehm 2012a: 179). All of these new issues bring the agency closer to the current EU institutions.

Europol is often involved in JITs to support Member States in the preparation and co-ordination of criminal investigations. The JIT principle was first included in the Treaty of Amsterdam (ex Article 30(2)(a) TEU) and it was later reinforced after the 9/11 terrorist attacks (Council Framework Decision 2002/465/JHA). Europol can participate in JITs under three conditions: (a) the involvement must be expressly requested by a Member State; (b) the JIT must include at least two Member States; and (c) the offence investigated must fall under Europol's mandate (de Buck 2007: 257). If these conditions are met, Europol can be part of an investigation team for a fixed period of time.

2 Europol's data exchanges within the EU

In addition to Europol's general purpose of supporting and strengthening national law enforcement authorities' action in the prevention and combat of crimes, Article 5 ECD lists a few other more specific tasks. One of these tasks is 'to collect, store, process, analyse and exchange information', usually sent by Member States. As a result, large amounts of personal data are currently stored in Europol's files. These are analysed by Europol officers and exchanged between its units, Member States and even third parties.

Europol offers strong data protection and data security safeguards in the processing of data. In fact, the JSB has described Europol's data protection framework as one of the strongest in the world, because the agency has 'strict, tailor-made rules and efficient supervision arrangements' (Joint Supervisory Body 2013a: 2). This section pays special attention to Europol's communication tool, the Secure Information Exchange Network (SIENA). It stands out for being a very secure system for data processing, and it also complies with the purpose limitation principle. Taking this as a premise, I scrutinise whether Europol's data protection regime could be used as a reference for Member States. This analysis also includes a study of the proposed Europol Regulation.

2.1 The increasing involvement of Europol in the data-sharing procedures within the EU

As noted above, Europol is currently the biggest AFSJ agency, covering any serious crime affecting two or more Member States, or the EU itself. Europol provides a platform for the exchange of criminal intelligence and information (COM(2012)

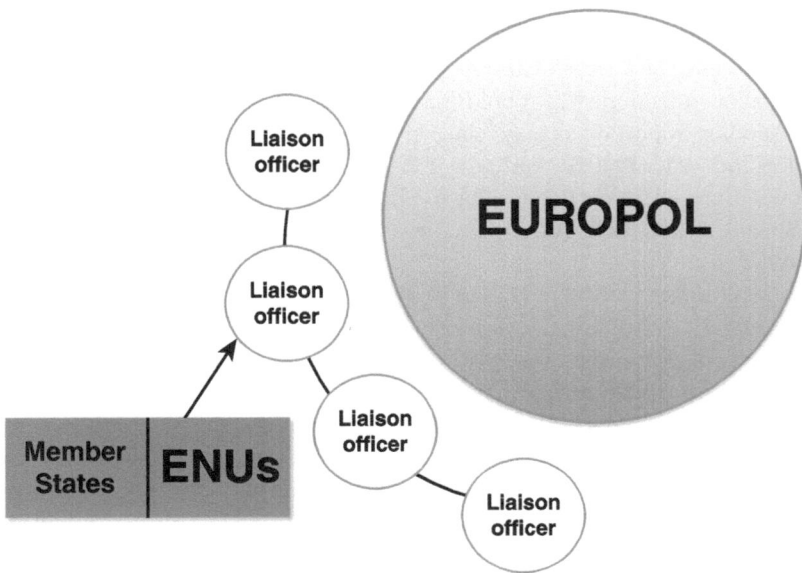

Figure 3.1

735 final), processing a large amount of data every day. A considerable part of such data is first collected by national law enforcement authorities,[2] which follow the rules in the Council decision on the exchange of information and co-operation concerning terrorist offences (Council Decision 2005/671/JHA). This act sets out the conditions under which the information has to be sent to Europol.

The common procedure for transferring information from a Member State to Europol is illustrated above.

As perceived from Figure 3.1, the contact point between Europol and Member States is usually through the so-called ENUs (Article 8 ECD), although Article 7(5) of the proposed regulation allows establishing contact with any 'competent authority of a Member State'. Thus, when it enters into force, Europol will be able to make direct contact with national law enforcement authorities without going through the national contact point. By having direct contact with law enforcement authorities in the Member States, Europol will also prevent clashing with police operations among Member States in cross-border investigations.

Each Member State has an ENU. They were introduced in 2010 with the adoption of the ECD. ENUs have access to the Europol Information System (EIS) when they need to search for information on individuals with factual indications or reasonable grounds to believe that they have committed (or will commit) criminal offences within the Europol's mandate. Before ENUs were established, such information was only accessible via Europol's liaison officers.

2 Data might also come from another EU agency or EU information system, private entities, third countries and international organisations.

Although, as Chapter 1 shows, Member States are free to choose the channel for exchanging information between them, ENUs are the only possible channel for exchanging information with Europol. ENUs are used in any case where Europol is involved, but they may also be used by Member States to exchange information bilaterally for crimes outside Europol's mandate. ENUs can exchange information directly or through the so-called Europol Liaison Officers, who are part of an ENU but stationed at Europol's headquarters (COM(2012) 735 final, pp. 5–6; COM(2013) 173 final, Article 8). Each ENU seconds at least one liaison officer to Europol in the Europol Liaison Bureaux, and there are currently a total of 160 liaison officers in The Hague (Council of the European Union 2014a: 20). They provide Europol with information of the particular Member State 24/7, and they assist in the exchange of information. Regarding the data access that liaison officers have to the national law enforcement's databases, it varies from one country to another. For instance, in some Member States such as Spain, liaison officers always need to contact the Spanish ENU in order to get access to Spanish police databases, whereas in Finland liaison officers have direct access to all Finnish databases.

Member States have no clear obligation to provide information to Europol under the ECD (Disley *et al* 2012: 47); and the agency does not have, in principle, access to Member States' national law enforcement databases. Member States are divided when it comes to transferring information to Europol for the prevention and investigation of crimes. Some of them are convinced of the added value of the agency and rely on the support that Europol can give to their own work (Vermeulen and Wills 2011: 17). They often request Europol's assistance during the investigation of a crime. Yet, other Member States do not provide Europol with sufficient information (EDPS 2013: 7–8), or they simply do not share information with Europol at all. This is mainly due to a lack of confidence and trust among such Member States about the added value that the agency can provide (Bures 2008: 498).

Law enforcement authorities of Member States can decide not to involve Europol in a criminal investigation by using other communication channels such as the Swedish initiative and Prüm decision. As seen in Chapter 1, these are multilateral EU instruments for exchanging criminal information among Member States. However, the use of the Swedish initiative and Prüm decision does not always exclude Europol. For instance, Europol is informed of a request made through the Swedish initiative each time this falls within the agency's mandate (Council of the European Union 2011a: 8). Likewise, Europol officials can issue a request using the Swedish initiative, in accordance with Europol's laws. In such a case, the channel used is either the liaison officers or the ENUs directly, and the information is transferred via SIENA. Also, specific handling codes in addition to the conditions established in the Swedish initiative have to be fulfilled for such requests (Council of the European Union 2011a: 4). After that, the information will be transmitted to the specific analysis work files (AWFs), the EIS or the Europol Operational Centre (Council of the European Union 2010: 9).

Europol also has a role in the use of Prüm decisions. In January 2012, Europol's Prüm Helpdesk and the Mobile Competence Team (MCT) were established. The purpose of both initiatives was to prepare a platform for experts, which would help Member States implement and run Prüm systems (Council of the European Union 2012a: 31). The MCT, operational since 18 July 2011, transferred all its activities to the Europol's Prüm Helpdesk in July 2013 (COM(2012) 732 final, p. 8). Hence, Europol is helping Member States exchange DNA, fingerprint and vehicle registration data that might then be shared with the agency.

Likewise, Europol has access to data obtained through VIS, SIS/SIS II, CIS and Eurodac.[3] This has raised concerns among privacy experts, who have argued that it might undermine the EU fundamental principles of purpose limitation and non-discrimination (Boehm 2012b: 342). However, in my view the main concern regards the national police authorities' data processing in the first place. Data processed by Europol goes through periodical auditing sessions, uses specific communication tools and applies a common level of protection for all types of information. In contrast, national law enforcement authorities use diverse communication tools and standards when they exchange VIS, SIS, CIS and Eurodac data with each other. Therefore, Member States could take Europol's infrastructures and systems as a model, as well as SIENA as default communication tool. This is examined in the next section.

2.2 The use of SIENA as default communication tool within the EU

2.2.1 Background

Europol has its own communication tool, called SIENA. It became operational in July 2009 and it is the backbone of Europol's infrastructure. It consists of a tailor-made messaging system, which carries no risk of interception due to its secure and user-friendly design (Disley *et al* 2012: 78).

SIENA is not the first communication tool used by Europol. Before 2009, Europol used a system called Information Exchange System (InfoEx). It was established in 1996 under the Europol Convention. However, in November 2005, with the prospect of a forthcoming legislative amendment in Europol, the idea for replacing InfoEx with a new application was proposed. SIENA was first discussed during the first half of 2007, and after an exhaustive privacy assessment by the JSB, it was approved by the Europol Management Board (MB) in July 2007. The designing of the new-generation communication tool commenced in October 2007. It offered a range of innovative functionalities such as the availability of the tool to the users of ENUs, Liaison Officers and Europol staff.

It can be seen above that Europol usually contacts Member States through ENUs in the terms of Article 8 ECD. ENUs use SIENA as the communication

---

3 Article 7 of VIS Council Decision 2008/633/JHA; Articles 41, 42 and 43 of SIS II Council Decision 2007/533/JHA; Articles 11(1) and 12(1) of CIS Council Decision 2009/917; and Article 7 of the Eurodac Regulation 603/2013.

tool with Europol. Likewise, SIENA is used by: (a) Member States' liaison officers; (b) seconded national experts; (c) Europol officials at Europol headquarters; (d) some colleagues in other designated competent authorities besides ENUs; and (e) some of the third parties with which Europol has concluded co-operation agreements (Disley *et al* 2012: 78). On 1 July 2009 SIENA became technically available for all ENUs, but Member States needed time for its implementation.

2.2.2 SIENA phases

SIENA has been evolving since July 2009. The first phase (SIENA v1.0, v1.1 and v1.2) was available until March 2010, at which time the second version of this tool (SIENA v2.0) was adopted. The new version introduced functionalities such as the extension to other designated authorities in Member States, and the access for third parties that had operational agreements with Europol. By mid-2011, SIENA v2.1 enhanced the availability to third parties holding a strategic agreement with Europol.

SIENA v2.2 was operational for the period 2012–2013. It included new functionalities such as: (a) the integration with national systems;[4] (b) the capability to multitask; and (c) the establishment of the European Multidisciplinary Platform against Criminal Threats (EMPACT) to set impact priority in the messages (e.g. messages referring to the Western Balkans).

SIENA v2.3 was implemented in the third quarter of 2013, and it introduced one major change: a Universal Message Format (UMF) Prüm form, through which a pdf form used for Prüm data exchanges was available within SIENA for Member States. That provided a glimpse of the future link between Prüm and SIENA, enhancing its use in investigations in which Europol was not directly involved. That also solved the lack of a common communication channel following Prüm hits (Council of the European Union 2014b: 7).

SIENA v2.4 incorporated the UMF II format. That was the second phase of the EU-funded project led by Europol called UMF. UMF is a structured data format in the SIENA messages that offers 'an additional service for those Member States that wish to automate parts of the workflows of international law enforcement cooperation' (Council of the European Union 2011b: 26). That phase of the UMF programme presented advantages in terms of cost savings, better use of resources, elimination of manual re-entry of data and reduction of copying errors (COM(2012) 735 final, p. 12).

In 2014, SIENA III was established. It enhanced interoperability between the national case management and the system by offering features such as faster searches and task assignment tools (Council of the European Union 2014c: 2). During 2015, the updated tool sought to integrate the Europol Analysis System (EAS), convert the UMF to a human readable format, prepare the embedding of

---

4 For the moment only Germany benefits from this functionality, being able to use its own national channel, the SIENA and Interpol channel all at once.

FIUs into SIENA and explore the upgrade of the tool to carry confidential material, among other issues (Council of the European Union 2015: 37).

Taking the above-mentioned into account, SIENA's evolution shows the clear intention of Europol to accommodate other EU channels like the Swedish initiative and Prüm in its own tailor-made communication tool. This tool brings national law enforcement authorities and Europol closer in the exchange of criminal information.

2.2.3 The scope of SIENA

Ninety-five per cent of Europol's information arrives through SIENA. It creates more than 38,000 SIENA messages per month (Council of the European Union 2014a: 13). The tool was originally developed for data exchanges between the agency and law enforcement agencies in the Member States (COM(2012) 735 final, p. 6), but a growing number of non-EU countries and third parties have been added to the system through the conclusion of co-operation agreements (Council of the European Union 2012a: 20 and 23).

Although in the majority of cases SIENA supports follow-up searches in the EIS, the tool can also be used for the exchange of information between Member States outside Europol's mandate (Article 8(4) of the Europol Regulation). For instance, in 2012 Member States used SIENA to exchange 222,000 messages; but only in 53 per cent of those was the information in the message shared with Europol (COM(2012) 735 final, p. 6).

Europol, the Commission and the Council are now encouraging Member States to use SIENA as the default system for exchanging crime-related information and intelligence (Europol 2012: 24; COM(2012) 735 final, p. 9; Council of the European Union 2014b: 2). In this sense, a Single Point of Contact (SPOC) will be established in every Member State, which will use all existing communication tools, including SIENA. An extended use of SIENA will not replace the use of other reliable channels for exchanging information among Member States (Council of the European Union 2013a: 7), but it will integrate all of them into a single communication tool.

2.2.4 Advantages of using SIENA as EU default communication tool

SIENA is mostly used for communications between law enforcement authorities and Europol, but it can also be extensively used for other data-processing systems in the future. In this sense, for instance, the Commission announced in January 2015 that the updated version of the EU PNR Directive will establish SIENA as the channel to exchange data among national PIUs, and also with Europol. In the same way, SIENA could be the tool for exchanging financial data according to the future TFTS, or even for exchanging data among intelligence services within the EU if they choose to use this tool.[5]

5 An exhaustive study of the intelligence services of the Member States and their role at the EU level is conducted in Chapter 4.

There are several advantages in using SIENA as the default communication tool by national law enforcement authorities. First, the system is in line with the privacy-by-design principle. As defined by the former EDPS Peter Hustinx, the principle of privacy-by-design means that 'controllers should be able to demonstrate that appropriate measures have been taken to ensure that privacy requirements have been met in the design of their systems' (Hustinx 2012). In fact, although this tool does not find any explicit legal basis in the ECD, the inclusion of the privacy-by-design principle and other data protection requirements have been present in SIENA since the very beginning. Throughout the different phases, SIENA has built a system that conforms to Europol's data protection and data security standards. For example, it only allows authorised staff to access the tool; and it processes specific categories of data in accordance to the purpose limitation principle. When a new SIENA request is launched by one of the authorised actors (e.g. if the Spanish ENU contacts the French Liaison Office for a child pornography investigation), a number of data categories need to be filled in. It includes the cybercrime area, EMPACT, crime-related content, handling codes,[6] reliability (e.g. A1), priority (high, normal, low), and the deadline (e.g. seven days).

Second, the increasing use of SIENA among Member States reduces the processing of mass data (e.g. bulk passenger lists) as a preventive measure. In Europol, mass data is only retained in very specific cases, and for a short period of time. Moreover, names included in mass lists are only disclosed after a positive hit. In contrast, if Member States use other communication tools such as regular email, there is no tracking of the amount of data processed, nor the period of time it will be stored in the particular server.

Third, SIENA is a multilingual interface, which permits operators at ENUs to communicate in their own national language (Council of the European Union 2014b: 5). This makes the system very efficient, since it does not require any translation of the messages, which might slow down a criminal investigation.

Notwithstanding the above-mentioned positive aspects, there would a few shortcomings if SIENA was established as the default communication tool within the EU. First, neither the current ECD nor the proposed Regulation[7] contains any mention of SIENA. This is a missed opportunity to regulate and enhance the use of the tool. Second, a problem encountered in the use of SIENA is that some Member States might prefer other channels instead. Some Member States do not see sufficient added value in Europol's tasks and findings, so they do not provide Europol with all the necessary information to fight serious cross-border crimes. These Member States prefer to use other channels such as Interpol,

---

6 There are currently three handling codes available with the following description: H1: Not to be used as evidence in a judicial procedure without permission; H2: No dissemination of the information without permission; and H3: any other restriction.

7 The ECD does not include any explicit provision of SIENA either. Even though it could have been included in the provision on AWFs, but this did not occur.

because it is more flexible and it includes the possibility for transferring judicial information (not only police information). Third, some Member States have not fully implemented the SIENA data protection features (Joint Supervisory Body 2013a: 4), and this technical obstacle impedes their use of the tool. Fourth, SIENA only exchanges information classified up to EU Restricted. It excludes any information filed as Secret or Top Secret – which makes it less likely to be used by intelligence/security services. In this sense, the Council has recommended increasing the SIENA confidentiality level in order to extend its use (Council of the European Union 2014b: 8). Lastly, another flaw of SIENA is that this tool offers a standardised channel to be utilised by all law enforcement agencies in the EU, but it excludes any information exchanged by intelligence services.

2.3. Europol's data protection regime

The compliance of SIENA with the privacy-by-design approach shows the significance that the right of data protection and privacy have for Europol. The agency claims to have one of the strongest data protection regimes in the world (Europol 2010: 4 and 11), with higher standards than those found in the majority of Member States. This section focuses on the examination of three main data protection safeguards in Europol: the compliance with the purpose limitation principle; the right of access, correction and deletion of data; and the external supervision by an independent body.

2.3.1. Purpose limitation principle

The current ECD processes personal data through two different systems: the EIS and the AWF. The former processes data introduced by Member States – and Europol itself in the case of third-country data – and it is used for cross-checking purposes. According to the last Europol General Report, information from nearly 71,000 people is held in the EIS (Council of the European Union 2014a: 17). The purpose limitation principle applies here, since the data processed belongs only and exclusively to either criminals or suspects of a criminal offence. The objective is to provide Member States with relevant information for future investigations involving such criminals or suspects of a crime.

Regarding the AWFs, they have a completely different *raison d'être*. It is a system that provides information within a specific criminal investigation, and supports either strategic analysis or operational cases. AWFs process information not only from criminals and suspects of a crime, but also from victims, witnesses and other relevant contacts. Yet, the AWFs are also structured in a way that complies with the purpose limitation principle.

There are currently two AWFs: the AWF for data on serious and organised crime (SOC) and the AWF on CT data. Each of these work files include different focal points or target groups separated by their crime area, as seen in the table below.

Table 3.1

AWF SOC		
MTIC	SUSTRANS	MONITOR
CANNABIS	PHOENIX	TWINS
COPPER	TERMINAL	CYBORG
HEROIN	CHECK POINT	COPY
SMOKE	EEOC	GNST

AWF CT				
HYDRA	DOLPHIN	TFTP	CHECK THE WEB	PIRACY

Today there are 25 different focal points,[8] many of which include target groups. Each focal point stores different types of data complying with the purpose limitation principle. The annex of each focal point regulation, developed by the Europol analysts themselves, details what types of data can be processed. For instance, in the focal point HEROIN, dealing with investigations related to heroin dealers and heroin trafficking, any data concerning an alleged victim is hardly justified as necessary for such investigations. In the same way, any sensitive data relating to the sexual orientation of a drug dealer is also considered unnecessary and, therefore, not processed. In contrast, for the focal point TWINS, which deals with child pornography cases, information about victims or the sexual orientation of the offender might be relevant for the investigation and, hence, processed.

Europol analysts working in focal points tend to follow the list of categories of data that they normally need to process during an ongoing investigation. Moreover, regular audits conducted by the Europol Data Protection Office (DPO) take place to supervise the adequacy of the data processed. One of the tasks of the DPO is drafting the audit plan for the coming year. It then scrutinises the selected focal point and verifies that the information processed is in line with the purpose limitation, proportionality and necessity principles.

Another mechanism – not foreseen in the legislation – which reinforces the compliance with the purpose limitation principle in both the EIS and the AWFs is the use of the so-called 'handling codes' for any information up to EU Restricted.[9] Every time a piece of information is sent by a Member State to Europol, an opening order is filled in, and the Member State has the competence to decide the restriction level applied for that particular information. This is possible through the handling codes. There are currently four handling codes available: (a) H0 or

8 Until 2011 there were 23 AWFs. Then they were reduced to two, and the concept of focal point and target groups was introduced. That new structure permitted an extended use of the Index Function, which is now able to search data among the different focal points in a common AWF.
9 There is currently a Europol initiative to allow handling codes up to Confidential.

no-handling, which permits the distribution to all Member States as long as it is necessary for the purpose of preventing and combating crimes; (b) H1, which prevents the information to be disclosed in judicial proceedings without the permission of the provider; (c) H2, by which cross-matched information cannot be disseminated without the permission of the provider; and (d) H3, which allows free text for other restrictions (e.g. only accessible for a specific target group).

The Member State originally providing the information to Europol is also in charge of deciding the level of classification – public, restricted, secret, top secret. That Member State has discretion in making that decision, and Europol cannot modify it without prior consent from the country (Abazi 2013: 14). Data access by Europol officials will depend on the level of security: officials with higher data security clearance will gain access to more classified information than those with low or no clearance.

2.3.2 Right of access, correction and deletion of data

The right of access is established in Article 30 ECD. According to this provision, individuals who want to access data that Europol stores about them need to contact the competent national authorities, normally the national DPA or a special police department. The procedure can be explained through the following hypothetical situation:

A German man, whose name is Paul, wants to access data about him held on Europol's databases. First, he needs to issue the request to the Bundeskriminalamt in Germany. He will be required to send a copy of his ID or passport and a letter with the data request by post. The Bundeskriminalamt will then notify Europol of the particular query within one month.[10] The agency will check all systems and

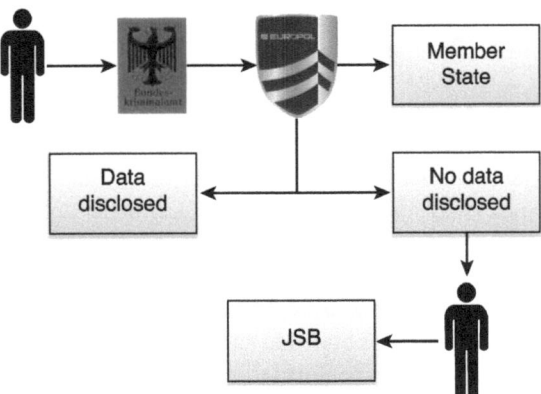

Figure 3.2

---

10 Some individuals contact Europol through their solicitor instead. This is also possible as long as the individual has signed a letter authorising it.

databases, and respond to Paul directly within the period of three months. If there is no hit, the agency sends a message to Paul explaining that there is no information held about him in the systems. If, on the contrary, there is a hit, Europol contacts the Member State that owns the information, which ultimately authorises the data disclosure. It might occur that there is an ongoing investigation in relation to Paul or that, by releasing it, national security is jeopardised. In such cases, the information is not revealed. Hence, Paul will only get access to his data if there is no objection by the country originally owning the data.

In case of a refusal, Paul can still appeal to the JSB, which will conduct an inspection at the Europol's premises, making sure that the request has been properly addressed. It is worth noting that the responsibility always lies with Europol, even if the agency has only followed orders from a Member State. If the JSB finds that Europol has failed to comply with the right of access, Paul may receive compensation for the damage.

Articles 31 and 32 ECD address the right to correct and delete information. The same procedure as in the right of access applies here. For instance, it could occur that Paul already knows that Europol has information about him, and has asked for the deletion of that information because it is not accurate. In this case, Europol will contact the Member State owning the information to determine whether it can be deleted. If the answer is positive, Europol will proceed to remove Paul's data from its databases. As in the right of access, the right to correct and delete information provide the possibility to appeal before the JSB. Yet, one of the problems detected is that, even once the information is corrected or removed from Europol databases, there is no efficient mechanism to certify that it has also been modified in the particular Member State.

2.3.3 Europol's oversight

Europol has a model supervisory scheme composed of two bodies: the Europol DPO and the JSB. Despite the existing complementarity between them, they play different roles in the protection of the data processed by Europol, as examined below.

The DPO is part of the agency's staff and, therefore, carries out an internal form of supervision, which according to Article 28 ECD is independent from the rest of Europol's activities (Disley *et al* 2012: 5). The DPO has many mechanisms at its disposal to ensure that Europol complies with the data protection rules. In this sense, Article 28(4) ECD establishes that:

> If the Data Protection Officer considers that the provisions of this Decision concerning the processing of personal data have not been complied with, he or she shall inform the Director, requiring him or her to resolve the non-compliance within a specified time.

However, the position of the DPO is at times a difficult one. Despite its formal independence, the office's funds come directly from Europol's budget. Therefore, the DPO has a dual role. One the one hand, it must ensure compliance of the agency, working hand in hand with the analysts responsible for the processing of personal data, and advising them on the spot (rather than *ex post*). On the other hand, the DPO must offer loyalty to the agency.

Besides the DPO, Europol has another oversight mechanism via the JSB. Although some scholars have criticised the JSB for its lack of objectivity (Hillebrand 2012: 175),[11] this body is composed of representatives from national DPAs and is, therefore, completely independent from Europol. The JSB, operational since 1998, aims at reviewing that the processing of personal data from Europol to other parties is carried out according to the agency's data protection principles (Disley *et al* 2012: 96).

The JSB carries out periodic inspections and external audits with the purpose of verifying whether Europol has properly implemented the data protection rules. It is not a judicial body, so it cannot impose sanctions in a case where Europol infringes a rule. However, its reports have always had a great political influence. In case of a violation, Article 34(4) ECD establishes that the JSB will require the Director of Europol to address the issue. The JSB is also the only body entitled to decide whether a recommendation has been adequately fulfilled.[12]Furthermore, it submits periodical reports to the EP and the Council,[13] and carries out appeal functions for data access requests (Scherrer, Jeandesboz and Guittet 2011: 49).

2.4 Main features in the proposed Europol regulation

On 27 March 2013 the Commission launched a proposal for a Europol regulation, which will replace the current ECD (COM(2013) 173 final). One of the goals of the proposal is to increase the flow of information on crime to Europol (Council of the European Union 2013b: 3). Although this enhancement has raised concerns among Member States and scholars, the proposal should be perceived as a positive development for the following reasons: first, Europol has gradually built a co-ordinated and efficient infrastructure which connects all Member States in the prevention and investigation of crimes. Second, the agency offers high standards in terms of data security, mainly through the SIENA tool. Lastly, Europol's data protection safeguards are robust and strong, and the guarantees it offers to individuals are often higher than those in the national legal frameworks. Yet, the proposed regulation also introduces some issues of debate, which will be addressed in this section.

2.4.1 Enhanced powers of Europol

The Treaty of Lisbon has introduced significant changes with respect to Europol. The agency now has an explicit legal basis in Article 88 TFEU, whose

---

11 Especially when it approved the first Europol-US Agreement.
12 This could at times be an obstacle since Europol is not always capable of implementing the JSB recommendations, sometimes for budget reasons, sometimes for the lack of resources needed.
13 Unfortunately, JSB reports on data protection aspects are not public.

first paragraph is also found in the proposed Europol regulation.[14] Two new main functions of Europol are: (a) it co-ordinates investigations; and (b) it has broader powers to retrieve and process information.

The co-ordination role was given to Europol in December 2009, with the entry into force of the Treaty of Lisbon. Article 88(2) TFEU states that Europol has competence to co-ordinate criminal investigations together with the Member States. Keeping the same wording, the proposed Europol regulation establishes that Europol has the duty to 'coordinate, organise and implement investigative and operational action' in Article 4(1)(c). Yet, the Regulation does not establish particular rules on how Europol and the Member States should distribute their competences when they work together in an investigation (Joint Supervisory Body 2013a: 6).

The possibility for Europol to participate in JITs is kept in Articles 4(1)(d) and 5 of the proposed regulation, with a clearer wording than that found in the current ECD. JITs allow participants to access information stored in Europol's databases and, at the same time, Europol can obtain new information and add it in its systems. Another new feature is that there is no longer a need for prior arrangement if Europol wants to participate in JITs. This will facilitate the involvement of Europol in the investigations. In addition, Article 5(3) states that Europol will 'take measures to assist [Member States] in setting up the joint investigation team'. Although this paragraph is somewhat symbolic, it enhances the role of Europol and is necessary for Europol in relation to the JITs.

Europol's co-ordination role is found in several other provisions of the proposal. For instance, Article 4(1)(g) permits Europol to 'develop, share and promote specialist knowledge of crime prevention methods, investigative procedures and technical and forensic methods, and to provide advice to Member States'. Likewise, Article 4(1)(h) allows Europol to provide technical and financial support to Member States; and Article 4(1)(l) empowers the agency to develop centres of specialised expertise for combating certain types of crime (e.g. the current European Cybercrime Centre (EC3) or the office for counterfeiting). Article 6 on Europol's requests to initiate criminal investigations does not present many changes from the wording in the current ECD. The only new issue is the need to inform Eurojust in some cases (Articles 6(1) and (5)) and the one-month deadline for the Member States to initiate the investigation (Article 6(4)).

The proposal also enhances Europol's access to crime-related information. It is particularly foreseen in Article 7 of the proposed regulation. Article 7(5) introduces an obligation for Member States to provide the agency with information. Yet, the ownership remains with the Member States, so it will ultimately have to authorise such data access.

Within this context, Article 23(3) of the proposed regulation states that 'Europol may retrieve and process information, including personal data, from information systems, of a national, Union or international nature'. Under the current legal

---

14 Moreover, Article 88, para. 2(b) TFEU is reproduced in Article 4 of the proposed regulation.

framework, the agency can only access information that national authorities have introduced to Europol's databases.[15] However, the practice shows that several Europol Liaison Officers have access to national police databases in their own countries, according to their security clearance. Therefore, and despite the EDPS opposition to such provision (EDPS 2013: 24), it seems reasonable that the Commission adds a legal basis for this, underlining that it will be possible 'in so far as authorised by Union, international or national legal instruments'.

2.4.2 Data protection

Although the JSB has argued that the draft regulation might result in a weaker Europol data protection regime (Joint Supervisory Body 2013a: 2), data protection rules will not necessarily lose strength under this new act. One of the amendments to be highlighted is that, for the first time, data protection rules are all in one single instrument. Following the previous structure, this section examines whether the new regulation will comply with the purpose limitation principle; the right of access, correction and deletion of data; and the external supervision by an independent body.

A. THE PURPOSE LIMITATION PRINCIPLE

The proposal introduces a more flexible system for the processing of personal data, which does not require specific data systems as in the current ECD. Data processing will depend on dataset levels. According to the explanatory memorandum on the proposal, the reason for this change is 'to better establish links between data already in its possession and subsequently analysing them' (COM(2013) 173 final, p. 7). However, in line with the JSB argument, the reduction from 23 to two AWFs in May 2012 was created for this same purpose, and therefore the Commission's argument seems out of date (Joint Supervisory Body 2013a: 8). Particularly, Article 24(1) establishes that:

> Europol shall process data, including personal data only for the purposes of: a) cross-checking aimed at identifying connections between information, b) analyses of a strategic or thematic nature, c) operational analyses in specific cases.

From Article 24 it is deduced that the new data processing structure will consist of a single depository with different data set levels of processing. It will be only capable to store data for three specific purposes, namely, cross-checking, strategic analyses and operational analyses. The first debate encountered on this issue is that it is hard to see how the future single 'EIS' is going to function. The regulation does not include any indication on this issue other than stating that

15 This is also foreseen in Article 7(5) of the proposed regulation.

privacy-by-design will be introduced (Joint Supervisory Body 2013a: 9). Considering that the current ECD also complies with the privacy-by-design principle, the only difference in the proposed regulation is that the system will no longer apply as a large-scale tool, but rather in a small-scale manner.

The Commission has justified the introduction of this new approach by stressing that the technical separation between the EIS and the AWFs is inefficient, since 'data must be stored at least twice (or three times) with duplicated obligations for the data owner as well as for Europol to maintain (update, delete) the data' (SWD(2013) 99 final, p. 3). For this reason, the Commission has decided that data protection rules in the future Europol regulation will no longer be 'database-oriented', but data protection safeguards will be rather attached to each piece and type of data (SWD(2013) 99 final, p. 5).

Although there is a significant chance that the current Europol systems are replaced by a single depository, the agency might maintain the existing structure in the future. In fact, oversight bodies such as the JSB and the EDPS have recognised the compliance of the existing AWFs and the EIS with the purpose limitation principle (EDPS 2013: 10). They have also expressed doubts about a future new structure, since Article 24 is presented in a very broad and ambiguous way, and it needs to be concretised (EDPS 2013: 12–13). Specifically, the JSB has highlighted its opposition to this more flexible information technology (IT) structure, stressing that the purpose limitation and the necessity principles are already applied in the current ECD through the flexibility clause (Joint Supervisory Body 2013a: 2–3).

The second debate refers to the scope of Article 24, which limits the data processing to purposes of cross-checking, strategic analyses and operational analyses. In the current ECD there is a flexibility clause allowing the creation of new information systems other than those expressly foreseen in the law – however, these must be authorised by the MB, the Director and the JSB in the terms of Article 10(2) ECD. The fact that this clause has never been used to date confirms that the current system is sufficiently flexible (Joint Supervisory Body 2013a: 9).

A similar flexibility clause is not found in the proposed regulation. Many Europol officials argue that this limitation of purposes for data processing will be a step backwards for the agency, which seeks to enhance its competences and become more operational in the future. For instance, under the future regulation, Europol will never be able to create a public portal for 'most wanted people' (similar to that found on the FBI website). Such a portal does not correspond to any of the three purposes listed in Article 24(1), so it would never be possible under the proposed regulation.

Therefore, the Council has suggested an amendment that would include a fourth purpose allowing Europol to process information for 'facilitating the exchange of information between Member States, Europol, other Union bodies, third countries and international organisations' (Council of the European Union 2014d, Article 24(1)(d)). If accepted by the Commission and the EP, it would maintain the current existing possibilities under Article 10 ECD.

Article 25 also refers to the purpose limitation principle. This provision tackles the need for Member States, EU bodies, third countries or international organisations to decide for what purpose the information is processed. If they fail to do so, Europol will take the decision. The EDPS has expressed its opposition to leaving the decision in the hands of Europol (EDPS 2013: 25). However, this is already occurring under the current system: information introduced mainly by Member States arrives at the department O1 by default. Department O1 decides whether the information is relevant and, if so, it is distributed to the other departments (e.g. AWF focal point TWINS). If not, the information is deleted from the pool within a period of six months.

B. RIGHT OF ACCESS, CORRECTION AND DELETION OF DATA

Any individual whose data is stored in the Europol database has, as in the current ECD, the right to access, correct, delete and block data, the right to a judicial remedy[16] and the right to compensation for damages or unlawful data processing. The only difference from the current legal framework is that, in the proposed regulation, the appellate body will be the EDPS instead of the JSB.

For the rest, there are no changes on this issue. The only criticism on individual rights has been raised by the EDPS, which has suggested modifying the wording of Article 39 for a more plain language (EDPS 2013: 28). In my view, however, this provision does not present complexities as it is drafted. In fact, the practice shows that the data access procedure is working well at Europol. The DPO responds to all data requests in a clear and efficient manner, despite the high number of queries lately. In seven years the number of data requests received by Europol has increased from 10 to 600, but each of these requests has been properly examined on a case-by-case basis.

C. EXTERNAL SUPERVISION OF EUROPOL'S DATA PROCESSING

Europol's supervisory body will be modified under the proposed regulation. According to the proposal, the supervision of Europol's data processing will be conducted by the EDPS, replacing the current JSB. The main reason for this change is that Europol became a full EU agency in 2009. Before Lisbon, Europol was a third-pillar organisation subject to an intergovernmental convention ratified by all Member States in 1998. Therefore, its activities were supervised by an independent body, the JSB, in accordance with the convention and within the scope of the former third pillar.

The EDPS is today in charge of supervising the EU institutions and bodies' compliance with data protection rules – including AFSJ agencies such as Frontex and the new agency for large-scale IT systems (eu-LISA) (Regulation (EC) 45/2001). The only agencies that still have their own supervisory bodies are

---

16 The current ECD only allows the judicial redress for access, not for correction or deletion. In the proposed regulation any processing activity can be challenged to the EDPS and appealed to the CJEU. See Articles 49 and 50 of the Europol Regulation.

Europol and Eurojust. Therefore, the proposed Europol regulation (and also the proposed Eurojust regulation) will align the supervisory mechanisms of all agencies and bodies of the EU.[17]

The EDPS has participated actively in the drafting of the proposal, and has expressed satisfaction with the new Article 46 (EDPS 2013: 2). On the contrary, the director of Europol and many powerful countries such as the UK, Germany and Sweden have stressed their discontent about the replacement of the current JSB with the EDPS. The JSB has also highlighted its objection to giving the EDPS the sole responsibility for Europol's supervision. Instead, it suggests creating an independent structure with equal participation of each national DPA, the EDPS and the Europol DPO (Joint Supervisory Body 2013a: 3 and 10).

The EDPS's supervisory role will consist of carrying out prior checks,[18] consultations, complaint handling,[19] visits and inspections (EDPS 2013: 15). In addition, the body will authorise automated processing of sensitive personal data, investigate complaints lodged by data subjects and carry out 'joint supervisions' with national supervisory authorities in some cases. Lastly, according to Article 37(3) of the Europol Regulation, the EDPS will be informed if Europol stores data for more than five years.

Pursuant to Article 46(3)(f) of the Europol Regulation, the EDPS will have powers to rectify, block, erase or destroy data; to refer a matter to the CJEU, and even to impose temporary or definitive bans for data processing. This last new power has been received with criticism among Member States and Europol, and, therefore, the body has clarified that it will be, in any circumstance, a very exceptional remedy (EDPS 2013: 16). Articles 47 and 49(2) of the proposal refer to the national authorities' co-operation with the EDPS. These provisions are particularly relevant considering the EDPS's lack of experience in auditing and inspecting Europol. The fact that the legislator has foreseen the possibility for national experts (for instance, the current JSB members) to participate in these EDPS audits is thus seen as a positive development.

The proposed regulation also gives the EP stronger supervisory powers in Articles 53 and 54. This new role has its origins in Articles 88(2) and 218(6) TFEU. Since the Treaty of Lisbon, the EP has been co-legislator in the AFSJ, which means that the EP plays an important role in 'ensuring that these agencies fulfil their mandates effectively' (Vermeulen and Wills 2011: 19). Since the current ECD was adopted before the Treaty of Lisbon, these new EP competences are not regulated (Hillebrand 2013). Therefore, Europol's draft regulation incorporates several provisions promoting the co-operation between the EP competences and the NPs in the scrutiny of Europol.

Under the current ECD, the EP only controls Europol's policies, administration and financial aspects. Articles 62(2) and 53(1) of the Europol Regulation show that

---

17 The EDPS today supervises more than 60 institutions and bodies.
18 The EDPS has issued more than 600 opinions on prior checks to date.
19 The EDPS has received more than 650 complaints to date.

these competences are enlarged in the future Europol regulation. The proposal adds the following new tasks for the EP: (a) the MB will have to consult the EP (and the NPs) on the annual programme (Article 15(4)); (b) the EP (and the NPs) will receive strategic analysis, non-confidential threats, situation studies and evaluations and working arrangements from Europol (Article 53(3)); (c) the EP will be able to make requests for classified and sensitive non-classified information (Article 54);[20] (d) the EP will receive all activity reports from Europol: (e) the Director of Europol will send reports to the EP;[21] and (f) the EP will appoint the Europol's Executive Director (Article 56(2)).

It is yet unclear how the EP will actually adapt its infrastructures according to these new tasks. Some scholars state that the EP will create an oversight sub-committee of LIBE called the Parliamentary Scrutiny Unit, which will have access to privileged information (Vermeulen and Wills 2011; Abazi 2014: 1132). However, as Abazi points out, it might clash with the principle of originator control (Abazi 2014). According to this principle, Member States originally sharing confidential information with Europol will retain the powers to decide whether the information can be accessed by the EP or not. Therefore, the new EP scrutiny competence might be *de facto* limited.

Lastly, when the proposed regulation enters into force, the agency will fall under the CJEU's full jurisdiction. It conforms to Protocol 36 attached to the Treaty of Lisbon. Article 10(2) of that protocol specifically states that the amendment of an act adopted before the treaty will entail the applicability of new powers by the Commission – which will have competence to launch an infringement procedure – and the CJEU.

2.5 Comparison with data protection standards in the Member States

After examining the data protection rules in the current ECD and the future Europol regulation, this section compares Europol's provisions with data protection rules in some Member States. The particular Member States chosen for this study are Bulgaria, Finland, Greece, Poland and Spain.[22]

As shown in Table 3.2, law enforcement authorities of the Member States often use regular email or the telephone to communicate with each other during a criminal investigation. Some departments also have encrypted channels of communication, but not all of them. The problem with not having secured communication tools is that crime-related data can easily be intercepted or accessed by third persons.

One of the data protection principles ensured by Europol is the purpose limitation principle. According to this rule, personal data collected and processed

---

20 It is expected that both institutions will conclude a working arrangement on that issue in the future.

21 The Council has suggested that the appearance of the Executive Director before the EP will only be to discuss non-operational matters.

22 This choice is based on the interviews that the author conducted during 2013 and 2014 with several police officers of these Member States.

Table 3.2

	Communication channel	Purpose limitation principle	Retention period	Independent oversight body	Audits	Right of access, modification, deletion
Europol	SIENA	Yes	– As long as necessary – Reviews after 3 years	– Europol DPO – JSB	Yes	Yes
Bulgaria	– Email – Special encrypted channel	Yes	As long as necessary	No	Yes, annually	No
Finland	– Email – Telephone – Fax – Intelligence blogs – SIENA	No	It depends on the seriousness of the crime Automated deletion	– National Police Board – Parliamentary ombudsman	Yes, annually	Yes, once a year free of charge
Greece	– Closed secure network – Hard copies of documents – Telephone	No	Unlimited	No	Unknown	Unknown
Poland	– Email – Fax – Cryptofax – Special mail for secret information – SIENA/Interpol/Sirene channels	Yes	– As long as necessary – 10 years for intelligence	Data protection department	Yes, annually	Yes
Spain	– Sistema de información policial (SIP) – Radio conference – Telephone – SIENA/Interpol/Sirene	No	As long as necessary	No	Yes, every 2 years	Yes

for one purpose may not be used later for other unrelated purposes. Law enforcement authorities in the Member States do not always comply with the principle. In several countries, if a piece of data is introduced in the database, it remains in the system for 'as long as necessary'. Normally, police officers have different levels of clearance. Officers with high levels of clearance are able to access any data in the system relevant to their investigation, and use them for any 'necessary' purpose within the scope of their duties.

Only two of the countries examined in this study have data protection departments in charge of overseeing that information stored in the law enforcement database is adequately processed. The majority of countries do not have independent bodies that control data processed by law enforcement authorities. Annual audits are conducted, but it is not always clear by whom and how police databases are scrutinised. An example of adequate data protection audits is found in Finland. Finnish law enforcement authorities are subject to annual audit plans that define the amount, targets and the themes. Audits are carried out by the National Police Board Audit Unit. This unit conducts a comprehensive inspection, which includes an in-depth examination of data protection issues. Besides this, Finnish police offices have other type of audits, conducted by a specific police unit. Lastly, the collection of intelligence is controlled by the Finnish parliamentary ombudsman.

Most of the Member States offer citizens the possibility to access their personal data. However, the procedure is subject to broad limitations and it varies from one country to the other. In Spain, for instance, police officers have one month to respond from the moment they receive the request. Yet, according to the Spanish law, data controllers (police) can deny the access, modification and suppression of data if it jeopardises national security, the freedoms and rights of a third person or any ongoing investigation.

For all said above it can be concluded that, in the processing of information, both the current ECD and the proposed Europol regulation offer higher data protection standards than the majority of safeguards applied within the Member States. Therefore, in principle, the Europol data protection framework could be taken as a model for Member States in the future.

3 Europol's data exchanges beyond the EU

It is well known that 9/11 set in motion the creation of a global security infrastructure. The goal was to create a global system that would connect law enforcement authorities in different countries for the prevention of similar terrorist attacks. At the EU level, measures on issues related to criminal law and external relations fell under the scope of the intergovernmental competence – former second and third pillars. Yet, due to the increasing number of cross-border crimes and the fear of global terrorism, EU institutions started to propose initiatives within the scope of the external dimension of the JHA pillar. In this regard, on 21 September 2001, the European Council expressed its determination to elevate Europol to 'an effective information and intelligence exchange medium'

(Bures and Ahern 2007: 196). One of the EU goals was to achieve a coherent external relations' framework between Europol and third parties, as part of the overall EU external action (Council of the European Union 2005; Disley *et al* 2012: 107).

Today, Europol is not only the EU agency dealing with the largest amount of information within the EU, but it also has an important role with respect to the exchange of data outside the European territory. The agency exchanges more than 20,000 messages a year with third parties, retrieving personal as well as non-personal data (UK House of Lords 2008: 20–21). Consequently, external activities of Europol have not only led to the strengthening of the internal security architecture within the EU Member States, but they have also had an influence on the EU's external security decisions (Mounier 2009: 593 and 597).

The impact of Europol on external matters tackles both the CFSP and the AFSJ. Regarding the CFSP, Europol exchanges information with military agents within the context of EU's civilian CSDP missions. On the external dimension of the AFSJ, Europol has numerous co-operation agreements with third countries. These co-operation agreements will be precisely the focus of this section. Europol's co-operation agreements are separated from the international agreements signed between the EU as a whole and third countries. Yet, Europol's agreements have often positioned the EU security policy as a reference for third countries, since such third countries had to implement Europol's data protection standards as a condition for the agreement. Because of this, I will examine whether Europol is becoming a normative actor within the area of the EU external relations.

This section looks first at the current legal instruments used by Europol for the exchange of data with third parties, focusing on Europol's co-operation agreements. After that, it analyses the special relationship existing between Europol and the US. These parties have two co-operation agreements, one supplementing the other, signed in 2001 and 2002 respectively. In addition, Europol has developed a relevant role in transfers of financial data taking place between the European company SWIFT and the US DHS. The last part of the section discusses the proposed Europol regulation and the changes it introduces with regard to Europol's data transfers to third countries.

3.1 Europol co-operation agreements with third parties

Europol is not only in charge of giving support to the Member States in the prevention, combat or investigation of crimes, but it also has a legal personality to negotiate and conclude co-operation agreements with third parties as part of its external relations (Mounier 2009: 586).

The Council of Ministers is the European institution in charge of laying down rules governing Europol's external relations. In line with Article 42 of the former Europol Convention, the Council adopted on 3 November 1998 an act on the rules governing Europol's external relations with third states and non-EU related bodies (Council Act of 3 November 1998). That act established the following main features: (a) the possibility to incorporate liaison officers at Europol's headquarters; (b) the opportunity to organise missions by Europol staff to the relevant third states or non-EU related bodies; and (c) the possibility to establish regular meetings between Europol and third parties.

The act also regulated the participation of the Council of Ministers during the negotiations and adoption of co-operation agreements in Article 2. Particularly, the Council is first entitled to draft a list of the third states and international organisations accepted for starting negotiations with Europol. Then, the Council has to authorise Europol's Director to enter into negotiations with the specific third country. After the negotiations, which take around two years on average (Mounier 2009: 588–589),[23] the Council will also authorise the conclusion of the agreement. In that sense, current Article 23(2) ECD adds that co-operation agreements with third states may be concluded 'only after the approval by the Council [. . .] and, as far as it concerns the exchange of personal data, obtained the opinion of the Joint Supervisory Body via the Management Board'.

Europol co-operates externally with 18 non-EU countries to date: Albania, Australia, Bosnia & Herzegovina, Canada, Colombia, Former Yugoslav Republic of Macedonia, Iceland, Liechtenstein, Moldova, Monaco, Montenegro, Norway, Republic of Serbia, Russia, Switzerland, Turkey, Ukraine and the US (Council of the European Union 2012a: 105). As examined below, some of these countries have concluded an operational agreement with Europol, whereas others have only a strategic agreement in force.

The agency has also concluded agreements with nine EU bodies and agencies, as well as with three international organisations, including Interpol. It is also worth mentioning that Europol hosts liaison officers from nine non-EU countries and organisations, which are Albania, Australia, Canada, Colombia, Iceland, Norway, Switzerland, Interpol and some US law enforcement agencies. Regarding the future co-operation agreements with Europol, negotiations have recently started in Brazil, Mexico, Georgia and the United Arab Emirates (Statewatch 2013).

As for the exchange of information between Europol and a third party, the Council did not adopt specific rules on this issue until 2009, exactly one day before the Treaty of Lisbon entered into force. Particularly, Council Decision 2009/934/JHA establishes the implementing rules on Europol's exchange of personal data and non-personal data with third parties, including a list of third states and organisations with which Europol can conclude agreements.

Article 23(2) ECD states that 'such agreements may concern the exchange of operational, strategic or technical information, including personal data and classified information, if transmitted via a designated contact point'. There are thus two types of co-operation agreements that Europol can conclude with third countries and international organisations: (a) strategic agreements, which do not exchange personal data; and (b) operational agreements, which do allow the transfer of personal data. For exceptional situations, the ECD establishes the possibility to share information with third states without a co-operation agreement, in the terms of Article 23(8) and (9) ECD.

23 For instance, negotiations between Europol and Colombia took around two years.

3.1.1 Strategic agreements

Europol currently has strategic agreements with the following third countries: Albania, Australia, Bosnia Herzegovina, Canada, Colombia, Iceland, Macedonia, Moldova, Montenegro, Norway, Serbia, Switzerland, Liechtenstein, the US, Turkey and Ukraine.[24] A strategic agreement between Europol and a third state, as the name indicates, only allows the exchange of strategic and technical information. Strategic information includes, for instance, enforcement actions to suppress offences, trends in the methods used to commit them and threat assessments. Similarly, technical information deals with any data about investigative procedures, crime intelligence analytical methods and forensic police methods, to name a few. Any transmission of data related to an identified or identifiable person falls outside of the scope of these agreements.

Strategic agreements permit the designation of the National Bureau of Europol in the police directorate of the third country. This bureau acts as a national contact point and participates regularly in high-level meetings with Europol. It is also in charge of the majority of information exchanges between both parties. Interestingly, liaison officers of a third country can be appointed even if there is no operational agreement between Europol and the third country. For instance, this was the case of Colombia and Albania before 2013. Both countries had only strategic agreements with the agency but they had liaison officers at Europol's premises – yet, they did not process personal data.

Two other observations need to be made with regard to strategic agreements. First, these agreements normally include a provision prohibiting the onward transfer of the information shared to other third countries, unless there is prior consent by the providing party. Second, each contracting party will be responsible for the choice of the appropriate classification level of information as regards data security standards. In this sense, there is always a table of equivalences between the third country and Europol.

3.1.2 Operational agreements

It is usual that a third country first signs a strategic agreement with Europol and, a few years later, it concludes the operational and strategic agreement. By doing that, the third country makes sure that it has enough time to build an adequate data protection framework before operational relations with Europol start. Europol has concluded operation agreements with Albania, Australia, Canada, Colombia, Iceland, Monaco, Norway, Serbia, Switzerland, the US, Macedonia and Liechtenstein to date.[25] This type of agreements exchange information, including personal data, in the form of specialist knowledge, results from strategic analyses and crime prevention methods that can add value for investigations.

---

24 In addition, Europol has strategic agreements concluded with CEPOL, FRONTEX, ECB, EU, ECDC, UNODC, OLAF, European Network and Information Security Agency (ENISA), World Customs Organisation, European Monitoring Centre of Drugs and Drug Addiction.

25 Europol has also operational agreements with Interpol and Eurojust.

As in strategic agreements, operational agreements require the appointment of a national contact point in the third country. This contact point participates in high-level meetings with the agency, and ensures the exchange of information between both parties on a 24-hour basis. In addition, both parties agree on appointing one or more liaison officers, who will be located at the Europol's headquarters. Third countries and organisations with an operational agreement with Europol are also capable of accessing AWFs and focal points (Mounier 2009: 589). Therefore, these third countries are required to have adequate data protection standards before concluding an operational agreement with Europol.

In this sense, a provision extinguishing personal data transfers if the adequacy is no longer in place is included in these agreements. Clauses on accuracy and the purpose limitation principle also integrate the agreements. When a third country sends information to Europol, it specifies its purpose and access restrictions. Europol will then check whether the data is necessary for Europol's tasks and, if not (or no decision is taken within six months), it will be deleted.

Data protection rules included in operational agreements are similar to those in strategic agreements. For instance, operational agreements establish limits on the information sent to third countries. Moreover, they include clauses on individual rights. Any person has the right to access information collected by the government of the third country and transferred to Europol, but the agency needs prior consent from the supplying party before the release. Regarding data security issues, third countries need to ensure that personal data received from Europol is protected through technical and organisational measures. Lastly, as in strategic agreements, the supplying party is in charge of choosing the classification level of such information.

Europol can also sign working arrangements on a particular focal point with those third countries that have operational agreements with the agency. In this regard, Article 14(8) ECD allows Europol, under certain conditions, to invite experts from third countries or international organisations to be associated with the activities of an analysis group. For instance, Switzerland and Australia have recently joined the focal point 'Check-the-web'. These countries already have operational agreements with Europol, so the level of data protection in these countries is adequate. Lastly, third countries accessing a focal point need to provide analysis data that justifies the necessity of such access, and all members of the particular focal point have to agree unanimously on it.

3.1.3 Data exchanges between Europol and private parties

Europol can also exchange data with private companies. However, the agency does not have agreements or other arrangements with private entities. Therefore, the general rule is that information exchanged between the agency and private companies needs to be transferred via ENUs, never directly.

If the private company is not established within the territory of a Member State, the third state's regime will apply. For instance, Europol often needs to contact the credit card company Visa, located in the US. When that occurs, Visa sends the requested data to Europol via the US competent authorities (Disley *et al* 2012: 117).

As mentioned above, if the third country has a co-operation agreement with Europol, information from the private organisation is transmitted to Europol via the contact point of that state. However, if there is no agreement between Europol and the home (third) country of the private company, Europol can process data only if the organisation is on a list approved by Europol's MB. In addition, a memorandum of understanding and an opinion of the JSB are required (Disley *et al* 2012: 116).

3.2 Europol's receipt of information from third parties without an agreement

Europol does not need to conclude a co-operation agreement with a third party if the agency only wants to receive information from that country. It is regulated in Article 10(4) ECD, and Articles 19 and 20 of Council Decision 2009/934/JHA. These provisions state that when Europol only seeks to receive information from third parties, it can do it, even if there is not a co-operation agreement in place. The only condition is the flow of information has to be one-way only. If Europol does not only receive but also sends information to that third country, a co-operation agreement with that third country will be required.

This procedure permits Europol to receive information from any third country rapidly. It is an advantage in comparison to the two years on average that it takes for the conclusion of a co-operation agreement with third countries.

The following requirements take place for every receipt of information: (a) the assessment of the reliability of the source (Article 19 of Council Decision 2009/934/JHA); (b) the communication of any deleted or modified information to Europol (Article 20 of Council Decision 2009/934/JHA); (c) the communication of the receipt to Europol's DPO, the Director and the JSB; and (d) the deletion of any information that has been obtained in violation of human rights.

It is worth adding that Europol's receipt of information from a third partner without an agreement has to be addressed on a case-by-case basis. Therefore, if Europol receives regular information from a particular third partner, Europol will require the conclusion of an agreement with that partner.

3.3 Data protection rules for data transfers to third parties

One of the current debates regarding Europol's external relations refers to whether Europol data transfers to third countries comply with the same data protection standards as data transfers within the EU (Ruthig 2008: 112). This section answers that question, and it also examines Europol's influence on data protection laws of those third countries with which the agency has co-operation agreements in force.

Some scholars have raised doubts about the adequacy of data protection rules when Europol transfers data to third countries (Gless 2008: 346; Kaunert 2010:

661–662; Boehm 2012c: 210). Indeed, this is the impression given by Article 23 ECD. The provision regulates the relations of Europol with third states and bodies, but it does not include specific rules on data protection for Europol co-operation agreements.

Detailed rules on the transmission of personal data by Europol to third states and bodies are found in Council Decision 2009/934/JHA. It requires the establishment of an independent authority responsible for data protection matters in the third country (Article 5(4)); an agreement on confidentiality for transmitting classified information (Article 6(2)); the need for concrete provisions on the recipient of the data, the type of data to be transmitted and the purposes (Article 15); a limitation of transmission to the competent authorities (Article 17); and the obligation to include a clause for correcting and deleting data (Article 16). Besides it, any data exchange between Europol and a third country has to comply with the principles of the OECD and the CoE.[26]

From Council Decision 2009/934/JHA it is inferred that Europol data transfers to third countries are only allowed when: (a) there is an adequacy decision on the level of data protection; (b) there is an existing agreement between them; or (c) exceptionally, to protect the fundamental interests of a country, or to avoid an imminent threat (Ruthig 2008: 112). Therefore, the general rule is that Europol's data transfers will not take place in countries without an adequate data protection regime.

As seen above, there are two types of co-operation agreements: strategic and operational. For operational agreements, an adequate level of data protection is required – unless it is a 'ticking bomb' situation – (Europol 2010: 23). Europol has to examine the data protection regime in countries and organisations outside the EU before it concludes the operational agreement (Disley *et al* 2012: 112). In order to do so, the agency observes the nature of the data, the purpose for which the data is intended, the duration of the data processing, the general/specific data protection provisions and other specific conditions. The steps to carry out this assessment are the following.

First, a data protection questionnaire is sent to the third country. If the Europol DPO is not convinced by the answers to the questionnaire, a data protection study visit is arranged. This is usually a one-week visit at the institutions of the third country that will carry out the data transfers, as well as the DPA of the country. After that, the Europol's DPO drafts a report about the study visit.

As illustrated in Figure 3.3, the study visit report is sent to the MB, which forwards it to the JSB. Then, the JSB provides an opinion to the MB on the study visit report. The JSB opinion will allow the MB to adopt its own report. If the MB report is favourable, Europol enters into actual negotiations. Once the negotiations are finalised, Europol submits the resulting draft agreement to the MB. The draft is then forwarded to the JSB, which sends a second opinion to the MB. Finally, the MB forwards the draft, together with the JSB opinion, to the Council for approval (Disley *et al* 2012: 113). The conclusion of operational agreements

26 These are studied in detail in Chapter 5.

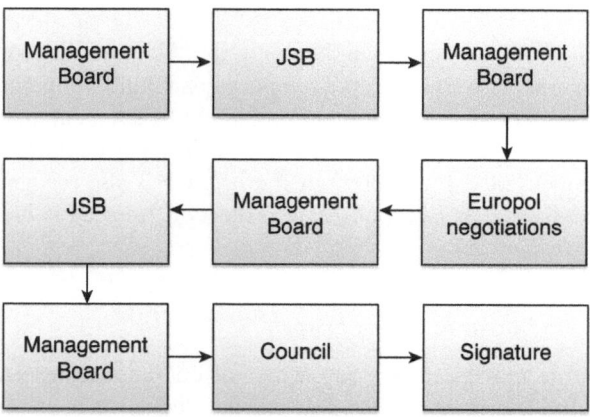

Figure 3.3

can take years. Yet, Article 23(8) and (9) provides a possibility for derogation from the general provision. Although the derogation has only been used once to date, it allows Europol to exceptionally transmit personal data to third parties without an operational agreement in urgent or exceptional cases.

The general procedure for Europol to conclude operational agreements is similar to that for international data transfers originating in a Member State. According to Article 31(2) of Directive 95/46/EC, the proof that a third country has an adequate level of protection starts with a Commission proposal, and it is then followed by opinions from the Art. 29 WP and the Art. 31 Committee.[27] After that, the EP can undertake a 30-day scrutiny and, finally, a decision is taken by the Commission.

In the terms of this procedure, the impact of Europol's data protection framework on third countries and international organisations has been notorious. Europol has become a key actor for exporting the European model and, particularly, the EU data protection standards. The reason for that is that Europol's external strategy presents less political pressure than the overall EU external strategy, so it becomes easier to negotiate with third countries. As a result, Europol has developed a role as normative actor. Third countries have often changed their domestic laws, adapting them to the European standards, in order to gain access to the agency's data (Mounier 2009: 589–593).

In conclusion, this section has demonstrated that Europol has been a norm exporter, influencing many third countries' data protection laws and principles. This influence has taken place during Europol's visits to the country, through guidelines sent by the agency to the third country, or by organising internships and training sessions at the Europol headquarters.

27 The Committee is established in Article 31 of Directive 95/46/EC and it is composed of representatives of every Member State who decide on matters like the adequacy decisions for third countries.

3.4 Special relationship with the US

The importance of a strong co-operation between the US and Europol is unquestionable. On several occasions Europol has participated in US operations that have resulted in the successful detention of criminals.[28] This section analyses the existing agreements between both parties, signed after the terrorist attacks that occurred on 11 September 2001. It explores whether the US is also recognising Europol's actorness, and whether Europol's data protection rules have had an impact on the US legal framework.

3.4.1 Co-operation agreements between the US and Europol

Europol has concluded a strategic and a supplemental operational agreement with the US. After the 9/11 terrorist attacks, Europol decided to make use of the emergency clause to share information with the US without having any agreement in force (current Article 23(8) and (9) ECD). However, the abusive use of the clause was strongly criticised and, therefore, the agency decided to formalise a data-sharing agreement with the US (Hillebrand 2012: 143).

The Strategic Agreement entered into force on 6 December 2001 (Agreement 2001). It was negotiated with very little time due to the urgency of the matter (Joint Supervisory Body 2001). That agreement was not seen as controversial since it did not allow the exchange of personal data. However, one year later a Supplemental Agreement was concluded between Europol and the US for the exchange of personal data (Supplemental Agreement 2002). On 16 October 2001, the former US President George W Bush sent a letter to the ex-president of the Commission Romano Prodi requiring access to all of Europol's information, including information on individuals (Statewatch 2001).

The Supplemental Agreement was concluded without first assessing the US level of data protection (de Busser 2009: 335). Consequently, the provisions of the Agreement do not correspond with the majority of operational agreements later adopted by Europol. For instance, in the US Agreement the purpose limitation principle can be circumvented if there is prior consent from the providing part, and onward transmissions of information are also possible. Moreover, there is no clear time limit for the data retention period, and individuals have no right to correct or delete their data. The negotiations for this operational agreement were tense. They raised strong criticism because of the low data protection standards, as well as the exclusion of the EP, NPs and NGOs from the negotiations (Hillebrand 2012: 145 and 183). Privacy experts feared that it could establish a precedent for other future co-operation agreements (Mounier 2009: 588). However, as can be seen below, it did not become the model for subsequent agreements.

---

28 See, for instance, the operation Joint Hammer, which included the involvement of the US Postal Inspection Service (USPIS), Immigration and Customs Enforcement (ICE) and the FBI. Europol was in charge with the analysis of the seized material, and it was co-ordinated by the DoJ. It was a success, resulting in 240 suspects identified, 61 child sex offenders arrested and 11 child victims identified.

There are several liaison officers established between the agency and the US.[29] Although the US removed its officials from the Europol headquarters at first, contact points were re-established in 2007 (Hillebrand 2012: 120). These come from the following US law enforcement agencies: Bureau of Alcohol, Tobacco, Firearms and Explosives (ATF); Drug Enforcement Administration (DEA); Secret Service (USSS); FBI; ICE; Internal Revenue Service (IRS); and USPIS. In addition, Europol has two liaison officers seconded at Washington DC (Council of the European Union 2012a: 19).

Therefore, Europol and the US authorities have been co-operating closely since 2001. They participate together in diverse joint projects,[30] developing trainings and information sharing.[31] SIENA is progressively becoming the tool of choice for exchanging operational information between both parties.[32] In particular, the US has become a key partner for Europol on issues related to terrorist financing (Council of the European Union 2012b), as examined in the section below.

3.4.2 The role of Europol in the TFTP

In June 2010 the EU and the US signed the second TFTP on the processing of financial data held by SWIFT. Europol has three main activities as regards the TFTP. The first is defined in Article 9 of the Agreement and it consists of allowing the US Department of the Treasury 'to spontaneously provide to Europol [. . .] the results of their processing of the data' (Europol 2011: 2). The second is established in Article 10 and it allows the agency to request searches of data obtained by the US authorities. The TFTP Unit (or O9), located at Europol's premises, is in charge of these two tasks. It is composed of three qualified staff members, and it has its own focal points to process data sent by the US (Europol 2011: 5).

The third and most controversial activity is described in Article 4 of the Agreement. It regulates Europol's verification process and consists of reviewing that requests specify the categories of data, their time limits, the geographical scope and the compliance with the necessity principle. Each request has 50 pages on average and, in most cases, they do not contain personal data.[33] The verification process is carried out by the operational officer, the Legal Affairs Unit and the DPO (Europol 2011: 4–5 and 7). Only if Europol authorises it will the designated provider (i.e. the SWIFT company) have the green light to send the information, in an encrypted format, to the US Treasury Department. In this sense, the EDPS

29 Article 8 of the 2001 Europol-US Agreement.
30 See, for instance, the joint project on countering violent extremism, where there is co-operation between the EU Member States, Europol and the DHS.
31 For example, in January 2013 Europol signed a letter of intent between ICE and the agency in which the two agencies committed to developing ongoing, co-operative efforts through support, training and information sharing on cybercrime, cyber fraud and online child sexual exploitation.
32 This has been recently promoted by the Council.
33 Except in particular investigations, for instance some requests with general references to Osama Bin Laden.

has complained that Europol is not a judiciary authority and therefore it should not be entitled to decide on the adequacy of the US requests (EDPS 2010: 5–6).

Europol has no access to the amount of data transferred to the US. The agency can only verify the request by taking into account other documents provided by the US. In addition, TFTP documents kept at Europol headquarters cannot be inspected by external supervisors such as the European Ombudsman without prior consent of the US authorities. The role of Europol as supervisory body is, therefore, very limited. In this regard, Ripoll Servent and MacKenzie have questioned the neutrality of Europol in the verification process. They state that 'Europol will almost certainly be pressured to maintain good relations with the US in order to successfully obtain TFTP leads, compromising its effective review' (Ripoll Servent and MacKenzie 2011: 397). Even if it is certain, Europol must still apply data protection safeguards during the verification process, concretised in Articles 5, 6, 7, 8, 12, 15 and 16 of the Agreement.

The TFTP Agreement also includes data security provisions. For instance, the US requests under Article 4 are classified as 'SECRET UE/EU SECRET' due to their high operational sensitivity and, therefore, highly secured. The majority of data exchanged between Europol and the US is channelled through the secure tool SIENA, which offers the possibility for additional future encryption measures (Europol 2011: 13–14). Unfortunately, a secure communication channel between Europol and the designated provider has yet to be established.

The JSB and the Commission oversee the implementation of the TFTP Agreement in the EU. In 2011 and 2012 both bodies found that the US had to issue more specific requests under Article 4 TFTP, and that the information had to be provided in writing. The US implemented these recommendations successfully (Joint Supervisory Body 2013b). In the US, the oversight comes from two EU independent supervisory authorities. They are in charge of checking that the information is processed according to the Agreement. In order to do that, they can access data, review searches and monitor the data protection rules, similarly to the role of the JSB within the EU.

The role of Europol in the TFTP Agreement demonstrates that the agency can also take part in EU international agreements for the exchange of data with third countries. The role of Europol for the control of TFTP data requests is particularly relevant, since it could lead the agency to participate in other future international agreements. For all that, it must be concluded that Europol plays a key role in data exchanges between the EU and the US.

3.5 Data transfers to third partners in the proposed Europol regulation

As mentioned above, on 27 March 2013 the Commission launched the proposal for a Europol regulation, which will repeal the current ECD. The proposed regulation includes new provisions on data transfers to third countries, the receipt of data from third countries, as well as the adoption and supervision of the co-operation agreements.

3.5.1 Transfer of personal data to third countries

Data transfers to third countries or international organisations are regulated in Chapter VI of the proposal. The general rule is that 'Europol may directly exchange all information, with the exception of personal data' (Article 29(2) of the Europol Regulation), unless it is expressly restricted in the sense of Article 25(2) of the proposal. In other words, transfers of personal data to third countries will be generally prohibited. Yet, in very exceptional cases and to the extent it is necessary for the accomplishment of its tasks, Europol will be able to transfer those personal data beyond the EU borders on a case-by-case basis. This is regulated in Article 31 and recitals 27–28 of the Europol Regulation.

In line with the current legal framework, Article 31 of the proposed regulation establishes three possible scenarios under which data can be exchanged between Europol and a third country. The first possibility is the existence of an adequacy decision, similar to that foreseen in Article 25 of Directive 95/46/EC for Member States' transfers to third countries. It will require a proposal by the Commission, in conjunction with an EDPS study on the national data protection standards. The EDPS will apply the same procedure as that established in Article 9 of Regulation (EC) 45/2001 for EU institutions and bodies not subject to Directive 95/46/EC. The Art. 29 WP, which will be re-named the European Data Protection Board, will also release an opinion on the agreement. After that, the EP will carry out a 30-day scrutiny, which will result in a recommendation. Finally, the Commission will adopt the decision. The average time for this procedure will be one and a half years.

A second option that will enable Europol to transmit personal information to a third country is the adoption of an agreement between the agency and the particular country pursuant to Article 218 TFEU. As established by Article 31(1)(b) of the proposed regulation, the international agreement needs to include adequate data protection safeguards. The conclusion of the agreements between Europol and third parties will be in the hands of Europol, as it is today. In line with the procedure in other EU bodies, the Commission will be the institution in charge of the conclusion of the international agreements between Europol and a third country.

The involvement of the Commission in Europol's activities is enhanced in the proposed regulation. Besides the new task of concluding international agreements, the presence of this institution at Europol's headquarters will be enhanced. Article 13 of the proposal includes the establishment of two members of the Commission in Europol's MB, which will be able to vote on Europol's future decisions. The Commission has already pointed out that it will still require the technical support of Europol on aspects relating to law enforcement, and that pre-existing international agreements will continue to be valid (COM(2013) 535 final, p. 6). It is, however, not fully clear how Europol will be involved in the procedure of Article 218 TFEU. In this regard, the JSB has argued that a legal basis for that should be included in the proposed regulation, ensuring that such additional tasks are in accordance with Europol objectives (Joint Supervisory Body 2013a: 8).

Also, the EDPS has claimed that the new procedure should require an EDPS report during the negotiations of an international agreement between the EU and third countries or international organisations (EDPS 2013: 20).

Finally, pursuant to Article 31(1)(c) it will be possible to transfer personal data to a third country if it has a prior co-operation agreement with Europol. The EDPS has asked for a transitional clause for this option, so that such existing agreements will be reviewed and aligned with the proposal within a maximum period of two years from the adoption of the regulation (EDPS 2013: 21). If this clause is finally introduced, the US-Europol Agreements will probably be revised. As stated above, such agreements do not fully comply with adequate data protection standards. Since many current co-operation agreements already include a mechanism to amend the scope of application of the agreements according to Europol's new mandate, the revision of existing Europol agreements in the future is highly probable.

Notwithstanding the three possible ways for transferring personal data to a third country, there is a carve-out clause for emergency situations in Article 31(2) of the proposed Europol regulation. If the proposal is adopted, it will derogate Article 31 ECD, requiring no formal assessment of data protection safeguards, either for cases of one single transfer, or for transfers of a set of data. If it is a single transfer, the derogation will take place after Europol's Executive Director authorises such transfers on a case-by-case basis. The data transfer will be authorised if: (a) it is absolutely necessary to safeguard the essential interests; (b) it is absolutely necessary to prevent imminent danger; (c) it is required on important public interest grounds; and (d) it is necessary to protect the vital interests of the data subject. Yet, despite the derogation, the Executive Director will not abstain from examining the data protection standards of the third country, informing also the MB.

If instead of a single transfer a set of data is transferred to the third country for an emergency situation, the derogation can only apply for one year maximum, and it will require an additional authorisation from the MB and the EDPS.

In order to implement a co-operation agreement or an adequacy decision, Article 31(1) will allow Europol to sign a working arrangement with the third country. As it is today, working arrangements need an existing agreement between Europol and the third country. However, the Regulation fails to define in what cases a working arrangement will not be allowed. It is thus unclear in what specific situations the adoption of these arrangements will and will not be pertinent.

One of the new uses for these working arrangements will refer to the EP data access to the EU Classified Information and sensitive non-classified information processed by or through Europol. Another new task of the EP will consist in scrutinising the adoption of such working arrangements (Article 53(3)(b) of the Europol Regulation). The next section discerns future EP tasks relating to Europol's external relations.

3.5.2 The enhanced role of the EP

Before Lisbon, the EP had a limited role in the adoption of agreements between the EU and third countries. That institution was consulted but its recommendations were not binding. In that sense, neither the former Europol Convention nor the current ECD conferred decisive powers to the EP. Article 26 ECD states that the EP should be consulted for the determination of the list of third countries with which the agency can conclude agreements (Wesser, Marin and Matera 2011: 295). It is not a coincidence that both Council Decision 2009/934/JHA on Europol's data exchanges with third parties and the first SWIFT agreement were adopted exactly one day before the Treaty of Lisbon came into force. The reason was to avoid the participation of the EP in the decision-making processes.

Since the Treaty of Lisbon entered into force the EP is no longer a mere consultative body. This institution now has competence to participate in the decision-making process for the conclusion of international agreements. For instance, in October 2012, Europol's MB proposed that Mexico, Brazil, Georgia and the United Arab Emirates be added to the Council's list, and the Council amended the list accordingly (Council of the European Union 2012c). Negotiations for operational agreements started with Mexico and Brazil in 2013 (Statewatch 2013). However, the EP voted against these initiatives arguing that the proposals for these agreements did not conform to EU laws (European Parliament 2013). The EP asked Europol's director and the MB to reconsider the proposal, and the negotiations were not started.

In addition to these new powers, when the proposed Europol regulation enter into force, the EP will have access to classified information processed by or through Europol (Article 54). Especially interesting will be the EP role as regards the TFTP Agreement. One of the past controversies regarding this agreement referred to Europol's refusal to send the TFTP inspection reports to the EP (Nielsen 2012). The constant dispute on document secrecy between Europol and the EP led to a decision from the General Court on 4 May 2012, Case T-529/09, *Council of the European Union v Sophie in 't Veld*, which was then appealed at the CJEU, Case C-350/12 P, *Council of the European Union v Sophie in 't Veld* (2014). Both courts were in favour of the EP document requests.[34] The Council argument that it would 'negatively impact on the European Union's negotiating position' did not convince the courts, which found that the Council had not properly established the risk of a threat to the public interest.

Although the new regulation will broaden the EP tasks relating to Europol, it is not clear yet whether these will also apply to the existing international agreements or only to those adopted after the regulation enters into force.

3.5.3 The lack of a SIENA provision

The tailor-made communication tool SIENA represents one of most secure measures created by Europol in order to exchange personal and non-personal data. Besides its use for data transfers between Europol and Member States, as well as among Member States themselves, there are today several third countries

---

34 Case T-529/09, *Council of the European Union v Sophie in 't Veld* (2012).

connected to SIENA. According to the last Europol General Report, 42 third parties are connected to SIENA – 13 directly and 29 indirectly – (Council of the European Union 2014a: 13).

When a third country uses SIENA as a communication tool, a message can be exchanged directly between the following actors: (a) Member States and Europol; (b) operational or strategic third parties and Europol; and (c) among operational or strategic third parties among themselves.

Norway and Australia were the first two third countries directly connected to the system, on 18 January and 7 April 2011 respectively. Ghana, Croatia and Iceland also joined the system that year. In 2012, nine other third countries connected to SIENA: the US, Switzerland, Serbia, Montenegro, Bosnia & Herzegovina, Albania, Turkey, Monaco and Canada. The tool is expanding its borders year by year.

Moreover, its use is no longer limited to third countries having operational agreements with Europol, but it is also offered to third parties with strategic agreements. Specifically, Bosnia & Herzegovina, Montenegro and Turkey are strategic partners of Europol and they use SIENA. Also, many US agencies are connected to SIENA.[35] The problem is that, although each of these agencies has a liaison officer at Europol, there is no contact point in the US territory.

The JSB has often underlined the necessity to regulate the use of SIENA as a messaging system between third parties (Joint Supervisory Body 2013b: 8). The body has also reiterated that SIENA is an adequate tool for exchanging information in terms of data protection and data security, including those communications sent beyond the EU borders.

However, there is no regulation of SIENA in the proposal. The absence of a SIENA provision in the proposed Europol regulation is particularly disappointing, since there are no rules to date about the exchange of data through this tool. Moreover, the inclusion of a SIENA clause in the proposal could have engaged other third countries to join it.

It has been seen above that a disparity currently exists within and beyond the EU regarding the channels and tools to exchange crime-related data. This could be minimised by establishing SIENA as the common default communication tool. The proposal underlines the importance of introducing privacy-by-design systems in Europol. SIENA definitely complies with the requirements to be considered a privacy-by-design tool. Yet, the proposal, which was the perfect context for it, has missed the opportunity to introduce specific rules on this tool.

3.5.4 Processing of data from third countries to Europol

As in the current legal framework, Europol will not need a co-operation agreement for receiving information from a third country. Nonetheless, the proposal

---

35 Particularly these are the ATF, DEA, FBI, ICE, National Criminal Intelligence Service (NCIS) and USSS.

includes a few new rules in this respect. First, in Articles 32(1) and 33(1) it expressly establishes the possibility to receive information from a private party in a third country. This will be feasible as long as one of the following conditions is met: (a) it is through a contact point of a third country with which Europol has concluded a co-operation agreement in accordance with Article 23 of Decision 2009/371/JHA; or (b) it is through an authority of a third country or an international organisation with which the EU has concluded an international agreement pursuant to Article 218 TFEU.

Second, the proposed regulation explicitly states that Europol will not process 'any information which has clearly been obtained by a third country or international organisation in violation of human rights' (recital 31 of the Europol Regulation). This new provision seeks to regulate what has been Europol's praxis for many years. For instance, negotiations with Russia for a co-operation agreement took a very long time due to the several violations of human rights by that country. Europol suggested many institutional and political changes as the conditions *sine qua non* for the adoption of a co-operation agreement with Russia. Today, the agreement has been concluded, but it still needs to be implemented. Lastly, the proposed regulation introduces specific evaluation codes on accuracy and reliability in Article 35, which will also apply for the information received from a third country or international organisation.

A related debate emerging from new Articles 24 and 25 needs to be highlighted. In the proposed Europol regulation, Article 24 makes a distinction between operational and strategic analyses. However, then Article 25(1) states that:

[A] Member State, a Union body, a third country or an international organisation providing information to Europol determines the purpose for which it shall be processed as referred to in Article 24.

Thus, a third country can discretionarily decide to send a piece of information to one or several Member States, but exclude Europol. Europol has no voice in deciding if certain information from a third country is necessary for its investigations, since the main objective of the agency is to support Member States in the prevention, combat and investigation of crimes, but it does not include the support of third parties. Therefore, any petition from Europol to be included in data exchanges between third countries and Member States is beyond the agency's mandate.

Finally, the Council has suggested including a paragraph in the proposed regulation that would allow the receiving of data sent by private parties in a third country with no co-operation agreement. The only limitation that the Council sets for that procedure is that Europol forwards the information to the Member State that has concluded an agreement with the third country (Council of the European Union 2014d: Article 32(1)(b)). Similarly, if Council's amendments are approved, Europol will be able to share data with private parties as long as the data subject has presumably consented to it, or if it is necessary for the prevention of an imminent threat (Council of the European Union 2014d: Article 32(3)(a)).

4 Shortcomings and limitations of Europol's data protection rules

As revealed in this study, Europol has become a comprehensive EU police actor due to its robust data protection framework. Europol's data protection rules are stronger than those applied in the majority of Member States and third countries. However, there are several issues today that impede such a scheme from becoming a reference for EU and non-EU countries. These are listed in the following paragraphs.

First of all, there is a lack of will from Member States and third countries have to share information with the agency. National law enforcement authorities often prefer to share information bilaterally rather than multilaterally (Bures and Ahern 2007: 222; Kaunert 2010: 656). They are reluctant to send data to Europol for several reasons. Sometimes these countries follow a rather 'national-minded' approach (Occhipinti 2013: 160), and sometimes they simply do not trust the agency (Rozée, Kaunert and Léonard 2013). Another reason is that some Member States do not believe that the agency offers any 'added value' to their national investigations. In this sense, many scholars refer to an inherent 'chicken-egg dilemma': Europol is not granted executive powers by the Member States; but it is precisely this limitation that causes the agency's lack of 'added value' (Bures 2008: 513; Bures 2011: 85–109; Léonard and Kaunert 2013: 9; Bures 2013). As a result, Europol does not make full use of all its capabilities and loses effectiveness as an EU police agency.

Second, Europol has no enforcing powers. This means that the agency has a very limited power over national law enforcement agencies' actions. An example of this is found in the paragraph suggested by the Council for the proposed Europol regulation. The Council suggests in Article 41 that 'if Europol becomes aware that personal data [. . .] are factually incorrect or have been unlawfully stored, it shall inform the provider of that data accordingly'. This is what currently occurs for data that Europol identifies as incorrect or out-of-date. Even if Europol modifies its database accordingly, there is no way to certify that the originating Member State has also amended the data.

Third, data processed by intelligence agencies is out of the scope of Europol. As examined in Chapter 4, a large part of the information processed for security reasons is collected by intelligence services of the Member States. For instance, in some countries police agencies are in charge of CT policies, whereas in others these fall under the scope of the intelligence services' tasks (Kaunert 2010: 656). Data collected by intelligence services is rarely shared with Europol, since the EU has its own supranational intelligence body called IntCen. Although IntCen and Europol have a co-operation agreement in force, Europol only assesses trends on a general level and it cannot conduct intelligence analysis outside the EU borders (Cross 2013: 391). Therefore, the participation of Europol in police investigations is constrained by the lack of access to information collected by intelligence services.

Lastly, there is a lack of convergence between some provision in the Police and Criminal Justice Data Protection Directive and those in the future Europol regulation. A confluence in the wording of both instruments is crucial to have a consistent EU data protection framework in the field of law enforcement. The new Directive, despite excluding Europol from its scope, impacts directly on the future Europol legislation. The necessity to align both instruments is in fact mentioned in recital 32 of the proposed Europol regulation:

> Europol should be autonomous and aligned with [. . .] Council Framework Decision 2008/977/JHA on the protection of personal data processed in the framework of police and judicial cooperation in criminal matters [to *be replaced by the relevant Directive in force at the moment of adoption*].

It is unclear what pushed the Commission to launch the proposal for a Europol regulation before the Data Protection Directive was in force. As the JSB noted, it would have been preferable to wait for the outcome of the data protection package (Joint Supervisory Body 2013a: 2 and 5). In any event, it is probable that ultimately the Europol regulation will not be adopted until the new EU data protection legal framework is in force.

5 Concluding remarks

Europol's co-operation with Member States has intensified over the years – especially since 2009, when the Treaty of Lisbon and the ECD entered into force. The first part of this chapter demonstrated that Europol's involvement in national police investigations is advantageous from a privacy perspective. The agency offers high data security and data protection safeguards for both Member States and individuals.

One of the data-sharing problems that Member States have experienced lately is that they do not have a common communication channel for transferring information. While some Member States have moved towards a more systematic use of the Europol channel (ENU), others continue to rely on the Interpol channel because of the traditional central role and ease of use of this instrument. Sometimes, such a multiplicity of available channels entails ineffectiveness at the EU level. Therefore, this chapter studied the possibility to centralise every cross-border data transfer for law enforcement matters into the SIENA tool. SIENA could ideally be the default communication tool for all data transfers, ensuring the same data security standards in any data exchange.

This study demonstrated that Europol includes higher data protection standards than many of the Member States. In particular, Europol has exemplary data protection rules on the right of access, correction and deletion; purpose limitation principle; retention periods; SIENA as privacy-by-design tool; data quality; and external supervision, to name but a few. These will be maintained in the proposed Europol regulation. This study examined the latest issues and controversies of this new proposal.

Third countries willing to conclude a co-operation agreement with Europol must first comply with the data protection standards of the agency. Europol has made several third countries align their legal frameworks to the Europol's data protection rules. In fact, negotiations between Europol and third countries are subject to much lower political pressures and lobbyism than an agreement adopted between the EU and third countries. Therefore, it is easier for non-US countries to find accordance with Europol than with the EU as a whole.

In light of the foregoing considerations, it can be concluded that Europol plays a key role in the global security environment. Its structure complements the existing networks of law enforcement officials for exchanging information within and beyond the EU. As Mournier noted in 2009, the agency 'exports European standards of policing and contributes to shaping local police systems' (Mounier 2009: 584). Therefore, the Europol data protection framework could be taken as a reference for all crime-related data exchanged among EU and non-EU countries. Yet, as pointed out earlier, intelligence services' data transfers do not follow the same data protection standards. This is examined in the next chapter.

Bibliography

Abazi, V, 2013, *Unveiling the Power over Europol's Secrets*, Amsterdam Centre for Law and Governance, Working Paper Series 4, Amsterdam, pp. 1–34.

Abazi, V, 2014, 'The future of Europol's parliamentary oversight: A great leap forward?', *German Law Journal*, vol. 15, no. 6, pp. 1121–1143.

Agreement Between the United States of America and the European Police Office, File n° 3710-60r2, 6 December 2001.

Boehm, F, 2012a, 'Information sharing in the Area of Freedom, Security and Justice – Towards a common standard for data exchange between agencies and EU information systems' in S Gutwirth, R Leenes, P de Hert and Y Poullet, *European Data Protection: In Good Health?*, Springer, Berlin, pp. 143–184.

Boehm, F, 2012b, 'Data processing and law enforcement access to information systems at EU level', *Datenschutz und Datensicherheit*, vol. 36, no. 5, pp. 339–343.

Boehm, F, 2012c, *Information Sharing and Data Protection in the Area of Freedom, Security and Justice Towards Harmonised Data Protection Principles for Information Exchange at EU-level*, Springer, Berlin.

Bures, O, 2008, 'Europol's fledgling counterterrorism role', *Terrorism and Political Violence*, vol. 20, no. 4, pp. 498–517.

Bures O, 2011, *EU Counterterrorism Policy. A Paper Tiger?*, Ashgate, Surrey.

Bures, O, 2013, 'Europol's counter-terrorism role: A chicken-egg dilemma', in C Kaunert and S Léonard (eds), *European Security, Terrorism and Intelligence. Tackling New Security Challenges in Europe*, Palgrave Macmillan, Basingstoke, pp. 65–93.

Bures, O and Ahern, S, 2007, 'The European Model of Building Regional Cooperation against Terrorism' in D Cortright and GA López, *Uniting against Terror. Cooperative nonmilitary responses to the global terrorist threat*, Massachusetts Institute of Technology Press, Massachusetts, pp. 187–236.

Case T-529/09, *Council of the European Union v Sophie in 't Veld* (GC, 4 May 2012).

Case C-350/12 P, *Council of the European Union v Sophie in 't Veld* (CJEU, 3 July 2014).

Commission Staff Working Document Executive Summary of the Impact Assessment on Adapting the European Police Office's Legal Framework With The Lisbon Treaty accompanying the document Proposal for a European Parliament and Council Regulation on the European Union Agency For Law Enforcement Cooperation and Training (Europol) and Repealing Council Decisions 2009/371/JHA and 2005/681/JHA, SWD(2013) 99 final, 27 March 2013.

Communication from the Commission to the European Parliament and the Council – Strengthening law enforcement cooperation in the EU: the European Information Exchange Model (EIXM), COM(2012) 735 final, 7 December 2012.

Council Act of 3 November 1998 laying down rules governing Europol's external relations with third States and non-European Union related bodies.

Council Decision 2005/671/JHA of 20 September 2005 on the exchange of information and cooperation concerning terrorist offences.

Council Decision 2009/371/JHA of 6 April 2009 establishing the European Police Office (Europol).

Council Decision 2009/934/JHA of 30 November 2009 adopting the implementing rules governing Europol's relations with partners, including the exchange of personal data and classified information.

Council Framework Decision 2002/465/JHA of 13 June 2002 on joint investigation teams.

Council of the European Union 2005, *A Strategy for the External Dimension of the JHA: Global Freedom, Security and Justice*, Doc. 14366/3/05, 30 November 2005.

Council of the European Union, 2010, *Guidelines on the implementation of Council Framework Decision 2006/960/JHA of 18 December 2006 on simplifying the exchange of information and intelligence between law enforcement authorities of the Member States of the European Union*, Doc. 9512/1/10, 17 December 2010.

Council of the European Union, 2011a, *Council Framework Decision 2006/960/JHA on simplifying the exchange of information and intelligence between law enforcement authorities of the Member States of the European Union ('Swedish Framework Decision') – Assessment of compliance pursuant to Art. 11(2) – Report*, Doc. 15278/11, 14 October 2011.

Council of the European Union, 2011b, *Europol Work Programme 2012*, Doc. 13516/11, 25 August 2011.

Council of the European Union, 2012a, *General Report on Europol's activities in 2011*, Doc. 10036/12, 24 May 2012.

Council of the European Union, 2012b, *Europol Work Programme 2013*, Doc. 12667/12, 17 July 2012.

Council of the European Union, 2012c, *Draft Council Decision amending the list of third States and organisations with which Europol shall conclude agreements*, Doc. 15951/12, 12 November 2012.

Council of the European Union, 2013a, *Draft Council Conclusions following the Commission Communication on the European Information Exchange Model (EIXM)*, Doc. 9811/13, 24 May 2013.

Council of the European Union, 2013b, *Proposal for a Regulation on the European Union Agency for Law Enforcement Cooperation and Training (Europol) – Discussion paper*, Doc. 10213/13, 29 May 2013.

Council of the European Union, 2014a, *General Report on Europol's activities in 2013*, Doc. 10426/14, 6 June 2014.

Council of the European Union, 2014b, *HENU Workshop on SIENA Implementation – Roadmap on SIENA implementation*, Doc. 10303/14, 28 May 2014.

Council of the European Union, 2014c, *Draft SPOC Guidelines for cross-border law enforcement information Exchange*, Doc. 6721/14, 20 February 2014.

Council of the European Union, 2014d, *Proposal for a Regulation of the European Parliament and of the Council on the European Union Agency for Law Enforcement Cooperation and Training (Europol) and repealing Decisions 2009/371/JHA and 2005/681/JHA – Presidency compromise text*, Doc. 8596/14, 7 April 2014.

Council of the European Union, 2015, *Europol Work Programme 2015*, Doc. 5250/15, 16 January 2015.

Cross, MKC, 2013, 'A European transgovernmental intelligence network and the role of IntCen', *Perspectives on European Politics and Society*, vol. 14, no. 3, pp. 388–402.

de Buck, B, 2007, 'Joint investigation teams: The participation of Europol officials', *ERA Forum*, no. 8, pp. 253–264.

de Busser, E, 2009, *Data Protection in EU and US Criminal Cooperation: A Substantive Law Approach to the EU Internal and Transatlantic Cooperation in Criminal Matters between Judicial and Law Enforcement Authorities*, Maklu Publishers, Antwerpen.

Directive 95/46/EC of the European Parliament and of the Council of 24 October 1995 on the protection of individuals with regard to the processing of personal data and on the free movement of such data.

Disley, E, Irving, B, Hughes, W and Patruni, B, 2012, *Evaluation of the Implementation of the Europol Council Decision and of Europol's Activities*, RandEurope, The Hague.

EDPS, 2010, *European Data Protection Supervisor Opinion on the proposal for a Council Decision on the conclusion of the Agreement between the European Union and the United States of America on the processing and transfer of Financial Messaging Data from the European Union to the United States for purposes of the Terrorist Finance Tracking Program (TFTP II)*, 22 June 2010.

EDPS, 2013, *Opinion of the European Data Protection Supervisor on the Proposal for a Regulation of the European Parliament and of the Council on the European Union Agency for Law enforcement Cooperation and Training (Europol) and repealing Decisions 2009/371/JHA and 2005/681/JHA, 31 May 2013.*

European Commission, 2004, *European Commission Action Paper in Response to the Terrorist Attacks on Madrid*, European Commission, MEMO/04/66, 18 March 2004.

European Commission, 2013, *Proposal for a Regulation of the European Parliament and of the Council on the European Union Agency for Criminal Justice Cooperation (Eurojust)*, COM(2013) 535 final, 17 July 2013.

European Council, 2009, *The Stockholm Programme – An open and secure Europe serving and protecting citizens*, 2 December 2009.

European Parliament, 2013, *Report on the draft Council decision amending Decision 2009/935/JHA as regards the list of third States and organisations with which Europol shall conclude agreements*, European Parliament, Doc. A7-0351/2013, 23 October 2013.

Europol, 2010, *Data Protection at Europol*, Publications Office of the European Union, Luxembourg.

Europol, 2011, *Europol Activities in Relation to the TFTP Agreement Information Note to the European Parliament 1 August 2010 – 1 April 2011*, File no. 2566-566, 8 April 2011.

Europol, 2012, *Europol Work Programme 2013*, 17 July 2012, www.europol.europa.eu (accessed 9 November 2015).

Gless, S, 2008, 'Zusammenarbeit von Europol mit Drittenstaaten und Drittenstellen' in J Wolter, WR Schenke, H Hilger, J Ruthig and MA Zoller (eds), *Alternativenentwurf Europol und europäischer Datenschutz*, C.F. Müller, Wissenschaft, pp. 346–363.

Hillebrand, C, 2012, *Networks in the European Union. Maintaining Democratic Legitimacy after 9/11*, Oxford University Press, Oxford.

Hillebrand, C, 2013, 'Guarding EU-wide counter-terrorism policing: The struggle for sound parliamentary scrutiny of Europol' in C Kaunert and S Léonard (eds), *European Security, Terrorism and Intelligence. Tackling New Security Challenges in Europe*, Palgrave Macmillan, Basingstoke, pp. 96–124.

Hustinx, P, 2012, 'Ensuring stronger, more effective and more consistent protection of personal data in the EU', *NewEurope*, 2 February, www.neurope.eu (accessed 9 November 2015).

Joint Supervisory Body, 2001, *Opinion 01/38 of the JSB in respect to the data protection level in the United States of America*, 26 November 2001.

Joint Supervisory Body, 2013a, *Opinion 13/31 with respect to the proposal for a Regulation of the European Parliament and of the Council on the European Union Agency for Law Enforcement Cooperation and Training (Europol)*, 10 May 2013.

Joint Supervisory Body, 2013b, *Implementation of the TFTP Agreement: assessment of the follow-up of the JSB recommendations*, Ref. 13/01, 18 March 2013.

Kaunert, C, 2010, 'Europol and EU Counterterrorism: International security actorness in the external dimension', *Studies in Conflict & Terrorism*, no. 33, pp. 652–671.

Léonard, S and Kaunert, C, 2013, 'Introduction – Beyond EU counter-terrorism cooperation: European security, terrorism and intelligence', in C Kaunert and S Léonard (eds), *European Security, Terrorism and Intelligence. Tackling New Security Challenges in Europe*, Palgrave Macmillan, Basingstoke, pp. 1–14.

Mounier, G, 2009, 'Europol: A new player in the EU external policy field?', *Perspectives on European Politics and Society*, vol. 10, no. 4, pp. 582–602.

Nielsen, N, 2012, 'EU hands personal data to US authorities on daily basis', *EUobserver*, 22 June, http://euobserver.com/22/116719 (accessed 10 November 2015).

Occhipinti, JD, 2013, 'Availability by stealth? EU information-sharing in transatlantic perspective', in C Kaunert and S Léonard (eds), *European Security, Terrorism and Intelligence. Tackling New Security Challenges in Europe*, Palgrave Macmillan, Basingstoke, pp. 143–184.

O'Neill, M, 2012, *The Evolving Counter-terrorism Legal Framework*, Routledge Research in EU Law, New York.

Proposal for a Regulation of the European Parliament and of the Council on the European Union Agency for Law Enforcement Cooperation and Training (Europol) and repealing Decisions 2009/371/JHA and 2005/681/JHA, COM(2013) 173 final, 27 March 2013.

Regulation (EC) 45/2001 of 18 December 2000 on the protection of individuals with regard to the processing of personal data by the Community institutions and bodies and on the free movement of such data.

Report from the Commission to the European Parliament and the Council on the implementation of Council Decision 2008/615/JHA of 23 June 2008 on the stepping up of cross-border cooperation, particularly in combating terrorism and cross-border crime (the 'Prüm Decision'), COM(2012) 732 final, 7 December 2012.

Ripoll Servent, A and MacKenzie, A, 2011, 'Is the EP still a data protection champion? The case of SWIFT', *Perspectives on European Politics and Society*, vol. 12, no. 4, pp. 390–406.

Rozée, S, Kaunert, C and Léonard, S, 2013, 'Is Europol a comprehensive policing actor?', *Perspectives on European Politics and Society*, vol. 14 no. 3, pp. 372–387.

Ruthig, J, 2008, 'Rechtliche Rahmenbedingungen der Tätigkeit von Europol – Bestandaufnahme Ausblick' in J Wolter, WR Schenke, H Hilger, J Ruthig and MA Zoller (eds), *Alternativenentwurf Europol und europäischer Datenschutz*, C.F. Müller, Wissenschaft, pp. 97–124.

Scherrer, A, Jeandesboz, J and Guittet, EM, 2011, *Developing an EU internal security strategy, fighting terrorism and organised crime*, European Parliament, Directorate General for Internal Policies, Policy Department C: Citizens' rights and Constitutional Affairs, Civil Liberties, Justice and Home Affairs, Brussels.

Statewatch, 2001, Letter US President George W. Bush to the ex-president of the Commission Romano Prodi, www.statewatch.org/news/2001/nov/06Ausalet.htm (accessed 9 November 2015).

Statewatch, 2013, 'The spider's web: Europol goes global in the hunt for intelligence and analysis', 5 March 2013, www.statewatch.org (accessed 10 November 2015).

Supplemental Agreement between the Europol Police Office and the United States of America on the Exchange of Personal Data and related Information, 20 December 2002.

UK House of Lords, 2008, *Submission by Europol, Select Committee on European Union. Call for Evidence*, File no. 3100-174, 28 April 2008.

Vermeulen, M and Wills, A, 2011, *Parliamentary oversight of security and intelligence agencies in the European Union*, European Parliament, Directorate General for Internal Policies, Policy Department C, Citizens' rights and Constitutional Affairs, Brussels.

Wesser, RA, Marin, L and Matera, C, 2011, 'The external dimension of the EU's Area of Freedom, Security and Justice', in C Eckes and T Konstadinides (eds), *Crime within the Area of Freedom, Security and Justice. A European Public Order*, Cambridge University Press, Cambridge, pp. 272–300.

4 Data safeguards for the intelligence collected and shared by Member States

The previous three chapters study systems used by law enforcement authorities (mainly, police officers) to process data within and beyond the EU. They examine the consistency between EU internal and external measures for data processing, as well as the impact they have on the EU fundamental right to data protection. Particularly, Chapter 3 suggests looking at Europol's legal framework as a guideline for establishing common data protection principles in the field of law enforcement.

However, in the field of security, data is not only processed for law enforcement purposes, but also by intelligence services. Despite the existing legal differences of data processed by intelligence services and data processed by law enforcement authorities, in practice, the line separating their tasks has become difficult to draw. In the past, the law enforcement authorities' methodology was clearly to 'see and strike', whereas intelligence services' functions were to 'wait and watch' (Svenden 2011: 523). In that sense, Germany still has a law of separation ('Trenungsgebot') that divides the roles between intelligence and police forces (Hillebrand 2012: 94). However, this division became more and more blurred over the years. The 'wall' that separated law enforcement agencies from intelligence services crumbled after 9/11 (de Busser 2010: 98). Today, police agents and intelligence analysts maintain regular contact, to the point that in some Member States (e.g. Spain), the intelligence community has a special department assigned to police agents, which allows direct contact between the two entities. In these cases, every time the intelligence agency gathers relevant information on a current or imminent crime, the centre informs police authorities, which will initiate an investigation based on that premise. The same occurs at the EU level with regard to the information sent from IntCen (intelligence centre) to Europol (law enforcement agency).

This chapter studies the main challenges that Member States have with regard to the regulation and control of intelligence processed within the EU. As a general rule, the EU has no capacity to cover standard intelligence service activities. Yet, there is a blurred line between intelligence services and law enforcement activities today. In this sense, the aim of this chapter is to identify whether the EU could have legal competence to adopt legislation on data exchanges among intelligence agencies. First, the Snowden revelations and the activities that intelligence services conduct within and beyond EU borders are studied. After that, a comparative study of intelligence agencies in France, Germany, Spain and the UK is conducted.

The choice of countries has been based on the locations where terrorist cells have been identified (Hamburg and Paris) and terrorist attacks have recently taken place (Madrid, London and Paris).

In summary, this study seeks to examine whether the lack of co-ordination of intelligence agencies, the systematic storage and data access by intelligence services and the divergence in external supervision mechanisms could negatively affect the establishment of global data protection standards.

1 Data processed by intelligence services

According to Article 4(2) TEU and Article 72 TFEU, data processing for 'national security' purposes falls outside of the scope of the EU laws. This purpose is also expressly excluded from data protection instruments such as Directive 95/46/EC or the Convention for the Protection of Individuals with regard to the Automatic Processing of Personal Data (1981 CoE Data Protection Convention) (Council of Europe 1981). Thus, national security measures are not protected by European privacy laws. But what exactly is 'national security'? A formal definition of this term is still missing in the EU laws.

Security policies in Member States are essentially organised through law enforcement authorities, intelligence services and military staff. Whereas the former has a role at the EU level through Europol and laws adopted under the AFSJ, the regulation of intelligence and military agencies remain, for the most part, in each Member State. However, the division of roles between law enforcement and intelligence services is not always clear, and it causes confusion about what the EU can and cannot regulate. As the 'Future Group'[1] of the Council of Ministers pointed out:

> While an exchange of information between national police forces is increasingly seen as common sense, the exchange of information between intelligence services creates a considerable challenge for the European Union.
> (Council of the European Union 2008: 38)

Unlike law enforcement authorities, which are subject to several EU laws (e.g. the recently annulled Data Retention Directive) and international agreements (e.g. the PNR Agreements), there is little Brussels can do to regulate laws governing intelligence services. Rules on these agencies are exclusively enacted by Member States.

In June 2013, an ex-analyst of the NSA, Edward Snowden, revealed numerous controversial activities conducted by the NSA. According to Snowden's documents, the NSA accesses millions of personal data from Americans and foreign citizens every day. That revelation sparked a controversial debate about the NSA, because these activities have been kept secret for a long time and they constitute direct violations of the right to privacy and data protection. For its part, the US government justified the actions by explaining that all data accesses were carried

1 Informal High Level Advisory Group on the Future of European Home Affairs Policy.

out according to proportionality and necessity criteria, and that the only goal was to fight the global terrorism that emerged after 9/11.

The Snowden revelations have questioned the legality of the US intelligence services' practices of mass surveillance. However, the US is not an exception. Most countries in the world are engaging in similar surveillance practices. There are many studies stating that internet surveillance programmes in the EU are equivalent to those of the NSA (Heumann and Scott 2013; Biermann 2013). Thus, in the EU (as in the US) a significant part of the information exchanged for the prevention and combat of serious crimes is collected by intelligence services.

Information processed by intelligence services is, in 85 per cent of cases, originally obtained through public sources and then transformed into intelligence (it is called Open Sources Intelligence (OSINT)). The other 15 per cent comes from private sources. They use software that allows them to crack passwords in a very short time. Hence, the main challenge of any intelligence agency is not the collection of data in itself, but rather the selection and analysis of the immense amount of data, and its transformation into useful intelligence.[2]

Thus, the main goal of analysts and experts of intelligence services is to provide useful knowledge rather that raw data (Taplin 1989; Lowenthal 1998; Davenport and Prusak 2000). However, on occasion, the over-abundance of information collected by intelligence services has been counterproductive. The Madrid terrorist attack of 2004 is an example of the inefficiency resulted of collecting too much information. Analysts of the Norwegian Defence Research Establishment (FFI) tracked a public document on the internet about Islamist terrorism. It included a detailed analysis of the Spanish political situation and a lengthy explanation of why the country should be seen as a target for Islamist terrorist groups after it aligned its policies to those in the US and the UK (Navarro Bonilla 2005: 10–11). Unfortunately, that document did not end up in the right hands to prevent the attack in Madrid. As this proves, only with a co-ordinated system is data collected by intelligence services a relevant tool for the prevention and combat of terrorism.

2 The blurry scope of national security and implications for the EU legislation

In the US, surveillance activities conducted on US citizens within the US territory but falling under the scope of 'national security' are not protected by the US Fourth Amendment. This exception was first established by the US Supreme Court in *Katz v United States* [1967] 389 US 347. Since then, the US Supreme Court has invoked the national security exception in numerous cases, in order to justify warrantless surveillance activities.[3]

---

2 There is no globally accepted definition of 'intelligence'.

3 *United States v United States District Court*, 407 US 297 (1972); *United States v Brown*, 484 F.2d 418, 426 (5th Cir. 1973); *United States v Butenko*, 494 F. 2d 593, 605 (3d Cir.1974); *United States v Buck*, 548 F.2d 871, 875 (9th Cir.1977); *United States v Truong Dinh Hung*, 629 F.2d 908 (4th Cir.1980); *In re Directives to Yahoo! Inc.*, 551 F. 3d 1004 (FISA Ct. Rev. 2008).

Similarly, in the EU, national security measures do not offer a full privacy protection for the EU citizens. Article 4(2) TEU excludes aspects related to national security from the scope of the EU legislation. This provision was introduced in the Treaty of Lisbon after the UK insisted that intelligence matters should not be part of the EU competences (Coolsaet 2010: 865). The clause expressly states that national security matters remain competence of the Member States. However, there is today no single accepted definition in the European and international treaties on what 'national security' covers (Article 29 Data Protection Working Party 2014b). Numerous scholars and politicians have offered definitions (Maier 1990; Mangold 1990: 1–14; Paleri 2008: 52; Sarkesian *et al* 2008: 4; Omand 2010: 9). Most of them agree that the term describes certain actions that society entrust to the governments to prevent adversaries from inflicting harm.

Security actions are often carried out by Member States, but this is not always the case. For instance, the EU is not a state, but it can still adopt security measures. As Matlary points out, the EU security policy 'is both de-territorialised as well as de-nationalised' (Haaland Matlary 2013: 23). Since 9/11, threats to security have been perceived as global. In that sense, the EP has noted that:

> While both the threats to national security and the responses to these threats have become increasingly globalised, accountability mechanisms have remained territorially bounded.
>
> (European Parliament 2013a: 4)

The global war on terror has reshaped the essence of the state and, consequently, the concept of 'national security' (Buzan 2007). Member States are no longer limited to their domestic security strategies, but they also implement national security policies adopted by supranational organisations, such as the United Nations (UN), NATO and the EU. In the EU, Article 73 TFEU establishes that it is the responsibility of Member States to co-operate and co-ordinate between themselves for the safeguarding of national security.

In the EU, the concept of 'national security' is thus intertwined with the terms of 'EU internal security' and 'EU external security' (European Parliament 2013b: 9). The EU regulates internal security matters as part of the AFSJ in Articles 67 to 89 TFEU, and external security issues as part of the CFSP (Articles 21 to 46 TEU). Instead, the regulation of national security issues falls under the exclusive competence of the Member States. The EU's role in this area would be purely co-ordinative, if any. For instance, one of the few examples of this limited EU role in national security matters is found in the regulation of the Schengen Information System.[4] Article 93 of Schengen Agreement Application Convention (SAAC) states:

> The purpose of the Schengen Information System shall be in accordance with this Convention to maintain public policy and public security, including

---

4 See Chapter 1, section 3.

national security, in the territories of the Contracting Parties and to apply the provisions of this Convention relating to the movement of persons in those territories, using information communicated via this system. (emphasis added)

The areas of national security, EU internal security and EU external security overlap with each other. Intelligence services are identified as the bodies in charge of national security matters in each Member State but, in fact, they have a role in certain supranational bodies too. For instance, within the scope of the AFSJ, the EC3 collects and processes cyber intelligence. The centre, established in 2013, is composed of national experts (police and intelligence agents) in the Member States, as well as representatives of other institutions such as the EEAS or the USSS. Moreover, as part of the EU external security, the intelligence centre IntCen[5] should be highlighted. IntCen is a central part of the EEAS, composed of representatives of intelligence services in the Member States. Hence, the centre's activities are related to national security.

For all said above, it can be concluded that the EU has *de facto* certain competences in the regulation of intelligence services' activities, despite the national security exception. The scope of Articles 4(2) TEU and Articles 72/73 TFEU needs to be concretised by the CJEU (Korff 2014: 38; Article 29 Data Protection Working Party 2014b). The Court is the EU institution that can better distinguish this concept from the similar terms of 'State security', 'internal security' and 'public security'. It can also discern whether the exemption of Article 4(2) has a general nature or if it applies only for certain activities of intelligence agencies.

The lack of precision of the national security exclusion may lead to abusive situations by law enforcement authorities with respect to the right to data protection. If all intelligence activities are considered part of the national security exclusion, it means that no EU data protection laws are applicable for these agencies. What is the purpose of protecting individuals' data collected by law enforcement authorities, if intelligence services can still freely break into their computers or intercept their calls? As Scheinin pointed out in 2009, the shift in tasks from law enforcement to intelligence agencies may serve as a way to circumvent the privacy protections in a Member State (Scheinin 2009: 11).

3 The significance of the Snowden revelations at the EU level

Since the summer of 2013, mass surveillance activities conducted by intelligence services became an issue of concern in the EU. The close co-operation that the NSA has with some Member States has called into question to what extent it violates the EU's right to data protection protected by the Charter of Fundamental Rights, the 1981 CoE Data Protection Convention, Directive 95/46/EC and Framework Decision 2008/977/JHA.

5 On IntCen, see Chapter 2, section 1.2.

This section studies the history of the NSA, the data collection programmes that the NSA uses and its secret co-operation with some Member States. It also examines the reaction to, and potential consequences of, the Snowden revelations with respect to the current EU-US data-sharing agreements.

3.1 The start of the NSA and ECHELON

The origins of the NSA date back to the end of the First World War. However, the NSA was not officially created until 1952, a few years after the establishment of the Central Intelligence Agency (CIA).[6] The NSA has its headquarters in Fort Meade (Maryland, US). This agency is bigger than the CIA and the FBI combined. The main building in Fort Meade has more than 95,000 workers and it classifies from 50 million to 100 million documents a year. During the first ten years after the establishment of the NSA, its existence was unknown among the general public. The history of this agency is based on secrecy. Analysts working there cannot reveal anything relating to the centre and they have minimal contact with the external world. The NSA is thus both the largest and the most clandestine of all US intelligence agencies.

Originally, the main purpose of the NSA was to provide detailed knowledge about the strategies and activities of the Soviet Union (Powers 2004: 239). It initially intercepted foreign communications in the political and military fields, but over the years the activities of this agency have expanded (Bamford 1982).

The NSA has used different methods to intercept telephone, fax and email communications. Initially, these interceptions were mainly conducted via microphones or laser equipment in small rooms, which sent out radio waves within an area up to 30 metres, and through wiretapping (European Parliament 2001: 30). The interception of radio signals was called SIGINT[7] and it was divided into two subsystems: COMINT[8] and ELINT.[9] The SIGINT system was based on several antennas that synchronised communications and electronic information with no awareness from the targets. This system was utilised during the Vietnam War in the 1960s and the Gulf War in 1990–1991 to spy on enemies (Powers 2004: 257). The NSA has also conducted interceptions via submarine cables, although this was rather unusual. That method was used, for instance, in 1971 when the American submarine Heli Bot recorded communications coming from a Soviet Union cable. The submarines had a magnetic system that allowed the reading of signals running through the cables. However, submarines were mainly used during wartime to eavesdrop on enemy communications (European Parliament 2001: 31).

---

6 The CIA was created in 1947 with the aim of detecting terrorist threats, and it was a direct consequence of the US failure after the Pearl Harbour attacks.
7 SIGINT comes from 'SIGnals INTelligence' and it is obtained from electronic signals that produce foreign communication systems, radars, etc.
8 COMINT comes from 'COMmunications INTelligence' and it is a subcategory of SIGINT, which collects foreign messages and voice communications.
9 ELINT comes from 'Electronic INTeligence' and it collects intelligence through electronic sensors. It is used to detect nearby ships and aircrafts.

Two controversial operations came to light in the 1970s, after the Watergate scandal: Minaret and Shamrock. The Minaret operation started in 1967 and consisted of warrantless interception of domestic electronic communications. The NSA spied famous people such as Jane Fonda, Malcolm X, Joan Baez, Dr Benjamin Spock and Martin Luther King (Webb 2008: 459). More than 6,000 foreigners and 1,000 Americans were spied on during that operation ('Echelon the secret power' 2000). The Shamrock operation dated back to as early as 1945 and it consisted of NSA bulk collection of telegrams when one end was outside the US. The three largest telecommunication companies in the US – Western Union, RCA and ITT – provided the NSA with the transcriptions of all telegrams arriving and leaving the country every day. That information helped the agency identify left-wing individuals who demonstrated against the war. The information collected was then sent to other US authorities such as the FBI, the CIA, the USSS, the Bureau of Narcotics and Dangerous Drugs (BNDD), and the Defense Department. That practice was carried out for four decades, until a Senate committee chaired by Senator Frank Church made it public (Webb 2008: 460). The report issued by Senator Church explained that the NSA collected 150,000 communications a month, which meant that at least one message was intercepted every 45 minutes.

After the Watergate scandal, there was a big debate about the two operations and thus the NSA decided to terminate them. However, a more powerful system was still ongoing: ECHELON. In 1943 the UK and the US signed an agreement to share intelligence collected via signal interferences. The UK had the necessary equipment to read codified messages, so the country worked with the US in the deciphering of messages sent by their enemies, the Germans. They learned about the Germans' strategy and that helped them to win the war. Once the war was over, the two countries decided to sign a new secret agreement called UKUSA (in March 1946). According to Article 4(a) of that Agreement:

> The parties agree to the exchange of the products of the following operations relating to foreign communications: 01. Collection of traffic. 02. Acquisition of communications documents and equipment. 03. Traffic analysis. 04. Cryptanalysis. 05. Decryption and translation. 06. Acquisition of information regarding communications organizations, procedures, practices and equipment.

Later, three nations of the British Commonwealth joined the Agreement: Canada, Australia and New Zealand. Together with the US and the UK they formed the so-called '5-Eyes'. Other countries such as Germany, Japan, Norway, Denmark, South Korea and Turkey became third parties of the Agreement. All of them had a common enemy, the Soviet Union, so the intelligence agencies of the five countries started to co-operate closely. In fact, today they still have a special relationship with each other, as proved in the Snowden disclosures.

In the 1970s, intelligence services noticed that High Frequency (HF) waves could be easily intercepted. By locating a satellite in the right position in space, all communications could be easy intercepted. Thus, ECHELON was born.

ECHELON was the codename of a giant satellite called P415. The five intelligence agencies which had access to data collected by ECHELON were the NSA in the US, the Government Communications Headquarters (GCHQ) in the UK, the Communications Security Establishment (CSE) in Canada, the Defence Signals Directorate (DSD) in Australia, and the Government Communications Security Bureau (GCSB) in New Zealand. None of them could have created a global system such as ECHELON individually.

The initial objective of ECHELON was to intercept communications from the Soviet Union, but that goal expanded to the point that it currently intercepts and shares data from stations of commercial satellites around the world. In the last ten years, many revelations by former analysts working in these five agencies have spoken out. These confirm that from the 1980s, intelligence agencies started to track activists such as Green Peace, the Red Cross and Amnesty International; public figures such as the Princess of Wales, the Pope and Queen Elizabeth II; and even public bodies such as the governments of Quebec, France and Japan ('Echelon the secret power' 2000).

For many years, ECHELON was more powerful than the internet itself. It collected and shared more than two million communications per hour (Wright 2005: 199), and it was not subject to any regulation. Through giant satellite disks established at each intelligence agency, it could globally intercept telephone calls, fax, internet and email messages. Intelligence agencies received communications through specific antennas called 'radomes'. After processing the information, it was shared with other UKUSA members.

ECHELON not only collected millions of data, but also processed them. Several super-computers interconnected with each other scanned the information according to a list of key words that were integrated in the system. Each super-computer was known as a 'Dictionary' and its functions were similar to those conducted by a search engine today, but instead of scanning websites, it scanned landline and mobile phone calls. Every member in the '5-Eyes' had its own 'Dictionary'. They could modify the keyword list at their will. The super-computers had semantic intelligence and they filtered every word of a communication. If a word coincided with one in the list, the subjects of the communication automatically became targets. Then, that information was shared with other intelligence services via a global computer system called 'Platform' (Webb 2008: 455).

The activities of the NSA were ignored by the world for decades. The '5-Eyes' tried to hide the existence of ECHELON, but that task became harder after Minaret and Shamrock came to light. In fact, the Watergate scandal led to a reform of the NSA laws. In 1975, a special committee of the US House of Representatives called the Pike Committee made a list of recommendations that became the premise of the Foreign Intelligence Surveillance Act (FISA) of 1978. FISA was created to obtain evidence for foreign intelligence. That law established the creation of the Foreign Intelligence Surveillance Court (FISC), which issued warrants based on probable cause that the target was an 'agent of a foreign power'. The court had to authorise surveillance activities conducted by the NSA and the FBI. According to the Snowden documents, in 33 years (1979–2013) the

FISC received 34,000 requests, of which the court only rejected 11 (0.03 per cent) (European Parliament 2014a: 7).

As ECHELON was not subject to any regulation, the individuals whose data were intercepted did not have any protection, since they were not residents in the country where the interception took place (European Parliament 2001: 24). ECHELON was first revealed by the journalist Duncan Campbell in his article 'Somebody's listening', published in *New Statesman* in 1988 (Campbell 1988). The article was later complemented by the Nicky Hager (Hager 1996) and Steve Wright (Wright 2005) findings. All of these reports on ECHELON pushed the EP to constitute a temporary committee – not an enquiry committee – on the ECHELON Interception System on 5 July 2000. The committee lasted 12 months and it comprised 36 MEPs (Görlitz 2013; Piodi and Mombelli 2014: 19).

The results obtained by the committee were not especially fruitful. They could not confirm the statements made by Campbell and Wright on the economic espionage conducted through ECHELON. These authors explained in their reports that ECHELON was no longer used to defend the US against the Soviet Bloc but rather to spy on big companies such as Airbus or Thompson CFS. However, the EP limited its report to a call for Member States to ensure that intelligence services in their countries did not process competitive intelligence. The Parliament stated that these practices would interfere with the loyalty duty, the common market and the principle of free competition among states. As for the legal framework of ECHELON, the EP concluded that it fell beyond the scope of the EU laws since it was an instrument used in the field of 'national security' (European Parliament 2001:18, 22 and 80–82).

3.2 The NSA data collection programmes

ECHELON is not the only NSA system to have been uncovered. The biggest revelation on the NSA's secret activities came from Edward Snowden, an ex-analyst who disclosed more than 1.7 million US top-secret documents that proved the intrusiveness of the Agency since 2001.

After 9/11, former US President George W Bush announced that the country had entered into a 'war on terror'. In consequence, the powers granted to law enforcement and intelligence agencies needed to be expanded in order to prevent and combat terrorism. In that sense, the NSA Inspector General stated in a report:

> Here is NSA standing at the U.S. border looking outward for foreign threats. There is the FBI looking within the United States for domestic threats. But no one was looking at the foreign threats coming into the United States. That was a huge gap that NSA wanted to cover.
>
> (NSA 2009)

The 9/11 terrorist attacks were carried out by individuals from outside the US, in communication with people within the US (the 9/11 hijackers). Therefore, on 26 October 2001, the US Congress passed the Patriot Act (Pub.L. 56). This act lowered the threshold of the so-called 'FISA wall', which minimised the inter-action between law enforcement and intelligence agencies. Yet, after 9/11, former US President George W Bush decided to promote the communication between all security agencies. Section 215 of that Act enabled the US government to collect bulk telephone metadata of US citizens provided there were reasonable grounds that it was relevant for international terrorism or any foreign intelligence investi-gation. Metadata includes telephone numbers, the origin/destination of the call and the date of the call. These are stored for a five-year period.

A few years later, in 2008, an act amending FISA (FISAA) expanded the US government's powers for the collection and processing of foreign intelligence. In particular, section 702 of FISAA permits the government to target communications of non-US individuals 'reasonably believed' to be outside the US without a FISA warrant. The NSA only needs to send an annual report to FISC determining the targets for the coming year (Greenwald 2014: 4–5). As in section 215, most of the data collected is retained for five years in the NSA database.

For almost a year, Snowden downloaded top-secret documents while working in Hawaii at Booz Allen Hamilton. He then travelled to Hong Kong and shared the information with *The Guardian* and *The Washington Post*. The first programme disclosed by Snowden was PRISM. In general terms, PRISM operates under section 702 of FISAA and consists of collecting data from targeted individuals stored in the servers of eight major internet companies: Google, Yahoo!, Facebook, Pa!Talk, YouTube, Skype, AOL and Apple. Through PRISM, the NSA and the FBI exchanged information provided by those companies. These companies have co-operated with the US government (Greenwald 2014: 109),[10] and those that have sought resist it[11] have usually been coerced by the FISC. In 2011, FISC stated that the NSA was collecting 250 million internet communications per year under PRISM. The data is held for five years.

FISC comprises District Court judges who carry out FISA work as an additional part of their duties. The DoJ issues the application to a single judge, who will decide whether or not the warrant is issued. The threshold is set on the existence of probable cause. This decision can be appealed to the FISA Intelligence Surveillance Court of Review (FISCR) and, ultimately, to the Supreme Court of the United States. Originally, FISC judges just reviewed the facts for individual surveillance orders. Yet, following the Patriot Act in 2001, FISA judges increasingly also considered legal arguments. These judges had to make very difficult legal decisions and they generally heard only from the government. Their opinions are not public, so there is no opportunity for outside feedback (see Figure 4.1).

In the EU, the collaboration of TSPs with the NSA was condemned by the Art. 29 WP. Reports released by this group are not binding, but they have a great political impact on the EU institutions and Member States. Regarding the collaboration of Google, Facebook, Apple, etc with the NSA, the Art. 29 WP pointed out that they could be infringing the EU laws:

---

10 However, in the beginning they denied any knowledge of the existence of PRISM.
11 Exceptionally, in July 2013 Yahoo! won a case against the disclosure of users' data through PRISM.

Figure 4.1

Companies need to be aware that they may be acting in breach of European law if intelligence services of third countries gain access to the data of European citizens stored on their servers or comply with an order to hand over personal data on a large scale.

(Article 29 Data Protection Working Party 2014a: 7)

Other programmes used by the NSA under section 702 FISAA were based on interception methods. Companies were not aware of such practices, but foreign governments were. For example, through BOUNDLESS INFORMANT the NSA collected more that three billion phone calls and emails passing through US tele-communication systems (Greenwald 2014: 81 and 92). MUSCULAR is another interception programme, which collects traffic and content data of Yahoo and Google users (Peterson 2013). Similarly, RAMPANT-A is a programme that taps into cables and intercepts the content of phone calls, faxes, emails, internet chats and even calls using Voice over IP (VoIP) like Skype (Gallagher 2014a). UPSTREAM surveillance consists of collecting data as it transits a network in real time. Telephone and internet companies knew about the data collection but they had previously been compelled to sign a co-operation agreement with the NSA to lawfully permit that interception (Bowden 2013: 15). All of these programmes have not been claimed illegal because the NSA does not break into the servers of the TSP but only intercepts the communications as they are transmitted via fibre optic cables.

Programmes such as BULLRUN, CHEESY NAME, EDGEHILL and QUANTUMHAND have a more sophisticated nature. Through these systems, the NSA is able to break encryption technologies. For instance, BULLRUN is a decryption software that circumvents online protocols such as HTTPS. Likewise, CHEESY NAME singles out encryption keys and EDGEHILL is used to decode encrypted traffic of major IT companies. Lastly, QUANTUMHAND is a programme through which the NSA installs a malware in the target's computer and uses a fake Facebook account to access the target's computer (Gallagher and Greenwald 2014).

Once the NSA obtains the encrypted information, a programme called XKEYSCORE enables the agency to glean information from it. It is distributed in connection points across the globe (it has 150 sites and over 700 servers). This programme allows targets to be monitored in real time as they are writing an email or surfing the net (Heumann and Scott 2013: 5; Greenwald 2014: 157–158). The mechanism used by this programme consists of 'slowing down the internet' so that analysts can go back and recover sessions that otherwise would have been dropped by the front data. Content data is kept from three to five days, whereas metadata is saved for longer, for approximately 30 days. Much of the largest

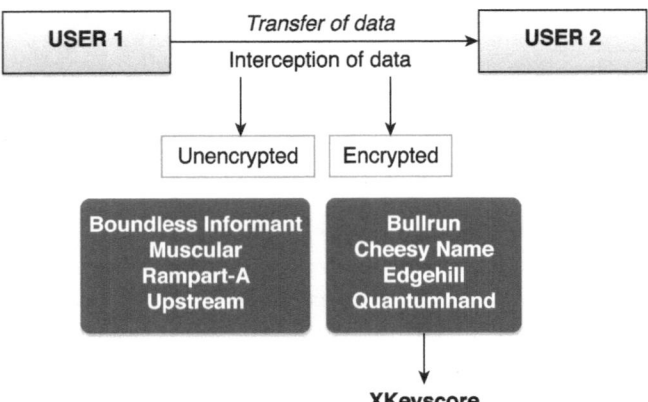

Figure 4.2

collection occurs in the UK under the basis of Executive Order 12333,[12] therefore it does not have US court oversight (see Figure 4.2).

Some of the programmes disclosed by Snowden are based on section 215 of the Patriot Act. For example STELLAR WIND allows the NSA to collect bulk metadata from a TSP, after a FISC order is issued. The metadata belongs to US and non-US citizens and the FISC order can be renewed every 90 days (Greenwald and Ackerman 2013). Data collected by the NSA through all of the above-mentioned programmes (and more) is stored in a 'broker', which is connected to a Google-like search engine. It is called 'ICReach' and enables the intelligence community to search for any name or piece of information it needs (Gallagher 2014b).

The NSA has always stated that it uses all these programmes for the prevention and combat of global terrorism. After the revelations, great criticisms were raised about the lack of efficiency of these programmes, which have not always led to the interruption of terrorist plots. In light of this criticism, the NSA felt obliged to explain in which cases these programmes had effectively contributed to stop terror plots. The NSA stated that section 215 programmes had detected 54 terrorist activities (Inglis 2013), whereas section 702 programmes had helped stop at least 42 attacks (Ledgett 2014). However, the agency has always used the case of Basaaly Moalin[13] to justify the effectiveness of section 215. As for the programmes established under section 702, the agency has usually mentioned the cases of David Coleman Headley,[14] Najibullah Zazi,[15]

12 EO 12333 covers any activity not considered 'electronic surveillance'. Activities within the scope of EO 12333 do not require a prior court order.
13 Moalin was a cabdriver from San Diego who provided US$8,500 to Al-Shabaab (Al-Qaeda affiliate) during 2007 and 2008.
14 Headley is a Pakistani-American who plotted to attack the Danish newspaper *Jyllands-Posten* in 2009. He was also involved in the planning of the 2008 terrorist attacks in Mumbai.
15 Together with Zarein Ahmedzay and Adis Medunjanon, Zazi plotted to bomb the New York subway system in 2009. Yet, studies say that it was not the NSA but the British intelligence that initiated the investigation.

Khalid Ouazzani,[16] Jamshid Muhtorov and Bakhtiyor Jumaev,[17] and Jihad Jane[18] as its principle successes.

In June 2014, the Office of the Director of National Intelligence revealed that 89,138 people were targets under section 702 FISAA in 2013 alone (US Office of the Director of National Intelligence 2014). Considering these numbers, one might wonder whether the 42 success stories really justify the fact that almost 90,000 people were exposed to the NSA's scrutiny. Moreover, another public debate questioned the work of the NSA after it was unable to prevent the Boston Marathon bombings in 2013 (Bergen *et al* 2014: 13–15).

The NSA has also explained that any interception made under section 702 undergoes executive, legislative and judicial oversight. The executive review is conducted by an independent inspector general, who carries out regular on-site reviews and sends reports to the Congress (NSA 2013: 3). The legislative oversight is conducted by the Intelligence Committee and the Judiciary Committee of the House of the Representatives and the Senate. As for the judicial review, the NSA has ensured that any interception or intelligence gathering needs prior order from FISC. Also, every 30 days, the NSA sends a report to FISC about the state of the investigation (NSA 2013: 6). However, this court has been highly criticised by pro-privacy experts and activists due to its secrecy; the poor information it gets to effectively assess the NSA activities (Heumann and Scott 2013: 6–7); the number of targets that a single order can involve;[19] and the low number of cases the court has rejected to date.[20]

The Snowden revelations sparked several legislative and political changes in the US. For example, the US Patriot Act is now expired and has been replaced by the USA Freedom Act, which ends the bulk collection of metadata in the terms of ex-section 215. Likewise, a list of five basic principles was released by key IT companies against the NSA mass surveillance (Davis 2013), and recommendations were published by the Privacy and Civil Liberties Oversight Board on sections 215 and 702 (Privacy and Civil Liberties Oversight 2014a, 2014b). The NSA has started to publish regular transparency reports (NSA 2014), and it now has a chief privacy officer (Kamen 2014), as well as a Review Group on Intelligence and Communications Technologies for the oversight of the agency. All of these changes are taking place in the US. Yet, the Snowden revelations have also had an impact outside the US territory and, especially, in the EU.

16 Ouazzani owned a small business in Kansas City and the NSA found that he provided tens of thousands of dollars to Al-Qaeda for many years.

17 Muhtorov and Jumaev, nationals from Uzbekistan, were accused of providing support to the terrorist organisation Islamic Jihad Union.

18 Jane plotted to kill the Swedish artist Lars Vilks because of his depiction of the prophet Muhammad.

19 Which can get up to 89,138 targets for a single order. See US Office of the Director of National Intelligence 2014.

20 As mentioned above, out of 34,000 requests, the court has only rejected 11.

3.3 Secret collaboration of the EU Member States with the NSA

Since 9/11, the co-operation of intelligence services in the EU with the US authorities has increased significantly. The common goal is to prevent a major terrorist attack. Today it is well documented that a few months before the 9/11 terrorist attacks many warnings came into the hands of the CIA and other intelligence services about Al-Qaeda's intentions, but they were not considered a threat (Bergen 2013). In July that year, an FBI agent in Phoenix claimed that terrorists could be attending flight schools in preparation for an attack. Around that time, the CIA informed former President George W Bush about a possible Al-Qaeda plane hijacking that would take place on 6 August 2001. Also, by early September three foreign intelligence services reported to the CIA that Bin Laden had ordered his four wives to urgently return to Afghanistan (Powers 2004: 362 and 388–389). None of these dots was adequately connected.

Following the attacks, the US government handed a list of recommendations to the CIA, the FBI and the NSA. It urged for the recruiting of more spies (especially those with connections to terrorist groups), as well as hiring new agents who could speak and translate relevant languages. From that moment, the NSA had to transform itself from a passive gatherer into a proactive terrorist hunter (Powers 2004: 411). In 2004, the Bush Administration released the 9/11 Commission Report through which it called other nations to engage 'in developing a comprehensive coalition strategy against Islamist terrorism' (9/11 Commission 2004). Consequently, national intelligence services within the EU committed to collaborating closely with the US government and, most particularly with the NSA, in the prevention and combat of terrorism and serious crimes.

As discussed above, the NSA has been maintaining a special relationship with four other English-speaking countries: Canada, Australia, New Zealand and the United Kingdom (UK). This collective group is known as the '5-Eyes'. The only EU country among the 5-Eyes partnership is the UK. A close co-operation has existed between the NSA and GCHQ, a British intelligence organisation, since the Cold War, when they signed the UKUSA Agreement (Powers 2004: 240). More recently, and according to the latest documents released by Snowden, the GCHQ receives 50 billion data messages per day through different programmes, some of which are provided by the NSA (Greenwald 2014: 100). The GCHQ does not need any warrant to access bulk NSA data (Privacy International 2014). One of the most controversial systems the GCHQ uses is the above-mentioned PRISM. Through this programme, the GCHQ is technically able to circumvent any formal British legal procedure and obtain data collected by the main TSP located outside the country (Gellman and Poitras 2013). As mentioned in previous chapters, it is not uncommon that law enforcement agencies informally contact TSPs in order to obtain users' data. The same occurs with respect to intelligence services. The Snowden documents reveal that TSP such as Verizon, British Telecommunications, Vodafone, Global Crossing, Level 3, Viatel and Interoute have long co-operated with the GCHQ providing it with users' information when requested.

Another programme used by the GCHQ is TEMPORA. Due to its privileged location, the UK hosts a quarter of all internet traffic in the world. In consequence, the UK is able to tap into dozens of undersea transatlantic cables and gather telecommunication data. TEMPORA was created precisely to collect and store such information. The Snowden documents unveiled that the NSA also has access to that data (MacAskill and Ball 2013; Nielsen 2013). A debate has arisen because TEMPORA is supposed to be used by the GCHQ to intercept foreign communications only. Yet, communications originating in the UK can still be intercepted by the NSA and then passed onto its '5-Eyes' partners, including the UK (Bunyan 2014: 13). In other words, through TEMPORA the GCHQ is able to obtain communications from British citizens, circumventing the prohibition established in the British laws.

Besides the GCHQ, intelligence services in other EU Member States have also been co-operating with the NSA. Specifically, these countries are Austria, Belgium, the Czech Republic, Denmark, Germany, Greece, Hungary, Italy, Luxembourg, The Netherlands, Poland, Portugal, Spain and Sweden (Greenwald and Aranda 2013a). After the UK, Germany is the Member State that has intercepted the most personal communications. Snowden used the following example when he told a German newspaper about the collaboration between Germany and the NSA:

> For example, we tip them off when someone we want is flying through their airports (that we for example, have learned from the cell phone of a suspected hacker's girlfriend in a totally unrelated third country – and they hand them over to us). They don't ask to justify how we know something, and vice versa, to insulate their political leaders from the backlash of knowing how grievously they're violating global privacy.
>
> (Edward Snowden interview 2013)

The collaboration between German intelligence services and the US has increased significantly since 9/11 due to the fact that Al-Qaeda established terrorist cells in Germany to prepare the attacks. The co-operation between the two countries dates back to the Cold War, when the US assisted German troops in Afghanistan (Bryant and Fontanella-Khan 2013). Today, the Federal Intelligence Service – the *Bundesnachrichtendienst* (BND) – mostly spies on foreign communications in countries such as Russia, Central Asia or the Middle East, but it has also permission to target Germans on a case-by-case basis (Farivar 2013).

However, the relationship between the US and Germany has been damaged since it was revealed that the NSA had been tapping the German Chancellor Angela Merkel's mobile phone for more than a decade (Lenoir 2013; Rawlinson 2013; Noack 2014). The surveillance began three years before she became Chancellor because the US wanted to gather information about the German position on the Iraq War (Lewis 2013). Germany has always had a special sensitivity towards issues concerning personal privacy and data protection due to its horrific experiences during the Nazi regime, and later by the East German secret police (Eddy 2013).

Another EU country that carried out enormous surveillance during 2013 is France. It collected data from more than 70 million French phones in only one month. The French intelligence community is divided into the *Direction de la surveillance du territoire* (DST), a domestic intelligence agency, and the *Direction générale de la sécurité extérieure* (DGSE), an external intelligence agency. The programme used to intercept communications is called US-985D, which targets both suspects and non-suspects. Phone calls and SMS messages registered by that programme have also been shared with the NSA (Follorou and Greenwald 2013). Ironically, one of the documents disclosed by Snowden reveals that France has also been considered a NSA target when the UN Security Council was preparing a resolution about the sanctions on Iran (Greenwald 2014: 144).

Another Member State that has been collaborating closely with the US is Spain. The co-operation between the two was reinforced in 2001. Two months after the 9/11 attacks, the former president of Spain, José María Aznar, gave the green light to the US intelligence services to operate on Spanish soil. In return, Aznar requested advanced interception equipment from the US government for Spain's *Centro Nacional de Inteligencia* (CNI). The documents leaked by Snowden show that the NSA intercepted data from more than 60 million Spanish citizens in only one month (Greenwald and Aranda 2013b). After the leak, the Spanish public prosecutor argued that such surveillance should take place without a prior court order. However, he added that it is especially complicated to learn more about the alleged violation since the interceptions are classified information and, consequently, the *Ministerio Público* has no access to them (Peral 2013).

This analysis demonstrates that intelligence services of Member States have individually consolidated a strong link with the US agencies. In return, the NSA equips all of these agencies with new technology and surveillance programmes.

3.4 EU reaction and consequences for the EU-US agreements

The Snowden disclosures put the spotlight on all of the current and future data-sharing agreements between the EU and the US. One of the main concerns of EU officials was that if data was collected by the NSA under section 702 FISAA then EU citizens had no redress mechanisms at all.

After the revelations, the former Vice-president of the Commission, Viviane Reding, sent a letter to the US Advocate General Eric Holder, asking several questions relating to the EU citizens' data that the NSA was gathering (Viviane Reding 2013). Likewise, the Art. 29 WP pointed out some aspects about PRISM that needed to be clarified (Article 29 Data Protection Working Party WP 2013). In order to find more answers, the Commission and the US government decided to create a transatlantic group of experts: the ad-hoc EU-US Working Group on Data Protection. Also, at the national level, governments of the majority of Member States launched initiatives to improve data security against intelligence services' intrusions (Bryant and Fontanella-Khan 2013; Kaufmann 2013).

Many aspects of the current version of the EU Data Protection Regulation have been questioned since the disclosures. In particular, there are two provisions of the GDPR that have been given special attention: ex Article 42 and Article 43a, suggested by the EP. Article 42 was included in the original draft of the proposal, leaked in December 2011, but it was later removed. Paragraph 1 stated:

> No judgment of a court or tribunal and no decision of an administrative authority of a third country requiring a controller or processor to disclose personal data shall be recognized or be enforceable in any manner, without prejudice to a mutual assistance treaty or an international agreement in force between the requesting third country and the Union or a Member State.

That provision was commonly known as the 'anti-FISA clause'. The US authorities intensively lobbied for the removal of the clause before the official document was released. The US considered that the anti-FISA clause would impede public regulatory agencies from accessing the data necessary for investigations and thus hinder the EU-US co-operation (US Federal Trade Commission 2011: 8). Consequently, Article 42 was removed from the draft.

Once the proposal was published, it was sent to the EP, particularly to the LIBE Committee, for inspection and the suggestion of amendments. The LIBE Committee made more than 4,000 amendments. Among them, it decided to include Article 43a, which has almost the same wording as the original Article 42. Since Article 43a has been finally added, the US authorities might have more difficulties in obtaining EU citizens' data through court orders, subpoenas, letters of request and letters rogatory (Wiese Svanberg 2014). Also, companies could be sanctioned if they transfer data to the US authorities outside the scope of a MLA treaty or a specific international agreement, or without the approval of a data protection authority. However, the real impact of the provision is unclear, considering that Member States' national security exclusion is maintained in the GDPR.

Current EU-US agreements have also been affected by the Snowden revelations. One of the consequences has been the annulment of the Safe Harbour Agreement by the CJEU (Case C-362/14, *Maximillian Schrems v Data Protection Commissioner* (2015)). That Agreement entered into force in 2000, when the Commission adopted the Safe Harbour principles to solve the problem of the lack of a complete data protection framework in the US (Commission Decision 2000/520/EC). The principles had the aim of complying with the adequacy requirement of Article 25 of Directive 95/46/EC. By the time the scheme was annulled, it included more than 4,400 certified companies based in the US. According to the Agreement, US companies implementing Safe Harbour principles complied with the adequacy standards in the terms of Article 25 of Directive 95/46/EC. However, some controversies arose already in 2013 when it was found that at least 10 per cent of the companies claiming membership to the Safe Harbour scheme were not actually listed there (COM(2013) 847 final, p. 7). Moreover, one of the NSA programmes disclosed, PRISM, showed that Safe Harbour did not prevent companies from transferring personal data to governments without EU approval.

After the revelations, the former Vice-president of the Commission, Viviane Reding, expressed concerns about Safe Harbour and issued recommendations in order to improve the legal framework (COM(2013) 847 final). Similarly, the Art. 29 WP released recommendations on the scheme in April 2014 (Article 29 Data Protection Working Party 2014c). For its part, the EP has taken a more drastic position calling for the immediate suspension of the scheme (European Parliament 2014b: 3).

Safe Harbour was recently annulled by the CJEU. The case arose after Snowden revelations, when the Austrian student Max Schrems started legal action before the Irish High Court because the Irish DPA had not stopped data transfers between Facebook Ireland and Facebook Inc. The Irish DPA claimed that Facebook complied with the Safe Harbor principles and, therefore, there was no reason to suspend its data transfers. The Irish High Court referred the matter to the CJEU for a preliminary ruling, questioning whether the Irish DPA had an obligation to examine the complaint regarding Facebook data transfers. On 6 October 2015, the CJEU annulled the Safe Harbour Agreement because it did not comply with the adequacy criteria for international data transfer in the terms of Article 25 of Directive 95/46/EC (Case C-362/14, *Maximillian Schrems v Data Protection Commissioner* (2015)) Safe Harbour has now been replaced by the EU-US Privacy Shield.

The Snowden revelations have also raised concerns about the current SWIFT Agreement. One of the documents disclosed by Snowden confirmed that SWIFT data have also been compromised. This revelation was met with huge disappointment among EU institutions, especially the EP, which had long fought to achieve adequate data protection standards for SWIFT. Therefore, the EP called for the immediate suspension of the Agreement. The MEP Jan Albrecht drafted an unofficial joint motion, pointing out that:

> Although the Parliament has no formal powers under Art. 218 of the TFEU to initiate a suspension or termination of an international agreement, the Commission will have to act if Parliament withdraws its support for a particular agreement.
>
> (European Parliament 2013c: para. 12)

Similarly, the former EU Home Affairs Commissioner, Cecilia Malmstrom, initiated formal consultations with the US in the terms of Article 19 of the SWIFT Agreement, as the first step towards a suspension of the Agreement. The Belgian and Dutch DPAs also investigated whether the NSA had been unlawfully accessing bank transaction data at SWIFT, but they finally concluded that there had been no violation (Dutch DPA 2013). SWIFT and Europol officials also arrived at the same result (European Parliament 2014b: 5). Therefore, the SWIFT Agreement has not been suspended for the moment.

The EU-US PNR Agreement has also been in the spotlight. The Joint Review for the implementation of the Agreement stated that during 2012–2013 the DHS made 23 disclosures of PNR data to the NSA (SEC(2013) 630 final, p. 16). However, the Joint Review stated that these were made on a case-by-case basis and according to the terms of the Agreement. What the Joint review did not mention is that those EU citizens whose data were transferred to the NSA lacked judicial and administrative redress (European Parliament 2013b: 14). It goes against the safeguards that the PNR Agreement endorses. Therefore, if it is found that there has been a violation due to the lack of redress, the Agreement could still be suspended, in accordance with the terms of Articles 24 and 25.

Lastly, a few words on the expected DPPA between the EU and the US. As seen in Chapter 2, negotiations for the DPPA have suffered an immense delay. They officially started in March 2011 but they are still ongoing. The main reason why these negotiations are at a standstill is precisely the issue of judicial redress for EU citizens. The former Vice-president of the Commission, Viviane Reding, tried to include a clause on this issue during the negotiations, but the US kept blocking the EU demands. The Snowden revelations have brought some changes to the negotiations in this respect. The US, which has always been leading the decisions on the Agreement, is now more willing to consider the EU suggestions on redress. In November 2013, Reding announced the US efforts to accelerate the completion of the Agreement (Reding 2013a). The EP has also highlighted the importance that the DPPA incorporates a clause permitting EU citizens to enjoy judicial redress, irrespective of where they have their residence (Baker 2013). Hence, it seems that the revelations have helped the EU negotiate the provision on judicial redress in the future proposal of the agreement.

In conclusion, trust needs to be rebuilt on both sides of the Atlantic. The revelations have clearly damaged the co-operation between the EU and the US in the field of privacy. As Reding pointed out 'We are not seen as partners, but as a threat' (Reding 2013b: 6–7). The Snowden revelations do not only involve the NSA. Similar activities take place in intelligence agencies in the Member States within the EU. For instance, most of the intelligence services in the EU do not require any prior judicial authorisation to get private information from foreign persons. This and other aspects are examined in the next section.

4 Systematic storage and access to data by intelligence services in the EU

The previous section shows that intelligence services of the Member States have maintained a close collaboration with the NSA. However, these intelligence services are also using massive surveillance programmes themselves, even if the information is not sent to the US. These programmes might violate the EU right to data protection, but due to their secrecy, it is not easy to get information about their actual functions and scope.

As seen in previous chapters, individuals of a Member State are able to go to the national and European police forces and request access to all information they keep about them. Yet, this right does not always exist for data collected and stored by intelligence services.

GCHQ in the UK has one of the most controversial legal frameworks in the EU. In 2013, the Interception of Communications Commissioner (ICC) released a report stating that it is lawful for GCHQ to intercept communications and acquire communication data (UK Interception of Communications Commissioner 2013). Two laws regulate the GCHQ functioning: the Intelligence Services Act (ISA) 1994 and the Regulation of Investigatory Powers Act (RIPA) 2000. The ISA sets rules about the warrant that the Secretary of State needs to give before certain actions. RIPA regulates all surveillance activities conducted by intelligence and law enforcement authorities. It establishes two types of interception warrants: the section 8(1) warrants and the section 8(4) warrants. They normally last six months and are authorised by the Secretary of State.

As for section 8(4) warrants (also known as 'certified warrants'), they allow the intercepting of external communications and are issued by the Foreign Secretary. Debates have been raised because of the broad certificates given by the secretary (Bunyan 2013). Section 8(1) warrants are required for the interception of content data stored in TSPs. Yet, if GCHQ seeks to access traffic data hold by these service providers, section 22(3) RIPA requires only an authorisation by a senior official. RIPA also serves as the legal basis for surveillance carried out by GCHQ via satellites and fibre-optic undersea cables. Since it does not involve direct contact with the TSPs, there is no need to send them a notice in the sense of section 33(4) RIPA. In fact, these interceptions are not authorised by a senior official, but they require section 8(4) certificates issued by the Foreign Secretary (Bunyan 2014; MacAskill *et al* 2013). However, UK laws on intelligence services need to be tightened up, since many questions are still unanswered about these interceptions – for instance, it is unclear from section 16(3) RIPA how domestic communications and foreign information are sorted out by the British intelligence services (Heumann and Scott 2013: 9; Bunyan 2014: 12).

Besides the interception of communications, intelligence services in the UK may obtain information through voluntary disclosures by private entities. According to sections 19–21 of the Counter-Terrorism Act 2008, even if someone volunteers to disclose information to the intelligence agency, such information still needs to pass the tests of necessity and proportionality before it is processed by the agency (UK Home Affairs Committee 2014: 10). However, these criteria might be very ambiguous at times, since there is no judicial or independent body in control of the compliance.

Systematic processing of data is also present in the French intelligence services. In fact, due to its overseas territories, France possesses the technical infrastructure to operate a global interception system without co-operating with foreign countries (European Parliament 2001: 11). The French Code of Criminal Procedure was amended in 2011 in order to enhance law enforcement and intelligence services' powers for the collection of data. This law authorises practices such as the decryption of protected computer data, numeric infiltration and the enrolment of online chatroom conversations (United Nations Office on Drugs and Crime 2012: 45–46 and 57). Likewise, the so-called *Loi de Programmation Militaire* (LPM), adopted in December 2013, enables French secret services to intercept any communication if it is authorised by the Prime Minister. Many debates have emerged with regard to this law, since its individual safeguards, adequacy and collected categories of data are undetermined (Champeau 2013). Lastly, another systematic collection of French citizens' data comes from the DGSE. The DGSE systematically collects the electromagnetic signals launched by computers and phones within the country, as well as the communications between France and other countries (Follorou and Johannes 2013).

The German Foreign Intelligence Services, BND, are based on a law passed in 1990 (BGBl. I S. 2954, 2979). This law authorises the BND to collect information from foreign communications and to request data obtained by TSP. Surveillance activities by German intelligence agencies are also regulated in the *Gesetz zur Beschränkung des Brief-, Post- und Fernmeldegeheimnisses*, also known as G-10 law (BGBl. I S. 1254, 2298). The law has been highly controversial since it provides additional surveillance powers to the BND, by limiting Article 10 of the German Constitution (protection of the privacy of correspondence, posts, and telecommunications). According to the supreme law, the BND can access letters and communications in order to avoid: (a) an armed attack; (b) an international terrorist attack; (c) illicit foreign trade transactions in goods, data processing programmes and technologies; (d) an unauthorised commercial shipment of narcotics into the EU; (e) the impairment of monetary stability in the euro zone; (f) international organised money laundering; and (g) commercial organised smuggling of foreign persons in the territory of the EU. The BND monitors international communications (mostly emails) through the largest German internet point Deutscher Commercial Internet Exchange (DE-CIX), located in Frankfurt. The agency identified 37 million communications in 2010 through DE-CIX, but the number was reduced after that year because the BND started to use other automatic filtering programmes (Heumann and Scott 2013: 12).

Germany has established some limitations for the BND surveillance activities. The German Constitutional Court declared in 2008 that secret online searches of private computers by domestic intelligence services were unlawful, and stricter conditions were imposed after that (Case 1 BvR 370/07). One of the changes was the amendment of G-10 Law in 2009, incorporating new safeguards and restrictions on surveillance (BGBl. I S. 2437). For instance, the collection of data about an untargeted individual's basic private life is now prohibited (Article 3a); the information on the private life of an individual that has been collected with no judicial supervision needs to be deleted (Article 5a); and new conditions have to be verified for the BND's transfer of intelligence to foreign public bodies (Article 7a). It confirms that data protection provisions are more visible in the G-10 Law than in other countries.

It can be concluded that intelligence services in Member States often have a *carte blanche* to collect and process information and turn it into intelligence. Data collected does not only belong to EU citizens under suspicion or linked to criminal groups, but it also includes data from innocent individuals.

5 Could the EU set up data protection standards for the exchange of intelligence?

Two interesting points have been examined in this chapter so far: the first refers to the rupture of the EU-US confidence since the Snowden revelations. From the moment the NSA's programmes and practices were disclosed, current and future agreements between the two parties have been called into question, and some members of the EU institutions have even suggested suspending them. These drastic statements have borne fruit: We see now a more flexible US government, willing to adapt to the EU demands in the field of data protection.

The second interesting issue seen in the previous section is that intelligence services' activities might hinder the effective establishment of global data protection rules in the field of security. Intelligence services, unlike law enforcement, are only regulated at the national level. There are no EU laws regulating the information processed by these bodies. As a result, EU data protection rules can be circumvented via intelligence services. This is particularly alarming if we bear in mind that the division of tasks between intelligence services and law enforcement authorities is becoming very diffuse today.

Taking all this into account, the third and final issue this chapter will examine is the possibility to approximate and harmonise EU data protection rules that affect national intelligence services, especially those provisions relating to individual safeguards and rights. These norms should not clash with Articles 4(2) TEU and 72 TFEU, which state that the adoption of laws on the safeguarding of national security is the responsibility of each Member State.

5.1 Lack of co-ordination of intelligence services within the EU

All Member States except for Ireland[21] have their own intelligence agencies, which act according to their specific domestic laws (Cross 2013: 391).[22] Intelligence agencies collect and analyse the data they deem necessary and, once it becomes intelligence, it is forwarded to national governments.

Espionage practices in Europe have their origins in ancient civilisations. Several historians of Greek and Latin civilisations have found documents revealing episodes of espionage during these periods. In the Middle Ages, such practices were improved by the inclusion of diplomatic services within governments, and the practice gradually developed over the centuries until the institutionalisation of intelligence services, and new forms of data collection and processing through cryptographic techniques became available. During the twentieth century, espionage became an extremely entrenched practice among European governments, who took advantage of the developments in signals intelligence technology that were made during that period. The First and Second World Wars, the civil wars in some European countries and the period of the Cold War were all characterised by the important role of secret services in gathering intelligence and counterintelligence related to rival countries. In contrast, the nineties was a

---

21 Functions of national security in Ireland are fully conducted by police forces.
22 Yet, not all Member States have the same level of experience as regards the collection and analysis of intelligence. The UK, Spain and Germany have a lot of experience in the intelligence sector, whereas newer Member States such as Poland and Slovenia are relatively inexperienced.

somewhat quiet decade for the intelligence centres. This is precisely why 9/11 came as such a shock.

The terrorist attacks of 11 September 2001 caused a revolution in the global intelligence society. Terrorists communicate globally and use all types of internet services (email accounts, fora, social media, VoiP systems, etc). Consequently, intelligence activities are no longer conducted at a state-to-state level, and coordination among public and private actors around the world is increasing. In particular, the US and the EU embarked on a significant joint effort to improve the co-ordination among its national communication systems by establishing a common political authority (Moret Millás 2005: 264).

Austria and Belgium suggested the creation of a CIA-style agency in the EU, but the other Member States did not support that initiative (Bures and Ahern 2007: 217). Nevertheless, two new bodies were established after the 9/11 terrorist attacks: the CTG and IntCen. The CTG is a forum composed of the parties of the 'Berne Club', namely, all EU Member States plus Switzerland and Norway. Their heads of security and intelligence services meet regularly in order to discuss data and analyses related to terrorism (mostly Islamic extremist terrorism) and to develop periodic threat assessments (Occhipinti 2013: 158–159). IntCen is the evolution of a previous European centre called Joint Situation Centre (SitCen). SitCen was created by the former High Representative of the CFSP, Javier Solana, one year before the 9/11 terrorist attacks, and it had three departments: the Operations Unit, the Analysis Unit and the Consular Unit. However, it did not tackle counter-terrorism issues at first.

After the attacks, SitCen enhanced its scope in order to examine internal and external threats related to terrorism and other serious crimes (Occhipinti 2013: 160). There were other attempts to improve SitCen capabilities after the attacks in Madrid (2004), London (2005) and Oslo (2011).[23] For instance, in 2005 the Analysis Unit established links with the CTG, which started to influence EU decisions on internal security matters (Mills *et al* 2011: 54–55). SitCen also recruited seconded analysts from Member States and internal security services (Busuioc and Groenleer 2013: 294), and it began to provide strategic reports to the Council of the EU and to Member States. These reports are usually in the form of signals intelligence (SIGINT),[24] human intelligence (HUMINT) and imagery intelligence (IMINT) (Svenden 2011: 536).

In April 2012, the EU re-named the body as 'IntCen'. IntCen's legal basis is not completely clear. The only mention of the centre is found in the Annex of EEAS Council Decision (Council Decision 2010/427/EU). Although not all EEAS instruments are part of the CFSP,[25] IntCen would probably fall under its scope. In

---

23 On 21 July 2011, Anders Behring Breivik detonated a bomb in Oslo and subsequently killed 77 (mostly young) people on the island of Utoya.

24 Particularly from France's satellites Helios and Pleiades, Germany's satellite SAR-Lupe and Italy's satellite Cosmo-SkyMed,

25 For instance, EEAS measures outside of the scope of CSFP tackle issues related to the neighbourhood policy, development, financial matters, the external dimension of human rights, environment, transport, etc.

that case, the current High Representative of the CFSP, Federica Mogherini, would be in charge of the centre. The other possibility is that IntCen uses Article 73 TFEU as its main legal basis. This provision does not belong to the CFSP, but to the AFSJ. This proves, once more, that the boundaries between the CFSP and the external dimension of the AFSJ are ambiguous. Moreover, IntCen does not only deal with external security matters, but it also carries out EU internal security functions. For instance, it co-operates with Europol and it drafts reports that it then sends to the Commission and the Council (Council of the European Union 2014a: 2). Therefore, the legal basis of the centre needs to be clarified. In that sense, in December 2013 the EP urged the Commission to present a proposal for a legal basis for the activities of IntCen (European Parliament 2013b: 25).

IntCen has recruited military intelligence and police analysts from Member States in order to increase the co-operation among national intelligence services (Cross 2013: 289). The tasks of the new IntCen have been viewed with optimism (Svenden 2011). Yet, the reality is that the competences of the centre are still very small, in comparison with those of a regular intelligence centre. In fact, the EEAS has made it very clear that IntCen is not an intelligence service, since the centre mainly provides information on crisis management situations. In addition, it does not have information collection powers or any operational role, and it only shares assessed intelligence among Member States, as well as with EU institutions and bodies (Mills *et al* 2011: 55–56).

IntCen has achieved a certain degree of intelligence integration within the EU. Some OSINT partnerships have been consolidated among some Member States such as Germany, Denmark, the Netherlands, the UK, Italy, Austria, Sweden, Norway, France and Belgium (Svenden 2011: 529). Member States have discretionary powers on the decision of whether to share information with the centre or not. In this sense, there is still a low level of political will among Member States to co-operate with the IntCen, and they are often resistant to share intelligence with the centre (Cross 2013: 288 and 400; Archick 2013: 3). Consequently, the 80 per cent of the intelligence stored by IntCen comes from only four EU-countries (Nielsen 2015).

There are many reasons why Member States are reluctant to share intelligence among each other. First, they do not always trust how other agencies are going to use the intelligence. They are very cautious about the risk of manipulation if they forward it. Likewise, they are often concerned about free-riding from others, or the loss of privileged influence if the intelligence circulates beyond the country. In addition intelligence services in the EU seek to establish a close link with the US government. Sometimes, they simply decide not to share information with other EU countries to maintain the privilege of enjoying a close co-operation with the US (Cross 2013: 390). Another reason for this lack of co-operation is the fact that there are no clear boundaries of what information should be collected by law enforcement authorities and what is to be obtained by intelligence services. In order to regulate these synergies between police and intelligence forces, in 2008 the Council suggested establishing networks of anti-terrorist centres in all Member

States, as well as enhancing the role of IntCen (Council of the European Union 2008: 38). Eight years on, this recommendation is still on the table.

5.2 Divergence in the oversight over intelligence agencies

In 2001, the EP released an analysis of the activities conducted by intelligence authorities (European Parliament 2001). Intelligence services are characterised as having a secretive nature and for collecting a large volume of data. The report highlighted the difficulties for evaluating the effectiveness of their activities, as well as their compliance with the laws. In particular, one of the recommendations made was the establishment of an appropriate legal and parliamentary supervision over secret services in all Member States.

Today most (but not all) intelligence services within the EU borders are monitored by oversight bodies. Yet, these supervisory bodies are not all alike. They have different tasks and features depending on the Member State. Particularly, three main types of control are identified within the EU: (a) executive control; (b) parliamentary control; and (c) (quasi) judicial control. Sometimes this control will be *ex ante*, and sometimes it will be *ex post*. This section examines the intelligence oversight in France, Germany, Spain and the UK.

The executive (or non-parliamentary) control is found in the British, German and French oversight regimes. Concerning the British legal framework, RIPA states that interception by intelligence services in the UK[26] needs to be authorised by the Secretary of State. According to section 5(2) RIPA, the Secretary issues surveillance warrants as long as the interception is proportionate and necessary (Bunyan 2014: 17). In addition, section 5(3) RIPA states that such interception needs to pursue one of the following purposes: (a) national security; (b) the prevention or detection of serious crimes; (c) the safeguard of the economic well-being of the UK; and (d) giving effect to the provisions of any international mutual assistance agreement. In Germany, the BND has an obligation to report all activities to the Chancellery, the Ministry of Interior and the Ministry of Defence. At the same time, these bodies will report the activities to the *Parlamentarisches Kontrollgremium* (PKG). Moreover, Article 7(a) of the G-10 Law obliges the BND to get the Chancellery's approval before sharing information with any foreign intelligence agency. Lastly, in France procedures consisting of tapping cables require political authorisation from the Prime Minister (Loi n° 91-646, Article 4).

Control through parliamentary committees is the most usual oversight system within the EU. Classical parliamentary control consists of organising regular meetings in which several questions are posed to the Ministers. Although Ministers have the obligation to answer the queries, in practice they can decline to by arguing that it would jeopardise the national security of the country. The four countries chosen for this study have a parliamentarian system that supervises national intelligence services. They have chosen this type of control because of the

---

26 Intelligence services in the UK include the GCHQ, the National Criminal Intelligence Service (NCIS), the Security Service (MI5) and the Secret Intelligence Service (MI6).

idea that, since intelligence services are a political tool of the government, the control must also originate in the government (Ruiz Miguel 2007).

In the UK, the Intelligence and Security Committee of Parliament (ISCP) is the parliamentary body in charge of the British intelligence community. The oversight is *ex post facto*. The ISCP publishes annual reports and supervises that the agencies comply with their tasks, budget, effectiveness and limitations (Heumann and Scott 2013: 9–10). However, as pointed out by a member of the ISCP, the Committee also experiences some shortcomings in its supervisory activities (Rifkind 2014: 8). The Interception Communications Commissioner's Officer has also *ex post* auditing tasks. It has access to any information from intelligence services and law enforcement authorities and it releases recommendations for such agencies afterwards. However, there are numerous limitations in its oversight. For instance, the body cannot always be fully transparent because of the confidentiality agreements it needs to sign. Also, it is not always easy to reach an effective remedy, and errors and breaches are difficult to identify.

France did not implement a parliamentary oversight over intelligence services until 2007. That year the country passed a law (Loi n° 2007–1443) establishing the *Délégation parlementaire au renseignement* (DPR). However, the DPR has numerous limitations. For instance, this institution has no right to conduct investigations and it is not disclosed the details of the operational activities conducted within the centre (Mills *et al* 2011: 210). There are other oversight bodies in France, such as the *Autorités Administratives Indépendantes*, but their powers are also very small (Wolf 2013). In December 2013, the French government approved the Defence Bill 2014-2019, which enhances electronic surveillance for French residents (Texte adopté n° 251). Yet, it does not establish changes on intelligence oversight.

The German Constitution (GG) states in Article 45(d) that the German Parliament or *Bundestag* can establish special committees to scrutinise intelligence activities of the Federation. The aforementioned G-10 Law foresees in Article 5 that intelligence services will be subject to parliamentary control by two different institutions: PKG and the *G-10 Kommission*.

The PKG's tasks are described in the German Law on the Parliamentarian Control of Intelligence Services of 2009 (PKGrG) (BGBl. I S. 2346). It oversees the *Bundesnachrichtendienst* (BND), the *Militärischer Abschirmdienst* (MAD) and the *Bundesamt für Verfassungsschutz* (BfV) and it is composed of up to ten members set by the *Bundestag* at the beginning of each mandate. The German government has an obligation to inform the committee about the general activities of the intelligence services, as well as the most relevant ongoing operations at least once every six months. The committee also supervises the annual budget plan of the centres (Article 9(2) PKGrG) and it can even ask for a report on specific issues. Meetings are secret and closed-doors and they take place every three months on average (Article 3 PKGrG). All the information is then transferred to the *Bundestag*, which will ultimately decide whether the German government has complied with its obligations or not (Article 13 PKGrG).

The other parliamentary control over German intelligence services is the 'G-10 Commission', which is appointed by the PKG. The G-10 Commission was created by the *Bundestag* in light of the constitutional right to privacy of correspondence, posts and telecommunications of Article 10 GG. It comprises members of the *Bundestag*, who are in charge of deciding on the permissibility and necessity of surveillance activities conducted by German intelligence agencies (Schwartz 2012: 297). The objectives and functions of the G-10 Commission are regulated in Article 15 of the G-10 Law. Members meet at least once a month and they control that the agencies' collection, processing and storage of personal data is adequate. The G-10 Commission has access to any information it deems necessary, and it examines complaints issued by citizens on potential surveillance abuses. In contrast to the rest of the intelligence services analysed in this study, the BND offers the possibility for individuals to request access to their data (Heumann and Scott 2013: 13-14). Although the agency can always reject the request if there is an ongoing investigation, this right offers better safeguards for Germans than for the citizens of the three other Member States.

It is worth adding as for the German oversight intelligence framework that, after the Snowden revelations, the German *Bundestag* established a temporary Committee of Inquiry for the investigation of mass surveillance activities by the German secret service and its co-operation with the NSA. The committee was unanimously voted in by all parties in the parliament, and it is composed of eight members: four conservatives, two social-democrats, one socialist and one from the green party. It is a temporary committee and it is expected to be operational until 2017. The committee is conducting interviews with expert witnesses in the fields of national law, international law and technology. It also examines technical issues regarding the intervention of communications by intelligence agencies in Germany. Yet, this committee does not have access to documents that involve other intelligence services (e.g. documents related to '5-Eyes'), and its contact with Edward Snowden has been restricted.

Similar to the British, French and German systems, the Spanish Parliament is the institution controlling the activities of the CNI. Article 11 of the Law 11/2002 details the procedure for this control, which requires the appointment of the so-called *Comisión de Secretos Oficiales* (or Secret Funds Committee), as part of the Congress. This Committee has access to most of the classified information in the CNI. It also oversees that the budget provided to the centre is not misused.

The UK, Germany and Spain have established judicial oversight over intelligence services. The British intelligence community is monitored by: (a) the Independent Reviewer of Terrorism Legislation; (b) the ICC; (c) the Intelligence Services Commissioner (ISC); and (d) the Investigatory Powers Tribunal. The current Independent Reviewer of Terrorism Legislation is David Anderson. He is not part of the government and is in charge of issuing reports and recommendations about the functioning of the British intelligence community to ministers and the Parliament. According to sections 57 and 59 RIPA the ICC and the ISC provide independent quasi-judicial oversight *ex post* and they are appointed by the British Prime Minister. The ICC supervises warrants issued for the interception of communications and the disclosure of communications data. In contrast, the ISC controls the adequacy of warrants issued by the Secretary of State authorising intrusive surveillance. Both commissioners give assistance to the Investigatory Powers Tribunal when it is required for an ongoing investigation. The Investigatory Powers Tribunal is composed of nine senior members who hear complaints related to illegal surveillance. However, this tribunal has a very opaque nature: because it is not an independent judicial body (Biermann 2013), it cannot initiate investigations in its own, and its decisions are mostly secret (Heumann and Scott 2013: 9).

As stated in Article 19 GG, German intelligence services are also subject to judicial control, but only if basic rights are infringed. This judicial review has a limitation: Article 99(1) of the Code of Administrative Court Proceedings (VwGO) allows specific files or electronic documents to be classified as secret if they affect the interests of the Federation or the *Land*.

As far as the Spanish regime is concerned, since 2002 the CNI is subject to judicial oversight under the basis of Organic Law 2/2002. According to Article 12 of Law 11/2002 and the single Article of LO 2/2002, the Spanish Supreme Court can rule on cases regarding the infringement of the right to inviolability of the home and the secrecy of communications (Article 18(2) and (3) of the Spanish Constitution). If CNI activities clash with any of these constitutional rights, they require prior authorisation from a judge. When a court order is requested, the judge must verify that such activity is necessary for the goals assigned. Article 12 of Law 11/2002 must be read in conjunction with Article 74(a) of the CNI Statute, which establishes an obligation for the agency to act according to the Spanish Constitution and the rest of the national laws (Real Decreto 240/2013). Yet, even if this is the formal procedure to get information in Spain, the CNI has sometimes circumvented the prior authorisation from a judge.

It can be thus concluded that there are no common rules on oversight for data protection issues over intelligence services within the EU. From the analysis above it has been seen that some national systems are very lax (e.g. France), whereas others are highly protective. Therefore, minimum standards on oversight in all Member States would improve the data protection for the information processed by intelligence services. Regarding the ideal control system, some scholars have seen many advantages in having an executive or non-parliamentary control (Mills *et al* 2011: 90–91), whereas others opt for a dual parliamentary and judicial mechanism (Hillebrand 2012: 44–57). For instance, the EP has suggested a two-fold system: an *ex-ante* control by an independent magistrate, and an *ex post* parliamentary oversight (European Parliament 2013a: 5). For its part, the Art. 29 WP suggests making national DPAs responsible for supervising the activities of the intelligence services (Article 29 Data Protection Working Party 2014a: 10).[27]

In my view, the ideal situation would be to adopt one single instrument with common oversight rules for intelligence services in all Member States. This could only occur if an EU legal basis for such development was effectively established. In that case, the EU rules would operate as a lowest common denominator in all

---

27 It is already happening in 13 EU Member States: Austria, Belgium, Cyprus, Estonia, Finland, France, Germany, Ireland, Italy, Latvia, Luxembourg, Poland and Sweden.

Member States. Since parliamentary oversight is the predominant system among Member States – at least 18 out of the 28 Member States have implemented parliamentary committees (Mills *et al* 2011: 92–95), this could be the nature of the system. Any executive or judicial scrutiny would have a complementary role. Parliamentary committees would have access to all classified information – with the appropriate security clearance – (Mills *et al* 2011: 119 and 127–128) and they would oversee that the intelligence services' activities conform to the law and effectiveness criteria. Naturally, it is not a perfect mechanism, since these parliaments would lack sanctioning powers (Hillebrand 2012: 48), and there would be a risk of having too many parliamentary bodies involved in the scrutiny procedures (United Nations General Assembly 2009: para. 46). However, a single instrument could never be adopted today, since the EU has no legal basis to regulate oversight mechanisms for national intelligence services.

5.3 Current challenges at the CJEU and the ECtHR

As seen above, Article 4(2) TEU excludes national security matters from the competences of the EU so, according to this provision, national security issues are beyond the scope of the Charter of Fundamental Rights' scope and the CJEU jurisdiction, too (Korff 2014: 35). As for the Charter, Article 51 states that this is only applicable to EU citizens to the extent that Member States are implementing EU laws. Regarding the CJEU, Article 276 TFEU establishes:

> The Court of Justice of the European Union shall have no jurisdiction to review the validity or proportionality of operations carried out by the police or other law-enforcement services of a Member State or the exercise of the responsibilities incumbent upon Member States with regard to the maintenance of law and order and the safeguarding of internal security.

In accordance with that Article, the Court has no competence to examine preliminary rulings on operations undertaken by law enforcement authorities for the maintenance of 'internal security' (here equivalent to 'national security'). Nonetheless, there is still one issue under review by the CJEU within the field of public order and the safeguarding of internal matters: the compatibility of national security measures with EU law. The CJEU has reiterated that even if Member States retain exclusive competence on certain security measures, the Court can verify if these are appropriate and conform to the EU treaties.[28]

As mentioned above, a definition of what national security covers is urgently required. In this regard, Germany has recently suggested clarifying the concept of internal security 'in order to avoid overlapping with tasks assigned to

28 See Case C-265/95, *Commission v France ('Spanish Strawberries')* [1997] ECR I-6959, paras 33–35 and 56–57; and Case C-124/95, *The Queen, ex parte Centro-Com Srlv. HM Treasury and Bank of England* [1997] ECR I-81, para. 25.

intelligence services in order to protect the security of the State from internal threats' (Council of the European Union 2014b). The CJEU has stated in Case C-285/98, *Tanja Kreil v Bundesrepublik Deutschland* (2000) that 'public security' encompasses both internal and external security (para. 17). Yet, it is uncertain whether the term 'public security' is equivalent to that of 'national security'. The Court should thus demarcate the scope of Articles 4(2) TEU and 72/73 TFEU, similar to the rulings on the production and trade in arms, munitions and war material. In the field of defence procurement, the Court has always maintained a strict interpretation of Articles 346(b) and 347 TFEU (Koutrakos 2013). Likewise, a clear list on the specific national security measures should be established. This list would make it easier to determine whether certain operations carried out by intelligence services go beyond national security purposes. If so, the EU principles would still apply for those operations (Korff 2014: 41).

In fact, in Case C-362/14, *Maximillian Schrems v Data Protection Commissioner* (2015), mentioned above, the CJEU has indirectly tackled some intelligence services issues. It is true that the decision did not address the issue of 'national security' and it only indirectly referred to the alleged incompatibility of the intelligence services software PRISM with Article 8 of the Charter, Directive 95/46/EC and the 2000 Safe Harbor Decision. However, the Opinion that AG Bot on that case referred to the concept of 'national security' in several occasions. AG Bot stated that the wording of the derogations (i.e. national security, public interest and law enforcement requirements) was too broad and imprecise, and he questioned the compatibility of the national security derogations with the EU law (Case C-362/14, AG Bot 2015, para. 168 and 183).

Besides the Charter, any EU citizen can invoke Article 8 ECHR (right to respect for privacy and family life) against intelligence services' practices, as long as they have exhausted the national remedies. Although it is an exclusive competence of the Member States to legislate on national security matters, as Contracting Parties of the ECHR, national laws cannot violate the clauses of the Convention. Moreover, according to Article 52 ECHR, the Secretary General of the CoE can *ex officio* request information from the Member States in order to verify that they are complying with the provisions of the Convention. In January 2015, the Secretary announced that he would use these powers to obtain information about the intelligence services' activities of the Contracting Parties (Council of Europe 2015: 2).

The ECtHR has dealt with numerous cases concerning mass surveillance activities that clashed with Article 8 ECHR. According to the Court's jurisprudence, the interference could occur even when the information is available in the public domain,[29] when police install covert listening devices in someone's

---

29 Application no. 62332/00, *Segerstedt-Wiberg and Others v Sweden*, Judgment of 6 September 2006; Application no. 28341/95, *Rotaru v Romania*, Grand Chamber Judgment of 4 May 2000; Application no. 30194/09, *Shimovolos v Russia*, Judgment of 28 November 2011.

home,[30] and when a national judge or a public prosecutor issues certain wiretapping orders.[31] The Court has likewise concluded that mass surveillance activities can only be used as long as they pursue a relevant national security interest.[32]

The majority of cases brought before the ECtHR refer to police surveillance activities, but the Court has examined intelligence services' practices too. For instance, the case Application no. 33810/07 and 18817/08, *Association 21 December 1989 and others v Romania* (2011) dealt with surveillance activities of anti-government demonstrators by the Romanian Secret Service. Likewise, in the cases Application no. 5029/71, *Klass and others v Germany* (1978) and Application no. 54934/00, *Weber & Saravia v Germany* (2006) the Court examined whether the G-10 Act in Germany was contrary to the Convention.

There are currently two pending applications issued by British and Hungarian citizens before the ECtHR. As for the Hungarian application, it challenges the practices conducted by the Hungarian Anti-Terrorist Centre (TEK), which includes intelligence and law enforcement authorities. Hungarian citizens have claimed that TEK is allowed to spy on them with no prior court order (Application no. 37138/2014, *Mate Szabo and Beatrix Vissy v Hungary* (2014)). In the UK, several British activists lodged an application before the ECtHR in September 2013. They argued that the use of GCHQ programmes such as PRISM and Tempora (which have no legal basis in UK laws) was in breach of Article 8 ECHR (Application no. 58170/13, *Big Brother Watch, Open Rights Group, English PEN and Kurz v the United Kingdom* (2013)). However, the right to privacy of Article 8 is not absolute, and governments can conduct surveillance as long as it is 'necessary' and serves a 'legitimate aim' (Article 8(2)). In previous cases,[33] the ECtHR has stated that national laws allowing data processed by Member States need to specify the offences and categories of persons monitored; the duration for the surveillance; its purpose; and the oversight mechanism. Moreover, Contracting Parties have a positive obligation to ensure that private companies do not co-operate in abusive surveillance activities (Korff 2014: 33).

---

30 Application no. 35394/97, *Khan v the United Kingdom*, Judgment of 4 October 2000; Application no. 44787/98, *PG. and J.H. v the United Kingdom*, Judgment of 25 December 2001; Application no. 62617/00, *Copland v the United Kingdom*, Judgment 3 April 2007.

31 Application no. 11801/85, *Kruslin v France*, Judgment of 24 April 1990; Application no. 27798/95, *Amann v Switzerland*, Judgment of 16 February 2000; Application no. 71611/01, *Wisse v France*, judgment of 20 December 2005; Application no. 59842/00, *Vetter v France*, Judgment of 31 May 2005; Application no. 14838/89, *A. v France*, Judgment of 23 November 1992; Application no. 35623/05, *Uzun v Germany*, 2 September 2010, Judgment of 2 September 2010; Application no. 8691/79, *Malone v UK*, Judgment of 2 August 1984; Application no. 30181/05, *Pruteanu v Romania*, Judgment of 3 February 2015.

32 Application 62332/00, *Segerstedt-Wiberg and Others v Sweden*, Judgment of 6 September 2006; Application 5029/71, *Klass and others v Germany*, Judgment of 6 September 1978, para. 48; Application no. 30562/04 and 30566/04, *Marper v United Kingdom*, Judgment of 4 December 2008.

33 See, for instance, ECtHR, *Klass v Germany* (1978), *Liberty and Others v the UK* (2008); *S and Marper v United Kingdom* (2009); *Gillan and Quinton v United Kingdom* (2010); *Kennedy v UK* (2010); and *Brunet v France* (2014).

In general, no application could be admitted before the ECtHR if national court instances have not been exhausted first. However, in that particular case, the ECtHR has admitted the application without it first being examined by the Investigatory Powers Tribunal, since that tribunal does not afford an effective remedy due to its particularly secretive nature. A court decision for both the Hungarian and the British applications is still pending.

Because of the limited redress that individuals have at the European level against mass surveillance activities, some of them have opted for initiating national procedures instead. In this sense, proceedings started in 2014 in German, French and British courts about the lawfulness of the PRISM programme. On 3 February 2014, three German NGOs[34] lodged a criminal complaint before the German courts against the NSA and GCHQ about 'mass surveillance, illegal covert intelligence activities, violations of the basic rights to privacy, and obstruction of justice by tolerating and supporting illegal surveillance of German citizens' (EDRI 2014). In August 2014, in France, the International Federation for Human Rights (FIDH) and the French Human Rights League (LDH) filed a complaint before the *Tribunal de Grande Instance de Paris*. In the UK, Privacy International issued a complaint before the UK Investigatory Powers Tribunal (UKIPT) on 13 May 2014, challenging the use of hacking tools (particularly, Upstream and PRISM) by the British intelligence services.

The only court that has issued its decision to date is the UKIPT. The tribunal stated in December 2014 that the interception of the claimants' communications did not contravene Articles 8 and 10 ECHR and, therefore, no breach had been committed (Case no. IPT/13/92/CH, IPT/13/168-173/H, IPT/13/194/CH, IPT/13/204/CH (2014)). However, in February 2015 the UKIPT clarified that before the PRISM and Upstream disclosures, the regime governing GCHQ data processing originally contravened the ECHR but that it was now adequate.

From this examination, it can be concluded that the EU could eventually have a role in intelligence services' matters. However, there are legal and also political issues that stop the EU from legislating on intelligence services, under the assumption that their activities are part of the 'national security' exclusion. Yet, there is no clear definition within the EU laws of what this concept includes (European Parliament 2013d: 4).

Besides the current judicial cases involving national intelligence services, one might wonder whether IntCen could be reviewed by the CJEU. If we consider that IntCen falls completely within the scope of the CFSP, the general rule of Article 275(1) TFEU is that the CJEU does not have jurisdiction in the field of CFSP. Yet, there are two exceptions to this rule (Brkan 2012). One is the Court's jurisdiction on matters concerning the delimitation between areas. According to Article 24 TEU, the CJEU has:

---

34 The International League for Human Rights, Chaos Computer Club and Digitalcourage.

[J]urisdiction to monitor compliance with Article 40 of this Treaty and to review the legality of certain decisions as provided for by the second paragraph of Article 275 of the Treaty on the Functioning of the European Union.

Under this provision, the Court could decide whether IntCen falls completely under the scope of the CFSP or for only certain of its activities. For those actions adopted as EU internal security measures, IntCen could be subject to external supervision in the future. The body in charge of it may be composed of national DPAs (similar to the current JSB for Europol) or even the CJEU.

5.4 The relevance of Article 39 TEU

Article 39 TEU was included for the first time with the Treaty of Lisbon. This clause gives a possibility to establish specific EU rules on the processing of personal data for activities falling under the scope of the CFSP. As can be seen in Chapter 2, data processed by IntCen and data collected during CSDP missions are two of the activities that could be regulated under Article 39 TEU. This provision regulates 'the processing of personal data by the Member States'. IntCen does not currently have any operational role, and it cannot collect information by itself. The centre gathers representatives of intelligence agencies in the Member States for exchanging information and drafting terrorism assessment reports. In other words, intelligence processed in the centre comes directly from Member States and other EU bodies. Therefore, Article 39 TEU could certainly serve as legal basis for the activities of the centre.

The Council is the institution that would regulate IntCen's data processing activities. The kind of measure to be taken would not be a legislative act, since this is not permitted under the CFSP (Article 24(1) TEU). Instead, the Council should adopt a decision, which would be voted in unanimously in the terms of Article 31(1) TEU. Such a Council decision on Article 39 TEU, even if it constitutes an exception of the general data protection provision of Article 16 TFEU, would improve the current situation in which every Member State has its own legal framework, if they have any at all.

As mentioned earlier, IntCen connects both EU internal security and external security matters. In that sense, Salmi points out that the centre can 'also provide analysis of terrorism and other global threats that are reflected in the EU internal security' (Salmi 2014). Article 39 TFEU rules would only apply for external security issues. That information collected within the scope of the EU internal security, as part of the AFSJ, would conform the general rules on data protection as stipulated in Article 16 TFEU. In other words, intelligence exchanged through IntCen to prevent or detect EU threats would fall within the scope of the AFSJ and, consequently, it would be subject to Article 16 TFEU. In contrast, intelligence exchanged by the centre beyond the EU territory to investigate international threats will be processed as part of the CFSP. In such cases, Article 39 TEU – never used to date – could serve as legal basis.

Either way, it is clear that the EU has competence to establish rules for IntCen. A transparent mandate for the centre would surely increase the intelligence co-operation within the EU for the years to come.

6 Conclusions

The Snowden revelations about intelligence services' data collection and processing activities have caused great concern within the EU. The leaked documents show that not only is the NSA collecting massive amounts of personal data from untargeted individuals, but also that intelligence agencies in the Member States are carrying out these same practices within the EU. This chapter has identified some of these activities, scrutinising their potential infringement of the EU fundamental right to data protection.

This chapter has presented two different case scenarios in which intelligence services' activities may clash with EU citizens' right to data protection: (a) when foreign intelligence services collaborate with private companies and EU intelligence services to process mass data of EU citizens (section 3); and (b) when intelligence services in the EU process mass data of EU citizens (section 4). What both cases have in common is that EU laws are in principle not applicable.

Nevertheless, the EU has several forms of redress for EU citizens at the national, European and international levels against intelligence services' activities. At the national level, despite all Member States having oversight mechanisms over intelligence services' activities, these differ from one country to the other. In some countries, intelligence agencies have the power to access information lawfully without a prior court order, whereas in other countries more stringent limitations apply. A way to harmonise these oversight measures would be by clarifying the IntCen's mandate. This chapter suggests the use of Article 39 TEU to establish rules on the information exchanged by intelligence services through IntCen, including the data protection standards they would have to comply with.

The EU has assumed that 'national security' activities are those carried out by intelligence services and, consequently, its regulation and control is almost non-existent at the EU level. However, this chapter has showed that national security duties can be conducted by either intelligence services or law enforcement authorities. Police agencies have been taking on intelligence-gathering roles over the years and, therefore, the tasks of both types of agencies overlap at times. Likewise, although intelligence services have national security tasks, they may also conduct EU 'internal security' and 'external security' functions. Therefore, the 'national security' exclusion of Articles 4(2) TEU and Articles 72/73 TFEU needs to be clarified.

Lastly, even if no express provisions are currently found in the Treaty of Lisbon and EU secondary laws, intelligence services' activities of Member States need to comply with the ECHR and the Charter of Fundamental Rights. There are at the moment three pending cases involving intelligence services at the ECtHR and the CJEU. On the one hand, the ECtHR is examining whether British and Hungarian secret services' activities are infringing Article 8 ECHR. On the other hand, an Irish court has issued a preliminary ruling before the CJEU asking whether Facebook and other tech companies have infringed Articles 7 and 8 of the Charter by co-operating with intelligence agencies via PRISM. These might become landmark cases. They will not only show the effectiveness of data protection rules for EU citizens, but will also reveal to what extent EU laws might be enforceable against global tech companies (such as Facebook), secret services of the Member States (such as GCHQ) and even intelligence agencies beyond the EU borders (such as NSA).

Bibliography

9/11 Commission, 2004, *The 9/11 Commission Report 2004*, www.9-11commission.gov/report/911Report.pdf (accessed 5 November 2015).

Application no. 5029/71, *Klass and others v Germany* (ECtHR, 6 September 1978).

Application no. 54934/00, *Weber & Saravia v Germany* (ECtHR, 29 June 2006).

Application no. 33810/07 and 18817/08, *Association 21 December 1989 and others v Romania* (ECtHR, 24 May 2011).

Application no. 58170/13, *Big Brother Watch, Open Rights Group, English PEN and Kurz v the United Kingdom* (ECtHR, 4 September 2013).

Application no. 37138/2014, *Mate Szabo and Beatrix Vissy v Hungary* (ECtHR, 13 May 2014).

Archick, K, 2013, *U.S.-EU Cooperation against Terrorism*, Congressional Research Service, Report RS22030, pp. 1–24.

Article 29 Data Protection Working Party, 2013, *Letter to Viviane Reding*, Ref. Ares(2013) 2872799 – 13 August 2013.

Article 29 Data Protection Working Party, 2014a, *Opinion on surveillance of electronic communications for intelligence and national security purposes*, WP215, 10 April 2014.

Article 29 Data Protection Working Party, 2014b, *Working Document on surveillance electronic communications for intelligence and national security purposes*, WP228, 5 December 2014.

Article 29 Data Protection Working Party, 2014c, *Letter to Viviane Reding*, Ref. Ares(2014)1139376, 10 April 2014.

Baker, J, 2013, 'EU Parliament could block data sharing with the US', *CSO*, 19 November, www.cso.com.au (accessed 6 November 2015).

Bamford, J, 1982, *The Puzzle Palace – A Report on America's Most Secret Agency*, Houghton Mifflin, Boston.

Bergen, P, 2013, 'Would NSA surveillance have stopped 9/11 plot?', *CNN*, 31 December, www.cnn.com (accessed 5 November 2015).

Bergen, P, Sterman, D, Schneider, E and Cahall, B, 2014, 'Do NSA bulk surveillance programs stop terrorists?', *New America Foundation*, www.newamerica.org (accessed 5 November 2015).

Bickford, D, 2013, 'Judicial Scrutiny of Intelligence Agencies', European Parliament LIBE enquiry, 7 November, www.europarl.europa.eu (accessed 6 November 2015).

Biermann, K, 2013, 'German intelligence service is as bad as the NSA', *The Guardian*, 4 October, www.theguardian.com (accessed 10 November 2015).

Bowden, C, 2013, *The US surveillance programmes and their impact on EU citizens' fundamental rights*, Policy Department Citizens' Rights and Constitutional Affairs, European Parliament, Doc. PE 474.405, Brussels.

Brkan, M, 2012, 'The role of the European Court of Justice in the field of Common Foreign and Security Policy after the Treaty of Lisbon: New challenge for the future' in

PJ Cardwell (ed), *EU External Relations Law and Policy in the Post-Lisbon Era*, Springer, Berlin, pp. 97–118.

Bryant, C and Fontanella-Khan, J, 2013, 'US spy scandal sparks EU privacy fears', *Financial Times*, 15 October, www.ft.com (accessed 6 November 2015).

Bunyan, T, 2013, 'Interception Commissioner fails to report on Section 8(4) certificates authorising GCHQ's mass data collection', *Statewatch*, www.statewatch.com (accessed 6 November 2015).

Bunyan, T, 2014, 'GCHQ is authorised to "spy on the world" but the UK Interception of Communications Commissioner says this is OK as it is "lawful"', *Statewatch*, www.statewatch.com (accessed 6 November 2015).

Bures, O and Ahern S, 2007, 'The European Model of Building Regional Cooperation against Terrorism' in D Cortright and GA López (eds), *Uniting against Terror. Cooperative Nonmilitary Responses to the Global Terrorist Threat*, Massachusetts Institute of Technology Press, Massachusetts, pp. 187–236.

Busuioc, M and Groenleer, M, 2013, 'Beyond Design: The evolution of Europol and Eurojust', *Perspectives on European Politics and Society*, vol. 14, no. 3, pp. 285–304.

Buzan, B, 2007, 'What is national security in the age of globalisation?', *Utenriksdepartementet*, www.regjeringen.no (accessed 5 November 2015).

Campbell, C, 1988, 'Somebody's listening', *New Statesman*, 12 August, www.newstatesman.com (accessed 5 November 2015).

Case *Katz v United States* [1967] 389 US 347.

Case C-285/98, *Tanja Kreil v Bundesrepublik Deutschland* (CJEU, 11 January 2000).

Case 1 BvR 370/07, German Federal Constitutional Court (*Bundesverfassungsgericht*, 27 February 2008).

Case no. IPT/13/92/CH, IPT/13/168-173/H, IPT/13/194/CH, IPT/13/204/CH (UKIPTrib, 13_77/H, 5 December 2014).

Case C-362/14, *Maximillian Schrems v Data Protection Commissioner* (CJEU, 6 October 2015).

Case C-362/14, *Maximillian Schrems v Data Protection Commissioner*, Opinion of AG Bot, 23 September 2015.

Champeau, G, 2013, 'Les députés enverront-ils l'article 13 de la LPM au Conseil Constitutionnel?', *Numerama*, 11 December, www.numerama.com/ (accessed 5 November 2015).

Commission Decision 2000/520/EC of 26 July 2000 pursuant to Directive 95/46/EC of the European Parliament and of the Council on the adequacy of the protection provided by the safe harbour privacy principles and related frequently asked questions issued by the US Department of Commerce.

Council Framework Decision 2008/977/JHA of 27 November 2008 on the protection of personal data processed in the framework of police and judicial cooperation in criminal matters.

Communication from the Commission to the European Parliament and the Council on the Functioning of the Safe Harbour from the Perspective of EU Citizens and Companies Established in the EU, COM(2013) 847 final, 27 November 2013.

Coolsaet, R, 2010, 'EU counterterrorism strategy: Value added or chimera?', *International Affairs*, vol. 86, no. 4, pp. 857–873.

Council Decision 2010/427/EU of 26 July 2010 establishing the organisation and functioning of the European External Action Service.

Council of Europe, 1981, *Convention for the Protection of Individuals with regard to Automatic Processing of Personal Data*, CETS No. 108, 28 January 1981.

Council of Europe, 2015, *Parliamentary Assembly, Committee on Legal Affairs and Human Rights Mass surveillance Report*, Rapporteur: Mr Pieter Omtzigt, Doc. AS/Jur (2015) 01.

Council of the European Union, 2008, *Report of the Informal High Level Advisory Group on the Future of European Home Affairs ("The Future Group")*, Doc. 11657/08, 9 July 2008.

Council of the European Union, 2014a, *3354th meeting of the Council of the European Union (Justice and Home Affairs)*, Doc.12243/14, 30 July 2014.

Council of the European Union, 2014b, *Proposal for a Directive of the European Parliament and of the Council on the protection of individuals with regard to the processing of personal data by competent authorities for the purposes of prevention, investigation, detection or prosecution of criminal offences or the execution of criminal penalties, and the free movement of such data – Chapters I, II and V*, Doc. 15659/1/14, 19 November 2014.

Cross, MKC, 2013, 'A European transgovernmental intelligence network and the role of IntCen', *Perspectives on European Politics and Society*, vol. 14, no. 3, pp. 388–402.

Davenport, TH and Prusak, L, 2000, *Working Knowledge: How Organizations Manage What They Know?*, Harvard Business School Press, Boston.

Davis, W, 2013 'Tech companies call for privacy oversight after latest NSA revelation', *Mediapost*, 1 November, www.mediapost.com (accessed 5 November 2015).

de Busser, E, 2010, 'EU data protection in transatlantic cooperation in criminal matters. Will the EU be serving its citizens an American meal?', *Utrecht Law Review*, vol. 6, no. 1, pp. 86–100.

Directive 95/46/EC of the European Parliament and of the Council of 24 October 1995 on the protection of individuals with regard to the processing of personal data and on the free movement of such data.

Dutch DPA, 2013, 'Data protection authorities have not found any violations at SWIFT', *Press Release Dutch DPA*, 8 May 2013.

'Echelon the secret power', 2000 (video file), www.youtube.com/watch?v=KJGe5FB2HIY (accessed 12 November 2015).

Eddy, M, 2013, 'For Western allies, a long history of swapping intelligence', *The New York Times*, 9 July, www.thenytimes.com (accessed 5 November 2015).

EDRI, 2014, 'German govt and intelligence agencies face penal charges for spying', *EDRigram newsletter – Number 12.3*, 12 February 2014.

'Edward Snowden interview. The NSA and its willing helpers', *Spiegel*, 7 August 2013, www. spiegel.de (accessed 6 November 2015).

Erstes Gesetz zur Änderung des Artikel 10-Gesetzes (1. G10uaÄndG k.a.Abk.), 30 July 2009 (BGBl. I S. 2437).

European Parliament, 2001, *'Report on the existence of a global system for the interception of private and commercial communications (ECHELON interception system) (2001/2098(INI))'*, Doc. A5-0264/2001 PAR1, 11 July 2001.

European Parliament, 2013a, *Democratic oversight of Member State intelligence services and of EU intelligence bodies*, Working Document 5, 12 December 2013.

European Parliament, 2013b, *Draft Report on the US NSA surveillance programme, surveillance bodies in various Member States and their impact on EU citizens' fundamental rights and on transatlantic cooperation in Justice and Home Affairs*, Doc. PE526.085v01-00, 2013/2188(INI), 23 December 2013.

European Parliament, 2013c, *Joint Motion for a Resolution on the Suspension of the TFTP agreement as a result of NSA surveillance*, Doc. PE519.345v01-00, 23 October 2013.

European Parliament, 2013d, *The relation between the surveillance practices in the EU and the US and the EU data protection provisions*, Working Document 3, Doc. PE524.632v01-00, 12 December 2013.

European Parliament, 2014a, 'Edward Snowden testimony to the European Parliament', March 2014, www.europarl.europa.eu/document/activities/cont/201403/20140307 ATT80674/20140307ATT80674EN.pdf (accessed 5 November 2015).

European Parliament, 2014b, *US Surveillance activities with respect to EU data and its possible legal implications on transatlantic agreements and cooperation*, Working Document 4, Doc. PE524.633v01-00.

Farivar, C, 2013, 'German NSA has deal to tap ISPs at major Internet exchange', *Ars Technica*, 7 October, http://arstechnica.com/ (accessed 5 November 2015).

Follorou, J and Greenwald, G, 2013, 'France in the NSA's crosshair: Phone networks under surveillance', *Le Monde*, 21 October, www.lemonde.fr (accessed 5 November 2015).

Follorou, J and Johannes, F, 2013, 'Révélations sur le Big Brother français', *Le Monde*, 4 July, www.lemonde.fr (accessed 6 November 2015).

Gallagher, R, 2014a, 'How secret partners expand NSA's surveillance dragnet', *The Intercept*, 18 June, https://firstlook.org/theintercept/ (accessed 5 November 2015).

Gallagher, R, 2014b, 'The surveillance engine: How the NSA built its own secret Google', *The Intercept*, 25 August, https://firstlook.org/theintercept/ (accessed 5 November 2015).

Gallagher, R and Greenwald, G, 2014, 'How the NSA plans to infect 'millions' of computers with malware', *The Intercept*, 12 March, https://firstlook.org/theintercept/ (accessed 5 November 2015).

Gellman, B and Poitras, L, 2013, 'U.S., British intelligence mining data from nine U.S. Internet companies in broad secret program', *The Washington Post*, 6 June, www.washingtonpost.com (accessed 5 November 2015).

Gesetz über den Bundesnachrichtendienst (BND-Gesetz – BNDG), BGBl. I S. 2954, 2979, 20 December 1990.

Gesetz über die parlamentarische Kontrolle nachrichtendienstlicher Tätigkeit des Bundes (Kontrollgremiumgesetz – PKGrG), BGBl. I S. 2346, 9 July 2009.

Gesetz zur Beschränkung des Brief-, Post- und Fernmeldegeheimnisses (Artikel 10-Gesetz – G 10), BGBl. I S. 1254, 2298, 26 June 2001.

Görlitz, N, 2013 'Le droit d'enquête du Parlement européen', *Cahiers de droit européen 49*, pp. 783–820.

Greenwald, G, 2014, *No Place to Hide: Edward Snowden, the NSA, and the U.S. Surveillance State*, Hamish Hamilton, London.

Greenwald, G and Ackerman, S, 2013, 'NSA collected US email records in bulk for more than two years under Obama', *The Guardian*, 27 June, www.theguardian.com (accessed 5 November 2015).

Greenwald, G and Aranda, A, 2013a, 'El CNI facilitó el espionaje masivo de EEUU a España', *El Mundo*, 30 October, www.elmundo.es (accessed 6 November 2015).

Greenwald G and Aranda A, 2013b, 'La NSA espió 60 millones de llamadas en España en solo un mes', *El Mundo*, 28 October, www.elmundo.es (accessed 6 November 2015).

Haaland Matlary, J, 2013, *European Union Security Dynamics. In the New National Interest*, Palgrave Macmillan, London.

Hager, N, 1996, *Secret Power – New Zealand's Role in the International Spy Network*, Craig Potton Publishing, New Zealand.

Heumann, S and Scott, B, 2013 'Law and policy in Internet surveillance programs: United States, Great Britain and Germany', *Stiftung Neue Verantwortung*, vol. 25, no. 13, pp. 1–17

Hillebrand, C, 2012, *Networks in the European Union. Maintaining Democratic Legitimacy after 9/11*, Oxford University Press, Oxford.

Inglis, JC, 2013, 'Strengthening privacy rights and national security: Oversight of FISA surveillance programs: Hearing before the S. Comm. on the judiciary', 113th Congress.

Joint Review of the implementation of the Agreement between the European Union and the United States of America on the processing and transfer of passenger name records to the United States Department of Homeland Security accompanying the Report from the Commission to the European Parliament and to the

Council on the joint review of the implementation of the Agreement between the European Union and the United States of America on the processing and transfer of passenger name records to the United States Department of Homeland Security, SEC(2013) 630 final, 27 November 2013.

Kamen, A, 2014, 'The NSA has a new, first time ever, privacy officer', *The Washington Post*, 28 January, www.washingtonpost.com (accessed 5 November 2015).

Kaufmann, S, 2013, 'Europe, lost on the digital planet', *The New York Times*, 14 October, www.nytimes.com (accessed 6 November 2015).

Korff, D, 2014, *'Expert Opinion prepared for the Committee of Inquiry of the Bundestag into the "5EYES" global surveillance systems revealed by Edward Snowden'*, Committee Hearing, Paul-Löbe-Haus, Berlin.

Koutrakos, P, 2013, *The EU Common Security and Defence Policy*, Oxford University Press, Oxford, pp. 257–278.

Ledgett, R, 2014, 'The NSA responds to Edward Snowden's TED talk', *TED2014* (video file), www.ted.com (accessed 5 November 2015).

Lenoir, F, 2013, 'United States tracked Merkel's phone since 2002: report', *Reuters*, 26 October, www.reuters.com (accessed 5 November 2015).

Lewis, P, 2013, 'NSA denies discussing Merkel phone surveillance with Obama', *The Guardian*, 27 October, www.theguardian.com (accessed 5 November 2015).

Loi n° 91-646, Contrôle de l'application de la loi relative au secret des correspondances émises par la voie des télécommunications, 10 July 1991.

Loi n° 2007–1443 (du 9 Octobre 2007) portant création d'une délégation parlementaire au renseignement, 9 October 2007.

Lowenthal, M, 1998, 'Open source intelligence: New myths, new realities', *Defense Daily International*, Special Reports, www.oss.net (accessed 10 November 2015).

MacAskill, E and Ball, J, 2013, 'Portrait of the NSA: No detail too small in quest for total surveillance', *The Guardian*, 2 November, www.theguardian.com (accessed 6 November 2015).

MacAskill, E, Borger, J, Hopkins, N, Davies, N and Ball, J, 2013, 'Mastering the Internet: How GCHQ set out to spy on the world wide web', 23 June, www.theguardian.com (accessed 6 November 2015).

Maier, CS, 1990, *Peace and security for the 1990s*, unpublished paper for the MacArthur Fellowship Program, Social Science Research Council, New York.

Mangold, P, 1990, *National Security and International Relations*, Routledge, New York.

Mills, M, Vermeulen, M, Born, H, Scheinin, M, Wiebusch, M and Thornton, A, 2011, *Parliamentary oversight of Security and Intelligence Agencies in the European Union*, European Parliament – Directorate General for Internal Policies, Policy Department c: Citizens' Rights and Constitutional Affairs, Brussels.

Moret Millás, V, 2005, 'El Centro Nacional de Inteligencia: Un aproximación a su régimen jurídico', *Foro Nueva época*, no. 2, pp. 249–295.

Navarro Bonilla, D, 2005, 'Introducción' in *El papel de la inteligencia ante los retos de la seguridad y la defensa internacional*, Grupo de Trabajo número 5/04, Dirección General de Relaciones Institucionales de la Defensa, Instituto Español de Estudios Estratégicos, Madrid.

Nielsen, N, 2013, 'EU asks for answers on UK snooping programme', *EUobserver*, 26 June, http://euobserver.com/justice/120656 (accessed 6 November 2015).

Nielsen, N, 2015, 'No new mandate for EU intelligence centre', *EUobserver*, 6 February, https://euobserver.com/justice/127532 (accessed 18 November 2015).

Noack, N, 2014, 'Yes, Berlin has its own spying scandals, but don't expect Germany to forgive the NSA', *The Washington Post*, 20 August, www.washingtonpost.com (accessed 6 November 2015).

NSA, 2009, *Inspector General Draft Report*, Doc. ST-09-0002, 24 March 2009, www. theguardian.com (accessed 9 November 2015).

NSA, 2013, FOIA Case: 71184B, DOCID: 4081031, 17 October 2013.

NSA, 2014, *NSA's Implementation of Foreign Intelligence Surveillance Act Section 702*, Director of Civil Liberties and Privacy Office Report 2014, 16 April 2014.

Occhipinti, JD, 2013, 'Availability by stealth? EU information-sharing in transatlantic perspective', C Kaunert and S Léonard (eds), *European Security, Terrorism and Intelligence. Tackling New Security Challenges in Europe*, Palgrave Macmillan, Basingstoke, pp. 143–184.

Omand, D, 2010, *Securing the State (Intelligence and Security)*, Oxford University Press, Oxford.

Paleri, P, 2008, *National Security: Imperatives and Challenges*, Tata McGraw-Hill, Delhi.

Peral, M, 2013, 'La fiscal pide el documento del espionaje de la NSA en España', *El Mundo*, 5 November, www.elmundo.com (accessed 6 November 2015).

Peterson, A, 2013, 'PRISM already gave the NSA access to tech giants. Here's why it wanted more', *The Washington Post*, 30 November, www.washingtonpost.com (accessed 5 November 2015).

Piodi, F and Mombelli, Y, 2014, *L'affaire ECHELON. Les travaux du Parlement européen sur le système global d'interception 1998–2002*, EPRS Service de Recherche du Parlement européen, Doc. PE 538.877, Brussels.

Powers, T, 2004, *Intelligence Wars: American Secret History from Hitler to Al-Qaeda*, New York Review Books, New York.

Privacy and Civil Liberties Oversight, 2014a, *Report on the Telephone Records Program Conducted under Section 215 of the USA PATRIOT Act and on the Operations of the Foreign Intelligence Surveillance Court*, 23 January 2014.

Privacy and Civil Liberties Oversight, 2014b, *Report on the Surveillance Program Operated Pursuant to Section 702 of the Foreign Intelligence Surveillance Act*, 2 July 2014.

Privacy International, 2014, 'Secret policy reveals GCHQ can get warrantless access to bulk data', 28 October 2014, www.privacyinternational.org (accessed 19 November 2105).

Projet de loi relatif à la programmation militaire pour les années 2014 à 2019 et portant diverses dispositions concernant la défense et la sécurité nationale, Texte adopté n° 251, 3 December 2013.

Rawlinson, K, 2013 'NSA surveillance: Merkel's phone may have been monitored "for over 10 years"', *The Guardian*, 26 October, www.theguardian.com (accessed 6 November 2015).

Real Decreto 240/2013, de 5 de abril, por el que se aprueba el Estatuto del personal del Centro Nacional de Inteligencia, BOE Núm. 89, 13 April 2013.

Reding, V, 2013a, 'Speech on data protection at the Delegation of the European Union to the United States of America' (online video), Washington DC, 18 November 2013, www. euractiv.com/video/eu-commissioner-reding-us-meetin-531789 (accessed 7 November 2015).

Reding, V, 2013b, 'Towards a more dynamic transatlantic area of growth and investment', SPEECH/13/867, 29 October.

Rifkind, M, 2014, *Intelligence Agencies in the Internet Age – Public Servants or Public Threat?*, Wadham College, Oxford.

Ruiz Miguel, C, 2007, 'Problemas actuales del derecho de los servicios de inteligencia', *Inteligencia y Seguridad: Revista de Análisis y Prospectiva*, no. 2, pp. 13–46.

Salmi, I, 2014, 'Multilateral intelligence cooperation in the EU', *Gnosis Rivista italiana di Intelligence*, no. 2, http://gnosis.aisi.gov.it/Gnosis/Rivista39.nsf/ServNavig/24 (accessed 14 November 2015).

Sarkesian, SC, Allen Williams, J and Cimbala, SJ, 2008, *National Security. Policymakers, Processes and Politics*, Lynne Rienner Publishers, Boulder.

Scheinin, M, 2009, *Promotion and protection of all human rights, civil, political, economic, social and cultural rights, including the right to development. Report of the Special Rapporteur on the promotion and protection of human rights and fundamental freedoms while countering terrorism*, General Assembly of the United Nations, Doc. A/HRC/10/3, NYC.

Schwartz, PM, 2012, 'Systematic government access to private-sector data in Germany', *International Data Privacy Law*, vol. 2, no. 4, pp. 289–301.

Svenden, ADM, 2011, 'On a "continuum with expansion"? Intelligence cooperation in Europe in the early 21st Century', *Journal of Contemporary European Research*, vol. 7, no. 4, pp. 520–538.

Taplin, WL, 1989, 'Six general principles of intelligence', *International Journal of Intelligence and Counterintelligence*, vol. 3, no. 4, pp. 475–491.

UK Home Affairs Committee, 2014, 'Post-legislative Scrutiny of the Counter-Terrorism Act 2008', Memorandum to the Home Affairs Committee, March 2014.

UK Interception of Communications Commissioner, 2013, 2012 *Annual Report of the Interception of Communications Commissioner*, HC 571 SG/2013/131, 3 July 2013, www.statewatch.org/news/2013/jul/uk-ann-rep-interception-of-communications-2012.pdf (accessed 6 November 2015).

United Nations General Assembly, 2009, *Report of the Special Rapporteur on the promotion and protection of human rights and fundamental freedoms while countering terrorism*, Martin Scheinin, A/HRC/10/3, 4 February 2009.

United Nations Office on Drugs and Crime, 2012, 'The use of the Internet for terrorist purposes', September 2012.

US Federal Trade Commission, 2011, 'Informal Note on Draft EU General Data Protection Regulation', December 2011.

US FISA Amendments Act of 2008, H.R. 6304 (110th), 19 June 2008,

US Office of the Director of National Intelligence, 2014, *2013 Transparency Report, Statistical Transparency Report Regarding Use of National Security Authorities – Annual Statistics for Calendar Year 2013*, 26 June 2014.

US Uniting and Strengthening America by Providing Appropriate Tools Required to Intercept and Obstruct Terrorism Act of 2001, 107th Congress, Pub.L. 56.

'Viviane Reding: "Data protection is a right"', *Al Jazeera*, 12 October 2013 (online video), www.aljazeera.com (accessed 6 November 2015).

Webb, DC, 2008, *ECHELON and the NSA*, IGI Global, Hershey.

Wiese Svanberg, C, 2014, 'The questionable legality and practicality of the EU's proposed anti-FISA clause', *Privacy Perspective*, 16 January, https://privacyassociation.org (accessed 6 November 2015).

Wolf, C, 2013, 'Is personal data better protected from government surveillance in Europe than the U.S.? Maybe not, *IAPP*, 20 June, www.privacyassociation.com (accessed 4 November 2015).

Wright, S, 2005, 'The ECHELON trail: An illegal vision', *Surveillance & Society*, vol. 3, no. 2/3, pp. 198–215.

5 The feasibility of global data protection standards for information processed for security purposes

Chapters 1 and 2 present the existing EU frameworks for data shared by law enforcement authorities within the EU and between the EU and third countries. The data protection challenges to which these give rise are also examined. As a response to these challenges, Chapter 3 suggests enhancing the use of Europol during cross-border police investigations. Europol has strong data protection and security standards, which Member States and third countries could also incorporate in their own legal frameworks. Despite this thesis being mainly focused on law enforcement data transfers, Chapter 4 examines data processing activities conducted by intelligence services. The reason for this is that law enforcement authorities work hand in hand with intelligence services, and the division of their activities has become more diffuse over the years.

So far, this book has suggested increasing the role of Europol and IntCen as a way to establish global data protection standards in the field of security. The final part of this book identifies other current international initiatives that put forward global data protection principles in the field of security. It presents an overview of the main instruments for establishing global data protection standards and it then discusses some shortcomings related to some of these initiatives.

In order to understand the necessity for common data protection standards in the field of security, a first assessment of the compatibility of mass surveillance activities with the public international law is conducted. These activities are mostly carried out by intelligence services (rather than by law enforcement agencies), as the Snowden documents have proved. After that, it analyses the principles enshrined in the *Recommendation of the Council concerning Guidelines governing the Protection of Privacy and Transborder Flows of Personal Data* (OECD 2013) (OECD Privacy Guidelines), the *Cooperation Arrangement for Cross-Border Privacy Enforcement* (APEC 2010) (APEC Privacy Framework), the UN Guidelines for the Regulation of Computerised Personal Data Files (United Nations General Assembly 1990), the Convention for the Protection of Individuals with regard to the Automatic Processing of Personal Data (1981 CoE Convention) (Council of Europe 1981) and the Convention on Cybercrime (Cybercrime Convention) (Council of Europe 2001a). Other general principles not linked to any international organisation will be also considered. This examination helps to identify which of these rules would bind security agents.

In sum, this chapter seeks to assess whether it is feasible to have data protection standards at the international level establishing rules that compel both law enforcement and intelligence services. If so, it determines what the ideal global data protection framework would be. It discusses, particularly, whether rules should be enclosed in one single law, a dual system, or a multiple legal framework.

1 Compatibility of mass surveillance systems with public international law

From the international law perspective, the debate on the lawfulness of intelligence services' activities is unresolved. Under public international law, espionage is neither permitted not prohibited (Aust 2014). But what about the specific mass surveillance activities that were exposed by Snowden?

If mass surveillance activities are seen as an 'intervention' in the terms of international law, then they are generally prohibited (Article 2(7) of the UN Charter). According to Article 51 of the UN Charter, the principle of non-intervention in customary international law may only be breached in times of war, and if the parties are engaged in armed conflict. Likewise, that 'intervention' could also be permitted if there is consent from the targeted State, as established in Article 24 of the UN Charter. The Snowden disclosures have proved that the NSA and the other members of '5-Eyes' have been spying on the governments of numerous countries such as Germany, Mexico, France and Brazil. When that took place, there was no armed conflict affecting these countries, and they never consented to that surveillance (Korff 2014: 4).

Another rule stemming from the customary international law is that an 'intervention' is prohibited if it takes place 'within the domestic jurisdiction of any state' (Article 2(7) of the UN Charter). Because of this rule, it becomes very difficult to condemn the activities conducted by the '5-Eyes' members. Since the communications are, in principle, intercepted from outside the country, the activities are not considered unlawful (Korff 2014: 6–7).

Nevertheless, the majority of surveillance activities that have been unveiled have not had other States as targets, but individuals. The customary international law regulates the possible breach of inter-State norms about respecting each other's sovereignty, but the question of the violation of individual human rights is dealt with as a separate issue. For these cases, international human rights law applies as a special branch of the public international law. Human rights laws protect individuals, not States, and they are characterised for being both treaty-based and customary. There are two specific UN laws on international human rights that include a provision on the right to privacy: the International Covenant on Civil and Political Rights (ICCPR) and the Universal Declaration of Human Rights (UDHR). Articles 17 ICCPR and 12 UDHR establish that:

1. No one shall be subjected to arbitrary or unlawful interference with his privacy, family, home or correspondence, nor to unlawful attacks on his honour and reputation.

2. Everyone has the right to the protection of the law against such interference or attacks.

According to these provisions, the UN High Commissioner for Human Rights (Office of the United Nations High Commissioner for Human Rights 2014), as well as the former and the current UN Special Rapporteurs on human rights and counter-terrorism (Scheinin 2013: 6; United Nations General Assembly 2014) have noted that mass surveillance programmes used by intelligence agencies are almost certainly illegal under international law. All members of the '5-Eyes' are parties to the ICCPR and the UDHR, but only the ICCPR has legally binding effects for its members. This Treaty was adopted by the UN in 1966 (but it did not enter into force until 1976) and has 167 States Parties, including the US.

The ICCPR is supervised by the Human Rights Committee. This committee is composed of several independent experts and it assesses whether the parties of the Covenant are complying with their obligations. In addition, it adopts General Comments on the interpretation of each of the ICCPR provisions. Unfortunately, the only General Comment on Article 17 ICCPR was released by the committee in 1988. In it, it was concluded that the idea of 'correspondence' needed to be extended to the digital sphere (United Nations 2008).

The main instrument that can be used to assess whether the NSA programmes violate Article 17 ICCPR is the privacy limitation test published by the former Special Rapporteur on human rights and counter-terrorism, Martin Scheinin, in 2009 (Scheinin 2009: para. 17). The test consists of seven points that, if complied with, could justify the limitation of any human right by the government. The specific requirements are the following: (a) the restriction must be provided by law; (b) the essence of the human right cannot be restricted; (c) the restriction must be necessary in a democratic society; (d) any discretion in the restriction must not be unfettered; (e) the restriction must be necessary for reaching a legitimate aim; (f) the restriction must obey the principle of proportionality; and (g) the restriction must be consistent with the other ICCPR rights.

As Scheinin explained before the EP in October 2013, the NSA mass surveillance systems fail to comply with 'several separate elements of the permissible limitations test' as regards the right to privacy (Scheinin 2013: 3). The failure was based on six elements: (a) the NSA programmes are not provided by law so they lack of a proper legal basis; (b) the essence of the right to privacy is violated because the collection of data does not distinguish among types and sensitivity of the information; (c) the interferences are not justified for the actual prevention of terrorism and other serious crimes; (d) FISA leaves room for unfettered discretion; (e) the intrusion is disproportionate in comparison with the results achieved; and (f) and the restrictions clash with other human rights besides the right to privacy like the right to non-discrimination (Article 26), the freedom of expression (Article 19), the freedom of association (Article 22) and the freedom of movement (Article 12).

The inconsistency of both US and UK security laws with other ICCPR rights is particularly visible as regards the right to non-discrimination. The RIPA in the

UK and the FISA in the US make distinctions between foreign and domestic communications. Consequently, there is a distinction between nationals (and long-term residents), and non-nationals. According to section 8(4) RIPA, 'external' warrants allow the collection of bulk data (Korff 2014: 21; Bowcott 2014), whereas 'internal' warrants do not permit it. Likewise, FISA discriminates non-US citizens, whose privacy is not protected by the US Fourth Amendment. In that sense, Korff suggested redrafting these laws to conform to Article 26 ICCPR (Korff 2014: 26).

The issue of extra-territoriality of the ICCPR is crucial for determining whether the '5-Eyes' activities have violated the Covenant or not. Most of the surveillance programmes that have been revealed by Snowden allow intelligence agents to access foreign communications without even moving from their headquarters. The internet has changed the way espionage works. Today, simply by installing software, analysts are able to break into any computer or tap any phone and collect all types of information.

That being said, NSA mass surveillance programmes will only be subject to ICCPR if extra-territoriality applies. The answer is not clear, since Article 17 ICCPR does not include any reference to its territorial scope of application, which means that the definition of the scope for the right to privacy is entrusted to Article 2(1) ICCPR (Scheinin 2014: 3). According to this provision, the Contracting Parties are obliged to comply with the rights of the Covenant 'within its territory and subject to its jurisdiction'. This has been the argument used by the US government to conclude that the surveillance of 'foreign' communications does not fall under the scope of ICCPR.

In contrast, the Human Rights Committee has long taken the position that the ICCPR applies extra-territorially. In 2004, the Committee released General Comments on the nature of the ICCPR obligations, in which it noted that rules included in the Covenant were *erga omnes*. The Committee added that the Contracting Parties must ensure the ICCPR rights to anyone 'even if not situated within the territory of the State Party' (United Nations Human Rights Committee 2004: para 10). The Committee has kept this position to date, giving rise to numerous cases that confirm the extraterritorial reach of the ICCPR.[1]

The International Court of Justice has also addressed the extraterritorial scope of human rights treaties, including the ICCPR. In its Advisory Opinion on the Wall built by Israel in the Occupied Palestinian Territory (OPT), it concluded that 'while the jurisdiction of States is primarily territorial, it may sometimes be exercised outside the national territory' (Cour Internationale de Justice 2004: para. 109).

Similarly, both the former and current UN Special Rapporteurs on the promotion and protection of human rights and fundamental freedoms believe that the ICCPR has an extraterritorial effect. On the one hand, Scheinin noted that positive State obligations may not apply outside a country's own territory, but negative obligations not to violate human rights apply everywhere and in respect of everyone (Scheinin 2014: 5). On the other hand, Emmerson stated that

---

1 For instance, *Lopez Burgos v Uruguay* (52/1979), *Sophie Vidal Martins v Uruguay* (57/1979) and *Guye et al v France* (196/1985).

States are legally bound to the Covenant and should offer the same protection to nationals and to non-nationals (United Nations General Assembly 2014: 17). According to these arguments, the US and the rest of the '5-Eyes' members have infringed the negative obligation of not violating individuals' right to privacy. Likewise, intelligence services' surveillance activities, even if conducted from home, are in breach of the right to privacy of Article 17 (Scheinin 2014: 7).

Assuming that the ICCPR applies extra-territorially, one last question needs to be answered: What are the legal remedies on public international law when a violation of the ICCPR occurs? The supervisor on the compliance of the ICCPR provisions is the Human Rights Committee. The UN adopted an Optional Protocol of the ICCPR, which allowed individuals within the jurisdiction of one of the Contracting Parties to issue a complaint for the alleged violation of any of the ICCPR provisions. Individuals need to exhaust all domestic remedies first, and the application cannot be examined by another international body (e.g. the ECtHR) at the same time. Also, it must be noted that the only '5-Eyes' members to have ratified the protocol are Australia,[2] Canada[3] and New Zealand.[4] Thus, since the US and the UK have not ratified it, no individual complaint against those countries could be issued today.

The Human Rights Committee can still evaluate the compliance of the ICCPR, even if the Contracting Parties have not ratified the protocol, through two other mechanisms: the inter-State complaint procedure (Article 41) and the mandatory reports that parties must submit under the Committee request (Article 40). The possibility to submit an inter-State complaint has never been used to date, but it would allow one State Party to complain about the violation of the Covenant by another party. For instance, it could occur that Germany or another targeted country starts an inter-State complaint procedure against the US. As for the periodical State reports, the Human Rights Committee has recently released concluding observations of the *Fourth Periodic Report of the United States of America* in which it expressed serious concerns about the NSA surveillance (United Nations Human Rights Committee 2011). On this matter, the Committee recommended that the US conform to the obligations of Article 17 ICCPR by specifying in detail the circumstances, duration, procedures and safeguards of the surveillance. In addition, the Committee urged a reform of the oversight system over surveillance activities and the inclusion of judicial supervision (United Nations Human Rights Committee 2014: 9). The legal nature of the Human Rights Committee Concluding Observations is imprecise. Some of the literature establishes that they constitute mere recommendations (University of Bristol and Arts & Humanities Research Council 2011: 1–2), whereas other scholars describe them as a 'soft law' instrument (Guzman and Meyer 2011; Icelandic Human Rights Centre 2010). Therefore, even if the Committee Concluding Observations might carry a

2 It was ratified on 20 September 1991.
3 It was ratified on 19 May 1976.
4 It was ratified on 26 May 1989.

considerable legal weight, it is not certain that they will shape the subsequent practice in the US as regards mass surveillance activities.

After this analysis it can be concluded that the ICCPR appears to be insufficient for the protection of the right to privacy against mass surveillance programmes used by law enforcement and intelligence services. In that sense, the Art. 29 WP proposed to adoption of an Additional Protocol to Article 17 in which the meaning of 'data processing' is clarified and its safeguards are guaranteed to all individuals (Article 29 Data Protection Working Party 2014a: 16). However, the proposal has not been successful. Others have urged the Human Rights Committee to adopt an up-to-date General Comment on Article 17 to codify and clarify the existing law, including on the issue of extraterritorial effect (American Civil Liberties Union 2014). This has yet to occur.

2 Initiatives to establish international data protection principles

After the examination of the international rules that could criminalise those mass surveillance activities conducted by intelligence agencies, it is crucial to explore whether there are also any international data protection principles that compel these agencies. If not, could any of the existing data protection legal frameworks be established globally in the future?

Previous chapters analyse the data protection rules adopted within the EU legal framework (i.e. those included in Directive 95/46/EC, Council Framework Decision 2008/977/JHA and Council Decision 2009/371/JHA (Europol Council Decision)). That analysis has confirmed that the EU has stricter data protection principles than other third countries. Likewise, it has concluded the EU does not apply the same rules if data is processed for commercial purposes, rather than for security reasons. It has also been shown that EU laws do not include, in principle, intelligence services. Because of these complexities, the EU can hardly become the model institution for a universal data protection framework today.

That said, it is necessary to scrutinise whether other international organisations would be in a better position to export their data protection principles worldwide. In this sense, the OECD, the UN and the CoE have included principles on privacy and data protection in their legal frameworks. Particularly, this section examines principles enshrined in the OECD Privacy Guidelines, the APEC Privacy Framework, the UN Guidelines for the Regulation of Computerised Personal Data Files, the 1981 CoE Data Protection Convention and the Cybercrime Convention.

2.1 OECD Privacy Guidelines

The OECD is the organisation that represents the major world economies. It released the OECD Privacy Guidelines in September 1980. The OECD Privacy Guidelines include principles such as the collection limitation, data quality, purpose specification, use limitation and accountability. Back in the 1980s, these

Guidelines had a crucial role since they served as the source of inspiration for other legal frameworks, such as Directive 95/46/EC in 1995; the Generally Accepted Privacy Principles (GAPP) in 2003, 2006 and 2009; and the APEC privacy principles in 2005.

In addition to the OECD Privacy Guidelines, in 2007 the OECD adopted a *Recommendation on Cross-border Co-operation in the Enforcement of Laws Protecting Privacy* (OECD 2007: 9). It was later developed by an Action Plan for the Global Privacy Enforcement Network (GPEN), which connects 22 privacy enforcement authorities from around the world. Unfortunately, neither the OECD Privacy Guidelines nor the GPEN have binding effects on the Contracting Parties.

Because of the massive growth of international data flows in the last 30 years, the OECD Privacy Guidelines urged the amendment of the rules. The review of the OECD Guidelines was officially announced during the Seoul Declaration for the Future of the Internet Economy in 2008 (OECD 2008). In October 2011 the OECD Working Party on Information Security and Privacy (WPISP) released the terms of reference for the review (OECD Working Party on Information Security and Privacy 2011). The review of the guidelines finally took place in July 2013 by a Privacy Experts Group of the OECD WPISP.

The 2013 OECD Privacy Guidelines incorporate new rules on data breach notification, risk management and interoperability activities through national strategies. All principles that existed in the 1980, however, remain unchanged (OECD 2013). This issue has caused different reactions among privacy experts: on the one hand, there are some scholars who agree with keeping the principles as they were in 1980; but on the other hand, there are those experts in favour of changing them. Regarding the latter, a study conducted by Cate, Cullen and Mayer-Schönberger in December 2013 suggested lowering the existing standards of privacy and data protection (Cate, Cullen and Mayer-Schönberger 2013). In particular, it proposed a reduction of the rules on data collection, as well as more focus on data processing guidelines. Moreover, that study noted that, instead of specifying the purpose by which certain data was used, rules on the 'not compatible' purposes should be included. In that sense, the authors proposed replacing the 'collection limitation principle' and the 'use specification principle' for a simple 'collection principle' and 'use principle'. Finally, they suggested including an 'enforcement principle' to ensure that all countries have the adequate laws and bodies to achieve effective compliance of the principles.

In contrast, a study released in March 2014 by Ann Cavoukian, Alexander Dix and Khaled El Emam suggested maintaining the current OECD principles (Cavoukian, Dix and El Emam 2014). The only change the authors proposed was the addition of the privacy by design principle. They also criticised the report of Mayer-Schönberger *et al*, arguing that the OECD rules needed to be reinforced rather than diminished.

It can thus be seen that, even after the revision of OECD Privacy Guidelines, many issues are still unclear. The 2013 OECD Privacy Guidelines came out in the same month Snowden exposed the mass surveillance conducted by intelligence services around the world. OECD rules only cover data processing activities within the scope of commercial or economic operations. Any data collected by law enforcement or intelligence authorities falls out of the competence of the organisation. However, the revelations have proved that a large amount of information collected by private companies for commercial purposes is later processed by governments for security reasons.

Because of this, my view is that the OECD guidelines could maintain the same foundational principles but they should include rules limiting the use and transfer of personal data collected by companies located in one of the OECD Contracting Parties (including the US, which is a member of the OECD). In any event, since the OECD Guidelines are not mandatory – although they are highly influential (Bygrave 2014: 50–51) – the possibilities to use this instrument for the establishment of global data protection safeguards are minimal.

2.2 APEC Privacy Framework

Another international organisation that has released privacy principles to be met by its members is APEC. APEC is comprised of 21 economies around Asia and the Pacific, which represent the 40 per cent of the world population and the 54 per cent of the world GDP (Kropf and Crompton 2013).

In the last ten years, APEC has brought great progress to the field of privacy. In November 2004 it established privacy guidelines that protected the information transferred among APEC economies. In particular, these guidelines established nine core privacy principles: preventing harm, notice, collection limitation, uses of personal information, choice, integrity of personal information, security safeguards, access and correction and accountability. However, the rules were non-binding and, hence, they could not be enforced.

Therefore, in 2010, the APEC guidelines were reinforced through the establishment of APEC Cross-Border Privacy Enforcement Arrangement (CPEA). It promoted the creation of Privacy Enforcement Authorities (PEAs) that would supervise data shared among APEC regions (APEC 2010). One year later, APEC announced the establishment of the CBPR system 'to reduce barriers to information flows, enhance consumer privacy, and promote interoperability across regional data privacy regimes' (APEC 2011a). Unlike the previous guidelines, these are mandatory for their members.

For a country to be part of the APEC CBPR system, it needs to first comply with the Charter of the Cross Border Privacy Rules Joint Oversight Panel, as well as a self-assessment questionnaire. The questionnaire is based on the nine APEC Privacy Principles mentioned above, and is reviewed by an APEC-recognised Accountability Agent, who assesses and enforces the laws (APEC 2011b: 3). The country must also have a PEA, as a public body responsible for enforcing the privacy law of the economy's jurisdiction.[5] A Joint Oversight Panel is the body in charge of supervising the adequacy of Accountability Agent and PEAs, with

---

5 That body could have the position of Accountability Agent and PEA at the same time.

powers to suspend them if they commit any irregularity (APEC 2011b: 9). It is composed of representatives from three APEC economies, who are appointed for a period of two years.

The first country to participate in the APEC CBPR system was the US in September 2012; and IBM was the first certified company in August 2013. The system is binding, so the countries and companies subscribing to it must have privacy policies consistent with the APEC principles. Unfortunately, there are today only four APEC economies (the US, Mexico, Canada and Japan) and five companies (IBM, Merck, Workday, Lynda.com and Yodlee) participating in the CBPR. The number of countries can, however, increase in the future. In fact, Australia is already on its way to joining the system (Heyder 2014).

A relevant issue of the CBPR is its similarity to the Binding Corporate Rules (BCR). The scope of the BCR is foreseen in the EU regulation on data protection. These rules will allow the establishing of standards within the EU for the transfer of data, irrespective of the data protection framework in the destination country (COM(2012) 11 final, preamble 83).

However, the CBPR and the BCR are not fully equivalent. On this issue, the Art. 29 WP published a study in February 2014 identifying the common aspects and differences between the CBPR and the BCR (Article 29 Data Protection Working Party 2014b). One of the main distinctions is that the BCR must be approved by national DPAs, whereas the CBPR have APEC Accountability Agents as supervisory bodies. There are companies such as Hewlett-Packard that have already adopted both CBPR and BCR. By increasing the number of private entities that comply with both BCRs and CBPRs at once, common minimum data protection standards could definitely be established on the global level.

In any event, as in the OECD principles, APEC privacy rules would never apply for information processed by individuals or governments. Consequently, even if the 21 economies decided to join the regime, it would hardly become a model to follow for global data protection principles, since its scope is very limited.

2.3 UN Guidelines for the Regulation of Computerised Personal Data Files

In 1968 the UN General Assembly released a resolution on the need to adopt data privacy legislation (United Nations General Assembly 1968). As a consequence, in 1990, after more than ten years of negotiations (de Hert and Papakonstantinou 2013: 281), the UN released guidelines concerning computerised personal data files (United Nations General Assembly 1990). This instrument establishes that personal information cannot be used for purposes contrary to the provisions of the UN Charter. These guidelines include privacy principles such as lawfulness and fairness, accuracy, purpose specification, non-discrimination, data security and interest-person access. They also require the designation of an independent supervisory authority, and they foresee sanctions in case of a violation.

The UN today has 193 members. Therefore, any law adopted under the framework of this organisation can already be considered 'universal'. However, the UN guidelines concerning computerised personal data files have been adopted by the UN General Assembly and, hence, they do not have binding effects. Moreover, they are guidelines that need to be implemented at the country's discretion. For this reason, these principles have often been under-used and undervalued (Bygrave 2014: 53).

Today, the UN Guidelines for the Regulation of Computerised Personal Data Files have been abandoned. They were created in 1990, but in the last 25 years enormous technological advances have taken place. These changes have made it a necessity to reform all existing privacy laws but, strangely, no amendment on the UN guidelines has been announced for the moment.

The UN Guidelines for the Regulation of Computerised Personal Data Files need to be updated. An alternative to this amendment has been suggested by Paul de Hert and Vagelis Papakonstantinou. These scholars proposed the creation of a new specialised UN Agency, similar to the World Intellectual Property Organization, to promote the principles (de Hert and Papakonstantinou 2013: 321). The same guidelines from 1990 could be utilised, but they would have a greater impact because they would fall under the scope of a specialised UN agency.

The only reaction on privacy changes under the UN legal framework has been recently launched by Germany and Brazil. In response to the Snowden disclosures, these two countries presented to the UN General Assembly in November 2013 a resolution claiming the expansion of the right to privacy internationally, as well as the end of the mass surveillance (United Nations General Assembly 2011). This resolution was replaced one year later by a new text, which claimed the limitation of metadata processing, among other particularities (Nichols 2014). The new resolution, which still needs to be voted in the UN General Assembly, is entitled *The right to privacy in the digital age*, and it specifies the States' obligations in the processing of data for security purposes (Ribeiro 2014). However, as with the 1990 UN guidelines, this resolution will be non-binding.

2.4 1981 CoE Data Protection Convention and Cybercrime Convention

For more than 30 years, the CoE has been participating in the creation of rules concerning the right to privacy and data protection among its Contracting Parties. As a general rule, Article 8 ECHR enshrines the right to respect everyone's private and family life and correspondence. More particularly, the CoE has two significant instruments: (a) the 1981 CoE Data Protection Convention (Council of Europe 1981); and (b) the Cybercrime Convention (Council of Europe 2001a). Both instruments have binding effects for its members, but while the 1981 CoE Data Protection Convention covers all fields of data processing, the Cybercrime Convention deals specifically with crimes committed by means of electronic networks. However, none of these Conventions has direct applicability for the individuals: every Contracting Party needs to adopt the necessary measures at the domestic level in order to enforce the principles enshrined in the Conventions.

The CoE has also released numerous recommendations tackling data protection issues since 1981 to date. However, these recommendations are not legally binding and, therefore, only the 1981 CoE Data Protection Convention and the Cybercrime Convention are examined in this section.

The 1981 CoE Data Protection Convention sets up minimum standards and values on the right to privacy that all Contracting Parties need to observe. According to Article 1 of the Convention, the right to privacy is guaranteed to individuals irrespective of their nationality or the place of residence. The Convention introduces principles referring to the duties of the parties, categories of data, safeguards for the data subjects, transnational data flow rules, mutual assistance provisions, and the role of the Consultative Committee, among others.

The 1981 CoE Data Protection Convention has been ratified by more than 40 countries (MEMO/12/192), becoming a reference for numerous national legislations that have adapted their privacy laws to conform to the CoE principles. Moreover, unlike APEC and OECD principles, these are applicable to both private and public sectors.

The Art. 29 WP found in 1998 that the 'adequacy' criteria foreseen in the Convention are almost equivalent to the adequacy conditions of Directive 95/46/EC (Article 29 Data Protection Working Party 1998). In fact, an Additional Protocol adopted in 2001 reinforced the weak points of the Convention, bringing it closer to Directive 95/46/EC (Council of Europe 2001b). Could the 1981 CoE Data Protection Convention set global privacy standards? As many academics have already pointed out, it is a very feasible option (Polakiewicz 2011). The following paragraphs discuss the reasons why these principles would comply with ideal territorial and temporal features.

With regard to the territorial scope of the 1981 CoE Data Protection Convention, the CoE is an international organisation constituted after the Second World War with the purpose of establishing common human and social rights among countries in Europe. Today, 47 countries are part of the CoE, 46 of which have ratified the 1981 CoE Data Protection Convention (Council of Europe 1981). Unsurprisingly, the majority of these countries are located within European borders. The fact that this international organisation is focused on one continent (Europe) could indeed cause problems in its use as reference for the establishment of global data protection standards. However, the 1981 CoE Data Protection Convention is open for accession to non-CoE parties. In that sense, Morocco and Uruguay joined to Convention in 2013, and other countries such as Mexico have already expressed interest in joining it in the future. Therefore, the clause for accession of non-members solves the territorial issue. The fact that the CoE is a Europe-oriented organisation does not impede the Convention's principles from gaining global relevance in the future.

The second issue of concern is the fact that the content of the Convention is, at first sight, outdated. Like the OECD Privacy Guidelines, the 1981 CoE Data Protection Convention was published in 1981, before the era of the internet. The original goals of the 1981 CoE Data Protection Convention have not changed today, but privacy has been challenged by phenomena that did not exist at the time it was adopted. In particular, the global technological evolution as well as the increasing number of counter-terrorism measures have led to massive collection, processing and storage of data, urging the amendment of all current data protection legislations. A small amendment in the 1981 CoE Data Protection Convention took place in 1999 to enable the EU to become a partner (Council of Europe 1999). As mentioned above, an Additional Protocol was included in 2001 with new provisions on transborder data flows and the establishment of DPAs. Yet, several gaps remained in the 1981 CoE Data Protection Convention (Bygrave 2014: 38–43), so a new thorough reform of the Convention was still needed. Therefore, a full reform of the Convention started to be discussed in 2011.

The proposal for the modernisation of the 1981 CoE Data Protection Convention was launched in January 2011 in the form of a public consultation (Council of Europe 2001c). Replies from governments, data protection authorities, NGOs, the private sector and professional associations were compiled by May 2011, and the report on the consultation was issued one month later. The document with the proposals for the new 1981 CoE Data Protection Convention was issued in November 2011 (Council of Europe 2011), and the Consultative Committee of the Convention released an official report with the most significant changes in January 2012 (Council of Europe 2012a). This was reviewed in March and April 2012 (Council of Europe 2012b; Council of Europe 2012c). The proposal for modernisation was finalised in December 2012, and the draft was then sent to the Committee of Ministers (Council of Europe 2012d). A specialised group called the Ad-Hoc Committee on Data Protection (CAHDATA) has been studying the proposal and suggesting amendments (Council of Europe 2014a). The third and last CAHDATA meeting took place on 1 to 3 December 2014 (Council of Europe 2014b). The modernised 1981 CoE Data Protection Convention has now been submitted to the Committee of Ministers, ready for adoption. Then, the Contracting Parties will need to sign it. As in the current 1981 CoE Data Protection Convention, there is a clause that allows non-Contracting Parties to access the Convention.

The new proposal includes several issues that need to be highlighted. First, the scope foreseen in Article 3 is broader than that in the current Convention. It applies to any processing of personal data, and not only to automated personal data files. Moreover, the proposal reinforces principles such as transparency, proportionality, purpose limitation, the right of access, the right to object, the right not to be subject to an automated decision, accountability and the duty to notify data breaches. As for the definitions, the term 'automated processing' is replaced by the wider concept of 'data processing'. The definition of data controller is also modified.

Article 12 on transborder data flows is particularly relevant for those countries who are non-Members of the CoE or have not ratified the Convention. An 'appropriate' level of protection in any transborder data flow will be presumed when data is transferred between Contracting Parties. However, according to paragraph 4, a procedure will be required to examine the appropriateness when the recipient is a non-Contracting Party. For instance, the US, being a non-Contracting Party, will not have the presumed 'appropriate' level of data protection, and will have to comply with Article 12(4) for every data transfer it receives from a Contracting Party (e.g. an EU Member State).

It is interesting that in previous versions of the proposal, third countries were required to have an 'adequate' level of protection, instead of an 'appropriate' level. It is not clear why the term has been modified, but this alteration might weaken the original data protection standards required for transborder data flows. As Greenleaf explains, the adjective 'appropriate' is not as strong as 'adequate', so the third country's compliance with some principles of the Convention would be here sufficient (Greenleaf 2013). While adequacy requirements can be found in Directive 95/46/EC and the future Data Protection Regulation, the term 'appropriate' is not defined in any other data protection law. Therefore, there will no longer be a formal equivalence between the EU and the CoE data protection frameworks.

Even if the national laws implementing the Convention involve national security issues,[6] Article 9a of the draft Convention States that the application of the Convention's rules can be restricted if the State has carried out an activity for national security purposes. Therefore, national security issues can be excluded from the 1981 CoE Data Protection Convention. Yet, there is another CoE Convention that does bind national security matters: the Cybercrime Convention.

The Cybercrime Convention (also known as the Budapest Convention) aims at combating all crimes committed through and against electronic networks. It was adopted due to the increasing number of digital crimes or cybercrimes, to the detriment of former 'conventional' crimes (van den Hoven van Genderen 2008). It is not an instrument directly promoting the right to data protection but it includes a few data protection safeguards such as the establishment of an independent supervisory body (Article 15(2)), the need for data retention rules (Article 16), data security measures (Article 19), and the use of mutual assistance procedures for transnational data exchanges (Articles 25 to 28), among others. In addition, the Cybercrime Convention establishes a low-intrusive mechanism to preserve crime-related data that is exemplary. It is called the 'quick-freeze' method and it consists of freezing data only after a connected crime has been detected.

As in the 1981 CoE Data Protection Convention, non-members of the CoE can still ratify the Cybercrime Convention. For the moment, six countries outside the CoE are part of the Convention: Australia, the Dominican Republic, Japan, Mauritius, Panama and the US. Furthermore, 11 other countries have already signed or showed an interest in acceding to it in the future. Therefore, the Cybercrime Convention complements the 1981 CoE Data Protection Convention by offering specific data protection rules in the field of law enforcement[7] in the internet age.

---

6 Currently, ten of the 45 members have been implementing the Convention, but they have excluded 'State security' matters.
7 Also in the field of intelligence, as seen below.

Considering the recent revelations proving that intelligence services can access unlimited information and interfere in all available communications, the Cybercrime Convention is of a special relevance. The Convention does not include a 'national security' exemption, so it also applies to certain intelligence services' activities. However, the problem is that the Cybercrime Convention does not explicitly cover all mass surveillance activities, but only those data interferences through computer systems. Therefore, it should be amended in order to cover any intelligence services' data processing.

The Cybercrime Convention could, if amended, establish universal data protection standards to be obeyed by law enforcement and intelligence authorities around the world. Today, 47 countries are already bound to the Convention, including the US, Panama, Mauritius, Japan, Dominican Republic, Australia and Sri Lanka. Also, the inclusion of an Additional Protocol on transborder data flows is currently being discussed. However, the prospects are not looking very positive for the moment. There is a risk that the new framework will soften the conditions for the exchange of crime-related data instead. As the former EDPS, Peter Hustinx, and the EP have warned, it could result in easier access of intelligence services to personal data (European Parliament 2013; Hustinx 2013).

2.5 Other global data protection principles

Besides the rules proposed by the OECD, the UN, the APEC and the CoE, there are a few other initiatives setting up global data protection and privacy principles. Particularly, the FIPPs, the Madrid Privacy declaration, the Charter of Digital Rights, the International Principles on the Application of Human Rights to Communications Surveillance (IPAHRCS) and the Tshwane Principles have been created for this purpose. Moreover, Australia, Canada and the EU already have their own core privacy principles. These are the Australian Information Privacy Principles; the Canadian Generally Accepted Privacy Principles (CICA principles); and Directive 95/46/EC and Council Framework Decision 2008/977/JHA in the EU.

Table 5.1 identifies the principles enshrined in each of these instruments. In order to get a complete overview, it also includes the OECD Privacy Guidelines, the APEC Privacy Framework, the UN Guidelines for the Regulation of Computerised Personal Data Files and the two CoE Conventions studied above.

As demonstrated in the table, the principles vary from one instrument to the next. Rules on notification, redress, data access, purpose specification, data quality, security, oversight, limited disclosure to third countries and the processing for special categories of data are included in almost all laws. Yet, there is no single principle common to all 13 documents.

In order to discern the most adequate instrument in the field of public security, the principles applying to public entities first need to be identified. In this sense, FIPPs, UN Guidelines, the Australian principles, Directive 95/46/EC, Council Framework Decision 2008/977/JHA, the Madrid Declaration, IPAHRCS, the Tshwane Principles and the two CoE Conventions apply to the public sector.

Table 5.1

	FIPPs	Australia IPP	UN guidelines	Canada GAPP	Dir95/46	CD2008	Madrid PD	Charter Digital Rights	IPAHRCS	Tshwane	2013 OECD	APEC	CoE Conv
Transparency	*	*					*	*	*	*	*		
Notification and/or consent	*	*		*	*	*	*	*	*	*	*	*	
Data access	*	*	*	*	*	*		*		*	*	*	*
Data correction	*	*				*					*	*	*
Redress and remedies	*		*	*			*	*	*	*			*
Purpose specification	*	*	*	*	*	*					*	*	
Use limitation	*	*	*	*	*	*					*	*	*
Data quality, integrity and accuracy	*	*	*	*	*	*			*		*	*	
Security	*	*	*	*		*		*		*	*	*	*
Accountability	*	*		*						*	*	*	
Auditing and Supervision	*		*		*	*	*	*	*				
Anonymity and pseudonymity		*						*					
Limited disclosure to third countries		*	*	*	*	*			*		*		*
Retention				*	*	*				*		*	*
Special categories of data		*	*		*	*		*	*	*			
Necessity and Proportionality					*	*					*		
Legality/legitimacy			*		*				*	*		*	*
Interoperability							*				*		

However, among these, only the Australian principles, Directive 95/46/EC, Council Framework Decision 2008/977/JHA and the two CoE Conventions are mandatory for the Contracting Parties.

Moreover, even if these five instruments compel public bodies, some of them exclude from their scope data processed for 'national security' purposes. These are particularly Directive 95/46/EC and the 1981 CoE Data Protection Convention. As mentioned in the introduction to this chapter, there is no clarity about what the term 'national security' includes.

The 'national security' exemption is also found in Article 4(3) TEU. As seen in Chapter 4, intelligence agencies' laws and principles are inexistent at the EU level. This is because the EU has always presumed that the activities of intelligence agencies were part of the 'national security' exclusion, while police and judicial bodies' activities were part of the AFSJ. Therefore, EU laws within the AFSJ involve law enforcement authorities, but not intelligence services.

The only intelligence agency that has openly claimed its compliance with privacy principles is the NSA. Particularly, the agency has stated that it implements six of the eight FIPPs: purpose specification, data minimisation, use limitation, data quality and integrity, security and accountability and auditing (NSA Director of Civil Liberties and Privacy Office 2014a, 2014b: 6). However, as observed above, FIPPs are not binding rules so they cannot be enforced.

In general terms, the establishment of a global data protection charter setting up common principles for intelligence services seems a very far-off goal for the moment. Some of the intelligence services are not even subject to a national regulation. In order to set up global data protection standards for these agencies, an alignment of the national laws constraining intelligence services is first needed.

The establishment of universal data protection principles for law enforcement bodies is much more feasible. Binding data protection rules for law enforcement authorities already exist in Europe and Australia. In the EU, law enforcement authorities are compelled by Council Framework Decision 2008/977/JHA and by the Europol Framework Decision. In Australia, law enforcement authorities are bound by Australian Information Privacy Principles.[8] However, it is difficult to turn such principles into universal rules, since they are based on specific territorial laws.

3 The ideal regulatory system for a global data protection framework

Despite the existence of all these instruments enshrining international data protection principles, there is no single study to date analysing what the most adequate legal approach would be. There are, today, more than a dozen different legal frameworks establishing data protection rules. Their coexistence is at times

---

8 However, there are some exceptions as regards the compliance of the principles by Australian law enforcement authorities.

confusing, since many of these instruments overlap in scope but they do not invoke the same principles. Also, some are non-binding whereas others have an obligatory nature for its Contracting Parties. Therefore, opposing the de Hert and Papakonstantinou's argument, which supports a 'multi-faceted international approach' (de Hert and Papakonstantinou 2013: 309), this book opts for a dual data protection approach.

My particular preference for a global data protection framework is a combination of the 1981 CoE Data Protection Convention and the Cybercrime Convention. As seen above, the principles these Conventions enshrine are binding for its Contracting Parties. Today 45 countries have already ratified the 1981 CoE Data Protection Convention, and a further 42 are bound to the Cybercrime Convention. The US has signed the latter and could eventually join the 1981 CoE Data Protection Convention since it is currently an observer on the CoE's committee.[9]

This two-fold system composed of the 1981 CoE Data Protection Convention and Cybercrime Convention would establish a robust data protection framework, providing even more consistency than the current EU data protection regime. The EU today has two main instruments that protect EU citizens' data: Directive 95/46/EC and Council Framework Decision 2008/977/JHA. Whereas the latter applies when the data processing is carried out within the context of law enforcement, the former applies for all other non-security matters. The same duality is found in the EU Data Protection Package released in January 2012. Again, it consists of two instruments: one in the form of a directive for law enforcement data exchanges; and a regulation for the rest of data-sharing operations. However, as seen in Chapter 4, no EU data protection rules are in force for intelligence services' activities.

In contrast, by choosing the 1981 CoE Data Protection Convention and Cybercrime Convention as global data protection instruments, all fields would be covered, including data processed by intelligence services. The 1981 CoE Data Protection Convention would apply for commercial and law enforcement purposes; whereas the Cybercrime Convention would be observed when intelligence services process information. This is also an ideal framework, since the majority of EU data-sharing instruments are already using 1981 CoE Data Protection Convention as a threshold.[10]

Another advantage in choosing the two CoE Conventions is that countries are not required to be CoE Contracting Parties to accede them. Thus, its success will depend on how non-EU Members perceive the Conventions. As an example, numerous non-EU countries and international organisations (UN, Organization

---

9 The non-EU countries with observer status are the US, Canada, Japan, Mexico, Israel and the Holy See.

10 See, for instance, Article 8 of the Swedish Initiative; Article 27 of the Europol Council Decision; and Article 25 of Council Decision 2008/615/JHA (Prüm).

of American States (OAS), African Union, APEC, etc) have participated in the negotiations for the modernisation of the 1981 CoE Data Protection Convention. In order to attract non-CoE parties it is important that the Conventions bring credibility, efficient functioning and enough mechanisms for implementation. Only after doing so could their principles have a global relevance in the future.

However, there is still a lot of work to do in the amendment of both Conventions. For instance, one of the current problems in the current Cybercrime Convention is that some Contracting Parties encourage TSPs to move their servers to third countries, which are not part of the Convention, in order to circumvent the law. Another issue that should be included in the amended Convention is a mechanism by which security actors could directly request data from TSPs and maintain the necessary safeguards for the individuals at the same time.

It can be concluded that the CoE is the primary candidate among all the existing international organisations for the establishment of data protection and global privacy standards. The organisation has the 1981 CoE Data Protection Convention, the Cybercrime Convention as well as Article 8 ECHR. After the appropriate amendments, these Conventions would cover all data protection fields, including intelligence security activities.

4 The EU's role in designing global data protection principles through the CoE

As seen in Chapter 2, although the EU is now gaining increasing relevance as an international actor in the field of security, such 'actorness' is not always strong in practice. The CFSP/CSDP and the AFSJ policies are still very much influenced by the interests of Member States and third countries.

In the area of data protection, continuous pressures from both private and public entities at the domestic and international levels have caused a lowering of the data protection safeguards in the EU. This has been seen in the current EU Data Protection Package, which is composed of two instruments: a regulation and a directive. The regulation establishes data protection rules for information processed in all fields except for law enforcement. The first draft of the regulation included a provision (ex Article 42), which prohibited a government from accessing data stored by a private company without a prior mutual assistance treaty or an international agreement. One month before the proposal was launched, the US government pushed the Commission to remove that clause, and it succeeded: the provision is no longer found in the proposal but it has been finally kept in the final version of the GDPR. Similarly, the new directive for data exchanged among law enforcement authorities has been softened because of political interests. First, the fact that the nature of the instrument is a directive and not a regulation means that there will be no uniformity among Member States in the implementation of its rules. Moreover, the new directive excludes sectoral data-sharing agreements as well as data processed by EU agencies such as Europol and Eurojust. Lastly, the proposal will not cover any data transfer conducted by IntCen and national intelligence services, since these are not considered part of the EU internal security policy.

Chapter 3 explains how, through Europol, the EU has influenced third countries to adapt their data protection laws as a condition for the adoption of a strategic/co-operation agreement with the agency. If, after a questionnaire, Europol has doubts about the adequacy of the rules in the third country, the agency will visit *in situ* the institutions in charge with the compliance of data protection laws and will advise about the necessary modifications prior to the adoption of the agreement. This procedure is much faster and more effective than that in the Police and Criminal Justice Data Protection Directive. According to Article 34 of the new directive, the Commission will also assess the adequacy of data protection rules in a third country before accepting international transfers. Yet, Article 36 allows the derogation of such adequacy in case of: (a) vital or legitimate interest; (b) immediate and serious threat to the public security; (c) prevention, investigation, detection or prosecution of criminal offences or the execution of criminal penalties; and (d) establishment, exercise or defence of legal claims. These situations, if interpreted broadly, could be used abusively to transfer massive amounts of data to any third country.

A similar carve-out provision for emergency situations is also found in Article 31(2) of the proposed Europol Regulation. However, if we compare these two Articles, we see that the list of cases included in the Europol Regulation is much more restrictive than Article 36 of the new directive.[11] Moreover, any derogation under the scope of the future Europol Regulation requires the approval of the Executive Director, the Management Board and even the EDPS, if the transfer is of a set of data. The same conditions do not apply for the new directive.

The EU has also used another mechanism to export high data protection standards without directly operating through its own instruments and institutions. This is the CoE. Despite it being an international organisation outside the scope of the EU institutional structure, the close link between both parties is unquestionable. In 2005, the ECtHR expressly stated that the EU provided human rights protection equivalent to that of the Convention (Application no. 45036/98, *Bosphorus Hava Yollari Turizm Ve Ticaret Anonim Đirketi v Ireland* (2005)). This presumption gained consistency with the inclusion of a provision for the accession of the EU to the ECHR in the Treaty of Lisbon (Blasi Casagran 2012: 79–83).

Regarding their data protection principles, the same equivalence has existed since the 1980s. In a disconnection clause, the 1981 CoE Data Protection Convention explicitly refers to the Commission's involvement in the negotiations, and its intention to conclude an EC instrument on the same subject:

> The Commission of the European Communities, which carried out studies concerning harmonisation of national legislation within the Community in relation to transborder data flows and possible distortions of competition, as

---

11 The reasons are: (a) it is absolutely necessary to safeguard the essential interests; (b) it is absolutely necessary to prevent imminent danger; (c) it is required on important public interest grounds; and (d) it is necessary to protect the vital interests of the data subject.

well as problems of data security, kept in close touch with the Council of Europe. The Commission decided to await the outcome of the work on this convention before deciding on its own action in the field of data protection.

(Council of Europe 1981: para. 16)

As prognosticated in the Convention, the first data protection instrument in the EU had much in common with its predecessor. In Directive 95/46/EC, the Commission had included exactly the same data protection principles as those in the 1981 CoE Data Protection Convention. At first glance, it may seem that the CoE influenced the EU, but in fact the Commission took an active role in designing the Convention that it would then cite as a reference in its own directive.

In 2001 an Additional Protocol was included in the 1981 CoE Data Protection Convention (Council of Europe 2001b). It incorporated provisions on supervisory authorities, and the adequacy criteria for data transfers to countries not part of the Convention. It is not a coincidence that similar clauses were already found in Directive 95/46/EC. The CoE clearly sought to base its Convention on the EU data protection standards. Unfortunately, the Additional Protocol has not been ratified by all Contracting Parties. At the time of writing, 36 countries have ratified this Protocol, and a further eight have signed it but are pending for ratification.

Finally, the same mutual influence occurred recently during the negotiations of the 1981 CoE Data Protection Convention's amendment. They started in January 2012, the same month that the Commission released the proposals for a new EU data protection framework. The EU participated actively in shaping the modernised Convention.[12] As in the EU Data Protection Package, the modernised 1981 CoE Data Protection Convention includes clauses on basic principles, sensitive data, data security, transparency, rights of the data subject, sanctions and remedies, data transfers to third countries and oversight. It has, however, omitted controversial provisions such as the 'right to be forgotten' or the new sanctions' system that includes the GDPR. The negotiations for the new 1981 CoE Data Protection Convention were subject to a lot less pressure from the US government and private companies than the EU Data Protection Package. And still, the EU played a key role in the final outcome.

As this section demonstrates, that there are alternative ways in which global data protection standards could adopt an EU 'style' without coming directly from EU instruments. Besides the Europol's role in exporting EU data protection standards, the CoE has also been the reflection of EU principles since the 1980s. There has always been a mutual influence between both organisations: the 1981 CoE Data Protection Convention has influenced Directive 95/46/EC; and now the EU Data Protection Package is influencing the modernised 1981 CoE Data Protection Convention.

---

12 'Commission to renegotiate Council of Europe Data Protection Convention on behalf of EU', European Commission, 19 November 2012, http://europa.eu/rapid/press-release_MEMO-12-877_en.htm (accessed 30 October 2014).

5 Conclusions

The great technological progress that has occurred in the last 15 years has prompted the need to establish global data protection principles for data processed for the prevention and investigation of crimes. This chapter has examined the feasibility of such principles.

There are many limitations found in the current proposals to establish a common data protection framework for information exchanged in the field of security. One of the obstacles seen in many of the initiatives for universal data protection principles is that some of them are not binding for its members, and other exclude activities conducted for 'national security' purposes. This study finds that only one international organisation could establish binding common data protection rules for both law enforcement authorities and intelligence services: the CoE. A combination of the 1981 CoE Data Protection Convention and the Cybercrime Convention would be the best option for expanding common data protection principles covering all sectors, including the field of security. These two Conventions already have more than 40 Contracting Parties, including all EU Member States and even the US in one of them. Once the modernised 1981 CoE Data Protection Convention is released, it could attract further third countries, bringing the institution closer to becoming 'global'. The EU has indirectly participated in the negotiation procedures of the 1981 CoE Data Protection Convention and its amendment. Therefore, through the CoE, the EU has found a way of exporting its own data protection principles, free of pressures from private and governmental interests.

It is essential to set up universal principles of data protection that bind any piece of information processed, regardless of its purpose. For data processed for security reasons, more accountability and control needs to be built up. Our history has shown that when governments have unlimited power, it can be easily abused. Therefore, basic principles need to be enforced to avoid abusive restrictions of human rights. Security cannot be used to justify a world in which individuals are permanently monitored by the State with no limitations. Any intrusion needs to be necessary and proportional in relation to the objective it pursues. There is no doubt that privacy is a universal right, so the adoption of a global instrument enforcing that right is the logical next step.

Bibliography

American Civil Liberties Union, 2014, *Privacy Rights in the Digital Age. A Proposal for a New General Comment on the Right to Privacy under Article 17 of the International Covenant on Civil and Political Rights: A Draft Report and General Comment by the American Civil Liberties Union*, March 2014.

APEC, 2010, *Cooperation Arrangement for Cross-Border Privacy Enforcement*, Doc. 2010/SOM1/ECSG/DPS/013, Data Privacy Subgroup Meeting, 28 February 2010, Hiroshima.

APEC, 2011a, *Leaders' Declaration The Honolulu Declaration – Toward a Seamless Regional Economy*, 12/13 November 2011, Honolulu.

APEC, 2011b, *APEC Cross-Border Privacy Rules System. Policies, Rules and Guidelines*, www.apec. org (accessed 16 November 2015).

Application no. 45036/98, *Bosphorus Hava Yollari Turizm Ve Ticaret Anonim Şirketi v Ireland*, (ECtHR, 5 June 2005).

Article 29 Data Protection Working Party, 1998, *Transfers of personal data to third countries: Applying Articles 25 and 26 of the EU data protection directive*, WP 12, 24 July 1998.

Article 29 Data Protection Working Party, 2014a, *Opinion on surveillance of electronic communications for intelligence and national security purposes*, WP 215, 10 April 2014.

Article 29 Data Protection Working Party, 2014b, *Opinion 02/2014 on a referential for requirements for Binding Corporate Rules submitted to national Data Protection Authorities in the EU and Cross Border Privacy Rules submitted to APEC CBPR Accountability Agents*, WP 212, 27 February 2014.

Aust, HP, 2014, 'Stellungsnahme zur Sachverständigenanhörung', Humboldt-Universität zu Berlin, 5 June 2014, www.bundestag.de (accessed 15 November 2015).

Blasi Casagran, C, 2012, 'The reinforcement of fundamental rights in the Lisbon Treaty' in S Dosenrode (ed), *The European Union after Lisbon*, Ashgate Publishing Ltd, Farnham, pp. 75–94.

Bowcott, O, 2014, 'Social media mass surveillance is permitted by law, says top UK official', *The Guardian*, 17 June, www.theguardian.com (accessed 16 November 2015).

Bygrave, LA, 2014, *Data Privacy Law. An International Perspective*, Oxford University Press, Oxford.

Cate, FH, Cullen, P and Mayer-Schönberger, V, 2013, *Data Protection Principles for the 21st Century. Revising the 1980 OECD Guidelines*, Oxford Internet Institute, University of Oxford.

Cavoukian, A, Dix, A and El Emam, K, 2014, 'The unintended consequences of privacy paternalism', Information and Privacy Commissioner Ontario Canada, 5 March, Ontario.

Council Decision 2009/371/JHA of 6 April 2009 establishing the European Police Office (Europol).

Council Framework Decision 2008/977/JHA of 27 November 2008 on the protection of personal data processed in the framework of police and judicial cooperation in criminal matters.

Council of Europe, 1981, *Convention for the Protection of Individuals with regard to Automatic Processing of Personal Data*, CETS No. 108, 28 January 1981.

Council of Europe, 1999, *Amendments to the Convention for the Protection of Individuals with regard to Automatic Processing of Personal Data [ETS No. 108] allowing the European Communities to accede of 15 June 1999.*

Council of Europe, 2001a, *Convention on Cybercrime*, CETS No. 185, 23 November 2001.

Council of Europe, 2001b, *Additional Protocol to the Convention for the Protection of Individuals with regard to Automatic Processing of Personal Data [ETS No. 108] regarding supervisory authorities and transborder data flows*, ETS No. 181, 8 November 2001.

Council of Europe, 2001c, *Public consultation, 'Modernisation of Convention 108: Give us your opinion!'*, www.coe.int/t/dghl/standardsetting/dataprotection/Consultation_Modernisation_ Convention_108_EN.pdf (accessed 15 November 2015).

Council of Europe, 2011, *The Consultative Committee of the Convention for the Protection of Individuals with regard to Automatic Processing of Personal Data, ETS No. 108. Modernisation of Convention 108: Proposals*, Doc. T-PD-BUR(2011) 27, 15 November 2011.

Council of Europe, 2012a, *The Consultative Committee of the Convention for the Protection of Individuals with regard to Automatic Processing of Personal Data, ETS No. 108. Modernisation of Convention 108: Proposals*, Doc. T-PD-BUR(2012)01EN, 18 January 2012.

Council of Europe, 2012b, *The Consultative Committee of the Convention for the Protection of Individuals with regard to Automatic Processing of Personal Data, ETS No. 108. Modernisation Of Convention 108: Proposals*, Doc. T-PD-BUR(2012)01Rev, 5 March 2012.

Council of Europe, 2012c, *The Consultative Committee of the Convention for the Protection of Individuals with regard to Automatic Processing of Personal Data, ETS No. 108. Modernisation Of Convention 108: Proposals*, Doc. T-PD-BUR(2012)01Rev2, 27 April 2012.

Council of Europe, 2012d, *The Consultative Committee of the Convention for the Protection of Individuals with regard to Automatic Processing of Personal Data, ETS No. 108. Modernisation of Convention 108: Proposals*, Doc. T-PD_2012_04_rev4_E, 18 December 2012.

Council of Europe, 2014a, *Convention 108 with Additional Protocol and Modernisation proposals, Working Document*, CAHDATA(2014)1, 25 March 2014.

Council of Europe, 2014b, *Convention 108 with Additional Protocol and Modernisation proposals, Working Document*, CAHDATA(2014)RAP03Abr, 3 December 2014.

Cour Internationale de Justice, 2004, *Consequénces juridiques de l'edification d'un mur dans le territoire Palestinien occuppé*, Advisory Opinion, 9 July 2004.

de Hert, P and Papakonstantinou, V, 2013, 'Three scenarios for international governance of data privacy: Towards an international data privacy organization, preferably a UN agency?', *I/S: a Journal of Law and Policy for the Information Society*, vol. 9, no. 3, pp. 271–324.

Directive 95/46/EC of the European Parliament and of the Council of 24 October 1995 on the protection of individuals with regard to the processing of personal data and on the free movement of such data.

European Commission, 2012, *EU-U.S. joint statement on data protection by European Commission Vice-President Viviane Reding and U.S. Secretary of Commerce John Bryson*, MEMO/12/192, 19 March 2012.

European Commission Proposal for a Regulation of the European Parliament and of the Council on the protection of individuals with regard to the processing of personal data and on the free movement of such data (General Data Protection Regulation), COM(2012) 11 final, 25 January 2012.

European Parliament, 2013, *The relation between the surveillance practices in the EU and the US and the EU data protection provisions*, Working Document 3, 12 December 2013.

Greenleaf, G, 2013, '"Modernising" data protection Convention 108: A safe basis for a global privacy treaty?', *Computer Law & Security Review*, vol. 29, no. 4, July/August, pp. 430–436.

Guzman, AT and Meyer, T, 2011, 'International Soft Law', *Journal of Legal Analysis*, vol. 2, no. 1, UC Berkeley, Public Law and Legal Theory Research Paper No. 1353444, http://ssrn.com/abstract=1353444 (accessed 15 November 2015).

Heyder, M, 2014, ' The APEC cross-border privacy rules – Now that we've built it, will they come?', *Privacy perspectives*, 4 September, https://privacyassociation.org (accessed 16 November 2015).

Hustinx, P, 2013, 'EU-US data sharing deal seen as NSA's potential spying option' (online video), 8 October, www.presstv.ir/detail/2013/10/08/328223/euus-data-sharing-deal-seen-as-nsas-potential-spying-option/ (accessed 15 November 2015).

Icelandic Human Rights Centre, 2010, 'Sources of International Law', www.humanrights.is/en/human-rights-education-project/human-rights-concepts-ideas-and-fora/part-i-the-concept-of-human-rights/sources-of-international-law (accessed 15 November 2015).

Korff, D, 2014, 'Expert Opinion prepared for the Committee of Inquiry of the Bundestag into the "5-EYES" global surveillance systems revealed by Edward Snowden', Committee Hearing, Paul-Löbe-Haus, Berlin.

Kropf, J and Crompton, M, 2013, 'The EU and APEC: A roadmap for global inter-operability?', *IAPP*, 26 November, www.privacyassociation.org (accessed 16 November 2015).

Nichols, M, 2014, 'Germany, Brazil push the U.N. to be tougher on digital spying', *Reuters*, 6 November, www.reuters.com (accessed 15 November 2015).

NSA Director of Civil Liberties and Privacy Office, 2014a, *NSA's civil liberties and privacy protections for targeted SIGINT activities under Executive Order 12333*, NSA Director of Civil Liberties and Privacy Office report, 7 October 2014.

NSA Director of Civil Liberties and Privacy Office, 2014b, *NSA's Implementation of Foreign Intelligence Surveillance Act Section 702*, NSA Director of Civil Liberties and Privacy Office Report, 16 April 2014.

OECD, 2007, *Recommendation on Cross-border Co-operation in the Enforcement of Laws Protecting Privacy*, 12 June 2007, www.oecd.org/dataoecd/43/28/38770483.pdf (accessed 6 November 2015).

OECD, 2008, Ministerial Meeting on the Future of the Internet Economy, 17/18 June 2008, Seoul.

OECD, 2013, *Recommendation of the Council concerning Guidelines governing the Protection of Privacy and Transborder Flows of Personal Data*, Doc. C(80)58/FINAL, 11 July 2013.

OECD Working Party on Information Security and Privacy, 2011, *Terms of reference for the review of OECD Guidelines governing the Protection of Privacy and Transborder Flows of Personal Data, Working Party on Information Security and Privacy*, Doc. DSTI/ICCP/REG(2011)4/FINAL, 31 October 2011.

Office of the United Nations High Commissioner for Human Rights, 2014, *The right to privacy in the digital age*, Doc. A/HRC/27/37, 30 June 2014, NYC.

Polakiewicz, J, 2011, 'International Data Protection Conference Convention 108 as a global privacy standard', Speech in Budapest, 17 June, www.coe.int (accessed 16 November 2015).

Ribeiro, J, 2014, 'UN committee calls on countries to protect right to privacy', *Pcworld*, 25 November, www.pcworld.com (accessed 16 November 2015).

Scheinin, M, 2009, *Promotion and protection of all human rights, civil, political, economic, social and cultural rights, including the right to development. Report of the Special Rapporteur on the promotion and protection of human rights and fundamental freedoms while countering terrorism*, General Assembly of the United Nations, Doc. A/HRC/10/3.

Scheinin, M, 2013, 'LIBE Committee Inquiry on Electronic Mass Surveillance of EU Citizens Hearing', European Parliament, 14 October.

Scheinin, M, 2014, 'To the Extent the ICCPR has Extraterritorial Effect, the Right to Privacy Is Not an Exception', written statement for Privacy and Civil Liberties Oversight Board's hearing on 19 March 2014, Washington, DC.

United Nations, 2008, *Compilation of General Comments and General Recommendations adopted by Human Rights Treaty Bodies Human Rights Committee, General Comment No. 16 (Article 17), para. 10*, Doc. HRI/GEN/1/Rev.9 (Vol. I), 27 May 2008.

United Nations General Assembly, 1968, *Human Rights and Scientific and Technological Developments*, Doc. A/RES/2450 (XXIII), 19 December 1968.

United Nations General Assembly, 1990, *Guidelines for the Regulation of Computerized Personal Data Files*, Resolution 45/95, 14 December 1990.

United Nations General Assembly, 2011, *The right to privacy in the digital age*, Doc. A/C3/68/L.45, 1 November 2013.

United Nations General Assembly, 2014, *Promotion and protection of human rights and fundamental freedoms while countering terrorism*, Doc. A/69/297, 23 September 2014.

United Nations Human Rights Committee, 2004, *General Comment 31, Nature of the General Legal Obligation on States Parties to the Covenant*, Doc. CCPR/C/21/Rev.1/Add.13 (2004).

United Nations Human Rights Committee, 2011, *Fourth Periodic Report of the United States of America to the United Nations Committee on Human Rights Concerning the International Covenant on Civil and Political Rights*, 30 December 2011.

United Nations Human Rights Committee, 2014, *Concluding observations on the fourth report of the United States of America*, 110th session, 10–28 March 2014.

University of Bristol and Arts & Humanities Research Council, 2011, 'Implementation of UN Treaty Body Concluding Observations: The Role of National and Regional Mechanisms in Europe', Summary and recommendations from the High Level Seminar held on 19–20 September 2011, Bristol.

van den Hoven van Genderen, R, 2008, 'Cybercrime investigation and the protection of personal data and privacy', Council of Europe, Directorate General of Human Rights and Legal Affairs, 25 May.

Conclusions

This book has investigated the possibility of establishing global data protection rules for data processed in the field of intelligence and law enforcement. In this regard, it has identified several challenges that need to be overcome for its accomplishment.

Chapter 1 determined that the creation of global data protection rules requires the EU to first harmonise its data protection framework within the AFSJ. This chapter offered an in-depth analysis on the state-of-play of the instruments and systems that the EU has adopted in order to process data for law enforcement purposes. There are at least nine different EU systems today (Prüm, the Swedish initiative, EIO, ECRIS, VIS, SIS, Eurodac, CIS, ENUs) that exchange information among law enforcement authorities in the Member States. In addition, four other EU systems are likely to be established in the future (EU PNR, TFTS, EES, RTP).

However, the EU data protection regime is rather fragmented. Each of these instruments has its own data protection rules, which in turn differ from the general Council Framework Decision 2008/977/JHA. Chapter 1 also identified some of the Member States' problems relating to the lack of implementation and usage of these instruments. Police authorities do not use the European information systems in a clear and consistent manner, and some of them do not have the systems fully operational yet. For instance, none of the Member States yet has the DNA data searches of Prüm up and running, or the technical infrastructure to use ECRIS. Therefore, under these circumstances, it is impossible to create a global data protection framework if the EU itself does not provide homogeneous rules for the exchange of law enforcement information.

Another challenge to overcome is the lack of an equivalent legal framework on data protection between the US and the EU. Chapter 2 delineated how the two parties have tried to overcome their legal differences by concluding numerous sectoral data-sharing agreements in the field of law enforcement. These are, in particular, the PNR Agreements, the SWIFT Agreement and the EU-US Agreement on the security of classified information. Moreover, negotiations for an umbrella EU-US data protection and data privacy agreement are currently ongoing. All of these instruments demonstrate the enormous efforts of both parties to reach a common approach in terms of data protection. However, in practice, all the existing EU-US Agreements on data protection matters differ from the EU legal framework for data exchanges in the field of law enforcement (i.e. Council Framework Decision 2008/977/JHA and the EU Police and Criminal Justice Data Protection Directive).

A third problem encountered in the creation of common global data protection standards is that any law would in principle exclude data exchanges carried out by intelligence services. Chapter 4 examined the increasing synergy between law enforcement and intelligence authorities. In the past, these two communities had very distinctive roles. While intelligence services were mainly conducting pre-emptive analytical tasks ('wait and watch'), police agents had an active role in enforcing the law ('see and strike'). Over the years, that division has become more and more blurred. Law enforcement agencies include analytical departments where police officers collect and process intelligence for the prevention of crimes. Similarly, many intelligence agencies have police departments within their headquarters, allowing a fluent communication between both entities.

Taking all of this into account, Chapter 4 scrutinised whether the EU could adopt laws and issue court decisions affecting data shared among intelligence services. As seen in Chapters 1 and 2, the AFSJ has rules concerning data exchanged among law enforcement authorities within and beyond the EU. The CJEU annulment of the Data Retention Directive case can be seen as one of the main EU achievements in the protection of data processed for law enforcement purposes. The court, for the first time, annulled an entire EU directive for being contrary to the provisions of the EU Charter. Articles 7 and 8 of the Charter are to be respected by any EU instrument that processes and shares data for the prevention, combat, investigation and prosecution of crimes. Also, the court stated that a directive must require Member States to implement it in a Charter-compliant way. This is significant for the future of a more centralised, EU-level, harmonised system and, perhaps, for the content of EU-third country agreements. However, the Charter does not apply for areas falling outside the scope of the EU, such as national security issues.

Article 4(2) TEU expressly excludes 'national security' matters from the competence of the EU laws. The concept of national security has been associated with intelligence services, but there is no clear definition of what the exact scope of this term is. Moreover, the EU has a new body called IntCen through which intelligence services of the Member States are able to meet and exchange information with each other. This implies that the EU currently has a certain degree of participation on intelligence services' matters.

For the establishment of global data protection rules, Chapter 3 suggested using Europol laws as a model. Europol currently operates on the basis of a council decision (ECD), although this will be soon replaced by a regulation. The ECD includes strong data protection provisions that refer to the right of access, correction and deletion; the purpose limitation principle; data retention data quality; and external supervision. Also, Europol uses the privacy-by-design tool SIENA to exchange information with Member States and third countries. Thus, Europol's laws offer strong privacy rules, higher than most data protection laws in the Member States. Therefore, this study proposes enhancing the role of Europol in cross-border criminal investigations, so as to increase the impact its rules and international agreements could have on EU and non-EU countries.

In fact, Europol has already been expanding its competences over the last ten years. It started as an intergovernmental organisation, regulated by a convention and with the purpose of supporting Member States' criminal investigations when it was required. Europol's powers also increased in 2008 when it became an EU agency. Once the current proposed Europol Regulation is adopted, the agency will acquire new competences. For instance, the proposed regulation establishes in Article 6 that Europol will be able to request the initiation of a criminal investigation by national units when it considers that it adds value. Member States will have a deadline of one month to reply on the initiative. If a Member State replies with a rejection, this will have to be accompanied by a reasoned justification.

However, the scope of Europol is limited to data shared among law enforcement authorities. Data exchanges among intelligence services are excluded from both the ECD and the future regulation. A way of clarifying intelligence services' activities would be by enhancing IntCen's role. IntCen was created in 1999 as a forum for exchanging sensitive information among intelligence services. At that time, it was called the SitCen and comprised only seven Member States. In 2012 the body was renamed IntCen and transferred to the EEAS. It has undergone organisational and structural changes but a concrete legal basis for its mandate has never been clarified. Chapter 4 suggested the use of Article 39 TEU as a legal basis to regulate IntCen's data processing activities.

The terrorist attacks that occurred in Paris in January and November 2015 could lead to the political will to reinforce Europol and IntCen's powers. Previous terrorist attacks in the EU have led to legislative initiatives, or the unblocking of the legislative processes. Enhancing the Europol and IntCen's mandate and including high data protection standards could give the EU a consistent data protection legal framework in the field of security. Intelligence services and law enforcement authorities in the Member States would then have a common body at the EU level, which would end the current divergences within the European borders.

Additionally, Chapter 5 examined the existing initiatives setting up international data protection principles that could regulate data exchanges for law enforcement purposes. These are specifically the Fair Information Practice Principles, the UN Guidelines, the Australian principles, the Madrid Declaration, the International Principles on the Application of Human Rights to Communications Surveillance, the Tshwane Principles, the 1981 CoE Data Protection Convention and the Cybercrime Convention. Yet, some of these principles are not binding for the Contracting Parties, and others exclude national security data transfers. After a substantial analysis, Chapter 5 focused on the principles of the 1981 CoE Data Protection Convention together with those in the Cybercrime Convention. Each of these two conventions has more than forty Contracting Parties today. A reformed version of these instruments (a modernised 1981 CoE Data

Protection Convention is about to be adopted) could serve as a reference for the establishment of global data protection rules among law enforcement and intelligence agencies.

National security issues are excluded from the scope of the 1981 CoE Data Protection Convention. The same exclusion is found in other instruments such as Directive 95/46/EC, Council Decision 2008/977/JHA and the Treaty of Lisbon itself. However, as mentioned above, neither the CoE nor the EU institutions have formally defined what 'national security' really means. If national security is associated with intelligence services activities, these will not be bound by the 1981 CoE Data Protection Convention, but the principles included in the Cybercrime Convention will still apply.

The level of data protection of the CoE and the EU is presumed equivalent. It is not a coincidence that all the principles in the 1981 CoE Data Protection Convention are also found in Directive 95/46/EC. Also, the Commission is currently participating in the modernisation of the CoE convention. Whereas Chapter 2 highlighted the US influence on specific EU international data-sharing agreements as well as the future EU-US Data Protection Agreement, Chapter 5 identified the EU's active contribution to the CoE data protection legislation. The EU has thus been expanding its data protection standards through the CoE. This close relationship could be the keystone for establishing strong data protection rules around the world.

This book has shown that the notions of privacy and data protection do not oppose the objective of security, but rather complement it. Chapters 1, 2 and 4 mentioned numerous mass surveillance programmes and systems consisting of collecting large amounts of data from untargeted individuals. Apart from the potential clash between these systems and the right to data protection, its effectiveness has been questioned. This was precisely one of the issues raised by the CJEU in the Data Retention case. The 'collect-it-all' approach risks overloading databases with irrelevant data, which could divert attention from crucial data. This over-abundance of data was an obstacle in the prevention of past terrorist attacks such as those occurred in Madrid and London or, more recently, in the 2012 Boston Marathon bombing. There was an available amount of intelligence, but it was improperly identified and processed.

The importance of privacy and data protection is underlined throughout the five chapters of this study. In the field of security, this right can easily be suppressed. 9/11 presented the ideal context to adopt measures that reduced privacy and enhanced security through laws such as the Patriot Act. These measures are mostly preventive in nature, and now they have become operational it is extremely difficult to remove them because there are always potential threats that justify them.

For society, the over-surveillance creates the false notion that there is always someone watching and monitoring our actions. In particular, governments believe that constant surveillance can reduce criminal activity because an individual's fear that someone might be watching may deter them from committing a crime. Jeremy Bentham first propagated the idea of 'permanent visibility' in the eighteenth century with his design for an institutional building called the 'panopticon'. His panopticon prison was to be a circular structure with prison cells surrounding a central tower (the 'inspection house') from which prison guards could view every cell. The central tower might not always be occupied by guards, but the fact that the prisoners could never know whether they were being watched or not would cause them to self-regulate their own behaviour. Although Bentham's prison was never built, the notion of continual control by the government is found in many other contexts today. As seen in Chapters 1 and 4, law enforcement authorities today have the means to monitor our daily lives with the help of the internet and phone companies. New technologies play a decisive role in the collection of information for criminal investigations. Chapter 1 also showed that private actors collecting information for their own commercial purposes may be required to hand over such data to police or intelligence agents. In order to restrict that phenomenon, the purpose limitation principle should be included in the future global data protection framework.

At the time of finalising this book, new EU security measures are in the pipeline. Following the terror attacks in Paris on 7 January and 13 November 2015 linked to the Islamic State, Member States of the EU activated their security alerts to the highest levels and have decided to adopt new counter-terrorism measures. Member States have established stricter border controls, and many of them are committed to incorporate national PNR systems for the collection of passenger data by 2016. Also, other Member States decided to enhance the power of the police, allowing them to intercept communications without prior judicial authorisation. These measures assimilate the controversial (and now expired) Patriot Act, adopted in 2001 after the 9/11 terrorist attacks.

At the same time, new data protection legislation in the field of law enforcement will soon be passed on both sides of the Atlantic. In the EU, a directive on data protection for police and judicial matters will replace the current Council Framework Decision 2008/977/JHA. In addition, more concrete EU instruments such as the proposed Europol Regulation and the EU PNR Directive will include new data protection provisions for data processed for law enforcement purposes. In the US, several Patriot Act provisions are going to expire in May 2015 so new debates on their necessity and proportionality will surely arise by then. Likewise, US President Obama recently announced that stronger safeguards would be included for data processed through the FISA and the EO 12333. Mainly, the US President seeks to end the bulk collection of data and to establish better oversight mechanisms for US intelligence agencies. Finally, the EU-US Data Protection Agreement is on its way, and it will set down minimal rules that both parties will need to comply with in the exchange of crime-related data. This agreement is likely to be compatible with the 1981 CoE Data Protection Convention, facilitating the establishment of data protection global standards in the future.

Current and future security measures need to strike the right balance between data protection and privacy principles. In June 2013, the Snowden revelations demonstrated that a lack of restrictions for security agents in the collection and processing of personal data could cause serious conflicts with individuals' fundamental rights. In particular, the exposé about the surveillance programmes used by the NSA has irrevocably damaged the trust that individuals, companies and governments all over the world once had for intelligence services. The current lack of confidence in security authorities will only be repaired by reinforcing accountability and individual rights. Hence, data protection rules at the global level are now more necessary than ever.

Index